GLOBALIZING
THEOLOGY

GLOBALIZING THEOLOGY

*Belief and Practice
in an Era of World Christianity*

CRAIG OTT AND
HAROLD A. NETLAND

EDITORS

Baker Academic
Grand Rapids, Michigan

Published by Baker Academic
a division of Baker Publishing Group
P.O. Box 6287, Grand Rapids, MI 49516-6287
www.bakeracademic.com

Printed in the United States of America

Library of Congress Cataloging-in-Publication Data
Globalizing theology : belief and practice in an era of world Christianity / Craig Ott and Harold A. Netland, editors.
    p.   cm.
   Includes bibliographical references and index.
   ISBN 10: 0-8010-3112-5 (pbk.)
   ISBN 978-0-8010-3112-0 (pbk.)
   1. Theology—Methodology. 2. Globalization—Religious aspects—Christianity.
  I. Ott, Craig, 1952– II. Netland, Harold A., 1955–
BR118.G58 2006
230.01—dc22
                                                  2006002737

To our brother, friend, and colleague
Paul G. Hiebert,
in grateful appreciation for his friendship, scholarship,
and example of Christlike character

Contents

Foreword

WILBERT R. SHENK

From the human point of view, there is no way we can engage with the gospel independent of culture. Our interaction with the gospel relies on human language, worldview, and cultural context. The Bible speaks forcefully to this point: "The Word became flesh and made his dwelling among us" (John 1:14). Scripture reveals the gospel to us in terms of the Triune God's actions in relation to a particular people in all the particularities of their time and place in the world over many generations. We are utterly dependent on human language to speak about the gospel. The gospel engages the full range and all facets of human experience through the narratives of countless people, each speaking in their own vernacular and from within their worldview.

Cultures are restless and dynamic. They rise and fall—flourishing for a time and then stagnating or disintegrating. New cultures arise to replace those that have disappeared. Over the past five centuries, modernity has transformed the world. One of the hallmarks of modern culture has been its universalizing dynamic. One consequence has been the development of an increasingly interconnected global system of relationships. Globalization per se is not new, but a new stage in this process toward an integrated world system has been reached. We have no choice but to recast knowledge and relationships in light of the processes of modern globalization.

At the time of the Protestant Reformation in sixteenth-century Europe, the cultures of the world were all essentially traditional. In traditional culture, people validate actions and practices by appealing to tradition. The emergence of modernity marked a fundamental change

9

by unleashing revolutions in knowledge, technology, political theory, epistemology, and the reorientation of all human endeavors to the future. Modernity was future oriented, and its focus was innovation. The eighteenth-century Enlightenment boldly claimed that its purpose was to discover universal principles, or laws, that would free humankind from the disabling constraints of backward-looking cultural contexts. The Enlightenment program would allow humankind to escape the drudgery of traditional societies by harnessing nature to create a new kind of world. Indeed, modernity has produced a powerful culture that has penetrated all aspects of human life and extended itself to every part of the globe. In this respect, globalization as a process and as a reality is a direct fruit of modernity.

The essays that comprise this volume are dedicated to examining from multiple angles the significance of this process of globalization for theology. The authors hold up mirrors that reflect back to us the fact that the vocabulary, conceptualizations, and institutional forms that have held our modern worldview in place no longer work as they once did. To get our bearings in this new situation requires that we let go of what is worn-out and turn to the hard work of discerning new ways of seeing.

The church has been an active participant in the formation of modern culture. Like every other aspect of Western society, the modern church has been profoundly shaped by modernity and, consequently, is caught up in the crisis that has overtaken the wider culture. Major intellectual breakthroughs along the way advanced the idea that the process of modernization had no limits. As a result, modernity was tempted to overreach. It was self-confident of its ability to identify universals that were independent of cultural context and time, and thus the fruits of modern knowledge could be introduced throughout the world for the benefit of all people. Modern Christians have been largely uncritical of modernity in this regard.

Nowhere were the limits of modernity exposed more starkly than in the cross-cultural situation. The Western insertion into other cultures—first in the form of geographical exploration and the creation of systems of trade, followed by conquest and colonization—set in motion aggressive attempts to modernize and Westernize the rest of the world. Frequently, the West did not read the cultural signals correctly. The apparent acceptance of things Western often disguised the undertow of resistance. Traditional cultures stubbornly stood against the universalizing intent of modernity. The fruits of modernity were appropriated selectively, and ancient cultures did not disappear when modernity came on the scene. Indeed, these primal cultures remained the indispensable vessel that carried global cultural interaction forward. They have proven to be far more durable than was presumed by the promoters of modernity.

The modern missionary movement played an active role as a midwife in introducing modernity—along with the Christian message—to other peoples of the world. But it is too simplistic to say that modern missions were merely the religious adjunct of modernity. As John King Fairbank pointed out long ago, the modern missionary movement, spanning more than two centuries, is the single most extensive experiment in intercultural relationships in human history. What has set it apart historically from all others has been the fact that the essential rationale of the Christian mission was unlike all other movements, including military, cultural, economic, or political conquest. Missionary success was measured by what was shared with the host people, not what was extracted and carried off. In the end, missionaries were forced to abandon the Enlightenment disdain of cultural context, for inherent in the gospel is the demand that people be able to appropriate God's Word to them in their own culture and language. The supreme expression of this commitment has been the translation of Scripture into the vernacular wherever missionaries have gone.

To engage in "globalizing theology" today means that we must guard the commitment to the particular and the local while taking account of the fact that we live with an intensified awareness of the global. If theology is to serve the church throughout the world, it must reflect this bifocal way of seeing; this becomes the vantage point from which we must rethink and revise theology conceptually, methodologically, and programmatically. Paul G. Hiebert, in whose honor this volume is being published, has been at the forefront of analyzing and interpreting this shift. These essays offer rich materials that suggest many of the themes and issues that will be involved in carrying forward the task of developing a theology that is faithful to God's revelation, missionally motivated, and appropriately contextual to the twenty-first century.

Preface

CRAIG OTT AND HAROLD A. NETLAND

Paul G. Hiebert, distinguished professor of anthropology and mission at Trinity Evangelical Divinity School, has repeatedly and prophetically emphasized in his writings the importance of globalizing theology. In honor of Hiebert's seminal contributions to missiology, 180 missiologists, theologians, and friends from fifteen countries gathered June 21–22, 2004, on Trinity's campus in Deerfield, Illinois, for the 2004 Trinity Consultation on Missiology. Under the theme "Doing Theology in a Globalizing World," the consultation took up a number of related issues that have been addressed by Hiebert. The papers presented at that consultation comprise the core of this volume. They were rewritten based on interaction during the consultation. Additional contributions were then solicited to further round out the discussion of this complex topic from a variety of perspectives.

It is the hope of the editors and the contributors that this volume will offer a worthy tribute to Hiebert for his nearly five decades of serving the church through teaching and writing, not to mention his landmark contributions to the fields of missiology, anthropology, and theology. While these essays had their origin at the consultation honoring Hiebert, this is much more than a collection of conference papers. There is thematic unity to the chapters, and the essays, individually and collectively, make fresh contributions that take us further down the road that Hiebert and others have mapped out. Perhaps others—particularly those in theological disciplines other than missiology—will be stimulated through these pages to consider more seriously the implications of world Christianity for theology and praxis and to enter a more global dialogue on theological concerns.

As with any work of this nature, numerous gifted persons were active behind the scenes helping to improve and complete the project. We wish to thank all those students and colleagues who gave helpful critique and encouragement in the writing of these chapters. Special gratitude is owed to Amie Jaworski, who tirelessly attended to countless details of organization and correspondence, facilitating both the original consultation and the completion of this book. We are also grateful for the enthusiastic support of Trinity Evangelical Divinity School in sponsoring the Consultation on Missiology. Finally, we express our appreciation to Jim Kinney and his colleagues at Baker Academic for their encouragement and support in bringing the project to completion.

While these essays will certainly not be the final word on the implications of our globalizing world for doing theology, it is our prayer that our understanding of both the theological task and the rapidly changing world will be enhanced through these reflections.

Introduction

Globalization and Theology Today

HAROLD A. NETLAND

The past century has brought about some unprecedented transformations in our world. Some, however, are more apparent than others. The pervasive impact of modern technology on transportation, communications, and medicine is obvious. Yet arguably of greater significance, though certainly less widely acknowledged, is the enormous change in the demographics of Christianity worldwide. Whereas in 1900 the majority of Christians were in Europe and North America, and Christianity was identified as a Western religion, today most Christians reside in the non-Western world,[1] and Christianity is in decline in much of Europe. Michael Jaffarian observes that "by continent, relative to population growth, in the twentieth century, Christianity saw amazing growth in Africa, strong growth in Asia, slight decline in North America, even slighter decline in Latin America, but more serious decline in Europe" (2002, 19; see also Johnson and Chung 2004). Referring to this shift in the global distribution of Christianity, Philip Jenkins states, "We are currently living through one of the transforming moments in the his-

1. There is no uniformly accepted or nonproblematic way of speaking of various parts of the world. Some use terms such as *two-thirds world, three-fourths world,* or *majority world* to denote the nations and cultures outside Europe and North America. While there is some variety in use among contributors to this volume, in general we use "Western" to refer to the nations and cultures of Europe and North America and "non-Western" for all others.

14

tory of religion worldwide" (2002, 1). Similarly, the editors of the *World Christian Encyclopedia* note that

> during the 20th century, in fact, Christianity has become the most extensive and universal religion in history. There are today Christians and organized Christian churches in every inhabited country on earth. The church is therefore now, for the first time in history, ecumenical in the literal meaning of the word: its boundaries are coextensive with the *oikumene*, the whole inhabited world. (Barrett, Kurian, and Johnson 2001, 3)

According to Lamin Sanneh, "Christianity is the religion of over two thousand different language groups in the world. More people pray and worship in more languages in Christianity than in any other religion in the world" (2003, 69).

But the rise of what we might call world Christianity[2] is part of a broader phenomenon, a series of ongoing processes and relationships affecting ever larger portions of the world that are lumped together under the rubric "globalization." Globalization, and the changes in the nature and distribution of Christianity worldwide in particular, is forcing many to reexamine basic questions about Christian identity and the relation of local Christian communities to other Christian groups and traditions. Some of the implications of this are being explored by missiologists in their concerns with world evangelization (see Hutchinson and Kalu 1998; Taylor 2000a; Tiplady 2003). Less attention, however, has been given by evangelicals to how these new realities affect an understanding of the nature and task of theology. But globalization and the emergence of world Christianity have profound implications for how we do theology.

2. Lamin Sanneh distinguishes between what he calls "world Christianity" and "global Christianity." World Christianity is "the movement of Christianity as it takes form and shape in societies that previously were not Christian, societies that had no bureaucratic tradition with which to domesticate the gospel" (2003, 23). World Christianity thus reflects the changing demographics of Christianity worldwide and the fact that the Christian faith is now "at home" in many diverse social and cultural settings, manifesting a variety of local expressions. Global Christianity, by contrast, refers to "the faithful replication of Christian forms and patterns developed in Europe" (2003, 22). Global Christianity, aligned with European Christendom, is closely linked to the economic, political, and cultural dimensions of globalization, which spread the influences of the West worldwide. Global Christianity suggests "that growing Christian communities of professing Christians around the world are evidence of the economic and political security interests of Europe, that churches everywhere are a religious expression of Europe's political reach, or else a reaction to it" (2003, 23). While Sanneh's distinction is an important one, his definitions are not adopted in this book. For our purposes, world Christianity and global Christianity are used interchangeably to refer to the fact that the church today is found in virtually every country of the world and is increasingly at home in diverse cultural and linguistic expressions, and thus that Christianity can no longer be identified as simply a Western religion or be defined in terms of its European and North American heritage.

This last point no doubt calls for some clarification. It is hardly controversial today to claim that the communication and local expression of the (unchanging) gospel of Jesus Christ must be adapted to changing cultural dynamics. Contextualization is thus now an accepted part of the missiological and theological agenda, even if lingering questions remain about what it means and how we should go about it. But to suggest that theology itself needs to be altered in light of the changing realities in our world will strike some as problematic, since this seems to replace the eternal verities of the faith with the shifting demands of history and culture.

To be sure, theology, properly construed, does deal with unchanging truths revealed by God, truths that apply to all peoples in all cultures. But theology must be distinguished from God's revelatory Word. While it is rooted in God's authoritative revelation and is to be engaged in through prayerful reliance on the guidance of the Holy Spirit, theology itself is a human activity and discipline, and thus it is subject to and reflects the characteristics of those who do theology. Theology is thus an ongoing conversation by fallible human beings, under the guidance of the Holy Spirit, who reflect on God's authoritative revelation in light of current realities. One of the more significant developments of modern times has been globalization, and thus the essays in this book explore implications of globalization for how we should think of theology as a discipline and the manner in which we should do theology. To clarify this focus further, it will be helpful to consider briefly what is meant by both theology and globalization.

Theology

We might begin by considering David Wells's discussion in *No Place for Truth* (1993). Wells suggests that we think of theology as comprising three elements: confession, reflection on this confession, and cultivation of a set of virtues grounded in confession and reflection. Each has implications for how to understand theology in a globalizing world.

Confession, according to Wells, involves what the church believes, namely, "the truth that God has given to the church through the inspired Word of God." Scripture, as the Word of God written, determines what is to be recognized as normative by the church, regardless of the historical or cultural location of particular Christian communities (Wells 1993, 99). Evangelicals maintain that God has revealed himself to humankind in an intelligible manner and that we are to submit to his revelation as truth, allowing it to control our beliefs, even when this truth may not be particularly palatable to contemporary tastes.

Theology also involves reflection, or "the intellectual struggle to understand what it means to be the recipient of God's Word in this present world" (Wells 1993, 99–100). Such reflection must be comprehensive in drawing on the totality of God's revelation in Scripture, making responsible connections between the various parts of Scripture and central themes relating to God's nature and purposes. It should also be shaped by the wisdom of the church in the past, learning from how the church in earlier times understood and applied God's Word in different contexts. Finally, "reflection must seek to understand the connections between what is confessed and what, in any given society, is taken as normative" (Wells 1993, 100).

Theology, then, involves responding to the question, What does it mean to be the recipient of God's Word in this present world? This question is always contextually located, for one always asks it from within a particular historical, social, and cultural location. Moreover, the denotation of "this present world" can vary, at times referring to the entire world and all that this entails, while on other occasions referring to a very specific local context (e.g., early twenty-first-century Japanese businessmen in Osaka).

Who is to respond to this question and thus "do theology"? Wells argues that this is to be done not primarily by the academy or professional theologians but by the church in conjunction with the academy. In other words, theology is not to be relegated to professional theologians alone but ought to be carried out by the church as a whole and is to be utilized in the service of the church. But here the changing realities in our world become significant. Until recently, most Christians were in the West, so that even if theology was understood as belonging to the church as a whole, it was naturally assumed that it was something in which the Western church was to engage. The fact that most Christians now are in the non-Western world clearly has implications for who does theology for the church.

Moreover, answering the question, What does it mean to be the recipient of God's Word in this present world? requires that we understand the world in which we find ourselves. To do this, we must draw on a variety of disciplines distinct from biblical studies, disciplines such as history, cultural anthropology, sociology, economics, religious studies, and so on. Doing theology, then, is a multidisciplinary activity requiring us not only to exegete the Word but also to exegete the contemporary world.

Wells's third component involves "the cultivation of those virtues that constitute a wisdom for life, the kind of wisdom in which Christian practice is built on the pillars of confession and surrounded by the scaffolding of reflection" (1993, 100). Although often neglected, this dimension is critical, for genuine theology cannot be merely an intellectual exercise but must also include that growth in wisdom that transforms not only the understanding but also our dispositions, attitudes, and conduct. In other words, theology should result in "the type of spirituality that is centrally moral in its nature because God is centrally holy in his being, that sees Christian practice not primarily as a matter of technique but as a matter of truth, and that refuses to disjoin practice from thought or thought from practice" (Wells 1993, 100). In doing theology, then, we cannot make sharp distinctions between theology and ethics, or between correct beliefs about God and right behavior with respect to God and our fellow human beings. This too has implications for theology in a globalizing world.

Globalization

Few concepts today are as controversial or as polarizing as that of globalization.[3] That the world is becoming increasingly interconnected is widely acknowledged, but the nature, causes, and implications of this are frequently contested. Peter Berger observes:

> There can be no doubt about the fact of an ever more interconnected global economy, with vast social and political implications, and there is no shortage of thoughtful, if inconclusive, reflection about this great transformation. It has also been noted that there is a cultural dimension, the obvious result of an immense increase in worldwide communication. If there is economic globalization, there is also cultural globalization. To say this, however, is only to raise the question of what such a phenomenon amounts to. (1997, 23)

While we cannot explore globalization in depth here, a brief overview of what the concept means is needed, since it plays such a central role in the essays that follow.

At the heart of the notion of globalization is awareness of an increasingly complex interrelatedness on multiple levels across traditional boundaries. Frank Lechner and John Boli state:

> We are witnessing the consolidation of a new global society. . . . After World War II, the infrastructure for communication and transportation improved dramatically, connecting groups, institutions, and countries in new ways. More people can travel, or migrate, more easily to distant parts of the globe;

3. The literature on globalization is enormous. For a helpful overview of current debates, see the collection of essays in Lechner and Boli (2004b) as well as the discussion in Waters (2001).

satellite broadcasts bring world events to an increasingly global audience; the Internet begins to knit together world-spanning interest groups of educated users. Such links are the raw material of globalization. . . . The world is becoming a single place, in which different institutions function as parts of one system and distant peoples share a common understanding of living together on one planet. This world society has a culture; it instills in many people a budding consciousness of living in a world society. To links and institutions we therefore add culture and consciousness. Globalization is the process that fitfully brings these elements of world society together. (2004a, xvii)

John Tomlinson speaks of globalization as "complex connectivity," by which he means "the rapidly developing and ever-densening network of interconnections and interdependencies that characterize modern social life" (1999, 2). Similarly, Anthony Giddens defines globalization as "the intensification of worldwide social relations which link distant localities in such a way that local happenings are shaped by events occurring many miles away and vice versa" (1990, 64).

But globalization is more than just the *fact* of worldwide interrelatedness; it also includes our heightened *awareness* of this interconnectivity and the effects of this consciousness on local patterns and identities. Malcolm Waters captures this aspect nicely in his definition of globalization as "a social process in which the constraints of geography on economic, political, social and cultural arrangements recede, in which people become increasingly aware that they are receding, and in which people act accordingly" (2001, 5).

Globalization is thus a multidimensional phenomenon involving politics, economics, science, technology, culture, and religion. Emerging in the fifteenth and sixteenth centuries, globalization grew out of the processes and institutions of modernization. The main patterns of globalization were shaped by the economic institutions and practices of free-market capitalism as well as the political alignments and agendas of the Western powers, as earlier world empires gradually were replaced by the modern nation-state. The Cold War realigned the world politically in terms of bipolar relationships—the first and second worlds representing the democratic/capitalist and communist/socialist nations respectively, with the third world resisting such political commitments. The collapse of the former Soviet Union and the end of the Cold War, however, ushered in a new phase characterized politically not by bipolar but by multipolar political relationships.

The interplay between the economic and political dimensions, and the dependence of both on developments in science and technology, is brought out nicely in Thomas Friedman's suggestion that we think of globalization in terms of three distinct developmental stages (2005,

8–11).[4] The first stage began with Columbus's "discovery" of the New World, thereby opening trade between the Old World and the New World, and lasted until roughly 1800. In this stage, "the key agent of change, the dynamic force driving the process of global integration was how much brawn—how much muscle, how much horsepower, wind power, or, later, steam power—your country had and how creatively you could deploy it" (Friedman 2005, 9). The second stage, roughly from 1800 until 2000, was characterized by global integration brought about by large multinational companies. Innovation and greater efficiency in transportation and telecommunications technologies—culminating in the PC, satellites, fiber-optic cable, and early versions of the World Wide Web—were what propelled globalization throughout the twentieth century.

But according to Friedman, sometime around 2000 we entered the third stage of globalization, which is distinguished not only by a much wider use of telecommunications technologies across the globe but also by the resulting empowerment of individuals—not just nations or multinational corporations—to collaborate and compete globally in unprecedented ways (2005, 10). Whereas the earlier stages of globalization were driven by European and American institutions and businesses, the current stage is resulting in a "flattening and shrinking of the world," a leveling of the playing field by removing previous barriers to participation. Friedman argues that increasingly globalization is driven "not only by individuals but also by a much more diverse—non-Western, nonwhite—group of individuals. Individuals from every corner of the flat world are being empowered" (2005, 11).

Globalization is often regarded as primarily a matter of economic relationships, for global interdependence is perhaps most apparent in economics (Robertson 1991, 282). Robert Schreiter observes that with the collapse of Soviet socialist systems in 1989 there has been a resurgence of market capitalism worldwide and an intensification of a global economic system characterized by "its ignoring of national boundaries, its ability to move capital quickly, and its engagement in short-term projects that maximize the profit margin" (1997, 7). Market capitalism is entrenched worldwide and has generated enormous wealth for some. Yet it has not alleviated the poverty of much of the world's population; indeed, the

4. Globalization is both sustained by and reflected in the astonishing recent developments in communications technologies so that messages and visual images can now be communicated virtually instantaneously worldwide. "Globalization has its own defining technologies: computerization, miniaturization, digitization, satellite communications, fiber optics and the Internet. . . . If the defining perspective of the Cold War was 'division,' the defining perspective of globalization is 'integration.' The symbol of the Cold War system was a wall, which divided everyone. The symbol of the globalization system is a World Wide Web, which unites everyone" (Friedman 1999, 8).

gap between the rich and the poor widens, and many contend that the great wealth of some has come at the expense of deepening poverty of the many. The economics of globalization thus invites wildly differing assessments. Some see economic globalization as essentially a positive development that will ultimately produce higher standards of living for most peoples (Micklethwait and Wooldridge 2004; Sen 2004; Dollar and Kraay 2004). Others regard it as profoundly unjust and undemocratic (Stiglitz 2004; Gray 2004; Barber 1996), "a code word for subordination to imperialism" (Petras and Veltmeyer 2001, 154), enriching some at the expense of many.

But globalization involves more than just economic and political inter-relationships; it also affects the culture. Indeed, Malcolm Waters argues that popular culture has shown a greater tendency toward globalization than either the political or the economic sector (2001, 125). Although local cultural distinctives remain, disparate peoples and places are today increasingly linked by common cultural symbols, institutions, values, and behavior. Such commonalities include the growing dominance of English as a means of global communication; eating habits induced by the global spread of the fast-food industry (McDonald's, Starbucks, Pizza Hut, Kentucky Fried Chicken); popular music, movies, and entertainment—what Benjamin Barber calls the "infotainment telesector," or the "wedding of telecommunications technologies with information and entertainment software" (1996, 60); educational systems increasingly patterned after the Western university model; and so on. Barber's identification of globalization with the culture of "McWorld"[5] suggests that globalization is producing one massive global cultural system. But such cultural homogeneity should not be exaggerated, for even with globalization, local cultural patterns do not simply disappear. Rather, the influences of globalization interact with indigenous social and cultural patterns in such ways that what results is not necessarily the elimination of the latter but rather fresh expressions in which the new coexists with, by transforming, the old. The local will always have a kind of priority over the global because, as Tomlinson notes, we are physically embodied creatures, inextricably rooted in particular localities (1999, 9).

Peter Berger (1997) distinguishes several dimensions of cultural globalism, including not only the "McWorld" homogeneity Barber alludes to

5. Barber describes McWorld as the increasingly global culture shaped by "onrushing economic, technological, and ecological forces that demand integration and uniformity and that mesmerize peoples everywhere with fast music, fast computers, and fast food—MTV, Macintosh, and McDonald's—pressing nations into one homogenous global theme park, one McWorld tied together by communications, information, entertainment, and commerce" (1996, 4). Barber is well aware of the fragmenting effects of globalization as well, and he devotes considerable attention to the "counter-globalizing forces" at work worldwide.

but also what he calls the "Davos culture,"[6] associated with economic globalization, and the "faculty club culture," which involves the "internationalization of the Western intelligentsia, its values and ideologies." The faculty club culture "spreads its beliefs and values through the educational system, the legal system, various therapeutic institutions, think tanks, and at least some of the media of mass communication" (1997, 24–25).

It is tempting to dismiss globalization as merely another name for the imposition of Western consumerist culture on the rest of the world—Western imperialism in its latest phase. But this is misleading, since the simple identification of globalization with Westernization confuses the question of the origin of modernization and globalization with that of their current status and effects (see Berger 1997, 26–27; Tomlinson 1999, 63–70, 91–92; Giddens 1990, 52; Robertson 1992, 27). Although globalization did emerge through the expansion of Western powers, and Western economic, political, social, and cultural institutions have been "exported" to the non-Western world, the resulting institutions and processes are today genuinely worldwide, and their influences move in all directions simultaneously. In thinking of globalization in Asia, for example, we must of course acknowledge the flow of influences from the West to the East. But as Koichi Iwabuchi shows, the growing Japanese economic and cultural influences throughout Asia, as well as the many Japanese influences on the West (consider the popularity of sushi or anime in North American culture), are also part of globalization (2002).

Some maintain that the presence of significant antiglobalization movements and the resurgence of nationalism and tribalism in certain sectors show that globalization is waning. But this conclusion is premature. It is true that even as globalization promotes increased interconnectedness and commonalities across traditional ethnic, religious, cultural, and national boundaries, powerful reactionary movements are also resisting globalization as simply economic or political oppression and are reasserting local identities (see Barber 1996, 155–216; Stiglitz 2004). Indeed, as Mark Juergensmeyer argues, the significant rise in religious violence during the late twentieth century can itself be seen as a kind of antimodernizing, antiglobalizing reaction (2003a, 146–47). But these reactionary responses hardly mean that globalization is declining. Roland Robertson notes that "antiglobal movements have inexorably become part of the globalization process itself. This is so because two primary aspects of globalization considered in its comprehensive, as opposed

6. The term is derived from the annual World Economic Summit, which meets in the Swiss luxury resort.

to its economistic, sense are rapidly increasing global connectivity, on the one hand, and fast-expanding and intensifying reflexive global consciousness on the other" (2003, 114–15).

World Christianity

The dramatic changes in the worldwide distribution of Christianity are also part of globalization. Although just over two centuries have elapsed since William Carey published his *Enquiry into the Obligations of Christians to Use Means for the Conversion of Heathens* (1792), the religious landscape of the world today is strikingly different from that of Carey's day. In 1800, Christians overwhelmingly resided in Europe, with newly formed Christian communities (especially Roman Catholic) increasingly found in the Americas and Asia.[7] The link between Christian identity, geography, and culture was strong, so that to be European was to be Christian—allowing, of course, for bitter disputes among Europeans as to just who was *really* Christian—while the rest of the world was heathen.

But with the formal disestablishment of Christianity in much of Europe, Christianity has experienced a steady decline in terms of both numbers of believers and the social significance of Christianity (see Bruce 2002; Jaffarian 2002, 18–20; Johnson and Chung 2004). Much of Europe is now culturally and religiously post-Christian. Moreover, although Christians, in the broadest sense of the term, continue to form the religious majority in much of the West, they share religious space with growing numbers of "religious others." The presence of non-Christian religious traditions has become so pronounced that Diana Eck of Harvard University states, "The United States has become the religiously most diverse nation on earth. . . . Nowhere, even in today's world of mass migrations, is the sheer range of religious faith as wide as it is in the United States" (2001, 4–5).

While Christianity has been declining in some parts of the West, however, it has experienced explosive growth in much of Latin America, Asia, and Africa. Harvey Cox, one of the few Western academics to recognize the significance of these changes, observes that

sometime around 1970 the demographic center of Christianity shifted. Since then the majority of the world's 2 billion Christians are no longer to

7. But as Andrew Walls reminds us (see chap. 3 in this book), from the first centuries of the church on, Christian communities have flourished in portions of North Africa, the Middle East, central Asia, India, and China, and this Christian presence, while somewhat diminished over time, continued throughout the medieval and early modern periods.

be found in old European and North American precincts of Christendom
but in Asia, Africa, and South America. It is startling to realize that the two
largest Christian countries in the world, after the United States, are Brazil
and Mexico (with Russia and China close behind). (2003, 17)

The growth of Christianity in Africa has been especially dramatic.
Lamin Sanneh states that in 1900, with Africa firmly under colonial rule,
there were 8.7 million Christians, about 9 percent of the total population
of 107.86 million (2003, 14–15). Muslims outnumbered Christians by
a ratio of roughly 4:1. "In 1962 when Africa had largely slipped out of
colonial control, there were about 60 million Christians, with Muslims
at about 145 million. . . . In 1970 there were 120 million Christians [in
Africa] estimated; in 1998 the figure jumped to just under 330 million;
and in 2000 to 350 million" (Sanneh 2003, 15, 41). Significantly, the
expansion of Christianity in Africa came *after* the end of colonial rule
(Sanneh 2003, 18).

These changes are part of the globalization of religions. Mark Juergensmeyer states, "Religion therefore has always been global, in the
sense that religious communities and traditions have always maintained permeable boundaries. They have moved, shifted, and interacted
with one another around the globe. . . . Religion is global in that it is
related to the global transportation of peoples and the transnational
acceptance of religious ideas" (2003b, 5). Christianity can be seen as
both an agent in and a product of globalization.[8] Christianity, through
the modern missionary movements of the nineteenth and twentieth
centuries, served as a significant instrument of globalization. That is,
by carrying the gospel worldwide and establishing Christian churches
in linguistic, religious, and cultural contexts in which they did not
previously exist, Christianity was instrumental in globalization. As a
result, a new sense of identity as Christians developed among diverse
local groups, one that transcended and relativized prior indigenous
markers of identity, thereby connecting as fellow Christians what
would otherwise have remained disparate groups. Peter Berger, for
example, claims that "a distinctive process of globalization is provided
by Evangelical Protestantism, especially in its Pentecostal version."
The remarkable growth of Protestant evangelicalism in Latin America,
Africa, and Asia "brings about a cultural revolution" in local social
settings.

8. Christianity is not the only religion to fit this description. Linda Learman states that
"we live in an era in which non-Western traditions, such as Eastern religions, martial arts,
and healing practices, have also spread around the world." Buddhists "are examples of
transnational and cross-cultural movements resulting from and shaped by globalization
but also making use of it" (2005, 1).

It brings about radical changes in the relations between men and women, in the upbringing and education of children, in the attitudes toward traditional hierarchies. Most importantly, it inculcates precisely that "Protestant ethic" that Max Weber analyzed as an important ingredient in the genesis of modern capitalism—a disciplined, frugal, and rationally oriented approach to work. Thus, despite its indigenization (converts in Mexico and Guatemala sing American gospel songs in Mayan translation) Evangelical Protestantism is the carrier of a pluralistic and modernizing culture whose original location is in North American societies. (Berger 1997, 28)

Berger maintains that "this type of Protestantism is creating a new international culture, increasingly self-conscious as such . . . with vast social, economic, and political ramifications" (1997, 28). The processes and institutions of globalization in general also shape linkages among Christians worldwide, producing a sense of being a part of a larger body of believers even as one remains rooted as a Christian within his or her local cultural and social context. The relationship between Christianity and globalization can be seen in the two primary institutions in the late twentieth century for linking Christians worldwide: the Lausanne Movement and the World Evangelical Alliance (formerly World Evangelical Fellowship). They too are not only products of globalization but also institutional factors further intensifying a sense of common identity and interrelatedness among Christians worldwide.[9]

Evangelicals and the Globalization of Theology

The past half century produced a steady stream of significant missiological congresses and consultations, including the International Congress on World Evangelization in Lausanne, Switzerland, in July 1974—arguably one of the most significant events for world Christianity during the twentieth century. The resulting Lausanne Movement promoted further consultations devoted to issues in global evangelization, including the Willowbank Consultation on Gospel and Culture (1978); the International Consultation on Simple Lifestyle (1980); the Pattaya Consultation on World Evangelization (1980); the International Consultation on the Relationship between Evangelism and Social Responsibility, Grand Rapids (1982); the International Conferences for Itinerant Evangelists (1983, 1986); Lausanne II, or the Second International

9. According to its official website, the World Evangelical Alliance is a network of churches in 121 nations and over 100 international organizations "joining together to give a worldwide identity, voice, and platform to more than 335 million Christians" (http://www .worldevangelical.org/wefinfo.html [accessed January 10, 2005]).

Congress on World Evangelization, Manila (1989); and the Forum for World Evangelization, Pattaya (2004). Similarly, the World Evangelical Alliance, especially through the Theological Commission and the Missions Commission, has held numerous consultations addressing theological and missiological issues confronting the global church, including the Theological Commission's consultation on the Unique Christ in Our Pluralistic World held in Manila (1992) and the Missions Commission's Iguassu Missiological Consultation held in Iguassu, Brazil (1999).[10]

Yet while the issues addressed at these many consultations were often theological in nature, individual presentations as well as consultation documents gave little attention to questions about the nature of the theological task itself and how this should be understood in light of global Christianity. Most of the documents seem to take it for granted that there is a consensus on what is meant by theology and acceptable theological method and that the task is simply to bring this to bear on particular issues in world evangelism.[11]

Since the 1970s, however, there have been calls for evangelicals to rethink theology in light of emerging global realities. For example, eighty-five evangelical leaders from seventeen countries came together in Seoul, Korea, in August 1982 for the Sixth Asia Theological Association Theological Consultation. The resulting document, "The Seoul Declaration: Toward an Evangelical Theology for the Third World," stated, "We urgently need an Evangelical theology which is faithful to Scripture and relevant to the varied situations in the Third World" (Ro and Eshenaur 1984,

10. The major papers from the Lausanne consultations are available in Stott (1997). For documents from the WEF consultation on the Unique Christ in Our Pluralistic World, see Nicholls (1994); for the Iguassu Consultation, see Taylor (2000b).

11. Several of the documents issued by the consultations implicitly acknowledge the need for some fresh thinking about how we engage in theology. The Willowbank Report, for example, while affirming the authority of inspired Scripture for all believers in all cultures, recognizes that Scripture is always read from within particular cultures and that local communities of believers must interpret Scripture from within their own contexts. This, of course, produces the tension between the local and the universal in theology, a tension that is acknowledged but not resolved in the report (see Stott and Coote 1980, 313–18). Similarly, the Iguassu Affirmation calls for a return to biblical theology and challenges missiologists "to engage in renewed biblical and theological studies shaped by mission, and to pursue a missiology and practice shaped by God's Word, brought to life and light by the Holy Spirit" (Taylor 2000b, 19). Furthermore, it recognizes the importance of including every part of the global church in the missiological task. "Only thus can our missiology develop the richness and texture reflected in the Scriptures and needed for full obedience to our risen Lord. We commit ourselves to give voice to all segments of the global church in developing and implementing our missiology" (Taylor 2000b, 20). Nevertheless, while the Iguassu Affirmation itself, as well as many of the papers presented at the consultation, are informed by theological reflection, little in the documents addresses explicitly the implications of globalization for doing theology. One of the few exceptions is the paper by Paul Hiebert, "Spiritual Warfare and Worldview," reprinted in Taylor (2000b, 163–77).

23). While acknowledging their "indebtedness to the creeds of the Early Church, the confessions of the European reformation, and the spiritual awakenings of the revival movements of modern times," the writers of the declaration dismissed much of Western theology[12] as irrelevant to non-Western concerns:

> Western theology is by and large rationalistic, moulded [sic] by Western philosophies, preoccupied with intellectual concerns, especially those having to do with faith and reason. All too often, it has reduced the Christian faith to abstract concepts which may have answered the questions of the past, but which fail to grapple with the issues of today. It has consciously been conformed to the secularistic worldview associated with the Enlightenment. Sometimes it has been used as a means to justify colonialism, exploitation, and oppression, or it has done little or nothing to change these situations. Furthermore, having been wrought within Christendom, it hardly addresses the questions of people living in situations characterized by religious pluralism, secularism, resurgent Islam, or Marxist totalitarianism. (Ro and Eshenaur 1984, 22–23)

Similar indictments have been voiced by others, and there have been some significant attempts by Western and non-Western evangelicals to rethink theology in light of the global realities of the church today (cf. Athyal 1980; Conn 1984; Dyrness 1990; 1992; 1994; Han 2002; Hwa 1997; Samuel and Sugden 1983).[13]

To appreciate the call to move beyond Western theology, it might be helpful to refer to two seminal articles by Paul Hiebert. In "Beyond Anticolonialism to Globalism" (1994a),[14] Hiebert suggests that since the European "discovery" of the rest of the world in the fifteenth and sixteenth centuries, the West has moved through three distinct stages in its ongoing encounter with peoples from other races, cultures, religions, and societies. While the stages can be considered chronologically as distinct historical eras, they can also be understood as representing distinct perspectives that need not correlate precisely with historical periods. They thus reflect distinctive ways in which Western churches

---

12. It is, of course, just as misleading to speak of "Western theology," as if all theologians in Europe and North America are alike, as it is to lump together all Asian theologians as doing "Asian theology." There is enormous variety among theologians in the West, in both their methodological approaches and their conclusions. But with proper qualification, such designations can highlight some distinctive tendencies within certain cultural groups.

13. Other publications address implications of globalization for the church and mission without dealing explicitly with the question of theology (see Stackhouse, Dearborn, and Paeth 2000; Tiplady 2003; Hutchinson and Kalu 1998).

14. The article was originally published in *Missiology* 19, no. 3 (July 1991): 263–82. It has been reprinted in Hiebert (1994a), and pagination references here are to the 1994 volume. Hiebert treats similar issues in his chapter in this book.

have struggled to come to grips with deeply embedded cultural, ethnic, and religious differences. They also suggest different understandings of the nature and task of theology.

The first perspective is that of the colonial era, in which European voyages of exploration and trade resulted in foreign settlements, missions, and Western colonial rule of much of Asia, the Americas, and Africa. The legacy of this era was mixed (Hiebert 1994a, 57). On the one hand, introduction of Western advances in medicine, education, science, and agriculture produced undeniable benefits. Moreover, through the sacrificial service of many missionaries, the gospel was carried to the ends of the earth, the Bible was translated into many languages, and the church became established globally. At the same time, the colonial era was steeped in presumptions of Western superiority, resulting in an arrogance that saw little need to take other cultures seriously or to understand them on their own terms. The colonialist paradigm tended to view theology, as conducted in the West, as comprising a systematic set of universal truths that apply to all cultures and thus simply need to be translated into local languages. Just as truth is universal, so too is there one theology for everyone in all cultures.

But as the West was forced to take ethnic, cultural, and religious others more seriously, the colonialist perspective came under attack. More sensitive voices rejected the Western sense of superiority and called for greater understanding of non-Western cultural dynamics. Such changes in perspective were both instrumental in bringing about and also reflective of the enormous social and political transformations accompanying the collapse of Western colonial empires after World War II. Hiebert notes that the anticolonial reaction had profound implications for Christian missions. Mission theorists and practitioners adopted more culturally sensitive approaches, as reflected in, for example, the call by Henry Venn and Rufus Anderson to plant indigenous churches that are self-supporting, self-governing, and self-propagating. Missiologists gave greater attention to the dynamics of culture. While much of this was a needed corrective to the excesses of the colonialist model, the anticolonialist perspective brought with it excesses of its own. Openness to other cultures often resulted in an "uncritical process in which the good in other cultures was affirmed, but the evil in them was left unchallenged" (Hiebert 1994a, 59). Emphasis on local settings in contextualization tended to ignore the broader, transcultural dimensions to the Christian faith. More positive approaches to other religions frequently resulted in uncritical acceptance of other religions, syncretism, and an emphasis on religious dialogue that had no place for evangelism. Pluralism and diversity characterized the approach to theology as well, resulting in the proliferation of multiple local, ethnic, or culturally specific "theologies" at the expense of any unifying framework transcending particular contexts.

Hiebert calls for the church to move beyond both the colonialist and the anticolonialist approach to embrace a responsible, global perspective that acknowledges both commonalities and differences among peoples and that admits both positive and negative elements of local cultures and religious traditions. The arrogance of the past is to be replaced by an incarnational witness that lives out the unchanging truth of the gospel in local settings. Moreover, the privileging of the West in the colonialist paradigm and the prioritizing of non-Western local contexts in the anticolonialist perspective are to be transcended by recognizing that all parts of the global Christian community have contributions to make to the rest of the body of Christ. Hiebert argues that while God's revelation is true and does not vary with cultural differences, our understandings of this truth are partial and incomplete, and thus any particular expression of Christian truth should be open to revision in light of God's Word and the corrective insights of others in the body of Christ.

Similar concerns are expressed in Hiebert's 1988 essay, "Metatheology: The Step beyond Contextualization" (reprinted in 1994c). In addition to the widely accepted "three selves" for non-Western churches—self-governing, self-supporting, and self-propagating—Hiebert advocates a fourth self: self-theologizing. "Do young churches have a right to read and interpret the Scriptures in their own cultural contexts?" (1994c, 97). Surely they do. But will not self-theologizing result in the proliferation of local theologies and thus the relativizing of theology? To avoid this, Hiebert calls for a "metatheology"—a set of procedures for Christian communities globally that enables local Christian communities to do theology within their own local contexts but in conversation with other Christians globally. Scripture remains the source and norm for theology. However, "Just as believers in a local church must test their interpretations of Scriptures with their community of believers, so the churches in different cultural and historical contexts must test their theologies with the international community of churches and the church down through the ages. The priesthood of believers must be exercised within a hermeneutical community" (1994c, 102–3).

Hiebert suggests that the product of such an ongoing process could be a "growing consensus on theological absolutes" (1994c, 103). But this consensus will emerge only through an extended conversation by all parts of the body of Christ as they reflect together on the implications of the Word of God for their diverse settings. Meanwhile, this process will be unsettling for some in the West.

For the moment this will disturb Western churches that see their theological formulations as complete and final. In the end, however, it can help us in the West see where we have sold out to our cultures and where Christianity is in danger of becoming a Western civil religion. It will remind us that the kingdom of God is always prophetic and calls all cultures toward God's ideals, and that citizens of that kingdom are to form living communities that manifest the nature of that kingdom. In such communities, understanding the Word of God must be an ongoing and living process that leads to discipleship under the lordship of Christ in every area of life. (Hiebert 1994c, 103)

The essays in this book are a response to Hiebert's call for the church to develop global perspectives on theology that combine the local or particular with what transcends particular cultural settings and is thus universal.

Globalizing Theology

The contributors to this volume all agree that the changing global dynamics noted above have implications for how we think about theology. Not all agree, of course, on how we should understand and respond to these implications. For example, throughout the essays, there is a tension between whether we should think of "global theology" as a finished product applicable to all Christian communities or whether we should speak rather about "globalizing theology" as an ongoing process. Most contributors emphasize the latter, although some also acknowledge the importance of the former.

But just what do we mean by globalizing theology? Without curtailing the discussion prematurely, the following might serve as a preliminary definition: Globalizing theology is theological reflection rooted in God's self-revelation in Scripture and informed by the historical legacy of the Christian community through the ages, the current realities in the world, and the diverse perspectives of Christian communities throughout the world, with a view to greater holiness in living and faithfulness in fulfilling God's mission in all the world through the church. Thus, theology is to be an ongoing process in which Christian communities throughout the world participate. While theologians from the West can be expected to continue to exert considerable influence in this conversation, non-Western participants should be full partners in the process. Furthermore, although the perennial concerns of theology will remain, the specific issues addressed by theologians should, to some extent, be shaped by the new realities of globalization.

It is important to note that, both in Western and non-Western contexts, there are distinct constituencies or "stakeholders" in the process of globalizing theology, each with somewhat different needs and expectations. For example, the following distinct communities are involved in some way with doing theology: (1) Christian pastors and laity in local churches; (2) denominational leaders; (3) administrators, faculty, and students at Bible schools and seminaries; (4) missionaries and mission agency administrators; and (5) professional theologians as members of academic guilds. The needs, expectations, and, to some extent, the understandings of what theology is vary with each constituency. Yet each constituency is legitimate, and we must avoid privileging one stakeholder at the expense of the others.

The chapters that follow are grouped into three categories. Part 1 sets out the challenges for theology posed by world Christianity and globalization. Tite Tiénou, who has been active in theological education at various levels in Western and non-Western contexts, issues a stirring challenge for the Western church and academic theologians to take seriously the changing nature of world Christianity. Tiénou claims that the provincialism of Western theology must be overcome but that this can happen only when the Western theological academy intentionally addresses systemic issues such as "the hegemony postulate," which governs academic theology. Cultural anthropologist Darrell Whiteman emphasizes the importance of utilizing multiple disciplines in doing theology in the context of globalization. He shows how the disciplines of anthropology and theology are brought into fruitful dialogue in several of the seminal writings of Paul Hiebert, with significant implications for globalizing theology.

No one is better qualified to reflect on the worldwide spread of Christianity and the implications of this for theology than the eminent historian Andrew Walls. Walls reminds us that from its inception Christianity has been crossing boundaries and moving into ever new environments. World Christianity today is the latest phase of this ongoing process. Reflecting on his experience of over half a century in academic life around the globe, Walls looks at the discipline of Christian history as practiced in the West and pleads for an approach that is less provincial and includes the story of the genuinely global expansion of the church.

The chapters comprising part 2 focus more explicitly on methodological issues in globalizing theology. Theologian Kevin Vanhoozer proposes a fresh and nuanced way of understanding theology as theodrama—the words and acts of the Triune God. "Theology is faith seeking theodramatic understanding. . . . Christians demonstrate their understanding of the theodramatic gospel by speaking and acting in ways that correspond to what God has done in Christ through the Spirit." Theodrama is guided by the "canonical principle," which insists that theology be appropriately rooted in Scripture, and the "catholic principle," which regards the ethnic and social diversity of the church worldwide as "the condition for an enriched and enlarged theological understanding," resulting in Christians "speaking and doing the same truth differently."

The tension between the global and the local in theology has already been noted. Are there principles or precedents in Scripture that provide guidance in addressing the relationship between local concerns and universal truth? David Strong and Cynthia Strong examine the Jerusalem Council in Acts 15 as an example of a "hermeneutical community" and derive from it some principles that should inform the contemporary discussion.

Another way to get at the tension between the local and the universal is to consider the nature of the early ecumenical creeds and their normative role for all Christians. But which creeds? And were not the creeds themselves the product of local Christians' reflection on issues emerging within their own times and places? In what sense, then, should they be normative for Christians at later times in different settings? Evangelicals typically appeal to the authority of inspired Scripture and the lordship of Jesus Christ as defining what is universal and normative for all Christians. But how are we to interpret Scripture and to understand the person of Jesus Christ? Evangelicals look to the christological formulations of Nicea (325) and Chalcedon (451) as setting the parameters for acceptable perspectives on Christ. But must all Christians, in all cultures and times, embrace these particular formulations? Steve Strauss provides a fascinating case study of Christology within the Ethiopian Coptic Church and its reaction against the Christology of Chalcedon, in which these issues are prominent.

Charles Van Engen picks up on the notion of glocalization—a concept developed by Roland Robertson and others (Robertson 1995; Tomlinson 1999, 197) to signify the dynamic interrelatedness of the global and the local in particular contexts—as a way of understanding the relationship between local communities of believers and the global church. Local churches are to be involved simultaneously in God's mission locally and globally—that is, they are to be "glocal" in their self-understanding and ministry.

Anthropologist Robert Priest reminds us that theology involves not only a proper understanding of God but also an accurate understanding of human selves. For the latter, the theologian must draw on not only God's revealed Word but also those disciplines—especially the social and human sciences—that enable us to understand people's actual lived experiences. Based on his own experience among the Aguaruna in Peru, Priest shows the significance of careful ethnography and the use of "experience-near" concepts for understanding human realities and unpacking biblical themes relating to sin. Priest's essay has powerful implications not just for missionaries in cross-cultural settings but for everyone engaged in doing theology.

Part 3 includes essays examining a range of specific issues connected with globalization and the church. M. Daniel Carroll R., an Old Testament scholar who has lived much of his life in Guatemala, focuses on the central place of economics in globalization, arguing that "globalization requires a hermeneutics of responsibility." He reminds us that "the hegemonic capitalism that largely defines our lives must be processed theologically, even as our theologies themselves need to be examined for any possible ideological captivity and/or potential to nurture alternative biblical perspectives and values."

Modernization and globalization have directly affected understandings of ethnic, cultural, religious, and national identity. In a richly textured historical and cultural discussion, Vinoth Ramachandra explores ways in which national and religious identities—Western, Eastern, British, Indian, Hindu, Christian, Muslim—were formed through the confluence of many factors in the nineteenth and twentieth centuries. Religion has been, and remains today, a powerful resource for nationalist movements.

But, of course, it is not only "religious others" who have been shaped by the historical and cultural forces of their times; Christianity, including the modern missionary movement, is itself subject to these influences. Given the dominance of the United States worldwide since World War II, the fact that American evangelicals have been at the forefront of the missionary movements of the past sixty years, and the widespread perception that in some sense America is a "Christian nation," we need to ask, What does it mean for American Christians to live as followers of Jesus in our globalizing world? (see Avram 2004). Ramachandra reminds us of ways in which Christian witness in India in the past was compromised through linkages—both perceived and real—between Christian missions and British colonialism. But he correctly points out that we are now living through another era in which Christianity is again perceived by many as a partner with a dominant political, economic, and cultural system—that of the United States. Many assume today that Christianity can be identified with American cultural values and foreign policy initiatives, especially as these are played out in the Middle East. Globalization means that these cannot be treated merely as domestic issues for Americans; they carry theological and missiological implications for the global church. Eloise Hiebert Meneses picks up where Ramachandra leaves off and issues a prophetic challenge to Christians in the United

States—the Rome of our time—to resist Christian nationalism by choosing Jesus over Caesar.

The globalization of the church includes the recent phenomenon of non-Western missionaries, or the genuinely worldwide expansion of missionary activity. Missions now is from everywhere to everywhere. James Plueddemann examines this development and the implications of it for both mission agencies and theological education. In a similar vein, Lois McKinney Douglas draws on her half century of involvement in theological education in various cultures for her reflections on challenges and opportunities for global theological education.

Anthropologist Paul Hiebert, in whose honor these essays were written, considers what paradigm should inform our understanding of missions and missionaries in the twenty-first century. Hiebert suggests that in our globalizing world, where boundaries are more fluid and all Christians—not just cross-cultural missionaries—encounter cultural and religious others, missionaries can serve a vital function as mediators. With their intercultural sensitivities, missionaries are "'inbetweeners,' standing between different worlds, seeking to build bridges of understanding, mediating relationships, and negotiating partnerships in ministry." One significant context for such mediation is in global theologizing, where a missionary can help mediate between those doing primarily local theologies and those more concerned with the universal dimension of theology as truth for everyone.

Editor Craig Ott concludes by summarizing some of the salient themes running through the essays. But Ott moves beyond summary to note what still remains to be done in globalizing theology and to offer some concrete recommendations for the future. As evangelicals, we are in the early stages of considering the implications of globalization for theology. But these essays provide grounds for hope that evangelical theology can indeed become more reflective of the Triune God we serve and the rich diversity of his global church.

Part 1

World Christianity and
Theological Reflection

1

Christian Theology in an Era of World Christianity

TITE TIÉNOU

Globalization, understood as the awareness "that the world is rapidly coming to be apprehended as 'one place,' . . . a totality wherein discrete selves, nation-states, and even civilizational traditions have their respective niches, each interconnected by complex, reticular relationships" (Garrett and Robertson 1991, ix), is not a new phenomenon. Today, however, the reality of globalization seems to be more evident for an increasing number of the world's population. Not surprisingly, this reality has generated publications on religion and globalization. A few examples will suffice here: *Religions/Globalizations: Theories and Cases* (Hopkins, Lorentzen, and Mendieta 2002), *Globalizing the Sacred: Religion across the Americas* (Vásquez and Marquardt 2003), *A Global Faith: Essays on Evangelicalism and Globalization* (Hutchinson and Kalu 1998), "Toward a Global Church History" (Shenk 1996), "Shifting Southward: Global Christianity since 1945" (Robert 2000), *The Next Christendom: The Coming of Global Christianity* (Jenkins 2002), *One World or Many? The Impact of Globalisation on Mission* (Tiplady 2003), and *Whose Religion Is Christianity? The Gospel beyond the West* (Sanneh 2003). These publications provide ample evidence of the "polycentric nature of Christianity" (Tiénou 1993) for academic and nonacademic readers. Polycentric Christianity is Christian faith with many cultural homes. The fact that Christianity is at home in a multiplicity of cultures, without being permanently wedded to any one of them (Tiénou 1993), presents for Christians everywhere a unique opportunity for examining Christian identity (Choong 1998; Shenk 2001) and Christian theology.

During the last two decades of the twentieth century, the Association of Theological Schools in the United States and Canada examined the effect of globalization on theological education in North America through its Task Force on Globalization.[1] In June 1999, the Association of Theological Schools adopted its *Guidelines for Evaluating Globalization in ATS Schools*. Globalization is currently an aspect of the "Characteristics of Theological Scholarship" of the "General Institutional Standards" of the ATS Standards of Accreditation (2002, 54). Yet as Donald Lewis says, globalization "appears to have become all things to all theologians" (1998, 37). Indeed, in spite of the attention paid to *Globalization and the Classical Theological Disciplines* (1993), Christian theology does not seem to be greatly affected by globalization. This may be due, in part, to the four meanings of globalization the Association of Theological Schools considers acceptable: "the church's universal mission to evangelize the world"; "ecumenical cooperation between the various manifestations of the Christian church throughout the world"; "dialogue between Christianity and other world religions"; and the mission of the church in its social and political dimensions (1999; Browning 1986, 43–44). Nothing in these four meanings of globalization suggests that it has a bearing on Christian theology itself.

With the foregoing in mind, I examine in the following pages the implications of globalization for Christian theology because "the task in the twenty-first century is to conceptualize theology in light of the fact that the Christian faith is global with multiple heartlands" (Shenk 2001, 105). The purpose here is not to propose a theological method for an era of world Christianity but to inquire about the conditions for a world conversation on Christian theology. I chose the present approach because world Christian theologizing cannot take place without worldwide conversation. For this reason, the following reflections seek to establish the framework for world conversation on theological method. I first state my convictions regarding the nature and purpose of the theological task. Second, I review the status of contemporary world Christianity. Third, I

1. The Association of Theological Schools in the United States and Canada devoted four issues of its journal, *Theological Education*, to globalization and theology: "Globalizing Theological Education in North America" (Spring 1986); "Global Challenges and Perspectives in Theological Education" (Autumn 1986); "Globalization and the Classical Theological Disciplines" (Spring 1993); and "Globalization and the Practical Theological Disciplines" (Autumn 1993).

examine the challenges of making Christian theology an endeavor and a conversation in which Christian theologians from the world community participate fully.

The Theological Task: Nature and Purpose

Theology is essential and indispensable for Christian living. This fact was recognized by nontheologian Dorothy L. Sayers (1969; 1980). For Christians, theology is necessary because it enables them to think and live Christianly so that they can love God fully, with heart, mind, soul, and strength. This implies that theologians should envision their task as one that helps "the faithful to think theologically, by which one basically means thinking Christianly" (Williams 2000, 161). This understanding of the theological task is grounded in the conviction that "theology is about making Christian decisions in critical situations" (Walls 2002a, 222). That may be the reason for what Tshishiku Tshibangu, a Catholic theologian from the Democratic Republic of the Congo, stated many years ago: Church life cannot exist without active theology (1987, 7: *"il n'y a pas de vie d'Eglise sans théologie en activité"*). Theologians, then, are called to foster active theology and to participate in sustaining it. They must do so by always remembering that Christian life needs participation in a community of disciples (Bonhoeffer 1954). Meaningful participation in a community of disciples requires that theologians live and work with humility as they seek to cultivate "creative fidelity" and "joyful performance" in Christ's followers (Vanhoozer 1995).

The development of active theology that nurtures "creative fidelity" and "joyful performance" grows out of the understanding that "Christian theology is not merely 'Christianity defensively stated.' It is also entrusted with the duty of 'Christian self-expression'" (Turner 1952, 16). Moreover, it takes for granted "the character of theology as Christian intellectual activity on the frontier with the non-Christian world, and hence as essentially communicative, evangelistic and missionary" (Bediako 1995, 259; see also Turner 1952; Bosch 1991). This character of theology helps legitimize what Wilbert Shenk calls "a new criterion of theological validity," whereby *"only theology that motivates and sustains the church in witness and service in the world deserves to be accredited"* (2001, 105, italics in the original). Consequently, the nature and purpose of the theological task require that it be a shared task because "Christian theology . . . is an intellectual enterprise by and for the Christian community" (Grenz 2000, 203). To say that the theological task is a shared one means that it cannot be done by one person or even a single group of people; the theological task is a communal one. The communal nature of the task applies to theological method also, for "method is not a set of rules to be followed meticulously by a dolt. It is a framework for collaborative creativity" (Lonergan 1972, xi). If it is granted that theological method "is a framework for collaborative creativity," then it is important to understand who, today, may participate in the theological task. This brings us to the second part of this chapter, namely, the shape of contemporary world Christianity.

Contemporary World Christianity: Where Is the Center?

Today, the people who should participate in the theological task come from a Christian community that is ever wider, since "the new reality of the Christian community can be fully appreciated only from a global perspective" (Shenk 1996, 56). We know, thanks to the works of numerous scholars (mostly missiologists and historians of world Christianity), that the Christian faith is no longer the faith of white Western people alone. David Barrett, Dana Robert, Wilbert Shenk, Lamin Sanneh, Andrew Walls, Kwame Bediako, and Philip Jenkins (to name only a few) have taught us that the center of gravity of world Christianity has shifted to the South.

Missiologists have known this fact for a long time, even though it may surprise the general population as well as many Christians. Indeed, in his 1989 Friends of St. Colm's public lecture, Andrew Walls stated that "the twentieth century has seen the most staggering development in the church for at least a millennium" (1989, 2).[2] For Walls, this "most staggering development" is the result of two major changes: the de-Christianization of the West and the Christianization of the non-Western world. Walls provides the following statistical evidence. "In 1900, 83% of the world's Christians lived in North America and Europe. Today [in 1989], something approaching 60% live in Africa, Asia, Latin America and the Pacific" (1989, 3). Note that this change occurred in less than a century. No wonder Walls could only come to the conclusion that "we have seen a massive change in the centre of gravity of the Christian faith, so that Africa has become one of its heartlands" (1989, 3). I sometimes refer to the change in world Christianity as the literal darkening of Christianity's complexion.

2. It is worth noting that before Jenkins's *Next Christendom* was published in 2002, readers of nonacademic publications had similar information available. For instance, *Christianity Today* featured the globalization of the Christian church in its November 16, 1998, issue with several articles dedicated to the theme "Now That We Are Global." In the general press, *Time* (Europe) focused on the growth of Christianity in Africa (February 2000).

The published literature on the southward shift of Christianity's center of gravity (including statistical documentation) tells only part of the story, for the darkening of Christianity's complexion cannot be fully documented in published form. For one thing, some of the documentation will remain inaccessible to scholars who read European languages exclusively. This is why documentation is needed on grassroots Christianity in Africa written in African languages or on Chinese Christianity written in Chinese. Moreover, much of the story of Christianity around the world remains untold. Commenting on the African situation specifically, Kwame Bediako suggests that "African Christianity must be distinguished from the literature on African Christianity" (n.d., 1–2). Similarly, world Christianity must be distinguished from the literature on world Christianity. Nevertheless, the literature on Christianity around the world provides sufficient information that things have changed dramatically. The change implies an increasing non-Western imprint on the Christian religion. We must, for this reason, keep in mind that "what at first glance appears to be the largest world religion is in fact the ultimate local religion" (Robert 2000, 56). We may therefore have to consider the adoption of a new vocabulary such as that suggested by Lamin Sanneh: "world Christianity" instead of "global Christianity." He writes:

> World Christianity is not one thing but a variety of indigenous responses through more or less effective local idioms, but in any case without necessarily the European enlightenment frame. "Global Christianity," on the other hand, is the faithful replication of Christian forms and patterns developed in Europe. (2003, 22)

Sanneh's distinctions may not persuade everyone, but it is a helpful description of two ideas: (1) Christianity is a world religion because it is a local religion, and (2) "flexibility at the local level, combined with being part of an international network, is a major factor in Christianity's self-understanding and success today" (Robert 2000, 56). These two ideas provide a good framework for understanding the reality of the Christian religion in the world today. This is why "world Christianity" has been used in this chapter.

The shift of Christianity's center of gravity is good news because it means that, as a global reality, the Christian faith is increasingly at home in many cultures and will not be imprisoned by any single culture. The good news, in this case, is that since people of color now represent the majority of Christians in the world, the perception of Christianity as a Western religion can be corrected. Making the case for Christianity on the basis that it is a worldwide global religion can, especially in Africa, erase the stigma of Christianity as a white man's religion. This will bring about apologetic dividends not only for Christians in Africa but also for those in Asia, Latin America, and the Pacific Islands. In other words, if Christianity is de-Westernized, Christians in Africa, Asia, and Latin America will be able to defend themselves when accused of being agents of Westernization and puppets in the hands of foreigners whose intention is the destruction of local cultures and religions.

The apologetic dividends of a non-European Christianity may also apply to the United States and some European countries. Sociologist R. Stephen Warner contends that the immigration of people of color into the United States "represent[s] . . . the de-Europeanization of American Christianity" (2004, 20), while Walter Hollenweger notes that "in many European cities there are more black, yellow and brown Christians coming together on a Sunday morning than white Christians" (2003, 94).

I am fully aware of the fact that many around the world continue to perceive Christianity as a Western religion. This perception does not, however, alter the reality that Christianity is now a local world religion. As Lamin Sanneh writes, "Christianity as a truly world religion [is] increasingly defined by the values and idioms of non-Western cultures and languages" (1997, 296; see also Robert 2000; Walls 1989). Yet one would not know that Christianity is increasingly non-Western if one reads publications such as Samuel Huntington's *Clash of Civilizations* (1996).

It is remarkable that in this book, published in 1996, Huntington states, "The West is now universally used to refer to what used to be called Western Christendom" (1996, 46). This statement seems to accredit the idea that Christianity is Western, especially if one accepts, as Huntington apparently does, the proposition that "religion is a central defining characteristic of civilization" (1996, 47). Western civilization, then, continues to be defined by the Christian religion.

Huntington does not mention a particular civilization pertaining to Africa. This is how Huntington deals with the African situation: "Most major scholars of civilization, except Braudel, do not recognize a distinct African civilization" (1996, 47). Huntington cites many reasons for the nonexistence of African civilization. Among the explanations given, of course, is the usual idea about "tribal identities" being pervasive in Africa. But what is most intriguing and interesting is the following statement: "Most significantly, European imperialism brought Christianity to most of the continent south of the Sahara. . . . Conceivably sub-Saharan Africa could cohere into a distinct civilization with South Africa possibly being its core state" (1996, 47).

It has been noted that "Huntingdon's [*sic*] hypothesized 'African civilization' has always been one of the least convincing parts of his argument" (Ranger 2002, 265). Be that as it may, what should one make of his assertion about Africa? Why has Huntington emphasized European imperial Christianity and not paid sufficient attention to the long presence of Christianity on the continent? Is it true that the presence of Christianity in Africa has obliterated African civilizations? If so, how can a distinct African civilization "cohere" around one of the most Christianized countries of the continent? Moreover, why did the presence of Christianity in Asia not produce the same effects?

Chee Pang Choong, from Trinity College in Singapore, provides an Asian perspective on some of the ideas expressed by Huntington. According to him, "Western or the West is . . . used rather broadly or loosely as a synonym for Christian or Christianity minus the 'Slavic Orthodox civilization'" (1998, 222). For Choong, this constitutes a serious problem because it only reinforces "the already common impression and prejudice in the non-Western world that Christianity is a Western entity rather than a cross-cultural and universal religion" (1998, 222). For Christians in Asia and Africa, then, Huntington's ideas provide arguments only for Asian and African critics of the Christian faith. This is because "the Christian population in Asia seems to have been ignored completely. Huntington seems to have failed to recognize the very important fact that the Christian population or 'map' worldwide has changed significantly since World War II" (Choong 1998, 223). In failing to acknowledge the worldwide nature of the Christian faith, Huntington and others only perpetuate the identification of Christianity with the West. As long as people continue to perceive Christianity as Western, the changes in world Christianity will not have the impact they deserve.

Major changes have indeed occurred in world Christianity. These changes are known by missiologists and historians of world Christianity and less known by Christians who are not in missiology and similar disciplines in the West. The southward shift of Christianity's center of gravity is hardly noticed or seriously taken into account by scholars who happen not to be Christian.

Non-Christian scholars may be able to ignore the shift in Christianity's center of gravity. For Christian scholars (even those in the West), ignoring this southward shift has detrimental effects. Christian scholars, especially the theologians among them, need to be aware of the change in Christianity's center of gravity because

the faith of the twenty-first century will require a devout, vigorous scholarship rooted in the soil of Africa, Asia, and Latin America, [for] the majority of Christians are now Africans, Asians, Latin Americans, and Pacific Islanders. . . . Christianity is now primarily a non-Western religion and on present indications will steadily become more so. . . . The most urgent reason for the study of the religious traditions of Africa and Asia, of the Amerindian and the Pacific peoples, is their significance for Christian theology; they are the substratum of the Christian faith and life for the greater number of the Christians in the world. (Walls 1997, 153)

In light of the foregoing, perhaps the question should be, Why has Christian scholarship paid so little attention to the "majority of Christians"? Is it because few Christian scholars, even theologians, agree with Andrew Walls that "the future of the Christian faith, its shape in the twenty-first and twenty-second centuries, is being decided by events which are now taking place in Africa, in Asia, and Latin America, or which will do so in the near future"? (1989, 3). What would happen to Christian scholarship and theology if all Christian scholars and theologians (from Northern as well as Southern continents) really believed that the future of Christianity no longer depends on developments in the North?

Acknowledging the fact that the majority of Christians are no longer Westerners is one thing. One may even concede that the demographic future of Christianity belongs to Africa, Asia, and Latin America. Does this also mean that the future of Christian theology and scholarship is being decided on these continents as well? One cannot presume a positive answer to this question in spite of the fact that Andrew Walls affirms that "the primary responsibility for the determinative theological scholarship for the twenty-first century will lie with the Christian communities of Africa, Asia, and Latin America" (2002a, 221–22). Take Africa as an example. Kwame Bediako says that "African Christianity has not attracted as much attention as its massive presence would appear to require" (1995, 263). Similar observations can be made about Asian and Latin American Christianities. Yet Bediako is hopeful. In spite of the current Afro-pessimism and views on Africa's marginalization in today's world, Bediako believes that "in one particular respect, and perhaps others too, Africa will not be marginalized, and that is in the field of scholarship, and specifically Christian and religious scholarship" (1995, 253).

I do not share Bediako's optimism fully. For me, optimism must be tempered by the following observation made by Walls in 1991:

In the last three decades literally hundreds of Africans and Asians have qualified at doctoral or equivalent level in Western theological institutions. Many of them did work of high quality in the process, and not a few contributed substantially to knowledge by their research. The expectation was that these would be the standard-bearers of the theological scholarship in the Southern continents. Clearly there were among them those who are standard-bearers in any company, who exercise an impact throughout the world. But equally clearly, the impact on scholarship of this core of highly qualified people, taken as a whole, does not seem commensurate with their talents or training. . . . But the rule of the palefaces over the academic world is untroubled. The expected publications do not materialize; or they have little international effect. And this seems to hold even in studies specifically directed to regional questions. (1991, 152)

I realize these words were written fifteen years ago. Has there been no improvement? Is the third world still marginalized in Christian scholarship and theology? While one cannot honestly say that the situation remains as Walls described it in 1991, it is also clear that Christian scholarship and theology are not yet endeavors in which scholars and theologians from Africa, Asia, Latin America, and the Pacific Islands participate fully. The theological scholarship from these new centers of Christianity still needs to make its mark in a substantial way. As Frans Wijsen writes:

> Often European theologians eagerly take up contextual theologies from Africa, Asia and Latin America, but they do not change their Western outlook and view of theology. They treat third world theologies as if they are exotic fruit to supplement their traditional European dishes. (2004, 173)

As long as this situation remains, there will not be full participation by the producers of these "exotic" theological creations.

Christian Theology as a World Endeavor: Challenges

The full participation of theologians and scholars from the new centers of the Christian faith presents a number of challenges. It may be useful, therefore, to review some of these challenges by asking the question, Why, to use Walls's words, is "the rule of the palefaces untroubled" in Christian theology and scholarship? In my mind, "the rule of the palefaces" continues because of the paradox observed by Kenyan theologian John Mbiti: "The Church has become kerygmatically universal, but is still theologically provincial" (1976, 8). Perhaps this paradox helps explain why relatively few people realize that the change in Christianity's center of gravity "has not only statistical but theological implications as well" (Frostin 1985, 127).[3] One may indeed acknowledge that the theological implications of this reality should lead to the development of Christian theologies from Africa, Asia, and Latin America (McGrath 2000). Nevertheless, the theologies of the Western "province" of the church continue their dominance, even if today "Western theological leadership of a predominantly non-western church is an incongruity" (Walls 2002a, 221).

3. This article, which was published in 1985, is an adaptation of a paper delivered at the seventh Nordic Systematic Theology Congress held in Copenhagen in 1983.

Christian theology and scholarship will remain provincial as long as some major challenges continue unaddressed. These include the following: the West's "hegemony postulate" (Frostin 1985), the West's self-perception that it is "the center," the perception of third world scholars as "purveyors of exotic, raw intellectual material to people in the North" (Kalilombe 1998, 19), and the "dialogue of the deaf" (Mazrui 1990) between the West and the rest of the world.

The West's hegemony postulate is the first important challenge we must face. The expression "hegemony postulate" comes from Per Frostin. He explains it in these words:

> In discussing Third World Theologies with Scandinavian colleagues, I have frequently encountered arguments of the following character: It is interesting that Third World Christians create new types of theology, but I can dialogue with them only on the condition that they state their critique of Western theology in a manner understood by me as scientific. In other words, the prerequisite of a dialogue is that the other party accepts "our" rules, since only these rules are genuinely scientific. This prerequisite for dialogue is . . . the *hegemony postulate*. (1985, 131, italics in original)

The West's hegemony postulate can be seen in other places. One may detect its presence in certain international gatherings. The 2001 Conference against Racism held in Durban, South Africa, is an illustration. Writing in the *Chicago Tribune*, Yvonne Scruggs-Leftwich states that the discord at the conference "was fueled by Western nations' determination to have their own way and to play by their own rules" (2001, sec. 8, p. 6).

The hegemony postulate may also appear in statements about the West's contribution to the world. Consider, for example, the opinion expressed by Robert Royal, then vice president at the Ethics and Public Policy Center in Washington, D.C.:

> Despite its many shortcomings and occasional atrocities, this Western dominance is providential. No better champion of justice, fairness, liberty, truth, and human flourishing exists than the complex and poorly known entity we call Western Civilization. The West, in the broadest sense of the term, produced both the New Testament and the Marquis de Sade, Francis of Assisi and Hitler. Yet, its rise has, in the main, been a blessing to the human race. The West's weakening or demise would pose a threat to many human virtues. Recovering and extending Western principles remain our best hope for a more humane world. For in these matters, there is no serious rival to the West. (1998, 17)

How does this view of providential Western dominance affect the participation of the third world in Christian scholarship in general and theological scholarship specifically? In my opinion, this view affects Christian scholarship whether its proponents are Christian or non-Christian. Can third world Christian scholarship be taken seriously by Christians, especially those in the West, who hold such a view? We may find a clue in what happened at the 1998 Lambeth Conference. African and Asian bishops were the majority at the 1998 Lambeth Conference of the worldwide Anglican Communion. Yet this did not prevent Bishop Spong of Newark, New Jersey, from dismissing the views of African bishops on human sexuality. As Lamin Sanneh reports, "He called those who did not agree with his progressive view on the subject backward and primitive in their reading of Scripture" (1998, 4). Bishop Spong's attitude illustrates the hegemony postulate as well as the West's self-perception that it is the center. This self-perception is the second challenge.

The West's self-perception that it is the center of scholarship is a corollary of the hegemony postulate. Here the assumption is that the West represents the center of scholarship and the rest (usually Africa, Asia, and Latin America) fits in the margins. This assumption is seen in the reflex of dismissing third world scholarship without real or adequate basis. So, for example, a seminary president in the United States can declare an African seminary "not a real seminary." I have encountered this on numerous occasions. The most recent one relates specifically to the West Africa Alliance Seminary, a seminary in Abidjan, Côte d'Ivoire, that I helped establish in 1993. I was dismayed to hear that the president of a U.S. seminary made this remark about it: "This school they call seminary in Abidjan is not a real seminary." My immediate question was How does he know? He had not visited the school at the time. As far as I know, he does not know French and is not acquainted with the details of academic life in the Francophone world. I find this remark puzzling. What is a "real seminary"? How does one determine its "reality" from a distance?

The West's self-perception that it is the center of scholarship is not limited to theology and Christian scholarship. It affects many academic disciplines. Commenting on literary studies, Christopher Miller writes, "The figure of the marginalized Africanist . . . is largely true to life. My contention is that Africa has been allowed to contribute almost nothing to the Western academy up to the present moment" (1993, 220).

Miller observes that "before the 1960s, Africa had been almost exclusively the province of anthropologists. Africans were seen more as cultural objects than producers of cultural interpretations" (1993, 219). We must not think that this view of Africans has disappeared completely. African scholars encounter it in Western academic institutions as they discover the contributions they are expected to bring. The nature of this contribution constitutes the third challenge.

Many third world Christian scholars have experienced the frustration of realizing that their contribution to the Western academy is that of "purveyors of exotic, raw intellectual material to people in the North" (Kalilombe 1998). In seminaries, this role fits more in mission studies or the practical disciplines. In the so-called theoretical disciplines of the theological academy, third world scholars often encounter "the hermeneutical strategy of negation at work," with the result that in biblical studies third world hermeneuts see "the systematic editing-out of their work" (Sugirtharajah 2003, 93). In this regard, I have often wondered if the real value of an African theologian to a Northern/Western seminary may not have more to do with his or her *Africanness* than with his or her expertise in a particular discipline. African scholars are forever asked to provide African comments and illustrations on all sorts of things. The Africans' scholarly expertise suffers in the long run. Consequently, "despite individual achievements and reputations, African scholarship is at best marginal, and at worst nonexistent, in the total intellectual and scientific endeavor in the world. . . . We have no choice but to produce what is ultimately a derived discourse" (Irele 1991, 63–64). This is a case of inclusion by marginalization. As long as this persists in Christian circles, Christian theologizing cannot be a world endeavor.

The "rule of the palefaces" continues in Christian scholarship and in theology for a fourth reason: the dialogue of the deaf between the West and the rest. In his *Cultural Forces in World Politics*, published in 1990, Ali Mazrui observed that America and the third world are engaged in a dialogue of the deaf. This characterization is applicable to the relationship between Western Christian scholars and those in Africa, Asia, and Latin America. Mazrui contends that in this dialogue of the deaf "Americans are brilliant communicators but bad listeners" (1990, 116). Today, America's bad listening skills prevent it from hearing the third world. Are Western Christian scholars better listeners than Mazrui's America? If they were, they would not continue the practice of marginalizing third world theologies and Christian scholarship. I see bad listening from Western Christians and theologians when, for them, the rubric "third world theologies" means that "the contextuality and historical process of their development are neglected and/or homogenized" (Sugirtharajah 2003, 163).

Moreover, according to Mazrui, the dialogue of the deaf between America and the third world is the result of what he calls six languages of American policy toward the third world. The sixth language, the English language (Mazrui 1990, 118), is the most relevant to our concerns here. English seems to be the language of global Christianity; it dominates international Christian conferences and international theologizing. According to Andrew Walls, "In 1910, English set out on its career as the successor to Latin as the international language of theology. The full implications of this for the world church remain to be faced" (2002b, 62). The present domination of English in international theologizing effectively closes the door to theologians who do not express their thoughts in that language. But can Christian scholarship and theology be truly global with one language in control? The use of English as the de facto language for international theological scholarship can only reinforce the dialogue of the deaf.

The dialogue of the deaf between the West and the rest is not limited to matters pertaining to theology. It is real especially in scientific matters, and it prevents Westerners from listening to people from the third world. Commenting specifically on Africa, Howard French says that "in matters of knowledge, science and medicine in particular, the outside world has never grown accustomed to listening to Africans, or respecting their knowledge of 'serious' matters" (2004, 64). Bad listening also occurs in other arenas. It can be seen, for instance, in the remarks made by Italian prime minister Silvio Berlusconi in Berlin on September 26, 2001. Uli Schmetzer of the *Chicago Tribune* reports him to have said:

> We should be conscious of the superiority of our civilization, which consists of a value system that has given people widespread prosperity in those countries that embrace it, and guarantees respect for human rights and religion. This respect certainly does not exist in the Islamic countries.
> The Italian Prime Minister added that he hoped "the West will continue to conquer peoples, like it conquered communism." (2001, sec. 1, p. 9)

Even though Berlusconi has tried to offer some clarifications, he has nevertheless revealed "bad listening" to the Islamic world.

We have seen that the changed center of gravity of Christianity is undeniable. We have also noted that the West continues to practice bad listening. These two realities create the overall context of Christian theologizing and scholarship in the world today. This context may be a partial explanation for the fact that in the West

> the adjectives Black, Asian and Latin American are more important than the quality of the theology they espouse. Assigning a collective identity enables the academy to view these theologies as a separate "other" and an "object" to be studied and assessed. (Sugirtharajah 2003, 163)

So in spite of the theological works produced by third world scholars, acknowledgment that Western theologians need "the experience and reflection of missionaries and missiologists" (Stackhouse 2000, 55; also Mouw 1994) calls for "the validity of multiple perspectives in theology" (Poythress 1987); pleas for contextualization as a method in systematic theology (Davis 1978; 1984); and recognition of the necessity of missiological theology (Henry 1988), missional theology (Hiebert and Tiénou 2002a), and intercultural theology (Hollenweger 1986),[4] which is "the theology of intercultural encounter in the context of multicultural societies and a globalising world" (Wijsen 2004, 171), "the global domination of Western theology remains largely unaddressed" (Shenk 2001, 98). Consequently, third world theologians are either pushed to the margins (Fernandez and Segovia 2001; Segovia 1996), or their theologies are perceived as threats to orthodoxy (Packer 2000). It is a well-known fact that "standard" textbooks of systematic theology either lack any reference to theologians of non-European descent or contain only passing references to some without significant interaction with their ideas. When third world theologies are given better treatment, they tend to be covered in an appendix (see Smith 1992). We are then left with this: the West claiming to produce universal theology and the rest wanting "to articulate a fundamental theology that will make [them] equal partners in the theological circles that determine what is theologically normative" (García 2001, 56). The net result of the "global domination of Western theology" is that we are prevented from wrestling with the fact that "any theology needs to attend both to its contextual and to its universal dimensions" (Schreiter 1997, 3). This situation makes us unable to transcend provincialism.

Today, authentic Christian theologizing and provincialism are incompatible. We can, therefore, ill afford to continue on a path where we have colliding "arrogant regionalisms" (Quéau 2001, 14) in current world Christian theologizing. Let us move forward, then, in Christian theology as if we truly belong together. But how do we do so? Habits formed over years, and even centuries, cannot change overnight. Change will require specific actions. One such action may be for Northern (Western) theologians/scholars and potential scholars to learn Southern languages (even minority ones) well enough so that they engage in scholarship not from a position of strength and power. To do so, Westerners will have to "work hard at practicing the skills that distinguish a human being from a corporation: genuine listening, empathetic accompanying, and patient suffering" (Bonk 2004, 97).

Another way forward is for us to engage in sustained international and interdisciplinary scholarship on matters affecting all of us. Christian identity can be a matter worth our consideration. Now, more than ever, "the question of Christian identity is . . . a global one" (Choong 1998, 225; see also Shenk 2001). Reflection on Christian identity is urgent in

4. The expression "intercultural theology" was first proposed in 1979 by H.-j. Margull, R. Friedli, and W. Hollenweger (see Hollenweger 2003, 90).

light of the complex issues raised by the change in Christianity's center of gravity.

There are, no doubt, many other issues that can only be adequately addressed through international and interdisciplinary scholarship. This was Harvie Conn's hope (1984) when he argued for a trialogue between anthropology, mission, and theology. It is also an important aspect of Paul Hiebert's legacy in that he advocated a metatheologial process involving God's worldwide church (1994b). Christian theology will not truly become a worldwide conversation unless "Harvie Conn's dream of a 'missiological agenda for theology, not a theological agenda for missions,'" (Griffiths 2004, 125) is fulfilled and unless Western theologians (and not only missiologists) become the dialogue partners of third world theologians. May God grant us favor, and may we see the day when "the whole people of God have a say in theological decision-making" (Hollenweger 1986, 28). When that comes, Christian theologizing will truly be an endeavor in which Christians from everywhere participate fully.

2

Anthropological Reflections on Contextualizing Theology in a Globalizing World

DARRELL L. WHITEMAN

Why can't a woman be more like a man?" quibbled the exasperated Professor Henry Higgins, speaking of Eliza Doolittle in the movie *My Fair Lady*. Eliza had come into Higgins's male-dominated world, and her presence was upsetting the proverbial applecart. Professor Higgins was well equipped to function in his own male academic world, but he did not know how to cope with the cognitive categories required to interact with women. In similar fashion, it is tempting for anthropologists to wish, "Why can't the world be more like our nineteenth-century imagination of it—a world with neat, well-defined categories of culture and people groups, each appropriately demarcated from other cultures and ethnic groups by clearly defined boundaries?" Bronislaw Malinowski's functionalism, for example, worked so much better in that world than it does in today's world, where globalization and postmodernism are wreaking havoc with our anthropological categories.

In the same way that Henry Higgins had to learn how to cope with Eliza Doolittle's female world, missiological anthropologists must learn how to function in today's globalizing world, with its compression of time and space, new categories of thought, and rapid culture change. For example, we have often been more comfortable as "bush anthropologists" stomping through the steaming jungle than we are trying to make some cognitive sense out of the concrete jungle of today's megacities, teeming with a diversity of cultures, religions, and economic classes.

Of course, a brief historical inquiry would quickly reveal that the clearly demarcated and well-defined categories of people, sufficiently isolated from other groups so as to make their study more amenable to anthropologists, never did exist in the nineteenth century, or in any century for that matter. The rapid pace of globalization today, however, has made it more obvious that cultures are changing and that culture itself is contingent, constructed, and contested (Rynkiewich 2002b) rather than the neat package for analysis that we often assumed.

Not only has globalization affected anthropologists and their study, but it has also become a reality the church can no longer ignore. The church must take seriously differences in cultures, ethnicity, gender roles, and social location if it is going to be an authentic representative of the kingdom of God on earth (cf. Tiplady 2003). This presents a huge challenge for many Christians who strive to be culturally relevant while remaining biblically faithful. At the same time that globalization has been erupting around the world, the center of gravity for the Christian church has been shifting South and East, away from North America and Europe, where it was once a dominant force and the primary center for sending out missionaries (Jenkins 2002).

This geographic and cultural shift has resulted in a plethora of new forms and expressions of Christian faith. David Barrett's (2001) last count in the recent *World Christian Encyclopedia* is thirty-four thousand denominations, an increase from twenty-three thousand in the previous edition twenty years earlier. Therefore, today we are confronted not only with differences in cultures, economic patterns, and political structures but also with a diversity of Christian expressions, and we struggle to know how the church in the West should relate to the church in the rest. How can we interact with non-Western Christians without trying to dominate them? What can we learn from them? How can we serve one another in a spirit of humility and openness, sharing wealth and resources without becoming paternal? And so the question of doing theology in a globalizing world becomes very timely indeed.

As an anthropologist, I wonder if there is any role for missiological anthropology in this changing world. Are anthropological insights still relevant? Can they continue to make a contribution to understanding how the gospel of our Lord and Savior Jesus Christ can be made known, understood, and followed in a wide diversity of cultures that are constantly changing? Anthropology does have an important contribution to make in contextualizing theology today, but it will not be the old salvage anthropology of yesterday that will guide us. It will be a more reflexive and chastened anthropology, one that confesses that colonialism did as much to shape our anthropological categories as it did to influence our mission practice and theology.

Many of the chapters in this volume are from a missiological consultation on doing theology in a globalizing world in which we honored Paul Hiebert's contributions to defining and explicating the issues surrounding the universal church that is found today in a multitude of cultural forms. Such an effort requires multiple perspectives and complementary models, a point that Hiebert (1999) in his commitment to critical realism has often made. The editors of this volume have wisely brought together theologians, biblical scholars, historians, missiologists, and anthropologists to discuss the challenge of doing theology in a globalizing world. My task in this chapter is to look at the topic through the lens of missiological anthropology and to ask the question, Does anthropology continue to have a role to play in contributing to our missiology in a postmodern world in which globalization is blurring the lines that categorize peoples and their cultures? This chapter argues that anthropology has an important role to play in shaping theology and missiology in the midst of globalization.

It is fitting to begin by looking at some of the anthropological contributions Hiebert has made that can contribute to our conversation of contextualizing theology in a globalizing world. This volume is dedicated to Hiebert's legacy and his pioneering work integrating anthropology, theology, and missiology, whereby he has already pointed the way forward in the present discussion. This chapter concludes with a look toward the future and notes how Hiebert's anthropological insights will help us work together, developing a biblically faithful, culturally relevant, and truly global theology that overcomes the hegemony of Western dominance and transcends the parochialism of local theologies, a concern that Hiebert himself has repeatedly expressed (1988; 1991).

Hiebert's Anthropological Contributions

Before Paul Hiebert joined the faculty of the School of World Mission at Fuller Theological Seminary in 1977, he was a professor of anthropology at the University of Washington in Seattle. In fact, one of the earliest articles of his that I read was published in the *Journal of Anthropological Research* in 1976 in which he compared traffic patterns in Seattle with traffic patterns in Hyderabad, India (1976, 326–36). He was looking for underlying patterns of how societies create social order. It would not be long before he would take that same strong analytical mind and apply a structural analysis to missiological concerns about Christian conversion, worldview difference, the concept of culture, and folk religions. His earliest missiological writing of which I am aware appeared as chapters in books: in 1967, "Missions and the Understanding of Culture" (Hiebert 1967), and in 1976, three chapters in part 2 on mission anthropology in *Crucial Dimensions in World Evangelization* (Glasser, Hiebert, Wagner, and Winter 1976). His earliest anthropological articles that had a significant impact on missiology appeared in 1978: "Missions and Anthropology: A Love/Hate Relationship," published in the nascent journal *Missiology*, and "Conversion, Culture, and Cognitive Categories," published in that creative but short-lived journal *Gospel in Context* (Hiebert 1978a; 1978b). Both articles soon entered the mainstream of missiological anthropology and were frequently cited.

I have been in a good position to see the influence of Hiebert's anthropological writing in missiology. Ten years after these important missiological articles were published, many of his ideas were becoming household concepts in the field. I saw this reflected in the hundreds of articles that came across my desk as editor of *Missiology* from 1988 to 2003. Moreover, in the twenty years I have been a professor of cultural anthropology in the E. Stanley Jones School of World Mission and Evangelism at Asbury Seminary and have mentored many doctoral dissertations, I have seen Hiebert's missiological articles and books cited more than any others, and his "Critical Contextualization" piece seems to be employed by students as a theoretical framework in more dissertations than any other concept. From the vantage point of a missiological editor and mentor of graduate students, therefore, I can attest to the fact that Hiebert's anthropological contributions to the field of missiology and to the theme of this book on contextualizing theology have been enormous. Let's look briefly at some of those contributions in the order in which they appeared:

1. "Missions and Anthropology: A Love/Hate Relationship," *Missiology* 6, no. 2 (April 1978): 165–80. In this article, Hiebert traces a brief history of the ambivalent relationships between anthropologists and missionaries as they both struggle with questions concerning what it means to be human and the perennial challenge of unity versus diversity. Missionaries and anthropologists have both depersonalized people, missionaries through their ethnocentrism and seeing people as objects for conversion, and anthropologists by not taking seriously people's own religious understanding.

The problem of unity versus diversity confronted missionaries as they struggled with how Christianity should relate to the variety of non-

Christian religions and how the gospel can be expressed amid cultural diversity. Anthropologists for their part turned to cultural relativism, and despite some efforts to search for cross-cultural universals, they extolled the uniqueness of cultures in an infinite variety of expressions. In this important article, Hiebert anticipated his later writings on epistemology and the shift toward critical realism in both science and religion, which he welcomed, noting that this shift "provides a more adequate basis for Christian witness to non-Christians, and for the unity of the international church in the midst of surface theological variations and multiple activities" (1978b, 178). Hiebert called for an end to the hostility between anthropology and mission: "With the growing awareness among anthropologists that they must face the overwhelming problems of a real world which missionaries have faced so long, and among missionaries that they must deal with people within their sociocultural contexts which anthropology has studied, a greater mutual understanding and exchange of ideas seems possible" (1978b, 178). In the past twenty-five years, we have seen this begin to come true, and in today's globalizing world, it is all the more important that cooperation and understanding between anthropologists and missionaries take place.

2. "Conversion, Culture, and Cognitive Categories," *Gospel in Context* 1, no. 4 (1978): 24–29. In this important article, Hiebert asked the seemingly innocent question, Can Papayya become a Christian after hearing the gospel only once? As soon as we respond, "Yes, of course," we are immediately confronted with the fact that the receptor does not necessarily hear the same things the communicator intends to say. This is because they have different cognitive categories by which they organize their world, and so a change in basic meanings often occurs. Hiebert, drawing on studies in mathematics and set theory, introduced the missiological world to the concepts of bounded sets and centered sets and then applied these to the problem of conversion.

Most of us who have grown up in conservative evangelical churches have been shaped by an understanding of conversion as a bounded set. We reinforced our identity as Christians by focusing attention on the boundary that distinguished us from non-Christians. For me, my Free Methodist boundary markers were clear: Christians did not smoke, drink, dance, go to movies, or play cards. It was all so simple and clear-cut. With this model, there was no ambiguity about who was and who was not a Christian. When Hiebert introduced the idea of "Christian" as a centered-set category, it was a conceptual breakthrough and a breath of fresh missiological air. This new way of thinking got us out of the logjam of static categories that did not square well with cross-cultural realities and gave us a dynamic way of understanding the process of conversion and discipleship. As I have taught this perspective over the past twenty years to both Western and non-Western cross-cultural witnesses, it has been one of the most liberating and powerful missiological concepts students have encountered. With the impact of globalization and post-modernism, which destroy neat, well-defined bounded-set thinking, this kind of centered-set thinking is important and timely. It enables dynamic thinking instead of static thinking about contextualizing theology in a globalizing world. It helps us focus more on what we share in common with Christians around the world (i.e., the fact that we are on a pilgrimage toward the same center, namely, Jesus Christ). The first priority in mission is no longer maintaining and protecting the cognitive categories and cultural forms we use to define our denominational distinctives. With centered-set thinking, the priorities are focusing on Jesus and encouraging people to make a change of allegiance to Christ, and then not interfering as the Holy Spirit guides them toward truth.

3. "Critical Contextualization," *Missiology* 12, no. 3 (July 1984): 288–96; and *International Bulletin of Missionary Research* 11, no. 3 (July 1987): 104–11. Another of Hiebert's concepts that can contribute to an under-standing of contextualizing theology in a globalizing world is his idea of critical contextualization. Found in an article by the same name, it has become a classic in missiological literature and is one of the most cited and used methods for enabling new Christians to deal with their tradi-tional culture and its non-Christian beliefs and practices. First published in *Missiology* in 1984 and then in 1987 in an expanded version in the *International Bulletin of Missionary Research*, "Critical Contextualization" outlines a method for a community of believers to evaluate and critique their culture in light of the gospel. In his 1987 article, Hiebert laid out the historical background in both science and mission that led to an era of noncontextualization, a period when colonialism and ethnocentrism dominated practice and thinking about Christian mission. As postmod-ernism began to spread its influence in the 1960s to the present day, it created a crisis of confidence in Enlightenment understandings of science and influenced missionaries and missiologists. They began to place a greater emphasis on "contextualization, not only of the church in local social structures, but also of the Gospel and theology in local cultural forms" (1987, 108). Hiebert (1987, 108–9) argues that this burst of enthu-siasm for contextualization as an antidote to the previous colonial era of noncontextualization resulted in too much uncritical contextualization. This tendency to baptize wholesale a convert's culture led, in turn, to a host of problems, including syncretism, a weakened view of sin and structural evil in a society, and an erosion of the core Christian claims about the truth of the gospel and the uniqueness of Christ. Often in an effort to remove the cross-cultural stumbling blocks to the gospel, the very offense of the gospel was also removed. Moreover, the focus on cultural

diversity and the uniqueness of each culture eclipsed an emphasis on working toward the unity of churches in different cultures.

In response to these and other problems, critical contextualization was a method whereby Christians could create a hermeneutical community and together could evaluate their own cultural practices and assumptions in light of their understanding of Scripture. This enabled them to accept much of their culture, since it was not intrinsically unbiblical. But it led to a rejection of aspects of their culture that were seen as inconsistent with their new Christian understandings, and in many instances, it enabled converts to take traditional cultural forms and fill them with new Christian meanings, thus developing truly indigenous forms and expressions of Christianity.

Although Hiebert was aware of the need to use this model of critical contextualization as one way for local churches to connect with the universal, global church, he clearly noted that critical contextualization does not operate from a monocultural perspective. This model has nevertheless sometimes been used inappropriately to reinforce the local expression of Christianity at the expense of connecting Christians to the global body of believers. Also, the local hermeneutical community should find ways to share its insights with and learn from the global church, instead of remaining isolated from other Christians. Andrew Walls (1982, 99) said it well when he noted that an indigenous church is a place where Christians in a given culture should feel at home, but they should not feel so much at home there that no one else is welcomed. This model of critical contextualization becomes increasingly important in a globalizing world, but adjustments will have to be made. For example, the local hermeneutical community is no longer an isolated culture, if it ever was, cut off from the flow of ideas, images, objects, and people from elsewhere. The hermeneutical community itself is increasingly influenced by globalization, whether it is found in rural villages or urban centers.

4. "The Flaw of the Excluded Middle," *Missiology* 10, no. 1 (January 1982): 35–47. A fourth article contributes to a discussion of the interaction of anthropology with theology and missiology in a globalizing world. When this article first appeared on the missiological scene and quickly gained recognition as unusually insightful, I thought to myself, Why hasn't this been said before as clearly as Hiebert is now making the case? Hiebert, in his analytical critique, showed how the Platonic dualism we inherited as children of the Enlightenment had invaded the Western worldview. We have a two-tiered view of reality that distinguishes religion from science. Religion is limited to the sacred and concerned with issues of faith, miracles, and other worldly problems. In contrast, science, which is based on materialistic naturalism, is perceived to be

a secular activity, concerned only with the natural order and with this-worldly problems and things that can be empirically verified. This has caused us to miss an entire middle level of concerns in folk religion that deal with realities of this world that are unseen, such as the problem of ancestral spirits, demons, unexplainable tragedies, and so on. Hiebert called for a more holistic theology that includes an awareness of God in natural history and the natural order. He notes, "So long as the missionary comes with a two-tier world view with God confined to the supernatural, and the natural world operating for all practical purposes according to autonomous scientific laws, Christianity will continue to be a more secularizing force in the world. Only as God is brought back into the middle of our scientific understanding of nature will we stem the tide of Western secularism" (1982, 46).

As postmodernism made its impact on Western culture, calling into question many assumptions of the Enlightenment, spiritual warfare became a concern for increasing numbers of Western Christians. Many concerned with spiritual warfare found Hiebert's "Flaw of the Excluded Middle" just the ammunition they were looking for to help them make sense of the unseen but this-worldly beings and their activities and to give them a missiological rationale for power encounters against the demonic world. It is interesting that Hiebert warned against Christianity becoming a new form of magic, once this middle level was no longer excluded. He contrasted magic, which is based on a mechanistic worldview, with worship, which is rooted in a relational view of life. He notes, "The difference is not one of form, but of attitude. What begins as a prayer of request may turn into a formula or chant to force God to do one's will by saying or doing the right thing. In religion, we want the will of God for we trust his omniscience. In magic we seek our own wills, confident that we know what is best for ourselves. The line dividing them is a subtle one" (1982, 46).

Hiebert's insights into a biblical approach and theology of the middle level have become all the more important as postmodernism influences culture and globalization brings us closer to people who do not live with a dualistic worldview that separates the sacred from the secular.

5. "The Fourth Self," in *Anthropological Insights for Missionaries* (Grand Rapids: Baker, 1985), 193–224. Another important anthropological insight that contributes to the topic of globalization and theology is found in chapter 8 of Hiebert's *Anthropological Insights for Missionaries*. He argues that we must go beyond the familiar three-self formulae of Henry Venn and Rufus Anderson articulated in the nineteenth century that called for churches planted by missionaries to become as quickly as possible self-governing, self-propagating, and self-supporting. Hiebert says this is not enough. To this trilogy should be added self-theologizing.

He asks the question, "Do young churches have the right to read and interpret the Scripture for themselves?" (1985, 196).

Self-theologizing is the basis for doing theology in a globalizing world because it recognizes the necessity of every community of believers to connect the gospel to their own worldview and to address the problems with which they struggle. But in today's globalizing world, self-theology is not a license to develop theology in isolation from all others. In a globalizing world, this is not possible. Self-theologizing is the first step toward developing a transcultural theology that transcends cultural differences (1985, 217). According to Hiebert, the following principles must be taken into account: (1) The theology must be biblically based, (2) it must be supracultural in that it transcends the limits and biases of human cultures, (3) it must be historical in focusing on God's acts in history, (4) it must be christological, and (5) it must be Spirit led (1985, 217–19). The tension associated with contextualizing theology for a given context is that the theology can become culture-bound and parochial, which in turn can lead to warped theologies that even justify racism, discrimination, and oppression. This is why local theologies must undergo checks and balances and be in conversation with the global community across time and space.

There are many more anthropological insights that Hiebert has contributed to the topic of contextualizing theology in a globalizing world (e.g., "Beyond Anti-Colonialism to Globalism," 1991), but this sampling of his ideas helps us understand the breadth and depth of his thinking. While Hiebert has been writing the past thirty years, the world has undergone rapid and profound changes as a result of globalization. We will now turn our attention to a brief discussion of globalization.

Globalization and Its Impact

The introductory essay to this volume by Harold Netland presents some of the basic issues involved in understanding globalization and its impact on the way we do, or should do, theology today. That discussion need not be repeated here. Instead, the following contains a few additional observations.

A common misperception of globalization is that it is having such a homogenizing effect throughout the world that diverse cultures are melding into one global culture and that linguistic diversity is disappearing as English gains dominance in the global market economy. This half-truth concerning globalization gives too much credit to economic and technological factors and underestimates the importance of cultural and religious dimensions of human existence. Despite the fact that the world is becoming compressed in time and space because of globalization, we are also seeing a renewed interest in ethnic identity, local culture, and indigenous forms of local knowledge (cf. Robertson 2000). In other words, the celebration of the local has now become a global phenomenon, due largely to globalization. What does this mean for contextualizing theology? It means that local forms of worship and expressions and understandings of Christian faith will become even more important to local populations of Christians. Here is where anthropology has an important contribution to make. Anthropologists have often done their best research on a microscale of local populations rather than through deriving generalizations from the macroscale study of entire societies.

In all my reading, I have not yet found one accepted definition of globalization, nor is there consensus on its exact description. Nearly all would agree, however, that it is about the increasingly interconnected character of the economic, political, and social life of the peoples on this planet. Globalization is not an entirely new phenomenon. For example, the ancient Silk Road connecting Europe with China is an example of an early economic and cultural linking of diverse societies across large distances. It is interesting to note that this old form of globalization is taking on a new face as a mission movement in China is emerging that plans to follow the Silk Road back to Jerusalem with the gospel (Hattaway 2003). What *is* new about globalization today is the speed, the scale, the scope, and the complexity of global connections. Millions of linkages and networks have emerged that involve multiple interdependent flows of a greater variety of goods, services, people, capital, images, information, and diseases (United Nations Center for Human Settlements 2001, xxx). Depending again on how one sees this interconnectedness, it is a phenomenon primarily of the latter part of the twentieth century. In fact, the term *globalization* first appeared in English in 1959. We use the term today to refer to what began happening in the latter part of the twentieth century. The twentieth century and the dawn of the twenty-first century is the period of concern when dealing with contextualizing theology in a globalizing world.

Three interconnecting processes have shaped globalization. The first is economic, the second is political, and the third is technological. Let's look briefly at each of these.

A single world economy. With the collapse of communism and the end of socialism in much of the world, beginning in 1989, there has been a worldwide expansion of market capitalism. This form of capitalism now extends around the world. It is characterized by its ignoring of national boundaries, its ability to move capital quickly, and its engagement in short-term projects that maximize the profit margin. This form of capitalism has generated great amounts of new wealth, but it has not helped much to ease the poverty of the majority of the world's population. While some have been fabulously enriched, many more are not better off and have been driven deeper into poverty and misery. With the increase in wealth, the disparity between rich and poor is growing worse in nearly all parts of the world, with roughly 20 percent enjoying the fruits of global capitalism and the rest struggling to hold their ground or slipping into deeper poverty.

The political process. Globalization has also had a political impact in the world. The most obvious example is the collapse of the bipolar political alignments that pitted democratic and capitalist countries against communist and socialist systems. The hallmark of this era was the Cold War. This situation began to change in 1989 with the fall of the Berlin Wall and the subsequent demise of communism in the Soviet Union and even the eventual breakup of the Soviet bloc. We now live in a multipolar political world, and threats to it and within it come from multiple sources, including terrorism that knows no political boundaries or alignments.

Technology. The third phenomenon, the technological, is the advancement in communications. Thanks to new communications technologies, messages and information can now be sent around the world almost instantly. Air travel makes the movement of persons and cargo rapid and relatively inexpensive. Just as the first two phenomena, a multipolar world and an interconnected economic system, have changed how we think of the world, the communications revolution of the second half of the twentieth century has reshaped how we perceive time and space. The communications technologies make possible a networking that increasingly eludes hierarchical control. Network has replaced hierarchy as a social model for communication. This is good news for Christians around the world who want to connect with one another and who desire to develop local theologies while at the same time staying in touch with the universal church.

The convergence of these three phenomena—global capitalism, a politically multipolar world, and communications technologies—creates what is known as globalization. But globalization also has a cultural and religious dimension, and hence we are forced to deal with the impact of globalization on the church around the world.

Amid all the debates and conjectures about what globalization is, there is a certainty about what it is not. Globalization, as it exists today, is neither Westernization nor imperialism. Although it has its roots in Western modernity, it is not simply a transference of Western culture around the world. Anthony Giddens (1999, 96) notes that the first phase of globalization was plainly governed primarily by the expansion of the West, and institutions which originate in the West. No other civilization made anything like as pervasive an impact upon the world, or shaped it so much in its own image. . . . Although still dominated by Western power, globalization can no longer be spoken of only as a matter of one-way imperialism. Action at a distance was always a two-way process; now, increasingly, however, there is no obvious "direction" to globalization at all, as its ramifications are more or less ever-present. The current phase of globalization, then, should not be confused with the preceding one, whose structures it acts increasingly to subvert.

At Asbury Seminary, our motto is taken from John Wesley, who claimed, "The world is my parish." Today, however, because of globalization, we are realizing that the world is *in* my parish (Rynkiewich 2002a). Globalization has come home to roost in our own backyard. Meanwhile, some students still think, "My parish is the world." We have to work overtime to help these students understand the global nature of the church and what we can and must learn from our brothers and sisters in Christ from other parts of the world.

Who Benefits and Who Loses Because of Globalization?

As we reflect on the need to contextualize theology today, we need to look briefly at who the winners and losers are in this globalizing world. Is globalization bad news for the entire church universal, or is it good news for some? In a fascinating article titled "Globalisation from a Grassroots, Two-Thirds World Perspective" (2003), Fiona Wilson helps us understand the impact of globalization from the perspective of the underside, those who are often marginalized.

The benefits of globalization are seen in the areas of communication and technology, the interlinking and opening up of the world, and benefits from products and services (Wilson 2003, 180). In a survey by Tearfund on the impact of globalization, most respondents noted the benefits of rapid and flexible communication and modern technology, especially the computer. It is easy to become euphoric about technological breakthroughs that lead us to believe evangelizing the world will now be easier and faster. However, we must never forget that there are seldom shortcuts to building interpersonal relationships through which the power of the transforming gospel may flow. How easy it is to think that technological solutions can take the place of interpersonal ones. But this is seldom the case. I am reminded of a story from Latin America in which a missionary in the 1930s wrote his supporters in the United States touting a new technological breakthrough that he was confident would make it possible to evangelize Guatemala in a matter of months. This new technological panacea was the megaphone!

Another benefit of globalization noted by these respondents was the idea of being interlinked in a wide network of relationships, enabling Christians to feel connected to the universal church and to discover the unity found among a diversity of Christians. This allows for local developments of theology that can be tested by interaction with a wider body of believers.

Despite some benefits of globalization, respondents nevertheless were far more vocal in their criticism of globalization and its harmful effects on their lives. Wilson says:

> The power and the injustice at the global level were pointed out in various ways. The lack of justice and equity, exploitation, the plundering of primary commodities, and the feeling that globalisation is out of people's control came across, especially in the responses from Francophone Africa. Respondents noted that the poor suffer, countries are unable to compete in the global markets, and inequality exists. The poor feel dominated by the rich, as the harmful effects of globalisation "advance at the pace of the giants." (2003, 181)

Here is a sampling of responses from respondents in various parts of the world (Wilson 2003, 182):

- "It is the law of the jungle: the strongest impose their laws upon the weakest" (Francophone Africa).
- "The rules of the game are dictated by the great/powerful for their own interests" (Francophone Africa).
- "We are becoming a more and more dependent society on the powers of the North—our country is being sold out" (Latin America).
- "My country is too poor, and I do not see how globalisation could bring good to my people. We are trailing behind the rich countries" (Francophone Africa).
- "The powerful have more and better tools to impose their opinions upon the poor" (Latin America).

Within the church, the harm of globalization was also seen. "The importing of all kinds of foreign teaching and styles of worship means that churches are conforming to non-traditional values and imported behaviour, and are not valuing their own cultural and church heritage" (Wilson 2003, 183).

Bulus Galadima states:

The church is still highly homogeneous in a world that is becoming increasingly heterogeneous. We need to learn to live as a global church, but race, ethnicity, class, and nation still divide us. The divisions within the church are a stumbling block to many unbelievers. Many Christians find their primary identity in their culture, ethnicity, or class rather than in their commitment to Christ. Racism and ethnicity are the greatest tragedies in the church today. (2003, 198)

The good news of globalization is that it is now easier for a hermeneutical community to exist that is global in scope and character, and people can test local expressions of Christianity against the universal body of Christ. The bad news is that people are likely to try to dominate the conversation from a position of power, which in turn creates a new form of ecclesiastical and theological hegemony. Once again, it will look like the West is trying to dominate the world, not with economic structural adjustment policies that create poverty but with theological arrogance.

Anthropology, Globalization, and Contextualizing Theology

I now want to bring together the two preceding discussions on globalization and Hiebert's anthropological insights to reflect on the future of doing theology and mission in a globalizing world and to suggest some contributions that anthropology can make to the enterprise. In what areas will globalization continue to have an impact, and in what ways will this present both opportunities and challenges to the church? Let me suggest three areas we must pay more attention to in the future.

First, because of the increasing poverty in the world that prohibits the poorest of the poor from reaping many benefits from globalization, microenterprise development efforts have sprung up that are empowering and enabling the poor to alleviate some of their poverty. One of the successful ventures in this area is the Grameen Bank of Bangladesh, which pioneered and popularized a methodology for extending small, collateral-free loans for self-employment to some of the world's poorest people. Founded in 1976 by a Bangladeshi economics professor named Muhammed Yunus, the bank by 2003 had loaned $4 billion to 2.8 million Bangladeshi villagers, of whom 95 percent were women (Bornstein 2004, 13).

While I am not advocating that the primary role of the church should now become that of a lending organization, I am suggesting that because of globalization there is a reason for Christian mission to focus more on promoting holistic transformation. Local theologizing must address issues of physical poverty along with spiritual poverty. Moreover, we in the wealthy West must be prepared to accept new discoveries and unexpected news in Scripture when it is read through the eyes of the poor. Here is another place where anthropology can be of help, for it will enable us to better understand how the social location of people shapes their worldview and how their worldview in turn influences their understanding of theology and shapes their Christian practices. A proper theological understanding of the kingdom of God will help us understand that all creation is waiting to be renewed and that holistic and integrated development done in the name of Jesus is part and parcel of the good news of the kingdom of God. Anthropological insights on culture change and development can greatly assist us as we discover ways to move forward in holistic mission. For example, many of our efforts to "help" the church in the non-Western world end up doing more harm than good. An example from the Solomon Islands comes to mind.

A well-known Christian nongovernmental organization from New Zealand wanted to provide portable sawmills to local churches so they could cut down valuable timber and have a more robust cash economy. The organization defined poverty as a lack of cash, and they saw cutting down trees for cash income as the solution to the problem. On both points they were mistaken. An anthropological investigation into the situation revealed that there was no poverty, even though there was little cash, because the land was rich and food was plentiful. Furthermore, the valuable timber was owned corporately by entire clans, not by individual persons. It became evident that the introduction of portable sawmills would sow disharmony among the people and create problems rather than meet needs. The organization's proposal to distribute sawmills was therefore rejected.

A second area of challenge and opportunity for doing theology in a globalizing world involves responding to the impact of urbanization on the global church. As urbanization and globalization come together in the megacities of the world, they present incredible opportunities but also tough challenges for the church. The economic impact of globalization is most readily seen in cities rather than in rural areas. In cities, we find the greatest disparity between the wealthy and the poor. In addition to economic diversity, the greatest amount of cultural and religious diversity is also found in cities. The plethora of cultural differences and ethnic groups makes it easier to create multiethnic churches reflecting kingdom values and thereby demonstrating to the world how unity in Christ can emerge out of a diversity of cultures and socioeconomic levels. Once again, this is where anthropology can be of tremendous help. Insights from urban anthropology can help us understand the tremendous rural to urban migration of people all over the world and why migrants are often more open to religious innovation when they move to the city. Anthropology can reveal how people move from rural kinship to urban social networks as the primary organizing principle of people in cities. We need contextual theologies appropriate to Christians struggling to survive in the megacities of this world, and this will require overcoming the frequent theological bias against the city.

A third area of challenge and opportunity for contextualizing theology in a globalizing world is charting a course through postmodernism with epistemological humility and confidence in the gospel, recognizing the social construction of our own worldviews in a world filled with enormous cultural diversity. Hiebert's insights are particularly helpful in this area. We are indebted to his writing about the epistemological shifts that have occurred in science and the implications this has for mission and missiology. It is perhaps ironic to suggest that anthropological insights can help us find a way forward out of the postmodern morass and contribute to doing theology in a globalizing world. The irony is because anthropology has contributed greatly to many of the postmodern concepts and language now in use. In fact, Walter Anderson goes even further and suggests:

> If any single occupational group deserves the credit—or blame—for bringing us into the postmodern era, it is the anthropologists. They created a new profession out of the study of otherness, and their findings have made it impossible for any literate person to believe that there is only one way of seeing the world. (1995, 53)

Missiologists need not be fearful of the realization that there are many ways to see the world. This need not necessarily threaten our faith and turn us into cultural relativists or religious universalists. The fact that so much of our reality is socially constructed does not lead to the conclusion that God is created in our own image and knows no existence other than that which we have created in our minds. Nevertheless, we need a theology that affirms the centrality of Christ in the world while also affirming the culturally diverse expressions that the body of Christ will necessarily take.

Anthropology can make significant contributions in this area of contextualizing theology, because it is always working with the tension between the particularities of culture and the universal patterns of human nature. In the same way that there are cross-cultural universals in all human beings amid the tremendous diversity of cultures, we should also expect to discover biblical values and perspectives that unite all members of the body of Christ, irrespective of their particular language, culture, social location, gender, or ethnic identity.

Conclusion

Revelation 7:9 presents a biblical image that I find the most encouraging in struggling with how to affirm the centrality of Christ in a culturally diverse world that is rapidly changing because of the influence of postmodernism and globalization. It is an image of unity in diversity. John writes:

> After this I looked and there before me was a great multitude that no one could count, from every nation, tribe, people and language, standing before the throne and in front of the Lamb. They were wearing white robes and were holding palm branches in their hands.

Revelation 7:9 provides an image of how the grand metanarrative that creates unity out of diversity will one day come to fruition. If this is a picture of what will someday be, why should we not begin now, while still on earth, to work to find a way of using our diverse cultures to bring a richness to our understanding of the gospel?

The picture we are given in Revelation 7:9 is of people from every ethnolinguistic group surrounding the throne of God, not worshiping God in English, or even English as a second language, but in their own language, shaped by their own worldview and culture. We can count on hearing over eight thousand languages when we are around that throne. The view we get of the kingdom of God is a multicultural view, not one of ethnic uniformity. One of the things we admire most about the gospel is its ability to speak within the worldview of every culture. To me, this feature is one of the empirical proofs for the gospel's authenticity and the truth of Christianity. This is also why theology must become contextualized in every cultural context while remaining biblically faithful and in conversation with the global hermeneutical community.

As we come to understand and appreciate the global church, we will be reminded that we do not have a privileged position when it comes to understanding and practicing Christianity. It cannot be the exclusive property of any one culture, for it refuses to be culture bound. It continually bursts free from the chains of bondage to cultural tradition. Japanese theologian Kosuke Koyama (1977) has reminded us that there is "No Handle on the Cross."

This chapter has suggested that anthropology has several important contributions to make to the challenges of contextualizing theology in a globalizing world. Bulus Galadima's words are a fitting conclusion to this discussion as he anticipates the possible ways we might respond to globalization.

The church can choose to respond to globalization in one of three ways. First, it can sharply reject all aspects of globalization as a worldly phenomenon (a fundamentalist type of response). Second, the church can accept globalization's relativism and pluralism, leading to a fundamental transformation of religious beliefs (a liberal type of response). Third, there can be an honest engagement of globalization's challenges in light of the eternal truths of the Christian message. In order for this last possibility to happen, we must identify the core of the Gospel. The seeming facile nature of this task is deceptive. It requires tact, creativity, and especially the enablement of the Holy Spirit. (2003, 201)

To this task we must turn, becoming more clear on what is the whole gospel for the whole world amid a diversity of cultures that are always undergoing change.

3

Globalization and the Study of Christian History

Andrew F. Walls

In Christian belief, salvation is a historical process. In some other religious traditions, notably those that have their origin in India, the historical process itself is the bondage from which humanity needs deliverance, and the insight that brings salvation is independent of the historical process. In the Christian understanding of the divine activity, salvation comes not only *in* history but *through* history; history is, as it were, the stuff, the material in which salvation takes place. Salvation is centered in the Christ event; yet even in the simplest forms of Christian affirmation, that event does not stand alone. It takes place as the climax of a long period of preparation; it leads to a long sequel. Had human history been irrelevant to or insignificant in the saving process, the incarnation might have immediately followed the fall. Instead, the story of the incarnation is organically related to several millennia of human history.

The early focus of that story is on the westward migration of a clan resident in Mesopotamia, the expansion of that clan into a nation, the rise of that nation to local glory, and its decline into colonial servitude, with many vicissitudes in between. This part of the story encompasses the emergence and collapse of several world empires and takes in much of the Middle East, the Mediterranean, and North Africa. But it is only the prelude; the Christ event, when it comes, is a history in itself, a history datable, as the Gospel of Luke makes clear, by the reigns of Roman emperors and the incumbencies of legates and procurators and satellite kings and high priests. That history, lasting some thirty years or so, is rooted in the long preceding history of the nation and cannot be adequately understood without it.

But the incarnation, though the climax of the redemptive process, does not mark its final act. It begins another phase of the history, which has so far occupied two millennia, seen other empires rise and fade, and taken the story across Europe, Asia, Africa, the Americas, and the Pacific. The evangelist Luke adds a second volume to his account of what Jesus did and taught. The Acts of the Apostles is a carefully constructed book, providing an account of the spread of Christianity to the heart of the Roman Empire. Once, however, Luke interrupts the Romeward flow of his story to take his readers to another international highway leading into the heart of Africa (Acts 8:26–39). With the story we know as that of the Ethiopian eunuch, he shows us that with the gospel all roads do not lead to Rome, that the gospel travels on other highways too, and that one day the stories will join up. And Acts is a manifestly incomplete book. It ends with Paul, the outcome of his appeal to Caesar unknown, teaching from temporary accommodation. The point is that the redemptive process does not end with Acts 28 or indeed with the apostolic age. It is an unfinished story, and we still have no sure means of knowing whether we are living in the very last days or in the days of the early church.

Salvation as a Historical Process

God has been in no hurry over the process of redemption. Its record stretches from early historic times to the present day and has been part of the history of every continent and of vast numbers of peoples. This has important implications for the Christian study of history and especially of church history.

The first implication is that the redemptive purpose of God is cross-generational. It is not completed in one generation, only in the totality of the generations. It was not completed in the generation of the incarnate Lord nor in that of his apostles. We should be wary, then, of using some later epoch—the Protestant Reformation, for instance, or the evangelical revival—as the defining description of the process. The redemptive process will not even be complete in the last generation of all, taking that generation in and of itself. What is only in germ, or even completely in one generation, may blossom in another and reach fruition in yet another. Prophets and psalmists kept this sense of generational continuity before Israel, and as a new age dawns, the first evangelistic appeal to go out from the church did not look only to the immediate hearers: "The promise is for you *and your children*," says Peter to the Pentecost crowds (Acts 2:39, emphasis added). Modern Christianity has become self-contained, and the potent sense of the ancestors has faded; we have lost the sense of "the God of Abraham, Isaac, and Jacob." Perhaps African Christianity will help to restore it as Africans increasingly assume leadership in the world church. Meanwhile, one of the vital tasks of the Christian historian is to convey the sense of salvation as a historical process. The great catalog of the ancestors of faith in Hebrews 11 closes with a remarkable statement. Neither Abraham nor any of the other heroes of faith has actually yet received what God promised them, because God has decided on a better plan—not for them but *for us*. Abraham, the writer argues, and all the other Christian ancestors, will not be made perfect, that is, complete, until the Christians to whom the Letter to the Hebrews is addressed are gathered into their succession. Extending it further, Abraham is waiting *for us* so that he can enter into his inheritance. The full significance of the great archetype of saving faith will be clear only when all the faithful are gathered in. The study of Christian history should display the kinship of Christians across the generations, for this is how the process of salvation works.

Mission history as a genre has particularly suffered from a one-generational focus. Much of the emphasis has been on the early period of evangelization, so that what passes for the church history of certain areas in Africa and elsewhere is merely a record of the establishment of churches. The attempt to obtain and record the testimony of the earliest converts is laudable and necessary, but it has often overshadowed what happened in later generations. The dimensions of Christian growth have often taken observers by surprise. When the members of Commission I made their report to the World Missionary Conference at Edinburgh in 1910 (and they included some of the best-informed and most-experienced people of their generation), they could think of the evangelization of inland Africa as hardly begun. They built their hopes for the Christian future on China, Japan, and India. How we need the history of those intermediate African Christian generations, comparative accounts of how people became Christians, and of what it meant to be Christian at different periods in that particular place.

A second implication concerns the record of the cross-cultural diffusion of Christianity. The progress of the generations is not simply important for biological ancestry. Historical development also displays—and here we come to a dimension of the subject to which Paul Hiebert has contributed significantly—the geographical, demographic, and cultural change in the composition of the Christian church. Cross-cultural diffusion is a recurring factor in Christian history; indeed, it may be said that, historically, cross-cultural diffusion has been Christianity's lifeblood. At several crucial points in Christian history, it would have been reasonable to predict that Christianity would become a marginal faith (as has occurred with Zoroastrianism) or would die out altogether were it not that it had crossed a cultural frontier and taken root among a different people. These geographical, ethnic, and cultural developments, like the generational movements already referred to, belong together in the cosmic salvific process, the divine plan of redemption. The last recorded question of the disciples to the risen Lord is, "Are you at this time going to restore the kingdom to Israel?" (Acts 1:6). It is a natural enough question for Jewish people who have been watching the triumphant progress of the Messiah. Nor does the Lord dismiss the question as entirely out of place or as reflecting a misunderstanding of his ministry; he merely tells them that times and seasons are in the Father's hands. The disciples as Jewish people naturally comprehended salvation in terms of the salvation of Israel. This was not wrong in itself, but the full salvation of Israel, involving as it did bringing into Israel huge numbers of those Israel called "the nations," was a many-splendored thing beyond their imagining.

It was the emergence of Gentile Christianity—the first crossing of a cultural frontier in Christian history—that enabled the Christian faith to survive the fall of Jerusalem and the destruction of the Jewish state. In the meantime, the two forms of Christian life had to live side by side in one church. The Epistle to the Ephesians reflects two ethnic and cultural communities in the church. Each had its own converted lifestyle, one utterly Jewish and Torah based, the other reflecting the conditions of the Hellenistic world of the Eastern Mediterranean but in converted form. There must have been many abrasive patches in churches made up of both groups, but the epistle makes it clear that the two communities belong together. They are each building blocks in the construction of the new temple; both are organs equally necessary to the functioning of the body of which Christ is the head. Indeed, as the epistle proceeds, we find that neither group can on its own realize the full stature of that body. We all come *together*, the apostle assures us, to the full stature of Christ.

At that time there were only two communities in the church (or churches) being addressed. Since then Christian cross-cultural diffusion has brought many more into the church, and our own day has seen the greatest proliferation of all. Each is to have, like Jew and Greek in the early church, its own converted lifestyle as the distinctive features of each culture are turned toward Christ. The representation of Christ by any one group can at best be only partial. At best it reflects the conversion of one small segment of reality, and it needs to be complemented and perhaps corrected by others. The fullness of humanity lies in Christ; the aggregate of converted lifestyles points toward his full stature.

The Cross-Cultural Dimension of Writing Christian History

The study of the past is always a cross-cultural exercise. Even when we share the ethnicity and language of the objects of our study, we do not share their world or their view of the world. They did not have options that are open to us; knowledge that we take for granted was hidden from them. Their minds were stored with things we have forgotten or never knew. They may have read our Scripture, but with different eyes, seeing different things as significant. If they shared the same theological tradition as we follow, it is unlikely that they understood or experienced it in the same way we do. The qualities needed in a historian are therefore the qualities needed for interpersonal cross-cultural encounter—the qualities, in fact, of a good missionary. The historian needs the sort of empathy that makes it possible to enter the world of other people, the preparedness to labor to see the world as people of another day saw it, to understand their language and the way they used it. The historian also needs to explore the available options as they appeared to them.

This much is true for any attempt at historical investigation. Any attempt to interpret Christian history by taking account of the chronological and cultural generations as potential building blocks of the new temple in its interpretation makes the need for such empathy still greater. Church historians can benefit from the Hiebertian virtue of cultural sensitivity.

For instance, a culture-sensitive reading of the history of Christian doctrine might reveal how the crossing of cultural frontiers develops and enlarges theology. This happens because entry into a new culture at any depth may both pose questions previously unconsidered and provide intellectual materials for pursuing those questions. As the early church entered the Greek world at greater and greater depth, it came to a new, fuller understanding of who Christ is than Gentile believers could ever have attained simply from essentially Jewish categories such as Messiah. The great creeds are the product of the new questions posed by deeper penetration of the Greek world of thought. When today we recite words like "God from God, Light from Light, Very God from Very God, begotten, not made, being of one substance with the Father," we are drawn out in worship. Yes, we realize that this is who Christ, the Jesus we meet in the Gospels, really is. But this discovery was the outcome of a long and painful process. The process involved attempting to think in Greek in a Christian way, asking Greek questions (questions that in another culture might seem irreverent and presumptuous), using indigenous categories and conventions of debate, making indigenous mistakes. When the process was complete, it could be agreed that it was all implied in Scripture, but it was only following indigenous mental processes that made the discoveries and in doing so brought classical Christian theology into being. Nor was there any loss, anything valuable to be given up; the word *Messiah*, for instance, still meant everything that it had always meant. But its translation and transposition into a new cultural setting had revealed new dimensions.

Similarly, Christian entry into the "barbarian" cultures of Northern and Western Europe following the collapse of the Western Roman Empire stimulated new thinking about Christ's atoning work. The practice of both Germanic customary law and codified Roman law raised issues such as the responsibility of kin for offenses committed by relatives and the relationship between compensation and offense that, when brought into interaction with the biblical material, reached classical expression in Anselm.

The Cultural Factor in Contemporary Theology

Attention to the cultural factor in the history of doctrine, its persistent raising of new issues for theology, could make it much easier to recognize and cope with some important aspects of the contemporary theological situation. The determining factor in the contemporary Christian situation is the cross-cultural diffusion of the faith, especially during the past century, so that Christianity is now a principally non-Western religion. We must therefore increasingly expect modern theological issues to arise from Christian interaction, at a level wholly new, with the ancient cultures of Africa and Asia. It could prove to be a period, like that from the late second to the mid-fifth century, of immense theological ferment and creativity.

Africa is already revealing the limitations of theology as generally taught in the West. The truth is that Western models of theology are too small for Africa. Most of them reflect the worldview of the Enlightenment, and that is a small-scale worldview, one cut and shaved to fit a small-scale universe. Since most Africans live in a larger, more populated universe, with entities that are outside the Enlightenment worldview, such models of theology cannot cope with some of the most urgent pastoral needs. They have no answers for some of the most desolating aspects of life—because they have no questions. They have nothing useful to say on issues involving such things as witchcraft or sorcery, since these do not exist in an Enlightenment universe. Nor can Western theology usefully discuss ancestors, since the West does not have the family structures that raise the questions. Western theology has difficulty coping with principalities and powers, whether in relation to their grip on the universe or to Christ's triumph over them on the cross. The reason is that it is hard for Western consciousness to treat them as other than abstractions. So Western theology has difficulty in relating personal sin and guilt and structural and systemic evil and sometimes offers different gospels for dealing with each or quarrels as to which has priority. Perhaps Africa, which knows so much about systemic evil and where the principalities and powers are not a strange concept, may open the way to a more developed theology of evil, as the issues already appearing in African pastoral practice are threshed out.

The presentation of Christian history, therefore, must reveal not only the chronological movement of the generations but also the demographic movements in the constitution of the church. This will reveal the movement of the Christian heartlands as a feature of Christian history. At different times, different regions and cultures provide the Christian mainstream, the representative Christians of that time. Were we able to assemble a group of representative Christians of the past, we might bring together Jerusalem apostles and elders with Nicene fathers, Irish monks, Victorian humanitarians, and African charismatics. We might reasonably claim that there is a relationship of historical continuity between such bodies of people, but we would have to acknowledge that these historically related groups of representative Christians often reflected quite different understandings of the Christian life. Each group would have practices and priorities that other groups would find strange, even repellent. By contrast, were we able to take five groups of representative Muslims from the centuries between the early Caliphate and the present day, there would be a good chance that they would at least be able to perform the Friday prayers together. Christian life and thought, taking as its norm the incarnation of the divine Word, requires incarnation, embodiment in the cultural specifics of a particular time and place. Generations may be utterly diverse, therefore, in their understanding and experience of the grace of God and yet belong together in the ultimate purpose of God. The full significance of any one of them is not clear without the others. Abraham is waiting for us before he receives the fullness of what was promised to him. In the meantime, making sense of church history is a cross-cultural exercise.

Reflections on World Christianity and the Academy

In considering the present situation in the teaching of Christian history, I hope that a degree of personal testimony may be forgiven. Humility and charity are scholarly, as well as Christian, virtues, and I can only ask further forgiveness if they are found to be lacking in what follows. I have spent more than half a century in academic life, holding posts in several African countries, in Britain, and in the United States and being privileged to be a visiting lecturer elsewhere in Europe and the Americas and in Asia and the Pacific. Some institutions where I have worked have had as their goal the good of the church and the preparation of the church's ministry; others have been public universities where religious and theological studies were conducted in the context of humanistic and scientific learning, with believer and nonbeliever working side by side.

Many things have changed over the half century; some, perhaps, have not changed enough. What has changed most over the course of my lifetime is the demography of the Christian church, the southward movement of its center. Europe and, to a lesser extent, North America have seen recession, while Latin America, some parts of Asia-Pacific, and especially Africa have seen growth, and all present evidence suggests that these trends will continue. The corollary is that African, Asian, and Latin American Christianity will become more and more important within the church as a whole and Western Christianity less and less so. Neither the churches of the North nor those of the South have yet taken in the full implications of this major movement of the Christian heartland, the theological academy perhaps least of all.

The children of darkness are in their day and generation often wiser than the children of light. Parts of the secular academy have been clearer eyed than the church or the theological academy. When I first joined the African Studies Association of the United Kingdom, I was one of only four members whose special field lay in religion. Among Africanists generally, religion meant African traditional religion (territory contested with the anthropologists) or Islam, though the study of African Independent churches, as they were then beginning to be called, might be allowed. My special concern, African Christianity in general, was widely thought of as missions and thus not really African at all but a branch of Western activity within Africa.

The situation is different today. Historians, not theologians, opened the way. The leading British historian of Africa, Roland Oliver, first (as far as I have noticed) pointed out what was happening in African Christianity. He had already written *The Missionary Factor in East Africa* (1952, note the title) when, in 1956, he produced a pamphlet titled *How Christian Is Africa?* This pointed out that Christians in Africa appeared to be increasing in geometrical progression, having doubled their numbers every twelve years or so since the middle of the nineteenth century. Then the Ibadan School of History, including the late Kenneth Dike and his successors such as J. F. Ade Ajayi and E. A. Ayandele, began to produce their groundbreaking studies. Their principal sources were mission archives, and they revealed their immense scholarly value and significance. (Before their time it had even been solemnly stated, as regards one area of Africa, that mission sources did not exist.) The Ibadan School showed that mission archives were sources for *African* mainstream history. They showed that Christianity had on occasion played a determinative part in that history and that Africans were determinative figures in Christianity as far back as the 1840s. They showed that the history of such an important country as Nigeria cannot be understood without an understanding of its Christian history. The contribution made by the historical sciences to the study of religion in Africa has been vital. When theological studies cut themselves off from other branches of learning, they lose opportunities to renew their own streams with fresh, clear water. This point has been illustrated more recently from the same example of Nigeria by the work of the historical sociologist John Peel. His main sources—and they have been revelatory—are the records of nineteenth-century missionaries who were themselves Yoruba-speaking Africans.

By contrast with forty years ago, I now find that my colleagues in African studies, even if personally secular in outlook, fully recognize the importance of African Christianity. Social scientists, trained in participant observation, find themselves in Africa engaging in prayer, however little previous acquaintance they may have with that activity. Political scientists see the importance of churches as viable forms of civil society and in some countries the only form that works. Specialists in popular literature have noted the phenomenon; I heard a learned paper that described the entire popular religion of Ghana as "religious fundamentalism." Where Africa is the focus of study in the secular academy today, there is widespread acknowledgment that, if one wants to study modern Africa, it is necessary to know something about Christianity. In the theological academy, however, there appears much less recognition that, if one wishes to study modern Christianity, it is necessary to know something about Africa.

All over the Western world, ministers are being trained and future theological scholars are being identified and taken to doctoral level and beyond without any idea of what the church of today, in which they are called to serve, is really like. The way that Christian thought is presented to them implies that it is a Western religion, or at least, if it did not start that way, it has now become one. Church history is a case in point. A common church history syllabus begins with what is called the early church. In fact, it usually deals only with the part of the early church that lay within the Roman Empire. By missing the early church beyond the Roman Empire, the syllabus also misses Asia and Africa. It also loses the chance to compare the experience of Christians in the Persian Empire, who never had a Constantine, with the experience of Christians in the Roman Empire, who did. Students are led to identify the "Great Century of Missions" as the nineteenth, without noticing that there are other great centuries in the missionary history of the church or instituting any comparison between the nineteenth and the ninth century. Even the Roman Empire in this syllabus soon becomes the Western Roman Empire. Yet in Protestant anxiety to ease the leap from Augustine (354–430) to Luther (1483–1546), the syllabus frequently omits a critical period of Western church history, the conversion period. So there is no study of the engagement between Christianity and the traditional religions of Europe, the very point where comparison of the experiences of African, Asian, and Western Christians can be most illuminating.

For the same reason, Western students often do not have the opportunity to reflect on how and why Western Christianity came to take the shape it did. They are left to assume that Western Christianity is a normative form of the faith, seamlessly connected with the church of the fathers. Even well-read, scholarly Western theologians are sometimes surprised at the statement that Africa has nearly two thousand years of continuous Christian history, or that nearly fifteen hundred years of Asian church history took place before Western missionaries arrived, or that the first preaching of the gospel before the king of northern England was roughly contemporary with that before the emperor of China. What Western scholars studied as the history of the church was in reality the history of the church in "our village." More seriously, nothing in their theological education has prepared them for intelligent participation in a church that is principally African, Asian, and Latin American in composition or enabled them to realize the changed place of Western believers within that church. Worse still, versions of such syllabi are, with the best intentions, exported to Africa and Asia. The impression they give there of the place of Christianity in history is utterly distorting, the picture of Christian history that they encourage among non-Christians is profoundly misleading, and the problems of relating this notional "general" history of the church with local church history are well-nigh insuperable.

Christianity has always been, in principle, global; this is not just a phenomenon of the twentieth century. It is arguable that the few centuries when Christianity was overwhelmingly Western actually represent an exception. A product of Western intellectual history has been translated into academic organization so that the history of missions has commonly been separated from the history of the church. There is no such division in reality; they are the same. We have seen that, in the purposes of God, the generations, cultural as well as chronological, belong together and complement one another. Surely they belong together in the study and teaching of church history.

Light is dawning in many places. The attempts at comprehensive church history writing are increasing. A shining example is the *History of the World Christian Movement* (2001) by Dale Irvin and Scott Sunquist, with the splendid accompanying book of documents. There is a growing need for scholarly writing and teaching on African and Asian church history, for use not just in Africa and Asia but everywhere. Research in African and Asian Christianity is now a core requirement, belonging to the mainstream of Christian studies. The past forty years have seen these fields transformed through fundamental research work on primary sources. Whole forests of doctoral dissertations have grown up; thousands of academic articles of varying quality have appeared. There is still abundant fundamental work of this kind to be done, but there is also an enormous task of synthesis, as the dissertations gather dust and the very journals in which the articles appeared cease publication. It is work needed not in Africa and Asia alone but for the good health of Christian history everywhere.

This raises a final word about sources and resources for this renewal of the study of Christian history.

Sources and Resources for Studying Christian History

In the early 1960s, I was involved in a program to collect church records in eastern Nigeria. We sought to persuade local churches to deposit whatever documents they held in a special archive. Many insisted that little would result, that these churches did not keep records, or that time and termite had destroyed them. In the event, hundreds of documents were brought forth and deposited in the archive: baptismal and marriage registers; records of services held, with a note of the preacher and text in each case; minute books of meetings; books recording decisions in disciplinary adjudications. Some of them went back to the 1890s. Here were records of seventy years of an African church, emerging, growing, worshiping, witnessing, sinning, repenting—and hardly a foreign missionary appearing anywhere. We made provision for the conservation of the documents and appointed an excellent young graduate (he later became Nigeria's first professor of church history) to record and catalog them. We talked of photocopying them, but such processes in those days were expensive—they could wait until next year. There was no next year. The Nigerian Civil War came. The building took a direct hit and was burnt to ashes. I walked in the ashes and saw not a leaf that could be recovered.

We cannot escape the possibility of catastrophe; that is the human condition. It is in the nature of civilizations—from the Assyrian to the American, from the tower of Babel to the skyscraper—to aim for permanence. It is of the nature of Christianity that we have no permanence, no abiding city, until the new Jerusalem comes down out of heaven at the last day. We have come to associate ideas of permanence with the normal conditions of theological scholarship. We have come to assume that scholarship will normally require comfortable, if not luxurious, surroundings and abundant, if not superabundant, resources. But there is no necessary connection between permanence or stability and research. The scholarship of Origen (185–ca. 254) was built up in an age of insecurity and persecution. The scholarship of Northern Europe in the age of its conversion was developed amid desolating wars, the literary conveniences of Augustine's day long vanished. Theology does not arise from the study or the library, even if it can be prosecuted there. It arises from Christian life and activity, from the need to make Christian choices, to think in a Christian way. The largest fields of Christian life and activity are now appearing in Africa, Asia, and Latin America, and we may expect, and indeed are already beginning to see, crucial theological issues arising there. This is where acute situations requiring Christian choice will be constantly arising, and new questions will be posed as the biblical materials interact at deeper and deeper levels with the cultures of Asia and Africa. Places in Europe and North America that we have come to regard as the leading centers of theological eminence may well retain large resources but become insignificant for the most critical tasks. After all, the great theological centers of the Christian world were at one time Antioch and Alexandria.

The new Christian heartlands have learned much about catastrophe: the wars, the natural disasters, the coups, the economic breakdowns, the IMF, the trade patterns. Many things conspire to divide the world between rich and poor. In African libraries, the journal subscriptions ran out long ago. Every year important books on Africa are published at prices no African institution can afford and that would swallow any African professor's salary for months ahead. Perhaps Africa, as happened in the days of Isidore and Bede, will develop new and different structures for pursuing Christian scholarship. Africa and Asia have some unique resources, gold mines for Christian history. There are abundant records—printed, manuscript, and oral—that no one has yet collected or recorded. And there are human resources. The Christian world now has people who know what it is to live in a first-, a second-, or a third-century church. That could mean better resources for understanding the patristic period than the Bodleian or the Vatican libraries can supply.

That does not mean we should court catastrophe or sneer at the garnered resources in the older centers. Modern technology opens possibilities of sharing resources so that the Bodleian and Vatican libraries do not need to be replicated elsewhere. Perhaps the test of real sharing within the body of Christ could be whether new heartlands could get greater access to the stockpiled scholarly resources of the West, not just the leftovers but the substance.

The truth is that Christian history can now be satisfactorily studied neither in the Western world alone nor in the non-Western world alone, neither in the North nor in the South on their own. Even in scholarship, the cultural generations, like the chronological generations, belong together and need one another to carry out their respective parts in the construction of the new temple.

Part 2

Methodological Issues
for Globalizing Theology

4

"One Rule to Rule Them All?"

Theological Method in an Era of World Christianity

KEVIN J. VANHOOZER

Mission and Method in Middle-Earth: The Rule of Reason

How can humans speak of God? *Who* gets to speak of God? *Why* just these voices rather than others? The history of philosophy may be a series of footnotes to Plato, but we dare not make the same claim about the history of theology. Plato's thought may warrant a chapter or so in the history of Christian theology, but it is hardly the whole story. Yet in middle-earth—the story beginning with the Holy Roman Empire and the Middle Ages and reaching into early and late modernity—the West awakened to find itself Greek. And since the fifteenth-century voyages of discovery, the West has cast its shadow over other lands.

There are not a few similarities between the contemporary global situation and the one J. R. R. Tolkien depicted in *The Lord of the Rings*. To be sure, Tolkien rejected the notion that his story was an allegory. Yet it is hard not to hear a distorted variation of "modern" in "Mordor" or to miss a certain parallel between "that hideous strength" of the one Ring and the monological rule of reason in the modern era of scientific method: In *techne*—instrumental reason—we trust. By and large, the

voices that we think are authorized to speak of God belong to those who
have been trained according to Western notions of theological reason.
But how does "system" play in the *global* shire?[1]

Mission in the Modern West: Discovery and Domination

Jürgen Moltmann dates modernity (what Germans call *Neuzeit,* or
"new time") from 1492, the year that marked the discovery and conquest
of America, the "new world." To discover something "always means at
the same time an appropriation of what is strange and alien" (Moltmann 1999, 6). A similar dynamic of discovery defines modern scientific knowledge: "The seizure of power over nature by means of science
and technology is the other foundation stone of the new world order"
(Moltmann 1999, 7). Discovery in the context of modernity means domination: political, intellectual, cultural. The modern West has effectively
colonized the world, in large part through the power of instrumental
reason. Indeed, it is no exaggeration to speak of the *mission* of modernity:
to gain a measure of control, through reason, of the world, of others,
even of God.

Some of the more distinctive features of modernity complicit, at times,
with this mission include capitalism, liberal democracy, and the scientific method. Each of these developments is a tangible expression of an
underlying confidence in reason to order our economic and political
life and to gain control over our natural environment. These profound
cultural and intellectual changes came to be reflected in modernity's
institutions, not least the university.

The modern university aspires to universal knowledge. It was a fundamental presupposition that the kind of learning that took place in the
modern university was a *generically human* enterprise: "Before entering
the university halls of learning we are to strip off all our particularities—particularities of gender, race, nationality, religion, social class,
age—and enter purely as normal adult human beings" (Wolterstorff 1996,
38).[2] Success in the modern academy is not simply a matter of what

1. Michael Hardt and Antonio Negri (2000) argue that a new kind of sovereign power
is emerging to replace the nation-state. They call this power "Empire" and claim that it
is nonlocalized: "Empire's rule has no limits" (xiv). The object of Empire's rule is "social
life in its entirety" (xv). While Hardt and Negri are thinking of global market and communication forces, and while they link these with postmodernity, a case could be made
that these forces are but extensions of the rule of instrumental (e.g., marketing, economic)
reason. Interestingly, their sequel (2004) pits the "multitude" ("the many," a centrifugal
globalizing force) against "Empire" ("the one," a centripetal globalizing force). As we will
see, a similar dynamic is unfolding with regard to first and third world theology.

2. Mark Brett notes that in Western democracies public life has been dominated
by a discourse that tends to "treat individuals primarily as equal citizens and economic

you know, much less of who you are, but of how you know it. Accordingly, method—the study of the right procedure for knowing—replaced metaphysics as modernity's "first philosophy."

It is startling to think that evangelical seminaries may be the misbegotten progeny of their medieval and modern parents. Yet biblical studies has indeed become a kind of *techne*, or technology, of the text. Fernando Segovia observes that students trained in historical-critical exegesis must divest themselves of their cultural identity and interpret like Eurocentric readers (1996, 479).[3] Systematic theology, likewise, has become a kind of *theoria*, or theory, of God and his relation to the world, a theory that appears not to be located in any particular historical or cultural situation. Are exegesis and systematic theology really exercises of universal reason?

The Madness in the Method: Against Theological Myopia

G. K. Chesterton's *Orthodoxy*, a defense of the Apostles' Creed, is an excellent refutation of the West's reliance on theoretical reason. His chapter "The Maniac" is especially relevant. According to Chesterton, "The madman is not the man who has lost his reason. The madman is the man who has lost everything except his reason" (1959, 19). Lunatic logic is compelling and constricting; the madman suffers not from inconsistency but from *too much* consistency. In the insane mind, facts fit together perfectly and explanations are complete, but only because the madman is "not hampered by . . . the dumb certainties of experience" (1959, 19). Madness is a matter of intellectual tunnel vision, of submitting to the power of an idée fixe: "His mind moves in a perfect but narrow circle" (1959, 20). The result: "The insane explanation is quite as complete as the sane one, but it is not so large" (1959, 20).

There is a touch of madness in the West's fascination with method. Method, after all, is only a formalization of insight. For example, consider the different insights that fund the structuralist and historical-critical methods of interpreting the Bible. The one focuses on the literary form of the text, the other on its original setting and background. To employ only one such method to the exclusion of all others is to fall prey to interpretative myopia. That way hermeneutical madness lies.

The most unmistakable mark of madness is the connection between "logical completeness" and "spiritual contraction." Such a combina-

---

actors—religions, culture, and ethnicity therefore being regarded as private matters" (1996, 3).

3. We may well wonder whether the grammatical-historical method of exegesis, favored in evangelical seminaries, fares any better.

tion produces a "narrow universality" (1959, 20). The question, then, is whether Western theological method is "insane" in the sense that it is too narrowly universal.[4]

What Chesterton says about the need for mystery and the imagination is also worth noting: "Imagination does not breed insanity. Exactly what does breed insanity is reason. Poets do not go mad; but chess-players do" (1959, 17). And again: "The poet only asks to get his head into the heavens. It is the logician who seeks to get the heavens into his head. And it is his head that splits" (1959, 17–18). The chief mark of insanity, then, is "reason used without root" (1959, 27). Or perhaps without clothes. The question is whether reason can flourish (and remain sane) without the nurture of a specific language, culture, and fiduciary storied framework. Western pride in the universality of reason—instrumental, theoretical, calculative rationality—may actually be a symptom of cultural insanity. The madness of Western rationality and methodology, then, consists in its lack of imagination, its being too generic and too narrowly universal.

Our Big Fat Greek Method: What Are They Saying about Western Theological Thought?

"The greatest single change that has come upon the Christian faith during the last century has been the demographic shift in its focus away from its traditional centres in Europe and North America" (Parratt 2004, 1). While some ethicists are wary of deriving an "ought" from an "is," most non-Western theologians do not hesitate to draw a theological prescription from this demographic description.

More and more people are asking whether, and why, Christian theologians from other parts of the world must play by Western Christianity's rules in order to do theology. The really significant dividing line is no longer that between conservative and liberal Western Christians but that between Western and non-Western Christians: "The first is connected with the rational, businesslike forms of secular, Westernized society. The second is rooted in a romantic, mystically minded, pietistic or pentecostal 'counter-culture'" (Barrington-Ward 1988, 288). Kwame Bediako speaks not only for Africans when he complains that "Western theology was for so long presented in all its particulars as *the* theology of the Church, when, in fact, it was geographically localised and culturally limited, European and Western, and not universal" (2004, 115).

4. Fernando Segovia speaks eloquently of the plight of non-Western students who, on entering a Western seminary or university, find that "neither the content nor the mode of discourse is their own" (1996, 485).

Non-Western theologies question the form, content, and categories that have become the default setting of academic theology. In this respect, non-Western thinkers have become surprising bedfellows with certain Western postmoderns. Both groups, despite their differences, agree on the need for a genealogical analysis of Western intellectual systems to unmask their apparent universality and on the need to listen to others.[5] And both groups agree that the West's discourse on God and salvation is ultimately only a "local" theology.[6]

Postmodernists like Carl Raschke "dehellenize" evangelical faith in an attempt to undo theology's dependence on categories taken from secular philosophy.[7] The most fundamental of these categories is the notion that knowledge is *theoria*, a "seeing" with the mind's eye, a metaphor that encouraged Western thinkers to subscribe to the subject-object distinction. To think, according to this received view, is a matter of a subject's "seeing" an object: "The goal of thought is to obtain a clear and precise picture of what one is viewing" (Raschke 2004, 213). The ensuing quest for objective knowledge led philosophers like Descartes to view the knowing subject as detached from the world, able to abstract from experience universally true propositions through various rational procedures. Scholastic and modern theologians quickly followed suit, viewing theology as the "science" of God's revelation in nature and Scripture. Postmodernity is largely a reaction to the subject-object distinction and to its concomitant assumption that truth can be discovered by induction and deduction. Such theoretical assumptions provoke a similar reaction on the part of non-Western theologians. At the first meeting of the 1976 Ecumenical Association of Third World Theologians in Dar es Salaam, the attendees

5. Kwame Bediako makes the intriguing claim that certain aspects of postmodernity "bear the marks of a primal world-view" (2004, 60).

6. The postmodern condition is perhaps best viewed in terms of an acute awareness of one's situatedness (e.g., in gender, culture, history, language, geography, etc. [see Vanhoozer 2005d]). Rebecca Chopp makes a similar observation, noting that Latin American, black, and feminist theologians "have made a convincing case for the situatedness of all knowledge" (1997, 421).

7. According to Diogenes Allen, "Christian theology is inherently hellenic because it could not exist as a *discipline* without the kind of intellectual curiosity which was unique to ancient Greece" (1985, 4). Allen acknowledges that other peoples too ask "Why?" but the Greeks did so "persistently and systematically." Allen goes on to say that the minds of the early church fathers were "hellenic," not because they happened to use a particular set of concepts but because they too persisted in questioning and prized coherence (1985, 5). Going beyond Allen, one might suggest that Hellenization provided the ripe intellectual moment for the birth of Christian theology just as the Pax Romana provided the appropriate political conditions for the spread of the gospel. At the same time, it is important to distinguish a purely intellectual curiosity from faith's more passionate quest for understanding. My thanks to Lisa Sung for drawing my attention to Allen.

issued the following statement: "We reject as irrelevant an academic type of theology that is divorced from action" (Chandran 2000).

The postmodern philosopher Emmanuel Levinas argues that the subject-object structure itself is intrinsically violent. He calls the attempt to know subjects theoretically to master the world of objects "Greek-think."[8] Greek-think seeks to totalize or swallow up everything into procrustean conceptual schemes in its effort intellectually to grasp things (an essentially violent gesture). What this really amounts to is the totalitarian move to recast the "other" in terms of the "same"—to think otherness in terms of our categories, our system of thought, our language: "The labor of thought wins out over the otherness of things and men" (Levinas 1989, 79).[9] Levinas echoes the sentiments of many non-Western thinkers when he accuses Western systems of ideas, values, and even theology of repressing and oppressing the other.[10] What Levinas wants is not a better method but an "ethics" that respects the irreducible particularity of the other.

Non-Western theologians believe that something like Levinas's totalization happened regularly in theology. Brahmabandhav Upadhyaya contends, for example, that the Greco-Roman concepts of classical theology were singularly inappropriate for Indian Christians. His solution was to employ Hindu philosophy instead, on the grounds that just as Greek thought was a vehicle for the truths of the gospel in Europe, so "the truths of the Hindu philosopher must be 'baptized' and used as stepping stones to the catholic faith" (cited in Parratt 2004, 10). From Taiwan, Choan-Seng Song complains of Western theology's enslavement to an either-or rationalist logic and of its concomitant lack of imagination (1990b, 19–23). Song believes that theology should begin with the heart, a "third eye" that transcends reason and opens up the mystery of Being.

8. I am somewhat ambivalent about labeling Western thought "Greek." Philosophy in one sense is but "a series of footnotes to Plato." Nevertheless, what we typically think of as Greek or Eastern Orthodoxy developed independently of theology in the West, so much so that we can ask, "What does Athens (or Rome, for that matter) have to do with Byzantium?" The fact is that Eastern Orthodoxy did not go on to become the *scientia* that it did in the Latin West, nor did it adopt the Cartesian subject/object dichotomy or the various hermeneutical theories that derive from it. Eastern Orthodox theologians themselves would surely object to being lumped under the rubric Western. I owe this point to a personal communication with Lisa Sung.

9. "Greek-think" is thus a metaphor for intellectual ethnocentrism, that is, for any form of thinking that attempts to describe the "other" in terms that are intelligible within one's own culture rather than in terms of the other's culture.

10. If procedural rationality is the formal principle of Western theology, metaphysics is its material principle, so much so that some have coined the term *ontotheology*. Ontotheology is the discourse of God in terms of "being." The present chapter focuses on the formal principle. For more on the development of metaphysical theology or theism, see Kärkkäinen (2004).

Such an approach is better suited to the "Asian intuitive approach to reality" (1990b, 62–64). Jung Young Lee is similarly critical of Western theology's captivity to Aristotelian logic because it is contrary to the both-and, yin-yang thinking of Asia (1979; 1995).

Others suggest that Western missionaries displayed "judaizing" tendencies by insisting (or at least implying) that Africans had to become honorary Europeans in order to become Christians: "For each culture, 'barbarians' differ. For Anglo-Americans . . . the 'Gentiles' may be Hispanics, Africans, Chinese, Koreans" (Spencer and Spencer 1998, 10). The Ghanian theologian John Pobee even sounds like Levinas when he speaks of "the North Atlantic Captivity of the Church" (cited in Stinton 2004, 112).

There is a natural if limited alliance, then, between the postmodern critique of modernity and the third world's critique of Western theology.[11] The question remains, How do we do theology "after the West"? The very notion of method may itself be too Western a category to embrace for some. It may be that theology in an era of world Christianity inhabits a situation "after method," that is, a situation in which no one method dominates. What characterizes much non-Western theology is the "dynamic search for self-identity, an identity which takes seriously the traditions and cultures in which it is located" (Parratt 2004, 8).

So the various peoples of middle-earth have banded together to combat the evil empire of Mordor: the power of the one rule. One purpose of this chapter is to situate today's Christian theologian by calling attention to the church's global context and to remind us that no language or culture has a monopoly on God, the gospel, or theology. This is an important and timely prophetic blast against the monstrous regiment of systematic theologians, in whose company I count myself.

It is undeniable that the church has entered a new era. The race of men is no longer dominated by the power of the one rule. The reign of the sovereign knowing subject, and of universal method, is coming to an end: "The time of European and Western monologue is over" (Escobar 2003, 136). But does it necessarily follow that systematicians must go the way of the Elves, whose time had ended, setting sail (appropriately enough!) toward the West?

11. The editors of the forthcoming *Global Dictionary of Theology* (Dyrness and Kärk-käinen) state that terms such as *third world, non-Western,* or *Southern* are ambiguous, inappropriate, and generally no longer helpful. However, many non-Western theologians themselves continue to use the rubric third world "as a self-designation of peoples who have been excluded from power and the authority to shape their own lives and destiny" (Fabella 2000c, 202). See also Parratt (2004, 12). Note, finally, the self-designation of the Ecumenical Association of Third World Theologians (EATWOT).

This chapter describes the contemporary situation and proposes a way forward for doing theology. The second section treats the recent "turn to context." Highlighting an interpreter's situatedness challenges the exegetical pretense to objectivity and universality. Yet the turn to context ultimately helps systematics to recover the pastoral and practical dimension of its theological interpretation of Scripture. The next section examines the phenomenon of world Christianity and notes some troubling tendencies with regard to theological method, in particular, two forms of a "bad global" theology. The fourth section stakes a "mid-Western" claim about the nature and task of theology that stems from the subject matter of theology itself: theodrama, the words and acts of the Triune God that culminate in God's reconciling all things to himself in Jesus Christ. This section sets forth the canonical principle that theology, regardless of its context, must accord with Scripture if it does not want to proclaim and perform some other gospel than that of Jesus Christ. The next section then sets forth a catholic principle and argues that the ethnic and social diversity of the church is the condition for an enriched and enlarged theological understanding that issues in performance knowledge: speaking and doing the same truth differently. The chapter concludes by offering criteria for "great performances" of the gospel and by suggesting ways that systematic theology can continue to serve the church in the global diaspora.

Doing Theology and "the Turn to Context": From Method to Experience, Proposition to Praxis, Ideas to Identity

"All theology is ultimately 'contextual,' that is it arises from a specific historical context and it addresses that context" (Parratt 2004, 2).

Systematic theology is the cognitive and passionate endeavor to know and love the God of the gospel and to demonstrate the understanding of faith in loving and obedient speech and action. Biblical interpretation is the "soul of theology." From the start, the central task of theology consisted of interpreting the Bible in new cultural contexts: Athens, Rome, North Africa, etc. Indeed, it has been said that church history is largely the history of biblical interpretation (Ebeling 1964). Classical theology is a text-based discipline, a matter of sustained biblical commentary or "marginalia."

In the medieval universities, the hitherto informal reading of Scripture for edification (*lectio*) was transformed into a formal method of argumentation on the basis of Scripture (*disputatio*). Theologians appropriated Aristotle's categories (e.g., substance, cause, form, matter, etc.) and fashioned them into a golden methodological calf, a metaphysical interpretative framework for discerning the meaning and truth of

Scripture (e.g., God = uncaused cause). Reformation theologians were less in thrall to Aristotle's categories but persisted in seeing theology in terms of textual exposition.

Twentieth-century evangelicals in Europe and North America largely agreed with Charles Hodge that theology is an inductive science. According to this view, the Bible is one's storehouse of facts, and doctrine is what results from one's examination of the data. To be precise, doctrine is for Hodge the propositional product that follows from one's deduction of the principles that govern the facts. Such Euclidean theology is fatally abstract; cultural contexts play no role in this one-size-fits-all theological method. David Clark (2003, 104) notes that the traditional view of hermeneutics—the set of rules and principles for proper interpretation—assumes the subject-object distinction (e.g., interpreter and text). Instead of profitable pastoral instruction, theologians begat system after system, exchanging their ecclesial birthright for a mess of propositionalist pottage. Laypersons in the church would perhaps have been within their rights to bring a class-action suit against systematic theologians for criminal pastoral and missiological negligence. (I offer the present chapter as partial reparation.)

The single most significant methodological development that stems from the changing demographics of Christianity is the new appreciation for context: "Context has . . . become primary for the theological task" (Parratt 2004, 8). Context is simply shorthand for seeing theology as ineluctably tied to and rooted in particular social, cultural, and geographical networks. It is context that gives theologies their specific *texture*: "Theologians construct their theology in their own language, from the particularities of a given time, place, culture, and social location" (Pedraja 2003, 13).

Biblical interpretation involves text *and* context, and issues not only in commentaries but in particular shapes of community life. Thanks to their new appreciation for context, theologians now see their task in terms of not only theoretical deliberation but also practical liberation. What I will call the "turn to context" has resulted in a more vital and practical interpretation of Scripture in which understanding is a matter of loving as well as knowing God with all one's heart, mind, and strength. The net result is a recovery and an enlargement of the ancient notion of the theological interpretation of Scripture. We turn now to examine some aspects of this epochal development.

The Turn to Context I: History and Tradition

The sea change in twentieth-century hermeneutics—the shift from epistemology to ontology, away from questions of method to questions of human being—has everything to do with context. To be sure, Christian theology is inescapably textual. David Kelsey rightly comments that some involvement with the Bible is "analytic" in being a Christian (1999, 89). Yet it is now widely accepted that one of the key presuppositions of the modern Western university—that the academy is engaged in *generic* human learning—is deeply mistaken (Wolterstorff 1996, 44). Interpreters are never disembodied minds but embodied persons, persons who are male or female, persons who inhabit a particular place in space and time and so are susceptible to historical and cultural conditioning. Is exegesis without cultural presuppositions possible? It is not. Biblical interpreters have identities that cannot simply be checked at the door upon entering the academy. A human being, we might say, is always *ethnic*, never generic.[12]

Hans-Georg Gadamer argues in his magnum opus *Truth and Method* (2002) that readers of the text are always/already situated in history and culture ("horizoned"). Moreover, such situatedness is not an obstacle to but the very condition of understanding. Gadamer believes that preoccupation with scientific method—with tools and techniques that supposedly yield universal and absolute knowledge—actually tends to detach and distance a reader from the matter of the text that is passed on through the ongoing conversation (tradition) to which the text gives rise. Hermeneutics for Gadamer is a matter not of method but of the conversation that we are.[13]

For Gadamer, understanding is a matter not merely of theoretical cognition but of one's whole-person involvement in the subject matter of the text. Understanding is a matter of "fusing" the horizon of the text and the horizon of one's present context. To locate understanding in this hermeneutic fusion is to dissolve the subject-object distinction. One could say (though he did not put it in quite these terms) that Gadamer discovered contextuality: "the influence of social, cultural, and historical context on one's thought" (Clark 2003, 54). Third world theologians, even more than Gadamer, have given a distinctly contextual twist to the famous hermeneutical circle. It is not simply a matter of the relation between the parts and the whole of a work, or even of the necessity of preunderstanding (e.g., preliminary idea of what the text is about). No, the contextual variation of the hermeneutical circle concerns the attempt to relate the "world of the reader" (one's political, cultural, social context) with the "world of the text" (McDonald 1990; Míguez 2000).

12. Definitions and concepts of ethnicity are both varied and contested and beyond the scope of the present chapter. For an introduction to biblical and contemporary understandings of ethnicity, see Brett (1996).

13. For a fuller discussion of Gadamer's theory of understanding, see Vanhoozer (2005a).

Theology in an era of world Christianity is still hermeneutical, but hermeneutics now means not "rules for interpretation" but "reading from one's lived experience." It is largely thanks to the twentieth-century revolution in hermeneutics that we can now see how the Western preoccupation with method blinded interpreters to their own cultural and historical assumptions. Third world theologians share a conviction that Western theology was largely unaware of and uninterested in context: "Philosophical abstractions, church doctrines, and biblical texts—rather than concrete situations and experience—were used as the starting point of theology" (Fabella 2000a, 58). Today, it is hermeneutically incorrect to claim that one's interpretations are immune to cultural conditions and hence applicable to all times and places. Accordingly, non-Western theologians spend as much if not more time examining the context as the biblical text. We turn now to examine two ways of attending to context.

The Turn to Context II: Society and Praxis

One factor in particular behind the universal pretensions of Western theology looms large: its preferred helping discipline, philosophy. Western philosophy has tended to trade in universals. In logic, the key categories are "all" and "none." In metaphysics, the key categories (e.g., actuality, possibility, necessity) pertain to all kinds of being and, indeed, to Being itself. Yet even these metaphysical categories did not arise in a vacuum but rather in a particular historical condition and cultural context. Furthermore, the struggle to assert one set of categories over another is often not merely theoretical but is linked to issues of power and control. Justo González, a Hispanic theologian, wonders for example whether the traditional understanding of divine perfection as immutability was not an attempt by those in privileged positions to justify the status quo (1990, 97). Some have wondered, then, whether formulas such as "one person in two natures" are the best way to identify Jesus Christ in Africa, Asia, and elsewhere. For most non-Westerners in the twenty-first century, the burning issue is not metaphysics but poverty.

Context, like the poor, we will always have with us. While Western theology was contextual in spite of itself, context has today become an independent and important issue in its own right. Contemporary theologies make contextual issues *explicit* in a way that was not traditionally the case. In turning to context, third world theologians now employ a different handmaiden: not philosophy but the social sciences. The key methodological issue is no longer that of right procedure (how?) but location (where?) and position (who?).

The turn to context also entails a new concern with practice. It is difficult simply to speak of God and the gospel—the good news about the love of God and the coming reign of God—in a context in which people are suffering from various forms of oppression. It is not enough simply to theorize; one must do something: "The practical or operational moment, largely ignored in classical and modern theology, is the privileged function in the theologies of the South for which 'acting' represents a constitutive moment of all true theology" (Boff 2000, 200). In light of this new emphasis, some think that liberation theology will be judged to be "the most influential movement of the twentieth century, possibly even since the Reformation" (Phan 2003, 26). It is a new way of doing theology, and it is proving popular in many regions of the world (e.g., Latin America, South Africa, Africa, Asia).

Clodovis Boff (1987, xxv) provides a helpful summary of liberation theology's common methodological core: see-judge-act. To begin with, to acknowledge context fully means analyzing ("seeing") the social conditions in which theology is done. Given our embeddedness in context, we are always-already socialized (e.g., socially formed), at least to some extent. At the same time, humans are not simply patients but agents, able to criticize and transform patterns of social interaction. According to Juan Luis Segundo, we must be careful not to read the biblical text in a way that simply supports the contextual status quo. If ideology is "meaning in the service of power," it is important to acknowledge that the Bible too can be pressed into ideological service. For Segundo, then, to enter into the hermeneutical circle means criticizing ways of reading Scripture that contribute to oppression: "The one and only thing that can maintain the liberative character of any theology is not its content but its methodology" (1976, 39–40).

For Gustavo Gutiérrez, theology is "critical reflection on Christian praxis in light of the Word" (1998, 11). To know God is a matter not of contemplation and deliberation but of doing justice and liberation. Praxis, a central notion in liberation theology, means more than action; it has rather to do with the fact that human beings are not autonomous subjects "above" history but rather embedded within an already politicized historical situation. In other words, praxis is not something we do that is outside us as much as the medium in which we live and move. Praxis is also the name for concrete practices—practices that characterize the reign of God—that transform the social medium as well. The praxis of faith is *in* history but not of it.

Increasingly, theologians in Africa, Latin America, and Asia are more interested in orthopraxis than orthodoxy. Theology must be relevant, and it must make a difference; it must address people's concerns, and it must transform the structures of everyday life. Andrew Kirk rightly comments, "It is crucial to the integrity of theology never to isolate its intellectual work from the call to be a force for the transformation of human life. . . . This is the message of theology from the South" (1997, 39–40). To turn to the social context, then, means to *see* (analyze the social situation), *judge* (discern God's reign), and *act* (practice the politics of the kingdom of God).

The Turn to Context III: Culture and Identity

To this point, we have seen that the turn to context stems from a dual necessity: the hermeneutical necessity to acknowledge an interpreter's situatedness in history and the praxis necessity to transform unjust social structures and dynamics. The third reason to turn to context is to rediscover one's cultural identity, itself a kind of liberation: "For Africans, liberation is necessarily an *act of culture*. Cultural resistance has been an effective weapon and tool in critiquing the entire colonial system" (Martey 2000, 127). Whereas the turn to the social context focuses on the *aim* of doing theology, the turn to the cultural context focuses on *materials* and *resources* for doing theology.

Here we have to consider an important new factor in third world theology, namely, the "dynamic search for self-identity, an identity which takes seriously the traditions and cultures in which it is located. . . . The agenda must come from the social world in which Christians now live" (Parratt 2004, 7–8). This third turn to context is best illustrated by African theology: "Africans focus on the Africanization of Christianity rather than on the christianization of Africa" (Fabella 2000b, 105).[14] There is a deliberate effort to make use of notions and practices that are part and parcel of Africans' worldview and culture. The "Final Communiqué" of the 1977 Pan-African Conference of Third World Theologians calls for a truly contextual theology: "Our task as theologians is to create a theology that arises from and is accountable to African people" (in Appiah-Kubi and Torres 1979, 193).

The turn to context as a resource for theology has itself raised material theological issues. Perhaps the most pressing is that of the status of African religions. Whereas Western missionaries had dismissed them as pagan, the present trend is to see African traditional religions as a hospitable "preparation for the gospel" (Mbiti 1972; Nyamiti 1994). The alternative is to ask converts to Christianity to stop being African. In

14. Kwame Bediako notes that there are in fact two distinct trends in African theology: the more liberation-oriented black theology and the one we are concerned with here, namely, the theological exploration of the indigenous cultures of the African people (2004, 49). I am conscious that "African," like "Asian," "Latin American," and even "North American," is a broad descripto. Each admits of many subspecies.

Kwame Bediako's words, "Without memory we have no past, and if we have no past, we lose our identity" (2004, 51). Theological method in Africa centers on the notion of cultural identity, on producing theology that is both African and Christian. Andrew Walls rightly comments that conversion is not about adopting someone else's pattern of life and thought but rather about "the turning towards Christ of everything that is there already, so that Christ comes into places, thoughts, relationships and world-view in which He has never lived before" (cited in Bediako 2004, 117).

What this means for doing theology in Africa today is that one can no longer simply dismiss as "primitive" traditional beliefs and practices. Indeed, in the 1990s, a number of African theologians began to do theology with African categories, building Christologies around notions such as "healer" or "ancestor" (John Pobee; Charles Nyamiti). A number of Asian theologians have similarly complained that Christian theology may be *in* Asia, but it is not yet *of* Asia. Here too the issue is that of identity, specifically, constructing Christian theology out of indigenous cultural resources. Accordingly, some have sought to answer Jesus' question, "Who do you say that I am?" by developing Christologies that draw on Confucian teaching about family relationships in order to present Jesus as the "eldest son" (Peter Phan) or, in parallel with African thought, the "ancestor par excellence." We see, then, that there is a properly *cultural* variation of the hermeneutical circle: a mutual interaction between the gospel and a particular culture whereby both are enriched.

In sum, the turn to context contributes both a formal and a material insight that provides some methodological common ground between various third world theologies. Formally, the turn to context involves (1) a hermeneutical principle: an attention to lived experience, especially that of the poor, as the *medium* in which biblical interpretation takes place; (2) a critical principle: an analysis of social structures and a praxis oriented to liberating transformation; and (3) a cultural principle: an attempt to make use of indigenous categories in order to convert people to Christ without destroying their memories and cultural identities.

With regard to similarities in content, the emphasis on divine compassion and justice may well be the new material principle that unites Latin American, African, and Asian theologies: "What brings the Third World together as Christian theologians is . . . the sense that God also shares in . . . the marginalization of non-people, and in the pain of the oppressed" (Parratt 2004, 11–12).[15] Philip Jenkins provides a helpful complementary

15. One could say that non-Western theology has recovered a new dimension of what Luther called the theology of the cross, whereas classical theism and theological method line up on the side of the theology of glory.

insight: "If there is a single key area of faith and practice that divides Northern and Southern Christians, it is this matter of spiritual forces and their effects on the everyday human world. The issue goes to the heart of cultural definition and worldviews" (2002, 123).

World Christianity: How *Not* to Go "Glocal"

To speak of world Christianity—Christianity extended in space and time—means simply that "Christianity cannot be understood exclusively from a Western perspective" (Lee 1999, 11). The shift in demographics and the turn to context should produce an effect on Western theological self-consciousness as well. If theology is to serve the church, the new challenge is how to give local expression to the understanding of faith while at the same time coping with globalization.

Globalization is a disputed concept. I use it here with two distinct senses, senses that refer to two ways of going global. In the first sense—call it good global—globalization is "a planetary consciousness, a deepened awareness of, and sensitivity to, the reality of increasing interdependence among the peoples of the world" (Clark 2003, 101). According to the second sense—bad global—globalization is a homogenizing process, the counterpart in culture and the marketplace to the notion that the Western university is a place of *generic* human learning.

Thanks to developments in travel and communications, both space and time have been compressed. These new technologies enable the bad global to swallow up the local, to repress particular differences for the sake of an all-embracing sameness, to compress the other into the same. The bad global is the power of the cultural "one" (homogenization); the good global is the awareness of the cultural "many."

The "glocal" is the point of intersection between the global and the local; "glocalization" describes the way in which people in a certain locale respond to globalization, the way the local goes global. Robert Schreiter distinguishes between "global flows" and "local logics" and wonders where and how theology fits in. Flows move across geographic and cultural boundaries, and Schreiter sees four global theological flows: liberation, feminism, ecology, and human rights (1997, 16). These concerns are universal, not in the Enlightenment sense that reason was considered universal but because of their ubiquity in addressing world-wide problems.

The question for theologians is whether to go with one of these global theological flows or whether to focus on one's local or regional concerns. To be sure, theology exists to serve the local church. But how can we get beyond a situation in which each local or regional branch of the church inhabits its own HUT (Homogenous Unit Theology)? Before offering a constructive proposal, we would do well to review three problematic ways of going glocal, three inadequate ways of doing local theology in a global context. The first underemphasizes the theological significance of local cultures, while the second and third represent pathological extremes in their response to the cultural variation of the ancient problem of the one and the many.

Christ and Context: Cultural Adaptation

The temptation of conservative theology is to conserve: to preserve the selfsame content in different contexts. If the message of the gospel is unchanging, then local cultural forms are merely vehicles for conveying the essential, permanent deposit of truth. Contextual theology, according to this view, is a matter of extracting the doctrinal kernel from its original cultural husk and then reinserting it in, or adapting it to, a new cultural husk. The key presupposition of this model is that the essential message is supracultural, able to be abstracted from its concrete mode of expression.[16] Contextualization, according to this view, is primarily a matter of communication: decoding and encoding.

How does it work? Typically, a missionary or theologian decodes the message of the Bible and extracts the revealed, supracultural proposition, then encodes the proposition into the local idiom and culture. As David Clark astutely notes, "This model presumes that contextualization happens only or primarily in the encoding stage" (2003, 112). What this abstraction-adaptation model forgets is that "any articulation of the allegedly transcultural principles still reflects the culture of the translator" (2003, 112). In its haste to move from the biblical text to contemporary context, this model overlooks the significance of the culture and context of the theologian doing the adapting.

Theology thus becomes a bad global that (1) insists on a kind of *kenosis,* or emptying out, of each local context of anything distinctive and specific to the culture and (2) ignores the powerful shaping influence of the theologian's own cultural location. Kwame Bediako cites as a case in point Byang Kato's biblicism, an approach that led him to reject the possibility that his local culture had anything positive to contribute to theology besides serving as a kind of inert husk, a passive vehicle that communicates truth from elsewhere (Bediako 2004, 55). Going glocal involves more, however, than putting "the thought forms of a

---

16. Stephen Bevans calls this the translation model (1992, chap. 4). I have avoided the term here largely because of Lamin Sanneh's different take on the phenomenon of vernacular translation.

contemporary missionary-sending culture in the linguistic dress of a receptor-culture" (Clark 2003, 113). It involves actually *doing* theology in the new context.

Exaggerating "the One": Religious Globalization

The centripetal tendency of globalization is to make of many one: "The mass media promote a global Western-style monoculture in food, dress, leisure, music, and sports" (Balasuriya 2000, 93). The most insidious effect of globalization is homogenization—of culture, of religion. More than semantics is at stake, then, when we distinguish between world Christianity—the variety of indigenous responses to the gospel through local idioms—and globalized Christianity, a product of a general hermeneutics of a largely generic religious experience.

A World Theology (Reat and Perry 1991) represents an extreme version of this homogenizing bad global tendency. The subtitle of the book is *The Central Spiritual Reality of Humankind*. The book itself examines the five major world religions and argues that each is an expression of one, common world theology. Essentially, the book takes what George Lindbeck calls the "experiential-expressivist" theory of doctrine and uses it to "solve" the problem of religious pluralism. Each religion, they argue, is a culturally specific expression of what is fundamentally an experience of the same spiritual reality.[17] Theirs is a lowest-common-denominator approach that necessitates a definition of "spiritual reality" as that which influences human behavior (whether existing or not, material or nonmaterial) insofar as it pertains to hopes and needs that relate to the meaning of life, "a phenomenon some call God" (Reat and Perry 1991, 2). Each of the world religions perceives one or more dimensions of humankind's spiritual reality, and thus they are mutually complementary. This world theology offers a set of categories that allow members of the particular religions to talk to and understand one another.

A similar offering, though somewhat more distinctly Christian, may be had in Ninian Smart and Steven Konstantine's *Christian Systematic Theology in a World Context* (1991), part of a series in World Christian Theology. Their stated goal is to present "the golden vision of a Christian faith in a way which will make it more accessible to citizens of the world" (1991, 25). Their major methodological move is to regard other religions as worldviews (systems of belief and practice) with the same status as secular worldviews (e.g., Aristotle, process philosophy) that theologians regularly, and happily, employ for their own purposes: "It

17. Similar attempts include Smith (1981) and the work of John Hick. See also Miller and Grenz (1998, 177–99).

is a strange thing that the Churches have so often been worried about religion-religion syncretism but relatively blind to religion-secular world-view syncretism" (1991, 39).

Smart and Konstantine affirm what they call the "Federal principle": a call for differing worldviews to work together for common goals such as peace and justice. They support the broader ecumenical movement "across faiths" (1991, 440). Their own formulation of Christian theology has room for Buddhist emptiness, the prophetic strand of Judaism, and the sense of the divine presence in nature common to Native Americans (1991, 430). It is all the more ironic, then, that their theology has no room for the Chalcedonian creed; a literal incarnation is altogether too exclusivist for their universalism panentheism.

Christian theologians who care about the revelatory and redemptive finality of Jesus Christ will be no more tempted by Smart and Konstantine's version of global theology than by Reat and Perry's. Yet the question remains, What should theology make of the world religions? How much continuity is there between categories from African or Asian religions and Christianity? In the context of third world theology, "ecumenical" can mean an approach that strives to take into account not only the riches of other Christian confessions but also the truth of other religions (Boff 2000, 199). So how far can we stretch "worldview ecumenism" before it breaks? This issue is especially pressing for Asian Christians but is increasingly the case for the rest of us as well.[18]

Syncretism—the mixing of pre-Christian religious tradition with biblical and Christian beliefs and practices—is one of the earliest and most enduring strategies for bringing about a certain kind of ecumenical globalization. As a theological method, syncretism raises two basic theological questions. The first concerns the locus of divine revelation: Where has God made himself known, and how? One theological warrant for syncretism to which many appeal today is the same as that offered by Justin Martyr in the second century: The pre-incarnate Word through whom all things were made is active throughout creation. The second question is whether the basic content of Christianity is altered in the process of borrowing and admixing various elements from other religions. For example, the *Evangelical Dictionary of Theology* states, "The Bible reveals syncretism as a long-standing tool of Satan to separate God from his people" (Imbach 1984, 1062). Many twentieth-century Western missionaries held a low view of syncretism as the indiscriminate

18. John Parratt suggests that, broadly speaking, each of the three continents of the third world has contributed something unique to Christian theology: "Latin America, the emphasis on liberation in the sociopolitical and economic dimension, Africa, the integrity of indigenous cultures and religions, and Asia, the need to do theology in a religiously plural context" (2004, 11).

combining of religions; like oil and water, they do not mix. However, the *Dictionary of Third World Theologies* has a different take on syncretism, seeing the process of integrating the gospel into cultural codes as an inevitable aspect of faith seeking understanding and locating syncretism even within the Bible itself (Duraisingh 2000, 192–93). Similarly, Robert Schreiter puts a more positive spin on syncretism, arguing that it is a matter of forming new identities out of ready-to-hand cultural elements (1997, 63).

Why, in principle, can theology borrow from Plato but not from primal religions? Why can Clement of Alexandria get away with suggesting that Greek philosophy was a pedagogue that led to Christ, while Bolaji Idowu is criticized for saying the same thing about African traditional religions? According to Kwame Bediako, "The efforts of Idowu, Mbiti and Mulago to demonstrate on the basis of the oneness of God and the pre-Christian African sense of God, that African Christian experience is not totally discontinuous with the pre-Christian heritage, fall within the approach to the Hellenistic heritage adopted by Justin and Clement" (2004, 71). The intent in each case, patristic and African, is to vindicate Christian theology by associating it with what is best in the culture that preceded it. How else to ensure that conversion does not become a matter of being "not Greek" or "not African"?

Can we assume that religions in general are revelatory or that primal religions, like John the Baptist, are preparing the way? Perhaps no more and no less than we can assume that secular worldviews are revelatory or that Plato's philosophy was a preparation for the gospel. If syncretism is a flawed method, its error lies not in mining philosophies and religions for true insights but in assuming that all religions and philosophies are ultimately about the same thing. Even a cursory reading of Scripture shows that the God of Israel had nothing to do with the idols of Canaan.[19] It is important to clarify that such borrowings usually come not in the form of a wholesale synthesis but rather as ad hoc assimilations, a kind of theological bricolage.

Uncritical syncretism is an instance of bad theological glocalization. Uncritical syncretism is perhaps best seen as a by-product of an experiential-expressivist approach to religion that continues falsely to presuppose that there is an underlying spiritual similarity between differing "surface" expressions. There is ample biblical evidence, however, that the fallenness of humanity inclines us to distort the truth and to chase after spirits of our own making.

---

19. It is also important to observe that the biblical authors appropriated indigenous notions (e.g., the Semitic name El' for God) and put them to their own theological work.

Theology must work with cultural elements, to be sure, but this requirement entails what we might call a *critical* syncretism.[20] The way forward today is what it has always been. In the words of André Benoit, "It is a question . . . of rethinking Christianity within the framework of a non-Western culture without, however, betraying or twisting it. That is to say that they must recover the usable elements in the native civilisations and reject the others. The Fathers did the same" (cited in Bediako 2004, 68). Happily, there are good historical precedents. Yet there are no logarithms to facilitate this process. What is needed is sound theological judgment, and workable criteria, with which to discern the appropriate from the inappropriate. We return to the question of criteria below. For the moment, suffice it to say that critical syncretism is a matter of Word and Spirit leading the church to see in culture new earthen vessels for the gospel.

Exaggerating "the Many": Theological Ethnification

The homogenizing impulse of bad globalization has led some to react, and to resist, by going local and reasserting cultural particularities. This is true in the church as well; there is a centrifugal force of world Christianity too. In light of both the real and the felt oppression by Western institutions and ideas, it is no surprise that many third world theologians choose to define themselves in contradistinction to the churches and theology of the West. B. Bujo (1992), for example, claims that African theology is a reaction to not being taken seriously by the West. Robert Schreiter defines ethnification as "the process of rediscovering a forgotten identity based on one's cultural ties" (1997, 23). This rehabilitation of the many has nothing to do with an anything-goes pluralism, however, but everything to do with recovering cultural identities. We need to grapple with the following question: Should every theology be an ethnic theology, or is theological ethnification an example of a bad local? Can ethnic theologies resist the temptation to become ethnocentric?[21]

The proliferation of ethnic theologies is one of the hallmarks of twenty-first-century Christianity. The *Dictionary of Third World Theologies* has separate entries for Aboriginal, African, African-American, American

---

20. I intend this to be a proposal similar to Paul Hiebert's notion of critical contextualization (see Hiebert 1987).

21. Ethnocentrism maintains "that beliefs and practices in another culture should, or cannot but, be interpreted according to the standards of one's own culture" (Craffert 1996, 449). According to Mark Brett, ethnocentrism "is only malign when it is combined with homogenizing political power" (1996, 17) and, we might add, when it causes divisions in the church.

Indian, Asian, Asian-American, and this is just the *A* list! There are also entries for Caribbean, Chinese, *Dalit*, Malaysian, *mujerista*, *minjung*, Taiwanese, Thai, and Vietnamese theology. Biblical interpretation may be the soul of theology, but the implication of these many ethnic theologies is that contextual difference may trump textual sameness. Should theology's primary loyalty be to text or to context? It is not a matter of excluding either element—as we have seen, each is integral to biblical hermeneutics—but rather of doing appropriate justice to both. What is actually at stake in the project of ethnic theology is weaving text and context into their right respective places in "the pattern of religious authority" (Ramm 1959).[22]

The task of theology involves both text and context. It is a matter of bringing the gospel to bear on the questions and issues of life and thought at specific times and specific places in the world. The contextual flavor of theology follows from its pastoral remit: to serve the local—a concrete instantiation of the universal—church. The question, however, is whether a theology that addresses concerns that arise in particular contexts and that expresses the gospel in meaningful and relevant ways in those contexts must become an *ethnic* theology.

There is surely something right in the insight that one need not cease being an African, Asian, or American when one becomes a Christian. One does not abandon one's native tongue to speak the language of heaven. Neither must one equate Christian conversion with the annihilation of one's culture or identity. What, then, is the significance of the gospel with regard to one's past and, in particular, to one's culture's corporate memory enshrined in foundation narratives that shape a people's present experience?

Choan-Seng Song believes that the most important skill for Asian theologians "is the ability to listen theologically to the whispers, cries, groanings, and shouts from the depths of Asian suffering humanity" (Phan 2003, 33; Song 1984, 3–24). Song interprets John 1:14—"The Word became flesh"—to mean that "the story of God became the story of Jesus that lives in our stories" (1999, 66). In particular, to know the stories of suffering people today is to find a point of identification with the story of Jesus: "The cross of Jesus and the cross of suffering men, women, and children are linked in God and disclose the heart of the suffering God" (Song 1990a, 122). Telling and listening to stories is prominent in the method of Korean *minjung*, African, feminist, and Hispanic theologies (to mention but a few). To what extent should stories of women, the poor,

22. According to Bernard Ramm, the "Protestant principle" of authority is "the Holy Spirit speaking in the Scriptures" (1959, 28). This is similar to what I refer to below as the canonic principle.

the marginalized—stories "from below," the "underside of history," as it were—serve as resources for theology?

There is a profound connection between telling one's own stories and naming oneself. To be called "primitive" or "barbarian" by another, for example, is to have one's identity determined from outside oneself. By contrast, ethnic theologies let a group's own identity emerge by telling stories that validate the group's own lived experience. It is nevertheless dangerous when one's own individual or corporate experience becomes the framework for interpreting one's faith. Ethnic theologians must guard against the temptation to build a tower of Babel in the attempt to make a name for themselves (Gen. 11:4). This way enthnocentrism lies.

For an increasing number of Western theologians who have made the so-called cultural-linguistic turn, theology has indeed come to resemble ethnography. According to this view, theology's task is to describe the rules embodied in the Christian community's life and language. Communities are the locus of theology, to be sure, but the norm for Christian theology should not be this or that believing community, even when the community in question is the "global majority" of Christians. Doctrinal truth is not decided by sheer numbers. Nor is theology derived simply from an analysis of Christian experience. It is important that the strength and virtue of non-Western Christianity—its desire for contextual theology—not degenerate into a form of corporate expressivism for which theology is no more than an expression of Christian experience. It was Schleiermacher, the father of modern theology, who defined doctrine as "religious feelings set forth in speech," and, while he was thinking of individuals, there is nothing necessarily to be gained by tying theology to the religious sentiments of the masses.

Location should never become the essential characteristic of Christian theology. Clearly, perceptions of God differ from place to place, culture to culture. But there is only one true God, and God is the same in Africa, Asia, and Latin America, even if our experiences of him are not. To what extent, then, should the doctrine of God be tailored for the Southern and Northern hemispheres? Is trinitarian theology, for instance, an example of a merely local theology? (For that matter, where did the doctrine of the Trinity originate? Africa? Asia? Europe?) Should not all the people of God strive to continue in their own situations the story of what the one God of Israel was and is doing through Jesus Christ? There is a danger in talk of American or African theologies of repeating the "I am of Paul" "I am of Apollos" mistake on a much grander, cultural scale.

The lived experience of this or that culture, along with the history and tradition of the church as a whole, has a legitimate role to play as a *secondary* theological source. The primary source, however, must remain Scripture. The Bible is the formative text with which all Christians, regardless of their cultural context, must ultimately grapple, the authoritative script that all Christians must perform, albeit in a diversity of culturally appropriate ways. The purpose of those stories "from below" is, first and foremost, to communicate the gospel of Jesus Christ and to help people identify with the stories of Israel and the early church, not to sustain or promote national or ethnic identities.[23]

When culture becomes the primary source for theology, a theologian becomes a witting or unwitting revisionist. In the West, revisionists (aka liberals) are those willing to revise the faith to make it more acceptable and intelligible to those in a particular cultural-intellectual situation (e.g., modernity).[24] It is awkward, however, to use the label in contexts where there is no established Christian tradition to revise. Ethnic theology begins to make more sense in situations in which people are trying to make sense of Scripture in terms of their own cultural and intellectual background, perhaps unaware of, or unable to connect with, the resources from two millennia of Western engagement with the gospel. Eventually, however, these groups will become aware of Christians in other lands. At that point, the issue becomes how to give expression to Christian unity: one faith, one Lord, one baptism, yes, but one theology?

Theology is always contextual. Yet we should resist the ethnification of theology if this means reinforcing parochialism or fostering a hermeneutics of advocacy on behalf of a particular interest group only. Nonetheless, ethnic theologies make a positive contribution to the catholic church insofar as their particular cultural vantage point gives them insights into Scripture that we would otherwise miss. It is therefore important to see ethnic theologies as local instantiations of the faith of the church universal, where "universal" stands not for something supracultural but for something multicultural, namely, catholic faith.

World Christianity is increasingly multicultural, and this presents yet another problem for would-be ethnic theologies. Rasiah Sugirtharajah writes, "At a time when societies are becoming more multicultural, where traditions, histories, and texts commingle, and interlace, a quest for unalloyed pure native roots could prove to be not only elusive but also dangerous" (2002, 197). One compelling alternative to ethnocentric theology is a multiethnic theology in which we do not let our qualifiers (e.g., African, North American, Asian) become our primary identifiers. An identifier is a form of social demarcation, a mark that distinguishes "us"

23. George Sumner's notion of final primacy proves helpful here (2004). The story of Jesus is the interpretive framework for interpreting stories of one's own group, not the other way around.

24. Conservative theologians who are unaware of their cultural conditioning can also become inadvertent revisionists to the extent that their lived interpretations owe more to cultural than to gospel values.

from "them." Our identities as Christians are found first and foremost in Christ. Cultural location and ethnicity are important, to be sure, but ultimately they do no more than qualify our fundamental identity.[25] We are not our brothers' and sisters' identical twins, but we do all belong to the same family. It follows that one's ethnicity should play an adjectival rather than a nominative role; it qualifies but does not constitute our fundamental identity as Christians. Our relation to Jesus Christ, and therefore to one another, through the Holy Spirit does that.

We should not forget that Western theologians repeatedly criticized aspects of the worldviews and cultures from which they drew as well. For instance, Aquinas accepted Aristotle's notion of fourfold causality but rejected his notion of the eternality of matter. The biblical authors often do something similar. There is an important lesson here for the rest of us: Theology may make use of the available cultural resources but not without assessing their appropriateness and fittingness as forms for biblical content. It is to this constructive task we now turn.

A Mid-Western Proposal: Doctrine as Dramatic Direction (the Canonic Principle)

What follows are "mid-Western" comments on the topic of theological method in world Christianity. Why "mid-" Western? Because (1) the West is currently undergoing several tectonic intellectual and cultural shifts (e.g., from modernity to postmodernity), (2) I am in the middle of them, and (3) the West is amid something bigger than itself. I also mean "mid" in the sense of halfway, even halfhearted. I am a mid-Western theologian who seeks to do theology amid the detritus of Western civilization. My passion for the gospel disposes me to be critical of my own culture, most of all for how it has strayed from its biblical moorings. At the same time, with African and Asian theologians, I have to believe that God's Word has been and still can be translated into *my* culture too.

The following proposal incorporates insights gleaned from Western and non-Western theologies alike. It accepts the broad *contextual* principle that

25. The postmodern Jewish cultural critic Daniel Boyarin criticizes Paul's Galatians 3:28 vision ("There is neither Jew nor Greek . . . for you are all one in Christ Jesus") for being motivated by "a Hellenistic desire for the One . . . an ideal of a universal human essence, beyond difference and hierarchy" (1994, 7). Paul spiritualizes Jewish particulars like circumcision in a gesture of "coercive sameness" (1994, 236). John Barclay, however, points out that Paul's vision of a new humanity was neither ideal nor abstract; on the contrary, "he was placing alongside the Jewish community another which was equally physical and embodied in social reality," an alternative community "which could bridge ethnic and cultural divisions by creating new patterns of common life" (1996, 210).

the people of God engage Scripture in and from their particular locations. It accepts the *critical* principle of Latin American theologians who interpret the Bible in ways that address situational injustice. It accepts the *cultural* principle of African theologians who forge theology out of indigenous materials. Yet above these three, it affirms a *canonic* and hence *christological* principle, namely, that the Spirit speaking in Scripture about what God was/is doing in the history of Israel and climactically in Jesus Christ is the supreme rule for Christian faith, life, and understanding.

The main proposal concerns the nature of doctrine and the purpose of systematic theology. It departs from the stereotypical portrait of systematic theology as an abstract theoretical "science of God" that works primarily with concepts and seeks instead to reorient systematic theology toward *sapientia* (wisdom) or *phronesis*: *practical* reason, *lived* knowledge. The proposal therefore employs drama theory rather than philosophy as its handmaiden. To anticipate, it views the gospel as essentially dramatic, the Bible as a script, doctrine as theatrical direction, and the church as part of the ongoing performance of salvation. It also insists that "theodramatic" reason is as imaginative-intuitive as it is analytic-conceptual and that theology's primary aim is to help disciples discern how best to "stage" the gospel of the kingdom of God in concrete situations.[26]

Theology as Faith Seeking Theodramatic Understanding

The method of theology must be adequate to its matter. (This is not an imperialistic imposition of one culture's ways of looking at things, just a true insight.) Theology's subject matter—God and his relation to the world; God's speech and action, especially as these culminate in the person and work of Jesus Christ—is theodramatic. The theodrama begins with creation, with God's bringing into existence through his Word and Spirit beings who are not God but who are nevertheless able to fellowship with God and share in God's life. The fall almost immediately introduces the major complication: sin, an opposition to the divine purpose for the created order. The theodrama really begins to take off, however, with the divine promise: "I will make of you a great nation, and I will bless you, and make your name great, . . . and in you all the families of the earth shall be blessed" (Gen. 12:2–3 NRSV). God makes good on his *promissio* thanks to the *missio* (sending) of Son and Spirit. Though Jesus is born "late in time," he is the climax of the theodrama and the definitive clue to its meaning. Hence, Jesus Christ is the "first truth" of Christian theology, the definitive revelation of God, humanity, and the evangelical action (Sumner 2004, 14–15).

26. I treat these issues at much greater length in Vanhoozer (2005b).

The God of Jesus Christ is a missionary God. Indeed, the whole theodrama is essentially missional, consisting in a series of historical entrances and exoduses (e.g., incarnation, crucifixion, resurrection, ascension, Pentecost). Moreover, because the gospel is the story of the speech and action of Father, Son, and Spirit (e.g., the economic Trinity), we may say that the drama *is* the *dramatis personae*. Theology is faith seeking theodramatic understanding. Christians ultimately understand God, the world, and themselves by reference to what God has said and done for Israel, the nations, and the entire cosmos in Jesus Christ. The drama of Jesus Christ is the climactic word/act of God and hence enjoys "final primacy" (Sumner 2004, 16). All other truths must be engrafted into and encompassed by the drama of Jesus Christ.

Drama adds to story and narrative the element of embodied witness. Christians demonstrate their understanding of the theodramatic gospel by speaking and acting in ways that correspond to what God has done in Christ through the Spirit. Doctrine, then, is direction for the church's fitting participation in the drama of redemption. Doctrine helps us to understand what has already been done (by the Triune God) *and* what remains to be done (by the Triune God and by us). The key point is that we prove our understanding of the theodrama by faithful and fitting performance here and now. So while our understanding of what to say and do here and now is predicated on our understanding of what has already been said and done as attested in Scripture, we also need to understand the present situation.

Doctrine is, in the first place, a species of scriptural reasoning that makes explicit the implicit story-logic and meaning of the biblical text. The primary aim of doctrine is to conform our thinking—including our imagination—to the world made new in Jesus Christ attested in Scripture. Doctrine serves the church by helping its members understand that they have been "thrown" (to use Martin Heidegger's existentialist terminology) on the world stage and what their role there is as actors. Faithfulness to the story of Jesus demands not that we recreate the situation of first-century Palestine—we could not do this even if we wanted to—but rather that we perform or continue the same gospel story in new scenes and new situations. Doctrinal directions are normed by Scripture but realized in contemporary contexts.

Viewing theology as theodramatic understanding enables us to address simultaneously the questions of biblical hermeneutics and cultural identity, for the dramatic model calls for speech and action that are faithful to Scripture yet fitting to specific contexts.[27] It is the concern

27. George Sumner makes a similar point and contends that the task of contextual theology is to assimilate what went before (e.g., traditional religion) in ways that respect the "final primacy" of Jesus Christ (2004).

for context that makes theology less like *scientia* (theoretical science) and more like *sapientia* (practical wisdom). Aristotle had a name for this kind of practical reasoning: *phronesis*. *Phronesis* is about knowing what to do in particular situations. Theology, too, is phronetic inasmuch as it is a matter of knowing how to fit rightly—in accordance with the script and with the situation—into the drama of redemption. Doctrine serves the church by helping to form disciples with good judgment ("the mind of Christ"), namely, with the ability to discern what is fitting for Christian disciples to say and do in particular contexts to the glory of God. No one system of theology is appropriate for all times and places. The church needs to theologize without ceasing, not because the gospel changes but because the historical stage, cultural scenery, and intellectual setting of the church, the company of gospel players, is constantly changing.

Theodramatic understanding is a particularly compelling image for the church's theological mission in an era of world Christianity. Christianity cannot be reduced to a philosophy or a system of morality or even a set of religious rituals. It is rather a theodrama. The gospel scripts God's words and God's acts before it scripts ours. Furthermore, the notion of theodrama is not essentially Western; it transcends geographical categories. While it is true that terms such as *theater, drama, tragedy,* and *character* come from the Greek, the *Oxford Illustrated History of the Theater* has chapters on the "Beginnings of Theater in Africa and the Americas" as well as a chapter on South Asian, East Asian, and Southeast Asian theaters (Brown 1995). We should not limit our notion of what theater is to the Western mode only (e.g., to what happens on stage after the curtain opens). Anthropologists view ritual and other types of cultural performances as theater too, and it is precisely by such theater that cultures pass on worldviews and traditions (Schechner 1989; Turner 1982).

A faith-seeking-theodramatic-understanding approach has distinct advantages over what we called earlier "our big fat Greek method" because it responds to the concerns that led third world theologians to make the turn to context. In the first place, the directive theory of doctrine sketched above responds to the 1976 EATWOT Dar es Salaam conference call for an "epistemological break" with Western academic theology: "We reject as irrelevant an academic type of theology that is divorced from action" (cited in Torres and Fabella 1978, 269). Faith seeks an understanding or *phronesis* that involves more than conceptual analysis or theoretical cognition. As Aloysius Pieris puts it, "We know Jesus the truth by following Jesus the way" (1988, 82). *Phronesis* heals the gap between what Clodovis Boff calls the "theoretical or speculative" methodological moment and its "practical or operational" counterpart.

Boff observes that the latter has been largely ignored in classical and modern theology but "is the privileged function in the theologies of the South for which 'acting' represents a constitutive moment of all true theology" (2000, 200). Both moments have a legitimate place in theodramatic reasoning.

Second, to determine what is fitting to biblical text and context demands not only exegetical skill but also imaginative insight. Theodrama "remythologizes" theology by encouraging disciples to take the *mythos* (Greek: plot) of Scripture as the storied interpretative framework by which to interpret everyday life. Ordinary life is indeed the scene in which our speech and action demonstrate the understanding of faith. It is therefore well situated to respond to what Philip Jenkins calls the greatest change in the next Christendom, namely, the rejection of "our Enlightenment-derived assumption that religions should be segregated into a separate sphere of life, distinct from everyday reality" (2002, 141).

Finally, a theodramatic perspective lends credence to Andrew Kirk's claim that "all true theology is . . . missionary theology" (1997, 50), for the whole point of doctrine is to enable and encourage a disciple's participation in the missions of Son and Spirit. In sum, doctrine provides direction for the church's faithful speech and action, direction for embodying the way, the truth, and the life in new situations. Doctrine trains and disciplines imaginations to develop a theodramatic habit of viewing everyday life *sub specie theodramatis* (from the perspective of the theodrama).

The Canonic Principle: The Story of Jesus as the Church's Authoritative Script

The Bible itself, rather than any one interpretation of it, is the ultimate locus of transcultural authority (Clark 2003, 120). *Sola scriptura*—the Reformers' way of articulating the finality of Scripture—is not only a principle but also a practice: the Spirit-enabled habit of submitting one's intellect, imagination, and life to the theodramatic action of which Scripture is the normative specification. The canonic principle is an acknowledgment that our way of following must correspond to the way of Jesus, that our stories must correspond to *his* story.

Christians demonstrate understanding of the biblical script, and hence of what God was doing in Jesus Christ, not through academic treatises and commentaries but through their individual and corporate lives: Christian speech and action are forms of *performative* knowledge. The canon is the measure of our Christian wisdom and so functions as a sapiential criterion. But we can and must go further. The canon is not merely some external system of theological checks and balances but an instrument of nurture, a means for cultivating (not merely assessing) Christian wisdom. It is through becoming apprentices of the canon that we learn to make judgments about how to speak and act in ways that best continue the story of Jesus Christ.

It follows that the primary story from which Christians derive their sense of what the world is like and of who they are is the story of God in Christ reconciling the world to himself (2 Cor. 5:19). The once-for-allness of the canon is a function of the once-for-allness of the history of Jesus Christ himself. Of course, one cannot appreciate what God was doing in Jesus Christ without understanding what God was doing beforehand in creation and in the history of Israel; hence, the Old Testament is just as much a part of Jesus' story as the New. Hence, the canonical text carries an authority that one's contemporary cultural context does not. Our deepest, truest identity is thus discovered in biblical narrative, not the so-called foundation narratives of this or that culture or this or that nation.

Improvisational Wisdom: Acting Biblically in New Situations

While the canon alone is the supreme authority for Christian life and thought, every fitting performance of the gospel must also take account of our present speech and action. Our particular context—our situatedness in language and tradition—is crucially important, for theology is essentially a matter of demonstrating theodramatic understanding by continuing the same evangelical action differently in new situations. Andrew Walls (1996, 25) describes the gospel as "infinitely translatable." Just so. But we must not only translate but also perform the gospel in new cultural terms without injury to its essential content.

The metaphor of performing a script does not exhaustively address the problem of having to speak and act in ways that fit new situations and address new problems. *Improvisation* is a more accurate term for the process of judging how to speak and act in new situations in a way that is both canonically and contextually fitting. Many evangelical theologians and missiologists will no doubt react in horror to this image. Is it not the heretic who improvises and innovates? We can probably add "fear of improvisation" to Hiebert's list of reasons why Western missionaries once practiced a form of noncontextualization (1987, 104–6). In fact, it is only a misleading picture of improvisation as an unscripted, clever, off-the-cuff performance that has prevented missionaries and theologians from admitting that *every* speech and *every* act after the closing of the canon are a kind of improvisation. A false picture of improvisation must not hold us captive.

Improvisation is actually a form of disciplined spontaneity.[28] Good improvisers are trained to resist the temptation of preplanning, that is, of deciding what one will say and do before the scene begins. Preplanning is tempting because most people want to stay in control of the action (parallels to the history of missions should be obvious!). Improvisers are also trained to resist the opposite temptation, namely, to ad-lib or to display individual cleverness. The best improviser is the one whose speech and action appear neither preplanned nor ad-libbed but rather fitting. Christian theologians improvise whenever their doctrinal directions appear fitting or obvious to one who fears God, to one whose reflex is to follow the Word in the Spirit of freedom.

Every improvisation begins with an assumption, with some premise about one's situation ("You're a movie star trying to leave a hotel without being recognized"). In a given situation, anything that someone says or does is an "offer": an invitation to extend the action and keep the play going. Offers can be either accepted or blocked. To accept an offer is to respond in such a way that maintains and develops the initial action. In the case of the theodrama, the basic action is God's promise to Abraham: "I will make of you a great nation" (Gen. 12:2 NRSV). The history of salvation is largely the history of divine improvisations on this covenantal theme.

Memory is actually more foundational for improvisation than originality. An improviser seeks not to innovate but to respond to the past (to various offers), for the future is formed out of the past. Improvisers have keen narrative skills. They keep the offered act in mind in order to move the scene forward; they reincorporate earlier material in order to provide continuity and closure. Improvisers thus remember the past and are responsive to the present. The difference between acting from a script and improvising is that the improviser is more dependent on what the other actors are saying and doing. This is especially the case when the action carried forward derives from the economy of the Triune God.

Theodramatic improvisation is, then, a species of what Hiebert calls "critical contextualization" (1987), or perhaps I should say *disciplined* contextualization, for improvising is less a methodical procedure than a kind of virtue, a kind of personal *habitus*, itself the result of training (e.g., disciplined spontaneity).[29] Consider that genuinely contextual theology is accountable both to the theodrama (and hence to canonical texts) and to the contemporary situation (and hence to particular cultural contexts).

28. For more on improvisation, see Johnstone (1989). For an intriguing application of improvisation to Christian ethics, see Wells (2004).
29. We can parse "disciplined creativity" theologically in terms of Word and Spirit: The Spirit's freedom is biblically formed.

To participate fittingly in the drama of redemption ultimately requires good judgment, not just common sense but a "canon sense" that understands what God is doing in Christ and a "context sense" that discerns how to bear compelling and faithful witness to the gospel in settings far removed from first-century Palestine. Theological judgment, then, requires an intimate knowledge of the script and of the contemporary situation as well as the requisite skills—or *virtues*—to improvise.

The history of Christian mission and theology alike is thus the history of theodramatic improvisation. Each shoulders in different ways the same task: to maintain the evangelical assumption, to continue the evangelical action by responding to the offerings of Word and Spirit in culturally (and intellectually) appropriate manners. The challenge is to perform the same theodramatic play on different stages and in different languages (and worldviews). The apostle Paul, to take an apostolic example, had to improvise the gospel for non-Jewish listeners in Asia Minor and Rome. The Council of Nicea improvised the doctrine of the Trinity in suggesting that *homoousios* was a fit concept to express the implicit logic of Scripture in terms appropriate to fourth-century Hellenistic culture.

And so it goes. As with the fathers, so with medieval and Reformation Western theologians and non-Western theologians today: "No Christian theology in any age is simply a repetition of the inherited Christian tradition; all Christian theology is a synthesis, an 'adaptation' of the inherited Christian tradition in the service of new formulations of . . . the subject matter of theology" (Bediako 2004, 68). Doctrines direct us to improvise new things to say and do that are nevertheless consistent with our canonical script. It may well be that Jesus as the "great ancestor" is as canonically and contextually fitting in contemporary Africa and Asia as *homoousios* was in the ancient Roman Empire.[30] After all, Luke does trace Jesus' lineage back to Adam, and Paul does identify Jesus as a "second Adam."

It Takes a Global Village: Christian Theology as World Endeavor (the Catholic Principle)

Christians come to an enriched understanding of our script—of Scripture—by seeing what other interpreters have made of it. We come to an enriched understanding of the faith by coming to appreciate how other

30. George Sumner's strategy for dealing with this issue (final primacy) agrees in substance with the present proposal, though he does not explicitly mention improvisation. He does, however, speak of "recapitulating" what went before in a culture (e.g., ancestorship) so that it is edited or spliced into the salvation history that culminated in Christ (2004, 199).

disciples in other times and places have improvised their theodramatic performances. This is *not* to say that anything goes. The canonic principle keeps us centered; the catholic principle (to be set forth here) keeps us in bounds.

There is no one surefire method for reading the Bible that guarantees the truth of the ensuing interpretation. As we have seen, coming to right theodramatic understanding is ultimately a matter of forming habits of good judgment—and not only of judging but of seeing and acting as well. Understanding the Bible involves more than exegesis; it involves our engagement in a catholic conversation about its meaning/significance and our active participation in some performance tradition. Doing theology in an era of world Christianity ultimately means taking part in a worldwide conversation about how best to understand—to perform—the biblical text.

The Need for Vernacular Performance: Regional Theater

The church has advanced its mission through the centuries precisely by translating the gospel into the languages, thought forms, and practices of other cultures. Andrew Walls and Lamin Sanneh have written powerfully about the "infinite translatability" of the gospel and about the importance of translating the Bible into the vernacular (Walls 1996; Sanneh 1989). Similarly, we can speak of the "infinite performability" of the gospel, that is, of the church's ability to render the theodrama actively in new situations, for what ultimately gets translated is indeed the theodrama: a pattern of evangelical speech and action, a way of truth and life.

There is a real need for vernacular performances of the gospel, for what we could call regional or community theater. The would-be disciple needs to know what it means to follow Jesus Christ here and now, in such and such a situation, in just this kind of context. Regional theater (e.g., African, Asian, North, South, and Latin American theology) shows us how to perform the biblical text in different settings. Better: Regional theater shows us what the text *means* here and now. It is crucial that we come to see cultural context not as an impediment to textual understanding but as its vital condition. To understand Scripture genuinely is to know what it means and how it applies here and now, not simply what it meant or how it applied there and then.

One's cultural context may, of course, distort Scripture. If we are unaware of our cultural conditioning, for instance, we may suffer from a kind of hermeneutical myopia that blithely but mistakenly reads Scripture through the framework of our own culture's truths and values. Those who cannot see their own cultural conditioning are doomed to repeat it. It is just here that Western systematic theologians have much to learn. Western theologians must be aware of the cultural beams in their own eyes before attempting to remove specks from non-Western eyes. It is ultimately for the sake of better biblical interpretation that Western theologians need to attend to how the Bible is being read and practiced in the non-Western world.

No one way of embodying the gospel—no one regional theater—is exhaustive of the truth and the life. Regional theologies, no matter how committed they are to Scripture, inevitably display the signs of the times and places in which they were framed. At worst, they can become frozen idiolects that render it difficult for one group to talk to another. Horatio Bonar complained that some of the seventeenth-century Protestant confessions, "in giving a lawyer-like precision to each statement, have imparted a local and temporary aspect to the new which did not belong to the more ancient standards" (cited in Pelikan 2003, 481). At their best, however, confessions are more than ephemeral performances, more even than a series of local theologies. Confessional theologies are rather "great performances"—responses to their own historical context that contain lessons for the rest of the church as well.

No one performance of the biblical script serves as either template or paradigm for all others. The Word of God is absolute; not so the interpretations of men and women. Western and non-Western theologies are equally regional, not universal, performances. This is why adjectives such as *African, Asian American, German Lutheran,* and the like must stay qualifiers rather than become identifiers. The name that identifies us is "Christian": one who is "in Christ." These other theological qualifiers are not to be despised, to be sure, but neither are they to be the object of national, ethnic, or denominational pride. On the contrary, they are relatively local expressions of something universal, cultural incarnations of a transcultural reality.

The local church is perhaps best viewed as a contextualized performance of the catholic church: the universal church made particular, visible, and concrete in a specific place and time; the people of God speaking and acting in a specific language and culture in creative fidelity to the gospel. Kwame Bediako's inference is correct: "Wherever the faith has been transmitted and assimilated are equally 'centres of Christianity's universality'" (2004, 116). Local companies can produce masterpiece theater too.

The Catholic Principle

The present proposal encourages us to see our churches (and our theologies) as local instantiations or contextualizations among other local instantiations of the biblical gospel and of catholic (*kath' holou,* "on the whole") orthodoxy. Doing theology in an era of world Christianity obliges us to recover catholicity, long a mark of the true church, as a mark of true doctrine as well (see Schreiter 1997, 127–33). On the one hand, what the church over time and across space has always believed provides an important check and balance to new developments. On the other hand, local theologies become great performances when they respond to specific cultural contexts and to new problems in ways that contain lessons for the whole church.

The ancient rule of faith, a summary of the main theodramatic plot, is the prototype of catholic theology. It is significant that Irenaeus, one of the first formulators of this *regular fidei*, was by no means ethnocentric in his understanding of orthodoxy: "Those who, in the absence of written documents, have believed this faith, are barbarians, so far as regards our language; but as regards doctrine, manner, and tenor of life, they are, because of faith, very wise indeed" (*Against Heresies* 3.4.2). And again: "But the path of those belonging to the Church circumscribes the whole world, as possessing the sure tradition from the apostles, and gives unto us to see that the faith of all is one and the same, since all receive one and the same God the Father, and believe in the same dispensation regarding the incarnation of the Son of God, and are cognizant of the same gift of the Spirit" (*Against Heresies* 5.20.1).

To be sure, the rule of faith was formulated in a concrete cultural-linguistic context. Yet the Taiwanese theologian Shoki Coe argues that it is precisely by taking the *concrete* situation seriously that theology becomes truly *catholic*. Catholicity is not a "colorless uniformity" but a coat of many threads and many colors (Coe 1980). Andrew Walls observes that the story of Jesus Christ "grows" as the church continues its global mission: "It is a delightful paradox that the more Christ is translated into the various thought forms and life systems which form our various national identities, the richer all of us will be in our common Christian identity" (1996, 54).

The ecumenical creeds and the orthodox tradition may reflect the cultural perspectives of the past—indeed, they certainly do—but it is important not to dismiss them for this reason. Newton's laws of motion were discovered in a particular place and time too, but this alone is no reason for dismissing Newtonian physics. Is it possible, then, that there is no difference in principle between, say, Archimedes' insight into why things float and Athanasius's claim—or to use more provocative language, *discovery*—that the Son is *homoousios* with the Father? We would do well to distinguish contextualism—the view that everything we say is *determined by and relative to* a particular context—from the more modest contextual claim that recognizes the cultural clothing of our speech and action but does not necessarily deny their transcontextual significance.

In the case of the rule of faith and the ecumenical creeds, moreover, we are dealing not merely with the insights of an individual but with the consensus of a multicultural communion. If the ecumenical creeds do indeed represent certain theodramatic "discoveries" (e.g., discoveries about the identities of the divine *dramatis personae*), then we need to respect them; there is no need for each Christian community to reinvent the theological wheel. To affirm the catholic principle, then, is to affirm the importance of reading Scripture guided by the ancient-contemporary rule of faith, a rule that is itself ultimately authoritative only because it is an apt summary of the main contours of the theodramatic plot at the heart of Scripture.[31]

At the same time, it takes many interpretative communities spanning many times, places, and cultures to appreciate fully the rich, thick meaning of Scripture: call it a "Pentecostal plurality." The rule of faith provides important but often only minimal guidance directing us to read the Old and New Testaments as a unified story and identifying the protagonists (e.g., the Triune God, Jesus Christ). There are many theological issues, however, that the rule of faith does not address. Learning how Africans and Asians read Scripture, then, helps us better to see the beam in our own Western eyes.

Western theology remains part of the catholic heritage of the church. It is important, then, not to take "non-Western" as an invocation of Aristotle's law of noncontradiction (*not* Western) or in the sense of anything-but-Western. Such a negative reaction would be understandable, of course, given the West's poor track record vis-à-vis the "other." Nevertheless, the Holy Spirit did not wholly abandon the West for two thousand years; non-Western theology must therefore not degenerate into a form of knee-jerk reactionism. The way forward is not non-Western but *more*-than-Western theology.

Toward a Dialogical Systematics: Enlarging Faith's Understanding

"The time of European and Western monologue is over" (Escobar 2003, 136). The need for theology to expand its Western categorical repertoire is becoming increasingly apparent, even in the academy. A number of new initiatives are now underway. The Center for the Study

31. A case can be made for seeing the ecumenical councils of the early church and the creeds they produced as themselves moments in the theodrama, divinely directed scenes that facilitated the right reception of Scripture in the church. Here we may recall the above-mentioned suggestion that the "hellenic" mind-set was a providential condition for the development of Christian theology: "He [the Spirit] will guide you into all truth" (John 16:13).

of Christianity in the Non-Western World at the University of Edinburgh is well established, and I have already made reference to the *Dictionary of Third World Theologies*. It is encouraging to learn of the forthcoming *Global Dictionary of Theology* to be published by InterVarsity and of the Christian Doctrine in Global Perspective series (also published by Inter-Varsity). In the series preface to the latter, John Stott and David Smith write, "What is needed now are more books by non-Western writers that reflect their own cultures" (in Escobar 2003, 7).

Whatever the locale, theology must strive to abide by the canonic and catholic principles. From within a particular culture, people study the canonical script and seek to discern how to continue the theodramatic action in such a way that it engages the issue of life in the present context. Eventually, Christians in one culture will want to discuss their understanding of the theodrama with those from another culture, "other" in space and/or time. The purpose of this discussion is not to foster copycat theology but rather to be challenged by an outsider's point of view. According to Mikhail Bakhtin, "It is only in the eyes of *another* culture that foreign culture reveals itself fully and profoundly" (1986, 7).[32]

David Clark makes much the same point in regard to what he calls "dialogical contextualization": "The conceptual grid of cultures where the gospel is still new may slash through the jungles of established theological habits and renew readings of Scripture in cultures where the gospel is long-established" (2003, 118). Such a "dialogical systematics"—a catholic conversation that employs different conceptual schemes to fathom the same gospel—can in this way serve the church as, to use Calvin's phrase, an "external means" by which God enlarges and edifies the society of Christ.[33]

Doctrine develops as the church encounters new challenges and seeks to say and do what is theodramatically fitting. Take, for example, the doctrine of atonement. This doctrine developed through attempts to express the saving significance of Jesus' death in different contexts: "Different codes will highlight different aspects of the message" (Schreiter 1997, 80). In the New Testament itself, Paul employs legal codes (justification), ritual codes (sacrifice), and social codes (redemption or manumission from slavery) to convey the saving significance of Jesus' death. "Today, African theologians and Pacific theologians are using initiatory codes to carry the message: Christ's death is his initiation into new life" (Schreiter 1997, 80). Recall Andrew Walls's comment that the gospel "grows" as it enters

32. "Outsideness" thus becomes a crucial principle for understanding oneself and others: "Outsideness creates the possibility of dialogue, and dialogue helps us understand a culture in a profound way" (Morson and Emerson 1990, 55).

33. The full title of book IV of Calvin's *Institutes* is "The External Means or Aids by Which God Invites Us into the Society of Christ and Holds Us Therein."

new contexts. This phenomenon—growth of understanding through contextualization—also serves as an example of what Bakhtin calls "creative understanding."

The dialogue about how to continue the same theodrama in different cultural settings is never ending. But it is not a dialogue of despair—ever wrangling but never coming to the truth—but of *deepening*: The catholic conversation about how to speak and act canonically leads to a fuller appreciation of the drama's significance and of the way in which the meaning of the gospel can be extended into new situations. In short, the dialogue between times and cultures is the condition of a *creative* understanding, where creative means not innovation ("We're making this up") but rather new insight ("This has meaning-potential we have not fully grasped"). Creative understanding is essentially a matter of understanding the same thing in a different context, thus understanding *more*.

No one set of concepts can articulate the whole truth of the biblical text. Neither can one point of view, one literary genre, or even one Gospel. The truth of Scripture is plural and polyphonic: It takes four Gospels and many kinds of texts to bear witness to the truth of Jesus Christ. Surely this fact about the Bible has a bearing on how we do systematic theology.

Missiologists often depict systematic theology as working with "relatively abstract and acontextual terms"—with "experience-distant" concepts (so Robert Priest in this volume). There are indeed many examples of such "systems," of monological conceptual schemes that borrow from some philosophy or other. As I have presented it here, however, the task of systematic theology is to promote theodramatic understanding. The aim is not to formulate a universal set of categories that will work anywhere, anytime but to cultivate certain intellectual, spiritual, and practical habits—certain ways of seeing, judging, and acting. In Tite Tiénou's words, "Biblical writings do not teach us concepts of God; they show us how people encountered God, learned to know him and walked with him" (1982, 441). In sum, the task of systematic theology is to train actors with good improvisatory judgment, actors who know what to say and do to perform and advance the gospel of Jesus Christ *in terms of their own cultural contexts*.

Scripture is the concrete deposit of theodramatic wisdom. In helping us to understand the logic of the biblical action, theology trains us to read our own situations *sub specie theodramatis*. Athanasius attended to Paul's language about the Son's "equality with God" (Phil. 2:6–11) and judged that *homoousios* said the same thing in his context that Paul was saying in his. What ultimately matters is not the conceptual formulation but the canonical judgment that it seeks to serve. Athanasius's choice of term demonstrated good theological judgment: He indicated the way, the truth, and the life in terms that were faithful to the script yet fitting and appropriate to his own cultural-linguistic context. What is important for our purposes is the principle that "the same judgment can be rendered in a variety of conceptual terms" (Yeago 1997, 93).

The moral for systematic theology is clear. No one interpretative community can mine all the treasures of the Word of God by itself. If biblical interpretation is indeed the soul of theology, then theologians had better attend to the global conversation. Reading Scripture with Christians from different parts of the world is invigorating; to be exact, it reinvigorates our tired concepts and categories. This chapter has suggested that the most important contribution of voices from the global South and East has been rehabilitating the importance of interpreting Scripture with the goal of achieving practical wisdom: performing the text in new contexts, staging parables of the kingdom of God wherever two or three are gathered in Christ's name.

Mission and Theology in Middle-Earth: The Rule of Truth

A sapiential systematics proceeds from faith seeking theodramatic understanding, displays both canonic sense and catholic sensibility, and aims at bearing faithful witness in word and deed to the revelation and redemption that reach their climax in Jesus Christ.

Truth and Method Revisited

Tite Tiénou (in this volume) is right to observe that the West's self-perception as the center of biblical and theological scholarship is merely a corollary of the "hegemony postulate," namely, the requirement to play by the West's rules, by what I have called the rule of reason or rational method. Neither the church nor theology should be ruled by Western methods, for the truth of the gospel is less a matter of methods than of *missions:* As God sent his Word and Spirit to bear witness to the truth, so he now sends the church. Theological claims are thus mission statements or, to be precise, statements on a mission, namely, statements that help direct the church to participate fittingly in the drama of redemption. It is far better, then, to speak of the rule of truth, where truth is a matter of theodramatic correspondence to what God is doing in Christ as authoritatively attested in Scripture (Vanhoozer 2005c).

The new era of world Christianity has had profound effects on the church, not least on theology's self-conception. Thanks to developments in the global South, we now realize that *all* theology is essentially missionary theology, arising out of the need to translate and incarnate the gospel in and into particular cultural settings. Just as important is the renewed consciousness that theology is something that is lived. Doctrinal truth must be not only systematized but also *shown;* stated, yes, but also staged and even suffered.[34]

Great Performances: The Question of Criteria

No one region of the church has a monopoly on faithful and fitting theodramatic performance. It comes as no surprise, then, to learn that Robert Schreiter considers the single most urgent question facing local theologies today to be how to discern what is genuinely Christian and what is not (1985, 99). Are there safeguards against what we earlier referred to as forms of bad global theology—approaches that err on the side of either exaggerating absoluteness (e.g., generic unity) or relativity (e.g., ethnic fragmentation)?

Schreiter himself proposes five criteria for assessing Christian identity (1985, 113–17). Interestingly enough, each criterion has to do with Christian "performance."[35] Schreiter's first criterion—the cohesiveness of Christian performance—comes closest to what I have called the canonic principle. Christian speech and action must be "according to the Scriptures," though this "according to" requires not literal replication but creative imitation—in my terms, improvising with the biblical script. Each of Schreiter's four subsequent criteria is a variation on what I have called the catholic principle. Theology should correspond to the prayer and praxis of the Christian community, and local communities must be willing to challenge and be challenged by other churches with regard to their respective performances.[36]

The present chapter argues that the most important criterion for maintaining the same gospel across different cultures is theodramatic corre-

34. The church is a "theater of martyrdom" (Vanhoozer 2005b) because when it bears witness to the truth it must also endure various kinds of suffering—social, political, physical—for its witness. In this it is doing no more than following the example of the Lord.

35. Robert Schreiter is referring not to the theater but to Noam Chomsky's distinction between linguistic competence and linguistic performance. The "one rule" that rules them all is, for Chomsky, a properly *grammatical* rule. Schreiter sees tradition as analogous to a language system, faith as analogous to linguistic competence, and the liturgy as analogous to performance. For Schreiter, creeds and confessions represent the grammar that is derived from well-formed performances. My own view is that Schreiter begs the question as to what counts as a well-formed performance. I submit that theology as a kind of grammar must attend first and foremost to canonical performances. It is these canonical performances, and the deep-seared judgments they represent, that are theology's ultimate authority.

36. In his later work, Robert Schreiter reaffirms the five criteria with virtually no change (1997, 82).

spondence. Theology is faith seeking understanding, and we have genuine understanding only when we are able to situate properly our particular contexts within the larger theodrama. Theodramatic correspondence is thus tied to theodramatic coherence: "The best interpretation is the one that accounts for all of the data in the most coherent way. This implies, of course, that incoherence is a chief indicator of when our interpretations are wrong" (Sparks 2004, 32). In the final analysis, however, no single method can guarantee such correspondence or coherence. On the contrary, discerning how to embody the gospel in new contexts requires not methodical procedures but sanctified persons, persons whose minds and hearts and imaginations are captive to the Word.

What ultimately gets translated, contextualized, or performed from culture to culture, then, is theodrama: the pattern of evangelical—gospel-centered—speech and action. How do we recognize theodramatic fidelity from one context to another? The operative term is *direction*. Doctrinal formulations must lead people in different contexts in the same basic direction, namely, in the way of truth and life as these are defined by the story of God's words and deeds that culminate in Jesus Christ. Theology that can do that is "warranted wisdom"; theology is warranted because it tells the truth and wise because it leads to shalom (Stackhouse 1988, 161). Truth and justice and the righteousness of Jesus Christ are the universal elements in the good news that must be embraced and embodied in and by every local church. The task of theology is to train speakers and doers of the Word, people who can render in contextually appropriate forms the poiesis and the praxis, the truth and the justice, of God or, in terms of the proposal set forth herein, people who can improvise the gospel of Jesus Christ.

Diasporadic Systematics: The Fellowship of the Rule

Christian identity stems from our common effort to speak and do the truth of Jesus Christ in our respective contexts, in full awareness that we are not the only truth seekers, speakers, and sufferers to do so. Though the fear of the Lord is the beginning of wisdom, humility is the principle of its continuation. The recovery of Christian humility in the West—not least among systematic theologians!—may be just the beginning of a new phase of theological wisdom informed by the attempt of Christian disciples in a variety of cultures and settings to follow the way of Jesus Christ. What is different about doing theology in an era of world Christianity is our awareness of how narrow *our* way of pursuing "the way" really is.

It can be disorienting to realize that there are many ways of pursuing the way. At the limit, this realization can provoke an identity crisis. And why not? The need to rethink and renegotiate cultural identity is one of the hallmarks of our present era. Postcolonial critics have a name for the increasingly common phenomenon of migrancy and inhabiting in-between space: diaspora.[37]

At least two books in the New Testament are explicitly addressed to those in the diaspora. James writes "to the twelve tribes scattered among the nations" (James 1:1); Peter writes to "the exiles of the Dispersion" (1 Pet. 1:1 NRSV). The term originally described Jews scattered throughout the world as a result of a series of exiles. In these epistles, however, Peter and James give voice to the Christian consciousness of being a pilgrim people, a nation of strangers (Feldmeier 1996, 241).

The present moment calls for a diasporadic systematics, for a way of doing theology that acknowledges a "diasporized" Christian identity as well as the "dispersal" of interpretative authority among the nations.[38] To do theology and to read the Bible with diasporadic consciousness is to recognize that one must never be too at home in any one culture. Whatever their passports, Christians are really resident aliens (1 Pet. 2:11). The people of God must never define themselves primarily in terms of their culture, nationality, or ethnicity. Stated positively, a diasporadic systematics will seek to be at home in many places and to cultivate a "mixed" identity. For example, Hispanic theologians have a notion of the *mestizaje*, a mixture of Iberians and the indigenous peoples of the Americas. One need not go so far as the philosopher José Vasoncelos to see this ethnic mixture as a precursor to a new humanity, a cosmic race (see Pedraja 2003, 79). And yet there is something especially fitting about this image when viewed in light of the eschatological newness of existence in Christ.

To be a Christian is to be an ambassador of the new age in the midst of the old. Indeed, it is the vocation of the church to be a "holy nation" (1 Pet. 2:9), a nation of strangers who are out of time and out of place in this world (the old age), for Christian existence is existence in Christ. As those who live in Christ, Christians are freed from their past and alive to a future hope; hence, they relate differently to the present. Leonhard Goppelt's comment on 1 Peter is telling: "To be strangers is the emblem of Christians in society, for this expresses sociologically the eschatological character of their way of life" (cited in Feldmeier 1996, 257n60). A diasporadic systematics will not lord the truth over others

37. Experiences of diaspora are becoming more and more common in our postcolonial era as more and more people slip through porous cultural boundaries. For a discussion of diaspora in relation to biblical interpretation, see Sugirtharajah (2002).

38. See Boyarin (1994, 257) for a somewhat different application of the model of diasporized identity, namely, as a way of combining a desire to maintain Jewish ethnic and cultural specificity in a context of deeply felt human solidarity.

from positions of power, however, but will instead witness to the truth from positions of weakness. After all, the mission of the church is to participate in a drama that has a cross for its climax. Accordingly, the church must be about the business of training actors for a theater of martyrdom: The church's mission is to bear suffering witness to the truth (Vanhoozer 2002).

Finally, a diasporadic systematics will aim to cultivate multiethnic fellowships of those united by a common concern to figure out just what faithful discipleship means in particular contexts (Tanner 1997, 153) and by a common conviction that the biblical script, together with the catholic tradition, provides reliable direction for God-glorifying performances. This fellowship gladly accepts the rule of the canonic and catholic principles, themselves servants of the rule of truth. The systematic theologian is to serve this fellowship of the rule. I can imagine no more exciting or urgent task for theology in middle-earth than that.[39]

39. Thanks to Mark Bowald, Hans Madueme, Harold Netland, Craig Ott, Michael Sleasman, George Sumner, Lisa Sung, Natee Tanchanpong, Tite Tiénou, and Dan Treier for their comments on an earlier draft.

5

The Globalizing Hermeneutic of the Jerusalem Council

DAVID K. STRONG AND CYNTHIA A. STRONG

The globalization of Christianity gives rise both to joy and to concern—joy, because it represents the fulfillment of mission's desire for the universal knowledge of God; concern, because it has created a pluralistic world of Christian belief and practice. This pluralism is nowhere better expressed than in contextualization, in which each cultural group has been encouraged to construct its own theology using questions and methods relevant to its own context. Contextual or local theologies have arisen from concern that the West has promoted its culturally specific theology as a universal theology, even though it has been deeply influenced by an Enlightenment perspective (Schreiter 1997, 2–3). As Paul Hiebert asks, however, "If now we must speak of 'theologies' rather than of 'theology,' have we not reduced Christian faith to subjective human agreements and thereby opened the door for a theological relativism that destroys the meaning of truth?" (1994c, 94). Is there a biblical method for global theologizing that respects local concerns but preserves universal truth?

The Jerusalem Council in Acts 15 illustrates just such a theological process. In appealing to this text, however, we must exercise care. Over the years, missiologists have repeatedly turned to this passage as a model or paradigm for contextualization (e.g., Kraft 1979, 341; Hesselgrave and Rommen 1989, 11; Whiteman 1997, 3). In so doing, they have invariably reduced circumcision and keeping the law to cultural issues. From an Old Testament perspective, however, circumcision related to the covenant, and to enter into the blessings of the covenant, Gentiles had to become Jewish proselytes. The council's participants thus wrestled with issues far beyond "simply the pressures of culture and ethnocentrism" (Wiarda 2003, 235). Moreover, the narrative in Acts focuses on a single strand of church history, stressing the movement from Jerusalem to the ends of the earth and the transition from the Jewish mission to the Gentile mission. In the process, Luke emphasizes continuous growth and harmony (Marshall 1971, 74; cf. 187). This is certainly true in Acts 15, so that Luke's primary intent is not to establish a precedent for contextualization. In fact, Timothy Wiarda questions whether the council can serve as a paradigm at all, since ancient and modern circumstances are so different. The council occurred at a major turning point in salvation history, close to the time of Christ and in the presence of the apostles, which makes an extrapolation to our situation extremely difficult (Wiarda 2003, 237–39; see also Shelton 2000). If we remain faithful to the intent of the narrative, therefore, we can only secondarily derive lessons from the council's actions (Fee and Stuart 1993, 105–12).

Having acknowledged this, the approach used by the Jerusalem Council reveals one successful way in which diverse Christian communities with different theological concerns achieved consensus. In so doing, it lends credence to the Anabaptist perspective that we must rely more on theological process than on dogmatic theological statements to establish objective truth. In such a hermeneutic, we guard against subjectivity by remaining faithful to Scripture, the leading of the Holy Spirit, and the check of the hermeneutical community (Hiebert 1994c, 100). The council illustrates precisely this process, simultaneously respecting contextual concerns and preserving truth and unity in such a way that the gospel could continue its advance. Thus, while not paradigmatic, the theological process employed at the council points a way forward in mediating between local and global theologies.

The Use of Scripture at the Jerusalem Council

The Jerusalem Council met to decide a hotly debated theological and missional issue. The theological issue involved soteriology; the missional issue related to the continued success of the Gentile mission. Jewish Christians from Judea had arrived in Antioch and demanded the circumcision of Gentile believers as a requirement for salvation (15:1).

Like-minded converts from among the Pharisees also added the demand that the Gentiles keep the Mosaic law (v. 5). In short, Jewish Christians expected Gentiles to follow the Old Testament pattern of eschatological pilgrimage by becoming Jewish proselytes in order to receive salvation. The Jerusalem Council therefore occupies a pivotal position in the book of Acts. Indeed, Acts 15 has been recognized as the turning point of Acts, for a different conclusion could have stymied the Gentile mission (Barrett 1998, 709–10). As Peter and then the entire council recognized, it was not Jewish culture but keeping the law that was a burden and a difficult yoke to bear (vv. 10, 28). Theological questions thus had great practical import for the success of the mission.

Faced with such vital theological questions, the council tested its theological decision against Scripture (vv. 16–18, 20). But how did it do so? It began by hearing testimony about God's work among the Gentiles as reported by Peter, Barnabas, and Paul (vv. 7–12). In fact, Pentecostal James Shelton views Peter's experiential testimony as determinative for James's interpretation of Scripture (2000, 243). On the contrary, however, the disagreement revolved around an interpretation of Jewish law (*halakhah*), which could be settled only on the basis of Scripture (Bauckham 1996, 154). James therefore evaluated Peter's testimony in light of Scripture, stating that his experience accorded with the words of the prophets (plural) (vv. 14–15). The scriptural evidence he cites (vv. 16–18) substantially follows the Septuagint version of Amos 9:11–12, which deals with the restoration of "David's fallen tent." David's tent has been variously interpreted as the life of Christ, culminating in his resurrection (Haenchen 1971, 448); the Davidic dynasty (Polhill 1992, 329); and the eschatological temple (Witherington 1998, 459) that becomes the church (Ådna 2000, 157–59). The Septuagint, however, differed significantly from the Masoretic text. In particular, the Hebrew text of verse 12 suggests that David's fallen tent will "possess the remnant of Edom and all the nations that bear . . . [Yahweh's] name," while the Greek text states that David's tent will be restored so that "the remnant of men and all the nations that bear my name may seek the Lord."

The use of the Septuagint has led many scholars to conclude that James's speech is a Lukan construction, since James, the leader of the Jerusalem church, could not possibly have used a Greek translation during a church council in Jerusalem (e.g., Haenchen 1971, 469; Barrett 1998, 728). Through careful textual analysis, Jostein Ådna has argued convincingly, however, that the Septuagint actually reflects a different but legitimate Hebrew textual tradition existing at the time. Moreover, as the council endeavored to build consensus between Antiochians using the Greek text and Judeans using the Hebrew text, James's use of a legitimate but alternate Hebrew reading that corroborated the Greek text would have been crucial (Ådna 2000, 143).

James, however, does not simply quote the Septuagint verbatim; he conflates it with allusions to Jeremiah 12:15–16; Hosea 3:5; Zechariah 1:16; and Isaiah 45:21 (Ådna 2000, 130–39). That is, James correlates several prophetic texts in such a way that they provide commentary on the contemporary situation of the Gentiles who are turning to God without becoming Jews. His selection of Amos is particularly important because similar texts, such as Isaiah 2:2–4; 66:18–21; or Zechariah 8:20–23, which foretold the pilgrimage of the nations to Zion, could conceivably still require that the Gentiles become proselytes and undergo circumcision. Jews looked forward to the eschatological pilgrimage of the Gentiles, and the Jewish Christians would be no different. James's recitation of Amos 9:12, however, precludes this. In Amos, the Gentiles bear God's name and stand in covenant relationship with him without first becoming Jewish proselytes (Bauckham 1995, 458; 1996, 169; Ådna 2000, 147–48). Using such an approach to Scripture, James supports Peter's, Barnabas's, and Paul's reports that God had accepted the Gentiles without their first becoming Jewish proselytes and being circumcised, and he concludes that the church "should not make it difficult for the Gentiles who are turning to God" (15:19).

Having made this pronouncement, James then instructs the Gentiles to abstain from the pollution of idols, fornication, strangled animals, and blood (v. 20). The prohibitions are identical in 15:29 and 21:25, except for the substitution of idol sacrifice for pollution of idols. This so-called apostolic decree, which is a misnomer, since Luke did not consider James an apostle, has occasioned all manner of debate (see Proctor 1996 for an excellent summary). Some commentators relate all four prohibitions to participation in practices surrounding pagan idolatry (e.g., Witherington 1998, 461–63), and thus forsaking such practices would be required of all believers for salvation (Barrett 1998, 733–34). According to this view, fornication is associated with temple prostitution, while strangled animals and blood refer to nonkosher meat from the sacrifices. Most commentators, however, relate the prohibitions in some way to Gentiles' maintaining sufficient purity to have table fellowship with Jews. This would reflect Peter's own concerns for ritual purity when he was sent by the Spirit to Cornelius (Acts 10), as well as the background to the debate over table fellowship in Galatians 2:11–13 (which we would place before the Jerusalem Council). On the one hand, some justify the decree in light of the Noachian commandments against idolatry, incest, nonkosher meat, and murder, which first appeared in Jubilees 7:20 and were incumbent upon all human beings. There is little in the text, however, that suggests a reference to Noah (Proctor 1996; Barrett

1998, 734). C. K. Barrett, on the other hand, prefers simply to view the demands as prohibiting idolatry, murder, and incest—three things, according to the rabbis, for which Jews must be willing to die—with the provision to avoid the meat of strangled animals added to enable table fellowship (1998, 734–35). The majority of commentators, however, relate the prohibitions to the regulations for Gentiles living in the land found in Leviticus 17–18. Ernst Haenchen, for example, notes that these four requirements applied to Gentiles living among the Jews, whereas circumcision did not (1971, 450n1). This view is particularly strengthened by the fact that Acts 15:16 alludes to Jeremiah 12:15–16, where the Gentiles dwell among God's people. Using Rabbi Hillel's interpretive rules, texts that used common terms were to be interpreted in light of one another, and Leviticus 17–18 refers frequently to aliens living among the Israelites. Thus, pollution of idols is paralleled by the prohibition of illegal offerings and sacrifices (Lev. 17:8–9); fornication relates to prohibited sexual relationships (Lev. 18); strangled animals and blood could simply be taken as synonymous, since eating blood was also prohibited (17:10, 12), or strangled animals could be viewed as a negative counterpart to the positive command to drain the blood of hunted animals (17:13). Taken in this light, the fact that Moses was read in synagogues throughout the empire on every Sabbath (Acts 15:21) justifies the impositions, because the requirements for harmonious fellowship between Jews and Gentiles were well known (Bauckham 1995, 458–67; 1996, 172–78; Ådna 2000, 159–61).

At this point, several observations can be made. First, commentators have struggled with the application of the prohibitions. Haenchen, for instance, attempts to retain the ritual sense (1971, 469). Because this understanding is so culturally specific, however, the Western text had very early omitted strangled animals and substituted a negative form of the Golden Rule, thus turning the entire decree into ethical instruction (Barrett 1998, 735–36). On the other hand, as William Larkin observes, "The decree deals in the main with practical matters of accommodation for unity, not adherence to a universally normative moral imperative" (1995, 219n). Understood in this light, the decree illustrates an attitude essential to any form of global theologizing: Christians must be willing to surrender their freedom and to abstain from those practices that offend those from other religious and cultural backgrounds.

Second, James's hermeneutical process differed significantly from the historical-critical approach employed by modern Western exegetes. For one thing, he drew together diverse prophetic texts to comment on his contemporary situation. For another, like Rabbi Hillel, he interpreted terms in one text by means of similar terms in other texts, a method of cross-referencing. Modern Western scholars, on the other hand, prefer methods requiring careful analysis of grammatical, historical, and cultural contexts, and Gilbert Bilezikian goes so far as to caution against cross-reference as a method (1993, 15). Another popular hermeneutics textbook introduces ancient midrashic and pesher methods alongside allegorical methods as less satisfactory ways to approach the text than the literal historico-grammatical method (Virkler 1981, 49–53). At the very least, therefore, we must recognize that church leaders from other cultures may prefer different interpretive methods, even as they remain committed to the authority of Scripture. It is not our intention to argue the merits of one hermeneutical approach over another but simply to point out that the church has interpreted Scripture differently at different times and places. Moreover, we concur with Pentecostal theologian John Christopher Thomas's observation that our rationalist approaches to interpretation have done little to produce consensus even among evangelicals (1994, 41–42). Ultimately, we must recognize that our theological understandings are always partial and influenced by personal biases, and therefore the believing community must constantly return to the anchor of Scripture to test and correct its beliefs and behaviors (Hiebert 1994c, 99).

Third, we should be encouraged that global theology can be achieved in spite of language barriers. James endeavored to bridge the gap between the Hebrew and Greek texts by coming to a common understanding of the meaning of the text that was amenable to both groups. Using careful, culturally appropriate exegesis, James revealed the intent of Scripture; missionaries Peter, Paul, and Barnabas testified to the Spirit's work in other communities; and church leaders adjudicated between competing theological views. Careful study of Scripture is thus important for contextualization, especially when distinguishing among competing theological perspectives and cultural concerns. Furthermore, theological decisions made in community and based on the unchanging foundations of Scripture can establish Christian unity across language and cultural barriers.

The Use of Scripture in Globalizing Theology

The use of Scripture at the Jerusalem Council provides an example for the globalizing church. In the first place, the very fact that the council reached consensus about theological issues with broad ramifications for the success of the Gentile mission holds promise that the modern church can also resolve other such conflicts. The council has demonstrated that it can be done. Without such hope, each local community could be excused when it turns inward and develops its own idiosyncratic theology, but with such hope, each segment of the church is challenged to engage other parts of the church.

Second, James's interpretive methods serve as a reminder that different cultures may use different hermeneutics while fully recognizing scriptural authority. Schooled in Bible study methods and expository preaching at Dallas Theological Seminary, one of us taught a Korean congregation the need to observe closely such things as subjects and objects, verb tenses, and antecedents of pronouns. After the first session, the pastor's wife remarked that his methods were "so Western." Still, there was no question in her mind that Scripture was authoritative and the final arbiter of truth. Likewise, most of the sermons we heard preached by Korean pastors were devotional, some utilizing the allegorical method, but there was no question in the pastors' minds that Scripture was to be obeyed.

Perhaps the clearest contemporary example of a global community grappling with the authority of Scripture is provided by the recent dispute over homosexuality within the worldwide Anglican Communion, of which the Episcopal Church in the United States is an autonomous member. The Episcopal Church (USA) ordained a practicing homosexual bishop, and after his confirmation, the bishop reportedly said, "Just simply to say that [homosexuality] goes against tradition and the teaching of the church and Scripture does not necessarily make it wrong" ("Gay Bishop Confirmed" 2003, 8). Reaction was swift, both inside and outside the United States. African bishops responded by threatening to sever fellowship with the Episcopal Church (USA). The Lambeth Commission, established to resolve the conflict, observed that "within our own Communion, some eighteen of the thirty-eight provinces of the Anglican Communion, or their primates on their behalf, have issued statements which indicate, in a variety of ways, their basic belief that the developments in North America are 'contrary to biblical teaching' and as such unacceptable" (2004, para. 28). In dealing with the crisis, the commission repeatedly affirmed the authority of Scripture (2004, para. 53–62). It also reaffirmed Resolution 1.10 of the 1998 Lambeth Conference to uphold faithfulness in marriage between a man and a woman and to counsel abstinence for the unmarried because this accorded with the teaching of Scripture (2004, 77–78). The commission further endeavored to distinguish between essentials and nonessentials (*adiaphora*) and to discern the reciprocal impact of the local and the global on each other. They concluded by chiding the North American church for unilaterally deciding such a divisive topic without the consultation and consent of the entire communion (2004, para. 134, 144). From a hermeneutical perspective, the conservative wing of the church follows a hermeneutic based on the finality of Scripture, whereas the liberal wing begins with the ideals of love, acceptance, and compassion and reaches different conclusions. Clearly, without mutual agreement on a final authority, hope of global theologizing between the two wings of the church may be lost.

Third, the decision of the Jerusalem Council illustrates the attitude essential to achieving more global understandings. As far as the Gentiles were concerned, the four prohibitions addressed cultural peculiarities of the Jews, but for the Jews, the practices were religiously offensive. The council therefore demanded that the Gentiles forego their freedoms for the sake of their Jewish brothers and sisters. Such an attitude would go far toward healing many rifts in the global Christian community and creating a more unified church, both in theology and practice. This would, for example, profoundly transform a missionary's understanding of his or her rights. Missionaries among Jews and Muslims would willingly embrace a kosher or *halal* diet rather than forcing converts to eat pork as a sign of conversion, and those among Jains would become vegetarians. Willingness to surrender one's rights would also aid in resolving the issues of power that plague multicultural missionary teams. North Americans, with their egalitarian, democratic values, chafe under the leadership of Koreans, who prefer the hierarchical and authoritarian leadership styles of Confucianism. Meanwhile, Koreans struggle to understand the nuances of *Robert's Rules of Order*. Mutual appreciation for one another's values, coupled with a willingness to be flexible as to which style is adopted, would create appreciation and unity within the global missions community. The Jerusalem Council thus provides the modern church with a significant key to globalization.

The Holy Spirit

Not only was the council accountable to Scripture, but it was clearly responsive to the Spirit's leading. The Spirit had been at work throughout the book of Acts, and John Christopher Thomas attributes the frequent references to God's work in Acts 15 to the activity of the Spirit. In particular, the Spirit performs the signs and wonders reported by Barnabas and Paul (Thomas 1994, 45). Only two verses, however, refer overtly to the work of the Holy Spirit. In the first, Peter refers to God's gift of the Spirit to Gentiles (15:8), an obvious reference to Acts 10:44, 47 and 11:17.

The second passage, which is less clear, has a significant bearing on our discussion. In their letter to the churches in and around Antioch, the apostles and elders declare, "It seemed good to the Holy Spirit and to us not to burden you with anything beyond the following requirements"

(15:28). Most commentators understand this to refer to the council's inner experience of the Spirit. F. F. Bruce, for example, concludes, "So conscious were the church leaders of being possessed and controlled by the Spirit that he was given prior mention as chief author of their decision" (1988, 298). C. K. Barrett likewise observes that they recognized the Spirit's direction in the development of the church's life, so that the harmonious unanimity of the council merely reflected the prior decision of the Spirit (1998, 744). Although Barrett acknowledges that none of the speakers claims to have spoken, been moved, or been filled with the Spirit, William Larkin goes so far as to call the decree "Spirit-inspired" (1995, 227) (similarly Polhill 1992, 335; Thomas 1994, 49; Witherington 1998, 469).

A minority voice, however, represented by John McIntosh (2002), claims that the leaders simply recognized the observable working of the Spirit. In other words, the council claimed nothing about their inner guidance or inspiration but simply recognized the discernible activity of the Holy Spirit. Three things within the immediate context pointed to the Spirit's initiative: Peter's testimony about the conversion and gift of the Spirit to Cornelius and his household apart from circumcision; Barnabas and Paul's report of the signs and wonders that had indicated the Spirit's acceptance of Gentiles apart from circumcision during their missionary journey; and James's scriptural support of God's intention to incorporate the Gentiles as his people. Indeed, the entire movement of Acts to this point verified the Spirit's intention regarding the Gentiles.

Viewed in this light, the activity of the Spirit in leading toward a more global theology is evident. The work of the Spirit would necessarily include demonstrations of the Spirit's transforming power through conversion and obedient discipleship, which could also be accompanied by signs and wonders. As in the case of the council, however, the Spirit must also grant discernment to those in dialogue, the ability to recognize God's work in the lives of others, and the ability to fathom the true meaning and application of God's Word. Such an approach would contrast with the purely inner approach of the first view, which easily pits conflicting local theologies against one another as each side claims Spirit inspiration for its decisions.

As in its use of Scripture, the council's approach to the work of the Holy Spirit provides an example for churches pursuing dialogue in the global body of Christ. Like the council, churches seeking communion with other churches worldwide would acknowledge the confirming signs and wonders of the Holy Spirit while at the same time seeking evidence of genuine conversion and obedient discipleship. The application of this principle to relationships with African Indigenous Churches provides a case in point. Characterized by charismatic leadership, prophecies, healings, exorcisms, and independence from Western missions and churches, the widely divergent AICs have provoked various responses (cf. Hiebert, Shaw, and Tiénou 1999, 359–64; Jenkins 2002, 47–53, 107–39). Since primal religion aims to secure meaning, success, and guidance in this life without necessarily addressing sin against the Creator (Hiebert, Shaw, and Tiénou 1999), genuine conversion would be indicated by conviction of sin, and obedient discipleship would manifest itself in the fruit of the Spirit. These would, of course, be expressed in culturally appropriate ways. One early believer in the animistic Korean context, for example, demonstrated genuine transformation by enduring persecution, rather than by performing the prescribed ancestral rituals, and by continuing to worship, study his Bible, and witness to his extended family (Shearer 1966, 147–48). Clearly, as in the case of the Jerusalem Council, those dealing with the AICs would also require the Spirit's discernment to correlate happenings within the churches with Scripture. Kwame Bediako, for instance, argues that the primal worldview sees the universe as a unified cosmic system that is essentially spiritual (2004, 89). Such a view, which avoids the Western dichotomy between natural and supernatural, actually seems closer to the biblical worldview. Relying on the Spirit's discernment while evaluating the beliefs and practices of the churches would prove rewarding for both parties in the dialogue.

The Hermeneutical Community

In resolving the conflict between the perspectives of Antioch and Jerusalem, as we have seen, the council bowed to the authority of Scripture and the unmistakable evidence of the Spirit's will, but it also clearly acted as a hermeneutical community. In this process, the narrowly ethnic Jewish community and the multiethnic Antiochian community reached consensus in spite of sharp dissension as they acknowledged their common experience, the authority of Scripture, and the Spirit's will.

Diversity within the Christian community in Antioch created the potential for conflict. Membership cut across geographic and ethnic, social and cultural boundaries. Luke describes it as a mixed congregation of both Jews and Greeks (Acts 11:19–20). The leaders themselves further indicate the community's diversity, with Hebrew, Greek, and Latin names, different homelands, and different social classes (13:1). Differences between two particular groups, however, lay at the heart of the controversy. From the time of the Old Testament, Jews had viewed themselves as God's chosen people. Everyone else was a Gentile and alienated from God (Bietenhard 1976, 790–95). The term *Gentile*, therefore, emphasized not simply a cultural difference but a deeply religious distinction. Conflict erupted when believers from Judea (which may denote ethnicity rather than simply geographical location [Barrett 1998, 698]) insisted that the Antiochians must be circumcised (15:1). When they took their case to the Jerusalem leadership, the delegation from Antioch encountered believers belonging to "the party of the Pharisees," who also insisted they must adhere to the Mosaic law (v. 5). These Jewish believers adhered to what Peter Davids calls "Torah piety," which he finds represented in the book of James (2001, 85). Their religious identity was inseparable from keeping the law. The Christian community of that day, like the modern global church, was thus divided geographically, socially, and culturally but especially by heartfelt religious convictions.

Still, in spite of its diversity, the Christian community was united by common experience. Both Jew and Gentile had experienced conversion (15:3, 7), the gift of the Holy Spirit (v. 8), and signs and wonders (v. 12). In testifying to these common experiences, Paul, Barnabas, Peter, and James repeatedly pointed to the fact that this is God's work (vv. 3–4, 7–9, 12, 14, 17). The community thus began by acknowledging a common set of experiences. In this light, Pentecostals rightly recognize the importance of experience in the hermeneutical process. They believe that the interaction of knowledge and experience is unavoidable and that true understanding will result in obedience to God's transforming Word (Arrington 1988, 388). Anabaptists similarly emphasize applying Scripture to life rather than simply formulating abstract theological systems (Hiebert 1994c, 99–100). The search for a more global theology, therefore, should begin with recognition of our common Christian experience.

In resolving the differences between competing local theologies, the early hermeneutical community also depended on the insights of its leadership. When the church in Antioch encountered conflict, it dispatched representatives to Jerusalem, in part because the recognized leadership of their opponents resided in Jerusalem (Larkin 1995, 219). The leaders were identified as "apostles and elders" (15:6). Barnabas and Paul received scant attention, perhaps because Luke did not consider either an apostle (Ådna 2000, 125). Instead, Peter spoke for the apostles, and James represented the elders. Clearly, as John Painter observes, James was the leader of the Jerusalem church, since he spoke last and spoke decisively. Both the apostle Peter, who led the Jewish mission, and Paul, who led the Gentile mission, appear to have submitted to the authority of James (Painter 2001, 31, 35–36). Moreover, the Jerusalem church held primacy among the churches (Painter 2001, 58). While the global Protestant church no longer has a primate church like the first-century Jerusalem church, it still has leaders of churches and missions. If Painter's observations are correct, the example of the Jerusalem Council calls into question the popular notion of strongly hierarchical apostolic leadership, at least by that name (see Shelton 2000, 246–47), as well as Ralph Winter's two-structure thesis, which views churches as relatively impotent in conducting missions and advocates the multiplication of mission structures (Winter 1971, 193–200). Instead, mission leaders like Paul and apostles like Peter deferred to a church elder.

Ultimately, the hermeneutical community reached a harmonious resolution. The leaders did not impose their will on the community. Other representatives accompanied Paul and Barnabas from Antioch (Acts 15:2) and apparently participated in the discussions (v. 12). This would have been essential in order for both sides to accept the final outcome of the debate (Ådna 2000, 143). At the conclusion of the council, "the apostles and elders, with the whole church," decided to send representatives to Antioch with the letter of instruction (v. 22); the letter itself testifies that they all agreed to this action (v. 25). The council thus achieved consensus. This is probably the most important point of the entire narrative, for the Gentile mission could now proceed unfettered with the approval of the entire church (cf. Wiarda 2003, 240–41).

The example of the Jerusalem Council as a hermeneutical community challenges modern church leaders. Leaders at the council trusted, respected, and submitted to one another to resolve their disagreements. How different this is from our contemporary penchant for abandoning the fray and going our own ways. Unfortunately, this attitude has even found its way into the schools and seminaries that prepare future leaders. There deep divisions exist between the schools of theology and the schools of mission. Mission leaders dismiss theologians as ivory-tower academics, while theologians dismiss missionaries as pragmatic heretics, but the need for careful dialogue between theologians and practitioners has never been more vital. Current debates over contextualized Muslim evangelism (Travis 1998; Parshall 1998) and churchless Christianity (Hoefer 2000) cannot be settled apart from a carefully considered biblical ecclesiology. Arguments about the nature of spiritual warfare and territorial spirits cannot be settled simply on the basis of phenomenology; they require careful biblical study. At the global level, Western evangelicals are still suspicious of liberationist views, even though evangelical leaders within poorer countries acknowledge the importance of liberationist concerns (Tano 1981). Like the leaders at the Jerusalem Council, contemporary leaders must surely commit and submit themselves to painful but necessary dialogue.

Finally, to achieve consensus in the global theological task, modern leaders will have to proceed along lines similar to those of the council. The council was able to arrive at a harmonious conclusion because it focused on common experiences. All present affirmed that they had experienced God's grace in Christ Jesus and that they had experienced the working of the Holy Spirit. Proceeding from this premise, they did not seek an abstract, monolithic theological statement in the manner of Greco-Roman philosophy but rather built on the Hebraic view of knowledge as intimately personal and interpersonal. While maintaining the specific and necessary truth of salvation by faith, they permitted freedom in nonoffensive practices. They thereby freed the gospel to expand into every cultural group. In contrast, evangelical churches have too often erected walls based on specific, abstract, and supposedly universal dogmatic theologies. In so doing, they have failed to build the very bridges that facilitate the globalizing process.

Conclusion

Can the church achieve a universal theology? Probably the best we can achieve is something more akin to Robert Schreiter's "global theological flows," that is, loosely linked groups that mutually appreciate and understand one another, even though they are not uniformly the same (1997, 16). To accomplish even this, leaders in the globalizing church must act as a hermeneutical community. Proceeding from the recognition of a common experience of salvation in Christ and the work of the Holy Spirit in their lives, they must engage deliberately to understand one another and to work toward consensus on the essentials of theology and practice while accepting local freedom in the nonessentials. Collectively, they must attempt to discern the work of the Holy Spirit in their various communities, all the while remaining committed to obeying Scripture. The advance of the gospel to the ends of the earth will certainly require contextualization to establish the relevance and uniqueness of the gospel and to recognize the identity and maturity of ethnic churches. The Jerusalem Council, however, serves as a constant reminder that truth and unity must be maintained in the process. This is the gauntlet, then, laid at the feet of the twenty-first-century church by the first-century church: Are we willing to work toward becoming a global hermeneutical community, each part of the body of Christ listening to the others?

6

Creeds, Confessions, and Global Theologizing

A Case Study in Comparative Christologies

STEVE STRAUSS

For much of church history, the creeds and confessions of the early church have served to unify Christians. Nicea (AD 325), Chalcedon (AD 451), and other early church councils produced statements of orthodox Christianity that have united churches of many cultural backgrounds and time periods. From the earliest days of the church, most Christians have viewed creeds and confessions as the "pure," normative distillment of biblical truth for all cultures and all times, as the glue that binds the church together, and as the plumb line against which all other theologies should be measured. In an era when the church is becoming increasingly global and local theologies have taken center stage, it is tempting to fall back on the creeds of the early church as the remaining point of theological unity for the worldwide church. It would give us a secure foundation if we could see the early confessions as universal for all Christians in every context and see agreement with these creeds as a test of unity and orthodoxy in an increasingly diverse church. After all, if we cannot unite around the Nicean statement about the Triune God or the Chalcedonian formula regarding the person of Christ, what is left to unite global theology? If any contextual theology expresses itself in a way significantly different from one of these creeds, can it still call itself biblical and Christian?

The creed endorsed by the Council of Chalcedon (AD 451) is especially important. The center of the Christian faith is the person of Jesus Christ, and basic to biblical orthodoxy is a correct understanding of who Jesus is. Most Christians around the world—Catholic, Orthodox, and Protestant—have found unity around Chalcedon's statement that Christ had "two natures, *inconfusedly, unchangeably, indivisibly, inseparably* . . . in one Person (*prosôpon*) and one Subsistence (*hypostasis*), not parted or divided into two persons, but one and the same Son" (Schaff 1877b, 62). Not all Christians, however, have accepted the creed of Chalcedon. The council followed centuries of conflict over the nature of Christ. Each phase of the conflict had brought greater clarity to the church's understanding of who Jesus was, and, for many Christians, Chalcedon was the successful climax of the process. Throughout the West, the council was given the status of "a binding document and a definition of faith which was not susceptible to negotiation," and Chalcedon became one of the foundational creeds for the Western church (Frend 1972, 49).

In the East, however, Alexandria and Antioch had become theological centers for two different frameworks for understanding Christ's deity and humanity. Theologians from Alexandria, such as Cyril, had emphasized the importance of the *unity* of Christ's person in a *single* nature. Those of the Antiochene school, however, had highlighted the completeness of Christ's humanity by stressing the duality of his human and divine natures. Though many church leaders in the East accepted the Chalcedonian formula, those who followed the Alexandrian model immediately and violently attacked its conclusions. Riots broke out in Alexandria (Frend 1972, 149), and the patriarch of Alexandria, Dioscorus, attacked the Chalcedonian formula as theologically deficient. In the hundred years following Chalcedon, aggressive, non-Chalcedonian missionary activity led to the establishment of "monophysite kingdoms" in Nubia, Armenia, and Ethiopia (Frend 1972, 296–315), and separate ecclesiastical hierarchies were established throughout the East.

Today, these churches are known as the Oriental Orthodox Churches, including the Armenian Apostolic Church, the Coptic Orthodox Church of Egypt, the Ethiopian Orthodox Church, the Syrian Orthodox Church in India, and the Syrian Orthodox Patriarchate. They are similar to other Orthodox churches in their theology and practice but with one important exception: their long-standing rejection of the two-nature Christology of Chalcedon and their commitment to a one-nature Christology. Oriental Orthodox Christology is usually labeled "monophysite" by Chalcedonians, but this label is rejected by the Oriental Orthodox themselves.[1] Rather than a peripheral doctrinal point, a theology of Christ's single, unified nature is central to their theological identity.

Most evangelicals around the world have generally viewed any Christology other than the two-nature, one-person Christology of Chalcedon as unorthodox and unbiblical. Is Chalcedon, then, a universal standard of biblical Christology against which all local Christologies should be measured? If so, how should evangelicals respond to the one-nature Christology of the Oriental Orthodox Churches? Is a Christology that explicitly rejects Chalcedon a false, unbiblical aberration? How can two apparently conflicting Christologies both be appropriate local theologies unless all attempts at a unified, global theology are abandoned?

In some countries where an Oriental Orthodox church is the dominant Christian faith, evangelical denominations have grown rapidly over the past four decades. In these countries, questions about Chalcedon are not theoretical; they present a living, dynamic study in comparative Christologies. Ethiopia is an example of one such country, where evangelicals now make up 18.6 percent of the population, while 55.5 percent are members of the Ethiopian Orthodox Church (Johnstone and Mandryk 2001, 244). How should evangelicals in countries such as Ethiopia express their Christology? By explicitly embracing the Chalcedonian confession, are they preserving an important, biblical truth, or are they building unnecessary walls between themselves and these indigenous Christian churches? What would be the implications of evangelicals using non-Chalcedonian terminology to express their Christology and to build bridges with this ancient Christian tradition? Would they be appropriately contextualizing their faith or abandoning a key biblical doctrine?

These crucial questions faced by evangelicals living among the Oriental Orthodox, such as in Ethiopia, are also relevant to theologians from other contexts. Though there is general agreement among many Christians as to which creeds are normative, from very early in church history, deep divisions also developed over which creeds were to be accepted. The debate between Eastern and Western churches over the insertion of the *filioque* clause into the Western version of the Nicene

1. Though monophysite means "one nature," the Oriental Orthodox reject the label for two reasons. First, they affirm that Christ was two natures united into one composite nature, not simply one nature. Second, the term *monophysite* historically and linguistically may imply that one of Christ's two natures was absorbed by the other. The Oriental Orthodox churches strongly affirm the full deity and the full humanity of Christ after the union of his two natures into one nature and so distance themselves from Apollinarianism and Eutychianism, views that hold that Christ's deity absorbed his humanity. The Oriental Orthodox will sometimes use the expression *miaphysis* to describe their position. They define *miaphysis* as "composite unity" to emphasize that Christ's deity and humanity preserved their essential attributes in the union of the two natures (Aymro and Motovu 1970, 96).

Creed, at the local Council of Toledo in 589, is the most well-known example, but disagreements exist over other creeds and confessions. A study of comparative Christologies in the context of a non-Chalcedonian church, such as in Ethiopia, will contribute to both Christology and an understanding of the role of creeds and confessions for theologians from other contexts as well.

Form and Meaning

One of the most helpful tools in analyzing comparative Christologies and the role of the ancient creeds and confessions is an understanding of the subtle relationship between form and meaning in symbols and communication (Hiebert 1989). On the one hand, insisting that a particular form always carries the same meaning across culture and time reflects a naive positivism that cannot be maintained in real life. For example, the vocable *bug* does not carry the meaning of "insect" in every language; in Amharic, it carries the meaning of the English word *sheep*. A kiss, walking hand in hand, a raised eyebrow, a wink, or comparing a person to a particular animal all carry different meanings in different contexts.[2] On the other hand, maintaining that any form can freely be substituted to communicate the same meaning is equally simplistic: It ignores the historical connection between forms and their meanings and the control that social groups maintain over symbols. For example, wearing a ring on the fourth finger of the left hand is a form that, in the North American context, carries the meaning that a person is married. It would require a major shift in historical direction and social expectations for this form to take on a different meaning (e.g., that a person was simply wealthy or liked jewelry) or to substitute a different form to communicate the same meaning (e.g., that all married people wear a certain kind of hat or a certain color of clothing). Based on a critical realist epistemology, Paul Hiebert points out that "the relationship between meanings and forms varies according to the nature of the symbol" (1989, 109).

Hiebert suggests that the relationship between form and meaning is best understood in terms of a continuum. At one end of the continuum, form and meaning are sometimes *arbitrarily linked*. This is perhaps best seen in linguistic forms. The sounds that represent the idea of a canine mammal may be *dog* (in English), *perro* (in Spanish), or *wesha* (in Amharic). There is nothing that inherently connects any of these sounds

2. One of my students in Ethiopia was nicknamed Ox by his classmates, which implied steady strength in that culture. I never had the heart to tell him it might imply dullness or a lack of initiative in another context.

to the idea of a canine mammal; the connection is purely arbitrary. Sometimes form and meaning are *loosely linked*. Some connection exists between the form and the meaning, but the link might be disconnected, especially in cross-cultural communication. For example, many agricultural societies link land and fertility with being female and link battle and violence with being male. However, these connections would not be made in every culture. Theologically, some would suggest that the connection between a woman wearing a head covering and expressing submission or modesty is loosely linked: A head covering communicates submission or modesty in some cultures but might be replaced with another form to better communicate the same meaning in another culture. Sometimes form and meaning are *tightly linked*. Though the two are not completely equal, it would be difficult to discard the form without in some way affecting the meaning. Bowing or falling prostrate is closely associated across cultures as signs of submission or reverence. Baptism would seem to be tightly linked as a symbol of identification with Christ and the washing away of sin in new birth. It would be difficult or impossible to communicate the full theological truths of baptism without the use of water. Finally, form and meaning are sometimes *equated*. For example, when a minister says, "I now pronounce you husband and wife," his words (the form) actually create a new relationship between a man and a woman. In certain sacramental theological systems, the use of specific words during baptism and the Lord's Supper are understood to create a new reality by actually conferring grace.

This continuum model of the relationship between form and meaning has profound implications for translation, hermeneutics, and especially the contextualization of theology. While contemporary theologians do not have the freedom to substitute any form to communicate the meanings of Scripture or the creeds and confessions of the church, neither should they slavishly insist on using the same exact form to express the same theological truth in different cultural contexts or different eras of church history. Instead, they must determine the extent to which a theological form and its meaning are linked.

Some forms in Scripture are so closely tied to meaning that they must be maintained transculturally to maintain scriptural meaning. Conversely, other scriptural forms are less tightly tied to meaning; a substitute form will more clearly and accurately communicate the same truth. For example, in some cultures, greeting Christian brothers with a kiss would decidedly *not* communicate the meaning intended in 1 Peter 5:14. Churches that do not practice Jesus' command that his disciples wash one another's feet (John 13:14) generally agree that, in contemporary culture, a different form better communicates the meaning Jesus intended in that text.

The form-meaning continuum is particularly relevant in determining the role of the ancient confessions and creeds for contemporary contextual theologizing. Rather than simply asking whether a church (or a believer) agrees with the form of an ancient creed, one must examine the form and the meaning of the creed and the proposed alternative *in the specific contemporary context*. The remainder of this chapter studies the Christology of one particular Oriental Orthodox Church, the Ethiopian Orthodox *Tewahedo*[3] Church (EOTC), and uses the form-meaning continuum as a tool in comparative christological theologizing. The form and the meaning of the EOTC's one-nature Christology is examined from historical, contemporary, and linguistic perspectives so we can better understand its relation to Chalcedon and the relationship of the ancient creeds to contemporary contextual theologizing. Only then can a decision be made as to whether the Chalcedonian *form* is the best way of expressing biblical *meaning* about the person of Christ in the Ethiopian context.

The Christology of the Ethiopian Orthodox *Tewahedo* Church

Historical Perspectives on the EOTC's Christology

Three historical episodes must be understood to appreciate the EOTC's commitment to one-nature Christology. First, one-nature Christology was at the center of the establishment of the Christian faith in Ethiopia. The Christian faith took root in Ethiopia in the third century when local inhabitants attacked a passing ship off the coast of what is now Eritrea, and two boys from the ship, Frumentius and Aidesius, were captured and sold to the highland Ethiopians. Eventually, Frumentius became the Ethiopian king's secretary, and Aidesius served as his cupbearer. The young men were committed Christians, and they took advantage of their high position to promote their faith, encouraging the Roman merchants in the Ethiopian capital of Axum to build Christian prayer houses. Ultimately, they were allowed to go free, and Frumentius returned to Alexandria, where he encouraged Athanasius to appoint a bishop for Ethiopia who would promote mission work there. Athanasius responded by appointing Frumentius himself, who returned to Ethiopia and spread the Christian faith (Jones and Monroe 1935, 26–31; Hable Selassie 1972, 112; Frend 1972, 305).

3. *Tewahedo* means "union" in both Ge'ez (the ecclesiastical language of the Ethiopian Orthodox Church) and Amharic (the most widely used national language among Orthodox and evangelical Christians in contemporary Ethiopia) and is used by the EOTC as a technical theological term to express its one-natured Christology.

The Ethiopian church's close link with Alexandria and its non-Chalcedonian Christology was further sealed in the late fifth century when a group of Syrian missionaries—the Nine Saints—came to Ethiopia. Fleeing persecution from Byzantine Chalcedonians, they also came as part of a program "of careful recruitment and selection by the (Monophysite) patriarchate of Alexandria" to promote non-Chalcedonian Christianity (Taddesse 1972, 23, 29).[4] From its earliest days, therefore, the EOTC found a significant part of its identity in its non-Chalcedonian Christology.

Second, non-Chalcedonian identity was even more firmly established as a result of two Jesuit missions to Ethiopia in the sixteenth and seventeenth centuries. The Jesuits made a concerted effort to draw the church of Ethiopia into the Catholic Church, especially trying to persuade the Ethiopians to accept the creed of Chalcedon. One Ethiopian emperor, Suseneyos, actually accepted a Chalcedonian Christology and converted to Catholicism in the seventeenth century, but further Jesuit demands[5] were too much for the country as a whole. There was a "genuine popular insurrection" (Brake 1977, 139) throughout the land, and Suseneyos began a bitter civil war to preserve the Catholic faith. After one battle, Suseneyos and his son, Fasilades, surveyed the carnage, and Fasilades remarked, "This is not a victory over Muslims or heathens, but over our own flesh and blood, our fellow-subjects, our fellow Christians" (Blyth 1935, 87).

Shaken by the bloodshed and division of his country brought on by the war, Suseneyos issued an edict in 1632 granting freedom to return to the traditional non-Chalcedonian faith. He then abdicated and died later the same year (Jones and Monroe 1935, 96–98; Yesehaq 1989, 55–56). When Fasilades took the throne, he banished the Catholic missionaries from Ethiopia with the words, "The flock of Ethiopia has escaped from the hyenas of the West" (Brake 1977, 153). Over a hundred years of contact with Western Christians left the Ethiopian Orthodox *Tewahedo* Church bitterly hostile toward Chalcedonian theology (Taddesse 1972, 29). Yesehaq, an Ethiopian Orthodox bishop, calls the Jesuits "anti-Christians" who "came on political missions carrying with them not the Almighty God, but almighty swords and guns that caused the deaths of hundreds of thousands of Ethiopians" (1989, 57). For many Ethiopian Orthodox Christians, Chalcedonian theology will always be associated with one of the most destructive attacks on truly Ethiopian Christianity in their country's history.

Third, during subsequent years, the EOTC was divided by fierce internal debate over the time and effect of Christ's anointing. The issues that

4. See also Hable Selassie (1972, 116) and Jones and Monroe (1935, 38).
5. The Jesuits insisted that all Ethiopian Christians be rebaptized, all Ethiopian churches be reconsecrated, all Ethiopian priests be reordained, and that Latin be used in all Ethiopian church services (Jones and Monroe 1935, 96–97).

divided the Ethiopian church into Union (*Tewahedo*), Unction (*Qebat*), and Three Births (*Sost Ledet*) factions can seem obscure and perplexing to Western theologians.[6] But "the purpose of the subtle argument on unction [i.e., anointing] in Ethiopian Christology is to demonstrate whether one accepts a duality of natures in Christ or not" (Tesfazghi 1973, 88). Ethiopian Orthodox theologians wanted to "ward off the ever present danger of the Catholic doctrine of the two natures of Christ" (Hyatt 1928, 102). The intense debate and its resolution at the Council of Boru Meda in 1878 in favor of the Union (*Tewahedo*) position further solidified the EOTC's intense opposition to any theological position that seemed to promote two natures in Christ and brought to a climax the historical development of Ethiopian Christology by ensuring that only a one-nature position would be regarded as authentically Ethiopian.

Contemporary EOTC Christology

What exactly does the Ethiopian Orthodox Church teach, and what do its adherents believe about the person of Jesus Christ? At the heart of the EOTC's Christology is a belief in the perfect *union* of the divine and human natures of Christ into *one nature*. At the moment of the incarnation, the human and divine natures of Christ united into one unique nature that was both fully human and fully divine. An example

6. Biblical texts (Luke 4:18; Acts 4:27; 10:38) and the very name "Christ" (Messiah, Anointed One) teach that in some sense Jesus was anointed. Chalcedonian theology has generally understood that Christ was only anointed (i.e., received appointment, power, and authority for ministry) *in his humanity* (Tesfazghi 1973, 73; Ayala 1981, 93). But the Ethiopian Orthodox Church had placed the single nature of Christ at the center of its teaching. Therefore, the question arose among Ethiopian Orthodox theologians, In what sense was Christ anointed? The *Tewahedo* (Union) position stated that Christ was anointed before birth when his two natures united into one nature. The anointing restored to Christ's humanity what was lost in Adam's fall (Jones and Monroe 1935, 110; Ayala 1981, 104). The *Qebat* (Unction) position believed that the *Tewahedo* had overly divided Christ. They seem to have taught that the anointing had brought about the union of Christ's two natures and that his divine nature absorbed his human nature, a Eutychian understanding (Brake 1977, 155; Ayala 1981, 104; Jones and Monroe 1935, 110; Tesfazghi 1973, 80–81, 96). The *Sost Ledet* (Three Births) position may have emerged as much as a hundred years later and argued that Christ "was thrice born: once from the Father from all time; once in the Incarnation in the womb of the Blessed Virgin; once through the subsequent action of the Holy Spirit (either still in the womb, or, yet more radically, in the River Jordan; opinion was divided). Here the tendency towards Adoptionism was clear" (Crummey 1972, 24–25). Misrepresentations of the competing positions, regional politics, and the triumph of the *Tewahedo* position (which has tended to paint the opposing positions in extreme terms) have made it difficult to determine the exact beliefs of *Qebat* and *Sost Ledet* historically, and at least one scholar (Ayala 1981, 109–17) contends that there were only two positions, not three. The position presented here is that embraced by the large majority of historians of the EOTC.

is a classroom desk that is a union of a table and a chair; it retains all the essential attributes of both a table and a chair, united in a single entity with a single nature. The EOTC officially emphasizes that the union of Christ's two natures into one nature was accomplished without the confusion of the attributes of the two natures. Christ's deity was still a perfect deity, not in any way diminished by his humanity, and Christ's humanity was still a perfect humanity, not in any way altered by his deity. Though sometimes accused of teaching that Christ's humanity was absorbed by his deity, the EOTC formally affirms that "the manhood of Christ was absolutely real and perfect" (Samuel 1970, 51; Aymro and Motovu 1970, 95–98).[7] The central focus of the union of deity and humanity into a single nature is demonstrated in the preferred name of the church: Ethiopian Orthodox *Tewahedo* (Union) Church.

The EOTC stresses not only the unity of Christ's single nature but also the unity of all of his actions. Everything Christ did, including dying on the cross, he did as a single, unified person (Poladian 1964, 258–59).[8] EOTC theologians express particular concern at the Chalcedonian tendency to attribute some of Christ's actions to his divine nature and others to his human nature, evidence, they believe, that Chalcedonians have fallen into the heresy of Nestorianism (Berhanu 1993, 48; Habte 1964–65, 160).[9] If Christ's suffering and death took place only in his humanity, they point out, his death did not accomplish the world's salvation. Bishop Yesehaq of the EOTC's diocese in the Western Hemisphere affirms that "all concerning Christ should be applied to His entire person as one Lord. . . . God suffered, God was crucified, God shed blood, God died, and God was risen up for the salvation of all men. . . . If God the Word had not suffered on the Cross, the Christian hope for eternal salvation is vanity" (1989, 103).

The importance of the perfect union of Christ's deity and his humanity leads to the characteristic of Oriental Orthodox Christology that has caused Chalcedonians to accuse them of Eutychianism, the belief that Christ's deity absorbed his humanity so that he was no longer genuinely and perfectly human. Ethiopian theologians and laypeople sometimes make statements that seem to indicate that Christ's deity so absorbed his humanity that his humanity was distinctly different from

7. Samuel's (1970) and Aymro and Motovu's (1970) books are both officially sanctioned by the EOTC to explain its beliefs and practices to a wider audience.

8. Bishop Terenig Poladian is a theologian from a sister Oriental Orthodox church commissioned to write an official essay explaining the EOTC's doctrine.

9. Nestorius was accused of teaching that Christ was essentially two persons, one divine and one human, sometimes acting as God and sometimes as man. Gobena Berhanu and Mariam Habte are EOTC theologians.

that of other people (Samuel 1970, 49). "God became man and *man became God*" is a common expression used by EOTC theologians and laypeople alike to describe the incarnation (Strauss 1997, 88, 138). This expression seems to imply that Christ's humanity was transformed by his deity; his humanity became a divine humanity. The EOTC believes that only by means of an absolute unity that made every part of Christ's person divine could deity die and so bring divine salvation to humanity (Berhanu 1993, 47). Though they maintain that "neither of the natures was assimilated by the other," they also insist that his "flesh was made divine" so that every part of Christ's person would be God, enabling him to provide perfect salvation for the whole world (Aymro and Motovu 1970, 95–96). But if Christ's humanity became divine, it would seem that it was unlike the humanity of other people, and only the death of a genuine human being could pay for the sins of other humans. It was the failure to attribute a full, authentic humanity to Christ that led to the condemnation of Apollinarius (in AD 381) and Eutyches (in AD 451). What to Western theologians looks like Apollinarianism or Eutychianism is, to the Oriental Orthodox, essential to preserving the salvific effectiveness of Christ's death.

As a result, questions remain as to whether the average Ethiopian Orthodox person understands that a Jesus who possessed "divine flesh" was genuinely human. Ethnographic interviews conducted in one Addis Ababa parish in 1995 and 1996 indicated that a significant number of laypeople and parish clergy felt that Christ was not authentically human (Strauss 1997, 134–41).[10] One parish priest, for example, said that Christ "took the image of man to teach us and show us how to live. But he was true God, *not* true man (Amharic: *eunetenya sew*)." This same priest was shocked at the suggestion that Christ could ever have become hungry or tired like an ordinary person. The tendency to doubt Christ's true humanity was graphically expressed by a sixty-year-old man who had studied Ethiopian Orthodox theology most of his life. He said that Christ became a man to teach human beings, but "he didn't come to dig. He didn't come to build a house. He didn't have our human nature (Amharic: *tebay*). He was our king, above us." It seems that his idea was that Christ was humanlike but that he did not come to do the common work humans do. A Christ who was not genuinely human, of course, was not able to bear the sins of human beings. In addition, in the Ethiopian context, overemphasis on the deity of Christ at the expense of his humanity has led to the strong sense that other mediators are necessary to approach God. Several subjects even linked the importance of approaching God

10. C.f. Strauss (1997, 100–171) for a full description of research methodology and findings.

through saints and angels to the fact that Christ was not fully human (Strauss 1997, 143, 157).

The Influence of Language

The EOTC's suspicion that Chalcedonian theology is really veiled Nestorianism is exacerbated by the implicit meanings[11] of the words for "nature" and "person" in Amharic and Ge'ez. Because a *baheriy* (nature) is a concrete idea that always expresses itself in an *akal* (person), to speak of two natures in Christ implies two persons. Wolde Kifle Kidan's Ge'ez-Amharic dictionary (n.d.) explains that while *baheriy* (nature) is not the same as *akal* (person), it always acts through an *akal.* They cannot be separated. One can never attribute an action to a *baheriy*;[12] a *baheriy* always has to express itself through its own *akal.* As EOTC theologian Gobena Berhanu explains, "A person *(akal)* without a nature *(baheriy)* or a nature without a person doesn't make sense. If there are two natures, there *must* be two persons" (1993, 48).[13] In addition, EOTC scholar Moges Alemayehu explains that, to the average Amharic speaker, saying that Christ has two natures implies "two contradictory ways of thinking, two contradictory frames of mind, as if Christ could quarrel with himself" (1995). The ramifications for christological understanding in Amharic or Ge'ez are clear: It is nearly impossible to speak of two natures *(baheriy)* and one person *(akal)* because "two natures in one person" sounds like Nestorianism to many Ethiopian Orthodox theologians and like a double-minded self-contradiction to many average speakers of Amharic or Ge'ez.

Evaluation

Comparative Christology

How does the form-meaning continuum help in evaluating the Christology of the EOTC and in answering questions about its relationship to Chalcedonian Christology? First, it is clear that, among the Ethiopian Orthodox, the form *Tewahedo* is tightly linked with Christology that is

11. For a discussion of the importance of understanding implicit as well as explicit meaning in translation and theologizing, see Hiebert (1985, 144–58).

12. As an example, Wolde Kifle Kidan (n.d.) says one does not speak of a sickle cutting grain but of a person cutting grain, because the sickle is only the instrument; the person is doing the cutting. In the same way that a person expresses himself through the sickle, so the *baheriy* expresses itself through the *akal.*

13. Translation from Amharic by author.

genuinely Christian and authentically Ethiopian. For many Ethiopian Orthodox, history has forged an almost patriotic link between *Tewahedo* Christology and loyalty to their nation against the incursion of foreign religious ideas. Chalcedonian Christology, on the other hand, has been closely linked with "the hyenas of the West." The tight link between the form *Tewahedo* and the meaning "authentic Ethiopian Christianity" means that it will be very difficult to substitute other forms and still communicate a Christian faith that can be genuine in the Ethiopian context. Those who use Chalcedonian terminology with the Ethiopian Orthodox will likely be perceived as heretical perpetrators of a dangerous foreign cult. Use of the term *Tewahedo* by Christians in Ethiopia who are not Ethiopian Orthodox would be an important way to demonstrate that their faith is compatible with authentic Ethiopian Christianity.

However, it must also be recognized that, while formally affirming the perfect deity and humanity of Christ, a *Tewahedo*, one-nature christological form carries the implied meaning with some Ethiopians that Christ was less than fully human. The concern of Western theologians over the centuries that speaking of only one nature raises the risk of diminishing either Christ's deity or his humanity has proven valid among some Ethiopian Orthodox. A *Tewahedo* form may be authentically Ethiopian, but it may also imply ideas that are not biblical. However, because of the linguistic and historical context in Ethiopia, the Chalcedonian form may also imply ideas that are not biblical. Rather than being a clear way of affirming Christ's perfect deity and perfect humanity, theologically it will often be perceived as Nestorianism, and linguistically it will often suggest that Christ was double-minded. A careful study of the meaning of the Chalcedonian form in the Ethiopian context helps theologians recognize that the Chalcedonian form will often be inadequate to communicate biblical meaning.

Christians from outside the Ethiopian Orthodox tradition who relate to the Ethiopian Orthodox could respond to this dilemma in one of several ways.[14] First, they could adopt the EOTC form, identifying their Christology as *Tewahedo* but attempting to emphasize the full humanity of Christ and his adequacy as the only mediator between God and human beings. Second, they could adopt the Chalcedonian form while seeking to distance themselves from Nestorianism and other unintended meanings. Third, some Ethiopian evangelicals have chosen to communicate their Christology without using either the *Tewahedo* or the Chalcedonian form. Instead, they have written entirely fresh christological confessions (i.e.,

14. Paul Hiebert's guidelines on critical contextualization provide alternatives for believers seeking to contextualize biblical theology and respond to local beliefs and customs: adopt, reject, substitute, and modify with new meaning (Hiebert 1987, 110).

new forms) that affirm the perfect union of Christ's full deity and full humanity. This theologizing has grown out of analysis of their context and has led to Christologies that are both biblical and contextual.[15]

The path chosen by these Ethiopian evangelicals illustrates an important lesson for worldwide theologizing. Specific theological forms may accurately reflect biblical truth for many churches around the world but may still be inappropriate for a specific local context. If forms come with historical or linguistic baggage that overly weigh them down with unintended meaning, it may be impossible to fill those forms with new meaning. In these contexts, it may be best to choose new forms rather than to insist on using a form that has proven acceptable elsewhere. At the same time, local theologians must be careful of too quickly adopting a local form because it is authentic and acceptable to the context. If a form carries meaning that is contradictory to biblical truth, then no matter how "at home" it may make the gospel (Walls 1996, 7–8), one should be cautious about embracing it. When some forms carry either unbiblical meaning or inappropriate contextual implications, the preferred solution will often be to use entirely new forms to communicate the biblical truth.

Global Theologizing across Cultures

When local theologians are developing new, locally appropriate forms to communicate biblical meaning, their insights will contribute to a richer, fuller understanding of biblical truth for the global church. As they understand why a form has proven unacceptable locally, they prod the worldwide church to more closely examine its own theology. As they develop new forms, they add color to the multihued tapestry of the worldwide church's understanding of the meaning of Scripture. Global theologizing[16]—the sharing of local theologies from around the world—enhances the theology of the worldwide church.

15. Christology classes at the Evangelical Theological College and the Ethiopian Graduate School of Theology, both in Addis Ababa, have been engaged in writing biblical, relevant Christologies for their context from 1996 to 2004. These confessions were written in Amharic so that they would interface with the difficult linguistic issues, but they have been translated into English. An example of one such confession states that "being perfect God, he fulfilled everything on earth that created [humans] cannot do. Being perfect man, except for sin, he showed his fleshly nature by becoming tired, trusting, becoming hungry, crying, and especially by dying. Christ's deity did not override-abolish [Amharic: sha-re] or reduce his perfect humanity. Neither did Christ's perfect humanity override, abolish, or reduce his deity. We believe these two dwelt together in harmony without conflict, perfectly united in one person" (Strauss 1997, 223–24; other examples can also be found in Strauss 1997, 236–39).

16. "Global theologizing" is not being used in the sense suggested by Lamin Sanneh as "the faithful replication of Christian forms and patterns developed in Europe" but in

Context both increases and decreases theologians' awareness of aspects of the biblical text. "In all cultures there are elements which conspire against the understanding of God's Word. . . . On the other hand, every culture possesses positive elements, favorable to the understanding of the Gospel" (Padilla 1980, 69). Because their context will both open their eyes and blind them to aspects of the biblical text, theologians from every context need one another. Listening to theologians from other cultures helps theologians see what they may have missed because of their own cultural, theological, or historical biases. It helps them make sure their theology reflects as many implications of the biblical text as possible. It helps them make sure they have not strayed onto theological ground that contradicts Scripture and the theology of the universal church. "All theologies, including those in the West, need one another: they influence, challenge, enrich, and invigorate each other" (Bosch 1991, 456). And as theologians from many contexts share their insights with one another, a richer, more biblical metatheology—a worldwide theology that reflects the insights of many local theologies—emerges (Hiebert 1994a, 93–103).

For example, examining the reasons why Chalcedonian terminology is unacceptable to the Ethiopian Orthodox forces Chalcedonians to recognize the potential Nestorian tendencies in the way they state their Christology. Chalcedonians have usually not hesitated to say that Christ did certain actions "in his humanity" or "in his deity." The Ethiopian Orthodox would respond, "A nature does not act; a person acts. Does not attributing any particular action of Christ to his human or divine nature alone imply that there were two Christs? Does not saying that Christ did anything exclusively as a human or exclusively as God have clear Nestorian implications?" It is well beyond the scope of this chapter to wrestle with the relevant Scripture passages and to suggest a christological confession that incorporates these insights. The issues of the Ethiopian context, however, compel Chalcedonians to rethink their theology and to suggest a theology that more fully reflects scriptural truth. The confessions developed by Ethiopian evangelicals that are both biblical and appropriate to their context will help point the way. The christological theologizing of Ethiopian evangelicals can contribute to a richer understanding of the meaning of Scripture, more accurate and relevant theologizing, and a clearer articulation of biblical truth for the worldwide church.

---

the sense of a worldwide sharing of many local theologies, each of which has developed directly from interaction with Scripture and is expressed "through more or less effective local idioms" (2003, 22).

Creeds, Confessions, and Global Theologizing across History

Christological theologizing in the Ethiopian context also contributes to a better understanding of the nature of all creeds and confessions. It demonstrates that even theological forms as precious and as biblical as the Chalcedonian confession must not be thoughtlessly accepted or discarded in fresh cultural contexts. No creed—even that of Chalcedon—is the *only* way to express biblical truth. Instead, the continuum understanding of the relationship between form and meaning must be carefully considered before accepting, discarding, or substituting the theological forms of any creed in a particular context.

Part of the contextual nature of all theology is its historical context. "All expressions of Christian doctrine are rooted in history and are, therefore, historically and culturally conditioned" (Muller 1991, 91). Creeds and confessions emerged from the doctrinal struggles of a specific time in history. "Creeds, as an expression of the confessional character of all theologizing, are 'historically situational.' They are human acts of confession of God's unchanging good news, addressed to specific human cultural settings" (Conn 1984, 242). The creeds and confessions of the church are, therefore, a form of contextual theology. They are local theologies addressing particular situations the church has faced.

At the same time, creeds and confessions reflect a desire to reach beyond the local context and to express universal truth that will unite and provide identity for the church across generations and cultures. Despite postmodern assertions to the contrary, Scripture and distinctly Christian theology throughout history assert that there is universal truth. God has revealed this truth most clearly and completely in Scripture. Though theologies are all contextual, they are also an attempt to reach beyond what is merely situational and reflect this universal truth. The creeds of the church are contextual attempts to do just that.

The nature of creeds as both contextual and universal theologies demands that the church neither ignore them nor unthinkingly parrot them. "Contemporary systematic theology, therefore, cannot afford simply to repeat the language that it has been given—nor can it afford to ignore the past and attempt to strike out in new and innovative directions and expect to achieve any results or lasting significance" (Muller 1991, 94). Because of the contextual nature of creeds, simply repeating them or restating them is not necessarily the same as understanding or affirming them. Faithfulness to the contextual *and* the universal nature of creeds will demand, first, carefully studying the context in which they were written, second, isolating the universal truth the creeds were seeking to express, and third, restating the truths in language that carries the same meaning in the theologians' own unique context. "Faithfulness to such doctrines does not necessarily mean repeating them; rather it requires, in the making of any new formulations, adherence to the same directives that were involved in their first formulation" (Lindbeck 1984, 81).

For example, evangelicals ministering among the Ethiopian Orthodox should feel obligated neither to repeat the Chalcedonian form (two natures, one person) nor quickly to abandon it. Instead, they should carefully study the meaning of Chalcedon in its context and the relevant Scripture passages, reflect on the complexities of their own context, and then make an informed decision whether to use the Chalcedonian form or to adopt a new form that more clearly and accurately reflects biblical truth in their context.

Contextual theologians in the present must study and use the creeds of the past, not in slavish repetition of their words and phrases to maintain the pretense of doctrinal purity but as past models of contextual theology. Even as they engage in global theologizing with respected theologians in other contexts of their own time, they should view creeds and confessions as respected contextual theologies from another historical context. The contribution of those theologies will be valuable. They may provide direction, clarity, or enrichment. They should not, however, preclude fresh articulation of biblical truth that is relevant—and may even be more biblically stated—for the contemporary context. Reference to the contextual theologies of the past is a form of global theologizing that provides today's church with an outside perspective on its own theology (Conn 1984, 204).

Conclusion

One of the rich blessings of Christians living in the twenty-first century is the privilege of learning from their brothers and sisters around the world. Each church in each context faces unique issues and so has a unique perspective on Scripture. No church, no matter how biblical its theology or rich its heritage, can afford to isolate itself from the fresh insights of churches from other parts of the world. And no matter how committed a church is to a particular theological creed or confession, it should never view that theological form as the only way that theology can be expressed. Creeds and confessions are expressions of biblical truth for specific times and places. They unite the universal church around a common history and serve as examples of theology that is both biblical and relevant. This is the sense in which the universal church *can* unite around the Nicean statement about the Triune God and the Chalcedonian formula regarding the person of Christ. They were accurate expressions of biblical truth for their own context, and they consequently provide the church in *every* context with an example of biblical orthodoxy.

But in another sense, no creed, no matter how biblical, can ever be the standard against which all other theologies are measured. Only Scripture itself can stand in judgment of any theological expression. The forms through which scriptural truth is expressed in creeds and confessions should not be equated with the truth itself. In certain cultures and situations, a *different* form might be the only way to express the *same* confessional truth. The theologizing of churches wrestling to express that truth in their own context makes a valuable contribution to the theology of the worldwide church.

7

The Glocal Church

Locality and Catholicity in a Globalizing World

CHARLES E. VAN ENGEN

In the twenty-first century, the church of Jesus Christ needs to become self-consciously what it in fact already is: a *glocal* church. This chapter argues that a healthy congregation of disciples of Jesus lives out its catholicity by intentionally and actively participating in Christ's mission in a *glocal* fashion; that is, it is active simultaneously in global and local mission that dynamically fosters the glocal interaction between the global and the local.

In the late 1990s, the word *glocal* was coined to express a new interweaving of the global and the local (see Rosenau 2003; Robertson 1995; Tai and Wong 1998). I have chosen to use the word *glocal* here as a way to signal a kind of simultaneity in the nature of the church of Jesus Christ that is at once global and local in a number of senses. I will suggest that in the twenty-first century the church of Jesus Christ needs to become more explicitly what it already is: glocal in its essence, glocal in its theologizing, and glocal in its missional calling.

A quick Internet search of the term *glocal* revealed 347 entries representing a wide-ranging diversity of uses, including in:

- education
- organizational management
- advertising and economics
- communication, cinema, and computers
- globalization studies
- human rights and social work
- religion
- missions

But the primary arena of interest in the interweaving interaction between the global and the local seems to be in the study of cities, as, for example in such works as *Global Networks, Linked Cities* (Sassen 2002) and *Global City-Regions: Trends, Theory, Policy* (Scott 2001). Of particular interest is extensive information on "The *Glocal* Forum" and its Global Metro City network, founded by Uri Savi with offices in Zurich and Rome. The network's website (http://www.glocalforum.org) affirms the following:

> Global Metro City—The *Glocal* Forum is a non-profit organization working to build a new relationship between the city and the global village with the aim of contributing to peace and development. Founded in 2001, the organization encourages global powers to have broader respect for local powers and cultural diversity in a process defined as *glocal*ization. . . . The *Glocal* Forum aims to create a more equitable balance between the global and the local through a new pattern of diplomacy—the diplomacy of cities. (info@glocalforum.org; see also http://www.wearethefuture.com)

The implications of the concept of the glocal have been noted by some leading observers of the contemporary church. Five years before the Indonesian tsunami of 2004, Leonard Sweet published his earthshaking book *Soul Tsunami* (1999), in which he described the unprecedented turn-of-the-century transformations taking place worldwide. Interestingly, Sweet titled one of the chapters of that book "Life Ring #8: Get *Glocal.*"

Sweet suggests that one's proactive life response to tsunami-size transition should include an effort to "get *glocal.*" Although Sweet does not provide a definition of the term, it seems clear that he is describing the glocal when he says:

> Before you leave the house in the morning, you experience how global this world has become. You make that first cup of coffee—but only with the help of four states and six foreign countries. Who owns Firestone? Japan's Bridgestone. Who owns Dr. Pepper? Britain's Cadbury/Schweppes. Who

pushes the buttons of the Pillsbury Doughboy? Diageo, a company created
by Guinness (what country owns Guinness?) and Grand Metropolitan.
"Globalization" is more than the preeminent economic trend of the 21st
century, with a thriving global investment culture. It is also a new way
of living and being in the world. It is hard to underestimate [*sic*] the *unprecedented* nature of this global civilization. We have an interdependent,
interlocked economic system in which everybody in the world participates.
Global integration is becoming almost universal, with the Net the main
medium. (1999, 121–22, italics in original)

I believe Sweet is emphasizing the glocal here, that is, the interrelation-
ship between the local and the global in their multifaceted, multidirec-
tional, interactive dynamic influence one upon the other.

A glocal perspective of the universe recognizes that the smallest stone
thrown into a pond causes ripples that shake the earth. And the smallest shift in the tectonic plates of the planet causes a wave that changes
the course of human history. In ecclesiology broadly conceived, and in
missional ecclesiology in particular, we have been accustomed to set the
local, the national, and the global over against one another. For example,
we tend to speak of a congregation's local or neighborhood context of
outreach, ministries, or mission. A local church has a task force or
committee specifically targeted toward the needs of the church's closest contexts. Until recently, denominations in North America typically
have had a "home mission board" and another "board of world/global
mission." This local-global split is in fact worsening in many (especially
mainline) denominations in the United States. Many local churches in
the United States are now devoting the lion's share of their time, attention, personnel, and money to the needs of the people located closest to
the church's building and are doing so by reducing and in some cases
curtailing altogether their involvement in national or global ministries
and mission. The primary exception to this might be some short-term
mission trips by the church's members, trips that may be more Christian tourism than mission. The concept of globalization has not seemed
to counteract this trend. On the contrary, much of the discussion of
globalization seems to set the global over against the local and then to
analyze the impact that global forces are having on local realities—often
with a rather protectionist attitude.

In contrast to this, a glocal perspective may help us move beyond discussions of modernity versus postmodernity (Van Engen 1996), beyond
questions of postcolonial global mission (Hiebert 1991), and possibly
beyond the controversies over globalization as such (see, e.g., Tiplady
2003). *Glocal*ization, rather, seeks to perceive the world through the lens
of the simultaneous interaction, the interweaving influences, the dynamic,
always-changing, multidimensional interrelatedness of the global and the

local. This dynamic interaction recognizes that what was once known as the local is itself an aspect of the global in the same way that a quark or an electron is part of the entire universe. And the glocal recognizes that what we once knew as the global can only be expressed concretely in and through the local. In fact, mission in the twenty-first century involves "an ascending, never-ending spiral" or "boomerang effect," as Willem Saayman has suggested.

> I would like to argue that an adequate missionary ecclesiology demands a rethinking of the concept of linear process in mission. I think the process and progress from church to mission to church should rather be seen as cyclical, and specifically as an ascending, never-ending spiral. From the very beginning, therefore, the progress is not in a straight line *away* from the "sending" church *to* some faraway unreached "mission field," but rather curving back to it throughout. If we stick to the injunction of Acts 1:8, I would argue that the movement is from Jerusalem to Judea and back to Jerusalem, to Samaria and back to Jerusalem, to the ends of the earth and back to Jerusalem, etc. Such an understanding, to my mind, better expresses the role of mutuality and interdependence as essential preconditions for the churches to carry out their missionary responsibility. This implies that the evangelizers must always be evangelized anew; to use a well-known metaphor: the missionary chickens must always come home to roost. Or, to change my metaphor: this is the essential "boomerang effect" of Christian mission. The "sending" church(es) can and may never be left unchanged by its mission, not if the church is truly missionary by its very nature. (2000)

I am writing this chapter during Holy Week. As I walk through the story of the passion and resurrection of Jesus the Christ, I am struck by the glocal significance of the crucifixion and resurrection of our Lord. The entire universe in time and space was transformed in the instant when Jesus, hanging on a Roman cross near Jerusalem in that "first" century, proclaimed, "It is finished" (John 19:30). And all of life and human existence was changed when the resurrected Jesus Christ whispered to his disciples on that Easter Day, "Peace be with you" (Luke 24:36). In both time and space, the local and the global are folded in upon each other and are interwoven through each other into themselves—and glocal eternity is forever in an instant totally transformed. How can I grasp this?

I find that thinking about the nature of the Internet helps me get my mind around this new vision of reality. Every illustration or analogy has limitations. But I beg the reader's indulgence to imagine the Internet as an analogy of the glocal church of the twenty-first century. In looking at the Internet in this way, I do not mean to examine the Internet merely as a location and a pathway for communicating the gospel—or for attraction and advertising by creating webpages. That is a different matter, and Shawn Redford, among others, has challenged us to rethink the mission of the church in relation to the Internet, a missional process that he called "Facing the Faceless Frontier" (1999). In what follows, I want to suggest something different. What would the glocal church of Jesus Christ look like in the coming decades if we were to examine it in terms of its structure and organization through the kaleidoscope of the Internet?

Gazing through this looking glass, I think of each local congregation, each group of disciples of Jesus ("where two or three come together in my name, there am I with them" [Matt. 18:20]), as a desktop PC. This local-congregation-as-PC, like the desktop on which I am presently writing this chapter, may have a cable or a phone line through which it could be connected to the Internet. This small *c* church (represented by my desktop computer) may involve 5, 50, 500, or 5,000 disciples of Jesus. In computer terms, my computer may differ from other PCs in terms of its memory capacity, storage space, brain power, interfacing capabilities, and so forth. But no matter the size, it is fundamentally a PC. Similarly, no matter the size of a local church, in its theological and biblical essence, it is still basically the corporate congregation of those who gather as disciples of Jesus Christ.

Moving to a second level of organization, I also have my PC networked in my home with two other desktop computers and a laptop. I have done this by running a special network cable from each computer to a router. When all four computers are up and running, I can access all the data on all the hard drives of all four computers simultaneously. But each PC has its own hardware and software structures, and I cannot actually run the other computers from the one on which I am presently typing.[1] This is analogous to a regional group of churches, or a regional judicatory. Such a group of like-minded local congregations needs networking hardware and software, an ecclesiastical structure and personal relationships that hold them together (loosely or tightly) and facilitate their interrelations and intercommunications. Each local congregation has its own leadership, governance, structure, and other internal systems, but there is some level of cooperation, fellowship, accountability, recognition, and empowerment among them. In computerese, they are a local network. The networking hardware may be as organizationally loose as a clergy association or a pastors' prayer group in a town, or it can be as tight as a Roman Catholic diocese or a Methodist district. The extent, depth, and

1. I could do this if I had the right software installed on each computer, and herein lies an analogy for various forms of ecclesiastical organization: Roman Catholic, Orthodox, and Protestant; episcopal, presbyterial, congregational, or New Apostolic Reformation.

structural cohesion of this network depend, of course, on the ecclesiastical polity to which that network of congregations ascribes.

This takes us to a third level of organization. Some years ago, when the Internet was in its infancy, many of us became greatly enamored with the idea of email. I was among the first fifty thousand or so to subscribe to AmericaOnline (AOL). AOL is, of course, now only one of many companies that offer access to their servers. Most universities in the world have their own servers to facilitate communication on their campuses. Similarly, City of Hope in Duarte, California, the large cancer-research institution where my wife, Jean, works, has its own internal server that integrates the communication and facilitates all the organizational, administrative, and interpersonal relations necessary to run an institution with nearly three thousand employees. In computerese, this is an intranet. I think of Western European state churches, American denominations, and national churches that arose in Asia, Africa, and Latin America during the twentieth century as types of intranet systems. Looking at the Roman Catholic Church globally, one might say that it is like a huge intranet. In Protestantism, although world federations, alliances, fellowships, councils, and conferences bring together various denominations and national churches that share similar ecclesiastical traditions, these do not function, in my mind, in a structurally tight enough fashion to be thought of as intranets. The Anglican/Episcopal network centered in the Lambeth Conferences might be considered a type of Protestant intranet, but even that has begun to unravel in recent years. In banking terms, when I access my bank account with an ATM card at my local branch, I access my bank's intranet. But when I use my VISA card in the ATM of another bank, I access the Internet.

As we deepen and broaden our thinking about the global catholicity of the church, we may begin to see the church of Jesus Christ as a kind of glocal Internet. The Internet is something ontologically different from anything I have described thus far. Especially after the invention of Internet computer languages, the Internet became the invisibly visible, organically structured pathway of glocal communication. In my home office, where I am now writing, I use a cable/modem that is essentially connected to the Internet 24-7. When I call up an Internet communication software, something almost miraculous happens. Instantaneously, my computer becomes a part of the Internet, and I, through my computer, become one small component of a phenomenally huge glocal electronic system. My desktop PC is no longer an autonomous, individual computer; neither is the Internet merely the sum of such individual computers. Rather, my PC is now an integral part of a much larger whole. I and my computer are the Internet. In other words, when I log on to the Internet, my PC becomes instantly glocal—it is simultaneously local and global.

It is a glocally integrated part of the interaction between the local and the global.

This is the level at which we need to think of the church of Jesus Christ today as glocal. Analogous to my PC's relationship with the Internet, when I gather with other Christians in the name of Jesus, I am in that instant gathering with the family of God that includes over 1.5 billion followers of Jesus, the very large family of which Paul speaks in Ephesians 3:14–21. Like my PC, my local congregation is now hooked in spiritually, organically, temporally, and spatially to all those who everywhere always have believed in Jesus Christ. As we gather to worship our Lord Jesus Christ, we are instantly interconnected with all other Christians around the globe who are in Christ. This is the glocal Church that exists "in the power of the Spirit" (Moltmann 1977). This glocal reality recognizes that the small *c* church is in fact an integral part of the large *C* Church. This fact transforms our understanding of the missional life of the local congregation. Such a local congregation is not just *pars pro toto* (a part for the whole, as this has been expressed in, for example, Orthodox ecclesiology); it *is* the whole in which it participates. The whole church is there in that local congregation, and that local congregation exists precisely because it is a part of the whole. The concept of the glocal, then, may offer us a new way of understanding the catholicity of the church. What follows explores this by considering that the church is glocal in its essence, its theologizing, and its mission.

Speaking of the glocal church, then, is a twenty-first-century way of expressing the older idea of the catholicity of the church. But to appreciate this, we need to review what the church has understood when it says that it is catholic or universal.

The Church of Jesus Christ in the Twenty-first Century Is Glocal in Its Essence

From its birth after Peter's Pentecost sermon, continuing in Paul's Gentile mission, demonstrating astonishingly rapid numerical and geographical expansion during its first century of life, and acquiring explicit expression in the apostolic fathers, the apologists, and the post-Nicene fathers, the Christian church demonstrated a commitment to gather men and women from the entire world into its fold.[2] For twenty centuries, the church has defined its essential nature by using four words to describe its attributes, with one of these having to do with its universality: "I believe in the one holy *catholic* and apostolic church."

2. Parts of this section have been adapted from Van Engen (1981).

Because of the universal scope of God's intention, because of the universal scope of Christ's lordship, because of the universal scope of the kingdom of God, the church of Jesus Christ has always understood itself as nothing short of universal. Because the great king, Jesus Christ, has dominion over all nations, the church has understood the scope of its missional task as including all nations. As Kenneth Cragg once said, "The Gospel has no native country" (quoted in Niles 1962, 248). The universal nature of the gospel has meant that the church could find its true self only as it became a global village open to, including, calling, and embracing all humans.

The universal motif of the offer of salvation to all persons and the incorporation by faith of all peoples, families, tribes, and nations in the people of God (Revelation) have been reiterated again and again in the history of the church. The New Testament church, the early church fathers, the monastic movement, and the Second Vatican Council each in its own way sought to give expression to the same basic truth. It is the will of God that all peoples should become increasingly related to him and his body, the church. This universal purpose is built into the very essence of what the church is as the people of God. The people of God are gathered from the entire world. As such, it is essential to their being that they participate in that gathering. As the people of God, the church participates in Christ as and when it participates in Christ's universal salvation, gathering people from all four corners of the earth to be his body, the church.

From its beginning, this Christian community, which called itself the church, had some very distinctive features. Prominent among these was the conception of the church as the communion of the Holy Spirit. Emphasized in the apostolic benediction, this could be understood as an early definition of the church: "The grace of the Lord Jesus Christ, and the love of God, and the fellowship [*koinonia*] of the Holy Spirit" (2 Cor. 13:14).[3]

Kenneth Scott Latourette (1967) posed the question as to the factors that might have been responsible for the church's amazing growth as a communion of the Holy Spirit. After enumerating various factors external to the early church, he concluded, "Never before in the history of the race had conditions been so favorable for the acceptance of any one faith by so large a proportion of mankind" (1967, 364). But Latourette pointed out that, alongside these external factors, one must also take into consideration an important internal one: Christianity was inclusive.

3. On this point, see Minear (1960) and Davies (1965, 55).

Whence came these qualities which won for Christianity its astounding victory? Careful and honest investigation can give but one answer, Jesus. It was faith in Jesus and his resurrection which gave birth to the Christian fellowship and which continued to be its inspiration and its common tie. . . . The early disciples unite in declaring that it was from the command of Jesus that the Gospel was proclaimed to all, regardless of sex, race or cultural background. (1953, 106–7)

Latourette observes that "from the outset [Christianity] possessed a strong sense of the essential unity of all believers and a desire to give that unity tangible expression in a body bound together by a common faith and by love" (1967, 364). This is the astounding quality of the early Christian church. The Christian church was not anything like the exclusivist, introverted, secret mystery religions of the day. Rather, Christianity, from the very earliest times, as in Peter's Pentecost sermon (Acts 2), perceived itself as a radically inclusive religion that aimed to proclaim its message and extend its fellowship to both men and women, slaves and free, Romans, Jews, Greeks, barbarians, and all persons who would receive it.[4] The church understood its growth in catholicity as an expression of its essential nature.

One of the earliest references to the early church's self-awareness in this vein can be found in the Didache.

As this broken bread (of the Eucharist) was scattered upon the mountains and was gathered together and became one, so let thy Church be gathered together from the ends of the earth into thy Kingdom: for thine is the glory and power through Jesus Christ for ever and ever. (Bettenson 1956, 70)

As we can see in the New Testament table of nations in Acts 2, the earliest notions concerning the nature of the church include some kind of universal or catholic idea. The church is not a church of only one race, one nation, or one language. It is a church "gathered together from the ends of the earth" (Pelikan 1971, 156).

This idea of the universality of the Christian church must be understood as the substance behind the word *catholic*, first used by Ignatius (c. 35–c. 107)[5] in his epistle to the Smyrnaeans. J. N. D. Kelly remarks:

As regards "Catholic," its original meaning was "universal" or "general" and in this sense Justin can speak of "the catholic resurrection." As applied to

4. Cf. the New Testament table of nations in Acts 2:9–11, as well as Paul's statements of this thesis in Rom. 1:14; 1 Cor. 12:13; and Gal. 3:28. On this, see Bosch (1980, 94–95).
5. On the origin of the word *catholic*, see Brauer (1971, 423), Küng (1971, 297), and Schaff (1950, 145).

the Church, its primary significance was to underline its universality as opposed to the local character of the individual congregations. (1960, 190)

At this time, there was still no difference in the minds of the early church theologians concerning the visible in contrast to the invisible church. This universal fellowship or communion was almost always conceived of as an empirical, visible society. This was the real, existing fellowship of Christ, called by the Holy Spirit, open to all people in all the world.[6] The church of the apostolic fathers was the "holy and universal church sojourning in every place" to which the Smyrnaeans wrote to tell about the martyrdom of Polycarp around AD 155 or 156.

The incipient ecclesiology of the early days of the church[7] was refined and at times distorted through the work of the apologists. The catholic church became more and more the true church as opposed to the heretics, and the fellowship, the gathering, became increasingly the institution and the hierarchy. Prior to the Council of Nicea, the apologists talked about the unity of the church as a quality that was to be seen in the earthly, empirical church. Cyprian, for example, stated, "He cannot possess the garment of Christ who tears and divides the Church of Christ" (Deferrari 1958, 102). Pelikan observes, "In making such an issue of the empirical unity of the church, Cyprian was expressing the conviction of the church catholic from the beginning" (1971, 159).

This view of the unity of the empirical church in both Irenaeus and Cyprian (as the spokespersons for their era) was directly related to the catholicity or universality of the visible church. Cyprian, for example, used the illustration of the sun with many rays and the tree with many branches to show that "the church is one which with increasing fecundity extends far and wide into the multitude" (cited in Deferrari 1958, 99). As a preface to stating the creed, Irenaeus said, "The Church, though scattered through the whole world to the ends of the earth, has received (the faith) from the Apostles and their disciples" (cited in Schaff 1877a, 13).[8]

Although the doors were closing slightly through the writings of these men so that heretics and schismatics were out, still the gates were wide open to the "multitudes" of Cyprian and the "whole world to the ends of the earth" of Irenaeus.

Kenneth Scott Latourette observed that in all probability the Gnostic and Marcion heresies speeded up the process by which the thinking of

6. J. N. D. Kelly cites Clement of Rome, Justin, Ignatius, 2 Clement, and Hermas in this regard (1960, 190–91).

7. J. N. D. Kelly refers to early Christian ecclesiology as being "far from consciously formulated" (1960, 190).

8. See also Bettenson (1956, 17, 121–26).

the early church fathers was crystallized in their concept of the nature and the unity of the catholic church (1967, 341–42). By the end of the fourth century, a definition had emerged that has been preserved surprisingly intact to this day. The Niceno-Constatinopolitan Creed stated, "And I believe in the one holy catholic and apostolic Church" (see Schaff 1877a, 28; Schaff and Wace 1974, 163; Bettenson 1963, 25–26; Schaff 1950, 536–37). To gain an understanding of the church's self-awareness as expressed in the creed, we must observe carefully the perspectives of those contemporary with it.

One of the most explicit of the Nicene fathers on this point was Cyril of Jerusalem (315–86). Cyril expressed the belief that the church was catholic, meaning universal, and thus to be distinguished from heretical gatherings (see Schaff and Wace 1974, 140; Bromiley 1978, 132). But this did not mean the church was exclusive, from which the heretics were withheld. Neither did this mean for Cyril that it necessarily was the institutional hierarchy that was catholic. That came later. For Cyril of Jerusalem, the witness of the cross reached out to the entire world (lect. xii, 40, in Schaff and Wace 1974, 93). This meant also that the gifts and blessings of the Holy Spirit were to be spread over the entire world (lect. xvi, 22, in Schaff and Wace 1974, 121). Cyril said:

> It is called Catholic then because it extends over all the world, from one end of the earth to the other; and because it teaches universally and completely one and all the doctrines which ought to come to men's knowledge . . . and because it brings into subjection to godliness the whole race of mankind . . . and because it universally treats and heals the whole class of sins. . . . And it is rightly named (ecclesia) because it calls forth and assembles together all men. (cited in Schaff and Wace 1974, 139–40)

Thus, it is of the essential nature of the true, catholic church that it should extend its blessings to all people over the entire world. Cyril's conviction was shared by many of his Eastern contemporaries, including, for example, John Chrysostom (347–407). As J. N. D. Kelly puts it, "The Church, he affirmed, is Catholic, that is to say, spread throughout the whole world" (1960, 42).

Augustine of Hippo (354–430) was "the most influential of the fathers of the Western Church" (Brauer 1971, 72). In fact, "in a manner and to a degree unique for any Christian thinker outside the New Testament, Augustine has determined the form and the content of church doctrine for most of Western Christian history" (Pelikan 1971, 293). His influence was no less determinative in ecclesiology than it was in other aspects of church doctrine. Augustine's idea of the church was a large one. Geoffrey Bromiley notes, "For Augustine the Church comprises not just the part that journeys here on earth, but also that part which in heaven has always from creation held fast to God, that is, the church of the holy angels" (1978, 113). Augustine's church is a universal community, or in the words of Juan Luis Segundo, a "congregation of the human race" (1975, 6). His is a dynamic view of the church as the *communio sanctorum,* "the eschatological community of salvation sent into the world. She is also *civitas Dei,* the 'City of God' on earth, the Kingdom, the institution of salvation" (Bosch 1980, 105).

We must keep in mind that for Augustine the church was the people—the elect on earth and in heaven. The church had not yet been reduced to hierarchy and institution, as it would be later. Augustine made the distinction, though not as radically as did the Reformers, between the invisible church of the elect, whom only God knew, and the more visible church that was "an admixture of good and bad alike and will remain so until the final consummation . . . the *corpus permixtum*" (Davies 1965, 258; see also Wiles and Santer 1975, 164–65; Kelly 1960, 413). This did not, however, negate for Augustine the fact that there is, has always been, and always will be only one church, one body, one communion of saints. Thus, when Augustine spoke of the vast numbers of Christians in the catholic church, and he used that as a defense of his own church over against the heretics, he was speaking primarily of people in the here and now, of the *communio sanctorum* in the world as he knew it.

Vincent of Lérins (died before 450), one of Augustine's contemporaries, is credited with formulating the Vincentian Canon: *quod ubique, quod semper, quod ab omnibus creditum est* (What has everywhere, always, by all been believed) (Brauer 1971, 849–50).[9] The "all" to which Vincent referred was not to be restricted exclusively to the clergy and the hierarchy of the church. Augustine also included the laity, especially in relation to the prayers of the entire church, which often reflected and gave expression to the apostolic tradition (Pelikan 1971, 339). Thus, in Augustine's thought, the "all" who were to seek theological consensus had to be as broad as the church itself.

Centuries later, Martin Luther affirmed, "'Christian church' is a name and 'Christian holiness' an entity common to all churches and all Christians in the world; therefore it is called 'catholic'" (*On the Councils and the Church,* in Luther 1955, 41). Thus, for Luther, the church universal was the church spread over the entire world:

> I believe that here below and throughout the world, there is only one Christian Church, the Church universal, and that this Church is identical with

9. Jaroslav Pelikan provides a helpful discussion of the Vincentian Canon (1971, 334–41).

the universal fellowship of the saints, i.e., the devout believers everywhere on earth. This Church is gathered, sustained and ruled by the Holy Spirit . . . and strengthened day by day through the sacraments and the Word of God. (cited in Eastwood 1958, 26)

And John Calvin echoed this by saying:

Often, too, by the name of Church is designated the whole body of mankind scattered throughout the world who profess to worship one God and Christ. . . . The Church universal is the multitude collected out of all nations, who, though dispersed and far distant from each other, agree in one truth of divine doctrine, and are bound together by the tie of a common religion. (1975, vol. IV, 1, 7, 9)

The idea of catholicity contains much more than simply the notions of geographical and numerical extension. It has also to do with cohesion, doctrinal continuity, and catholicity in a temporal sense.[10] Here, however, we should notice the theme that courses through Scripture from the time of Abraham: The salvation of God is meant for all people spread over the entire world. Further, it is important to notice that with the restoration of the notion of the church as a people of God, the communion of saints, the Reformers again gave this geographic and numerical universality its proper weight in ecclesiology. The Reformers were followed in this by all of Protestantism. The fact that the church is the communion of saints and includes all races and languages spread over all the world was also stressed, for instance, in several of the evangelical creeds.[11] Remarkably, even though some of these creeds are set forth by strongly separatist groups, they still emphasize this facet of the essence of the church. Thus, for the Reformers and their progeny, the church as the communion of saints is composed of people of every race spread

10. This is emphasized by Karl Barth, who states, "The adjective 'catholic' means general, comprehensive. . . . Applied to the Church it means that it has a character in virtue of which it is always and everywhere the same and always and everywhere recognizable in this sameness, to the preservation of which it is committed. . . . Where it does not exist and is not recognizable in this sameness, where it is not concerned to preserve it, where it is not 'catholic,' it is not the true Church, the Church of Jesus Christ. The term 'catholic' speaks explicitly of the true Church activating and confirming its identical being in all its forms. . . . From the geographical meaning of the word there had derived and still derives the wider sense in which the reference is to the relationship of the Christian community to the other natural and historical human societies. In essence the Church is the same in all races, languages, cultures and classes, in all forms of state and society" (1958, 1, 701–3; see also Küng 1971, 298–302).

11. See, e.g., the Belgic Confession, the Confession of the Waldenses, and the Second Helvetic Confession.

over the entire world who believe in Jesus Christ—and thus the church *is for* all humans in all the world.

Both Gustav Warneck and Samuel Zwemer made a point of this. For them, this meant that "the Reformation certainly did a great indirect service to the cause of missions to the heathen" (Warneck 1901, 11; see also Zwemer 1950, 208–11). In fact, Luther laid the very foundation of Protestant missions in this regard.

> Of course, Luther maintained with emphasis the universality of Christianity and its elevation above all kinds of limit, whether of place, time, rank, or nation. He was quite certain also that, according to the promise, the Gospel must speed through the whole world and reach all nations. . . . "All the world does not mean one or two parts: (Luther said), but everywhere where people are, thither the Gospel must speed and still ever speeds, so that, even if it does not remain always in a place, it yet must come to, and sound forth in, all parts and corners of the earth." (Warneck 1901, 12)

This is the cornerstone of Protestant mission. An emphasis on numerical church growth is an attempt to give historical and geographical reality to one of the most basic elements in the church's self-perception: The church is for everyone, everywhere, always. The numerical growth and the geographic and cultural expansion of the church over time must be understood as a movement that gives expression in the here and now to the catholicity of the church in its geographic, numerical, and temporal significance.

The Reformers viewed the church as being essentially created from and looking toward a gathering of people into the communion of the gospel. Luther first expressed this in thesis sixty-five of his Ninety-five Theses by presenting the gospel as a net. "Thus the Gospel treasures are nets, with which of old they fished for men of riches" (cited in Bettenson 1947, 190).

Calvin developed this idea a little further. He presented the church as a net and stressed that when one is at first fishing with the net, all kinds of fishes are caught, and it is only after having brought them in that they are separated (1975, vol. IV, 1, 13, 292). This serves to set in bold relief the aspect of the church's nature as a gathering and as a gatherer. Thus, "The Church universal is a multitude collected out of all nations" (1975, vol. IV, 1, 9).

The gathering motif taught by Luther and Calvin was given prominence in several of the creeds of the Protestant church, such as the two Helvetic Confessions, the Scottish Confession, the Heidelberg Catechism, the Westminster Confession, the Savoy Declaration of the Congregational Church, and the Baptist Philadelphia Confession of 1688 (Schaff 1877a, 219, 324, 458, 657–58, 721–23, 738–41, 874).

The numerical universality of the church should be understood as part of the gift of catholicity that has been bestowed upon the church—a gift that in itself constitutes a task. The numerical growth of the church is seen as a quality of the church turned inside out, a dynamic energy directing the church toward the world. The numerical growth of the church, in this way of thinking, is precisely the universal, catholic church seeking to be what is. This is not triumphalist self-aggrandizement. Rather, it is a characteristic of the very essence of the church as the gathering of the community of the Holy Spirit, open to all peoples, to the entire world, in all time. As Hans Küng put it, the catholic church must "keep on becoming Catholic" (1963, 377). Or in the words of Wilhelm Andersen:

> The Church should never become fixed at any one place in the world. She must be on her way to the ends of the earth in the certainty that His time is pressing. In this manner mission calls forth the end, the coming of the Lord himself. The theology of mission is, then, also its goal. Then it also becomes adoration of the Triune God. (1961, 313)

G. C. Berkouwer pointed out that the Great Commission is actually an expression of the church's catholicity (1976, 106). It is for this reason that the church must take the lead in being accessible and open to all people (Eastman 1971, 131). The church's universality is the intentional, centrifugal, totally outward movement of the church. The church is less than what it is called to be when there is a loss of this outward directedness of the people of God.[12] Ernest Best said, "Catholicity is of the essence of the nature of the church without which it is not recognizable as church" (1955, 193). Berkouwer echoes this:

> The riches of the Church cannot be understood unless the Church is in motion in the "going forth" (Matt. 28:19) that Jesus commanded as "the most profoundly necessary step." Therein it is clear that God loved the world (John 3:16), that He was in Christ reconciling the world to Himself (II Cor. 5:19), and that Christ is the Savior of the world (John 4:42). This is a continuing reminder of the *missio Dei*, the "mission of God," which radically excludes every religious or cultural absolutizing. (1976, 394–95)[13]

The nature of the church's universality means that it exists for all people, for the entire world, and it is called to be in every place, among every language, tribe, family, and culture. Thus, we must conclude that the universal church can be recognized by its deep desire, its profound

12. On this theme, see Barth (1958, 2–3, 767–72), Berkouwer (1976, 123, 392ff.), Goodall (1953, 188–91), De Ridder (1971, 214–18), Bavinck (1956, 526–28), Peters (1972, 27), Blauw (1962, 115–18), and Piet (1970, 18).
13. Berkouwer quotes here from Karl Barth. See Barth (1958, 2–3, 874).

commitment to extend its joy, love, and fellowship to as many persons, peoples, cultures, and nations as possible. The church that has lost this burning desire has lost something of its universality under God.[14]

The Church of Jesus Christ in the Twenty-first Century Is Glocal in Its Theologizing

As we enter the twenty-first century, we find ourselves in a new world. Acts 1:8 is now a reality. Members of the church of Jesus Christ, numbering more than 1.5 billion, are now literally witnesses of Jesus Christ everywhere in their Jerusalems, Judeas, Samarias, and their ends of the earth. We are all aware that the center of gravity of the Christian church has shifted from North to South, from West to East. Among other things, this shift means that mission sending is now polycentric: Cross-cultural missions send their missionaries from everywhere to everywhere.

But the shift in the center of gravity of today's Christian churches and missions also means that the church is no longer a monocentric and mostly monocultural enterprise concentrated in Western Europe or North America. The Christian church today reflects a monumental shift with regard to the appropriate agendas, categories, agents, methodologies, worldview assumptions, types of rationality, perspectives, and modes of articulation that influence its thought and life around the globe. The church is now a global/local (glocal) reality. The glocal Christian church today consists of everyone who confesses with the mouth and believes in the heart, who proclaims in word and deed, that "Jesus is Lord" (Rom. 10:9–13; 1 John 4:1–3).

Although the glocal church is one, it is made up of a multiplicity of radically different contexts locally and globally. We are now a world church comprising many members globally. Yet we are one church. In Ephesians, Paul's primary letter dealing with a missional ecclesiology, he writes, "There is one body and one Spirit—just as you were called to one hope when you were called—one Lord, one faith, one baptism; one God and Father of all, who is over all and through all and in all" (Eph. 4:4–6). As I have written elsewhere:

> The Christian church does not confess "holy catholic church*es*," or "famil*ies* of God" or "bod*ies* of Christ" or "New Israel*s*." In the biblical view of the church the plural only refers to geographical location of churches, not existential being of the church. In its essence there is only one church. In Ephesians *ekklesia* appears only in the singular. . . .

14. See "Lumen Gentium" in Flannery (1975, 350). See also Blauw (1962, 111).

As Karl Barth has put it, we cannot justify, spiritually or biblically, "the existence of a plurality of churches genuinely separated . . . and mutually excluding one another internally and therefore externally. A plurality of churches in this sense means a plurality of lords, a plurality of spirits, a plurality of gods." (Van Engen, 1991; quoting Barth 1958, 675)

Yet we are also many members. Paul affirms the church's oneness as a preamble to describing the pluriformity of the gifts of the Spirit that are each a part of the one body. "But to each one of us grace has been given as Christ apportioned it. . . . It was he who gave some to be apostles, some to be prophets, some to be evangelists, and some to be pastors and teachers, to prepare God's people for works of service, so that the body of Christ may be built up until we all reach unity in the faith and in the knowledge of the Son of God and become mature, attaining to the whole measure of the fullness of Christ" (Eph. 4:7, 11–13). So there is one church that is one body, but there are many members, many charisms, and many ministries given for the church's mission in the world. This pluriformity and polycentricity of the one church necessitate our learning to be a glocal church involving the simultaneous, constant, dynamic interaction between the local and the global.

We seem to not fully appreciate the far-reaching implications of this dialectical tension of diversity within unity in a globalizing world. Let me point out two illustrative implications of this new reality. These implications have been addressed in some depth elsewhere in this volume, so my discussion will be brief.

Both Theology and Theologies

Doing theology in a globalizing world requires theologizing that affirms both the oneness of the church and the multiplicity of gifts that make up that glocal body of Christ. Unfortunately, the tendency has been for the church throughout the centuries to emphasize one of these themes at the expense of the other. On the one hand, since Constantine, the Christian church has tended to do its theology from a predominantly monocentric and monocultural perspective, formulating a set of theological dogmas that were assumed to be universally true for everyone, everywhere, always. This produced the concept of theology as a singular noun understood as the systematic aggregate of a set of unchanging propositions. This monocentric view of doing theology dominated not only the Roman and Eastern churches but the various branches of Protestantism after the Reformation as well. This perspective also permeated Protestant missions for over 150 years during the time of colonial missions.

In reaction to the hegemony of the Western church in theology, many theologians from Africa, Asia, and Latin America have affirmed a polycentric perspective of theologizing. This has resulted in the more recent Protestant attention given to the cluster of issues associated with the contextualization of the gospel. The perspective of contextualization as local theologizing represents a constantly changing reciprocal interaction between church and context, between the global and the local. It is thus a process of glocal reflection that begins with an analysis of the historical situation and proceeds to a rereading of Scripture, which in turn leads to interactive theological reflection concerning the context: an act of theologizing that propels Christians to active engagement with the cultural, socioeconomic, and political issues extant in the context, in conversation with Christians in all other contexts.

The multiplicity of contexts and worldviews that constitutes the world church today, representing a diversity of cultural assumptions and agendas, makes it necessary to speak in the plural of local theologies. But we must simultaneously affirm that there is only *one* church of Jesus Christ. Neither of these two themes is acceptable alone. To view doing theology as the construction of one monolithic theology superimposed on all Christians everywhere violates the truth that God's revelation took place "at many times and in various ways" (Heb. 1:1) and has always been received within the categories of specific cultural contexts. On the other hand, the atomization of a plurality of local theologies violates the oneness of the church, the unity of the Holy Spirit, the singularity of the gospel, and the unity of all Christians who read the same Bible (see Bosch 1991, 427). Thus, neither monolithic uniformity nor atomized pluriformity are satisfactory approaches to doing theology in a globalizing world. Therefore, the challenge before us is to find a way to know God in context, that is, to do critical theologizing in a glocal fashion through reading the same Bible in the midst of multiple cultures.

Epistemological Recontextualization

The global shift in the center of gravity of the Christian church worldwide offers a second implication that profoundly influences the way we should do theology. Not only must we seek to reconcile "one theology–many theologies," but we must also consider how to recontextualize the gospel of Jesus Christ in situations in which multiple Christian groups are involved in theologizing, there are multiple generations of believers, and there are a growing nominalism and a secularization of the church and its theology.

The world has undergone radical changes that should alter significantly our approach to contextualization, changes that call for an epistemological approach that takes into account the glocal church involved in critical theologizing. With one-quarter of the earth's population claiming to be Christian in some fashion, and with two-thirds of that Christian population now found in the South and the East, the process of contextualization must also include an epistemological shift as Christians in the North and the West listen to and learn from their brothers and sisters elsewhere. That is, contextualization involves Christian churches in one setting sharing with other Christian churches the way they, in their own context, read the Bible and understand the gospel (see Phan 2003). Christians from everywhere need to share with other Christians everywhere how they are coming to know God in context. Each step forward, each "translation" (Sanneh 1989, 31; Walls 2002b, 72–81) of the gospel offers the possibility of discovering something about God as revealed in the Bible that no one has previously seen. "As the gospel continues to take root in new cultures, and God's people grow in their covenantal relationship to God in those contexts, a broader, fuller, and deeper understanding of God's revelation will be given to the world church" (Van Engen 1996, 88–89).

But this deepening and enriching of our understanding of God's revelation in the Bible are possible only if there is an ongoing conversation between the local congregations and churches and the church globally by way of a mutually enriching process of critical theologizing. Moreover, a fresh epistemological approach to contextualization in these new situations of ecclesial diversity must speak to the second, third, and fourth generations of believers in each location, generations that often involve increased nominalism and secularization. Without such an intentional, ongoing recontextualization, it is highly likely that future generations of the church will become Christian in name only (Gibbs 1994, 17–38).

The Church of Jesus Christ in the Twenty-first Century Is Glocal in Its Missional Calling

In its essence, the glocal church is universal—and universally incarnated in specific times and places. Furthermore, the church is glocal in its extension, a fact that implies two dialectical realities: Although there is one church, there are many churches, and although there is one Bible, there are many readings of Scripture.

Building on this reality, we can make two complementary observations: (1) The glocal church's theologizing is to be critiqued by the global church and informed, shaped, and critiqued by local churches. (2) All universal truths about God can be lived out only by a particular people and by specific congregations locally, and a local congregation derives its meaning as it is the local manifestation, the local concrete expression of, the universal glocal church of Jesus Christ. Such a glocal perspective was affirmed by the apostle Paul:

> Though I am free and belong to no man, I make myself a slave to everyone, to win as many as possible. To the Jews I became like a Jew, to win the Jews. . . . To those not having the law I became like one not having the law . . . so as to win those not having the law. To the weak I became weak, to win the weak. I have become all things to all men so that by all possible means I might save some.
>
> 1 Corinthians 9:19–22

And in Galatians Paul wrote:

> I am astonished that you are so quickly deserting the one who called you by the grace of Christ and are turning to a different gospel—which is really no gospel at all. . . . As we have already said, so now I say again: If anybody is preaching to you a gospel other than what you accepted, let him be eternally condemned!
>
> 1:6–7, 9

How does the glocal church maintain the dialectical tension between faithfulness to revelation and contextual appropriateness in its communication? How do Christian churches from diverse contexts listen to and learn from one another in order that they might know the same God better within their own contexts? Paul gives us an indication of a way forward in the way he develops his thought in Galatians 3 through 6. If we reread Galatians not from the point of view of law and grace (though certainly that is a major theme) but from the standpoint of Paul as a glocal critical contextual theologian, we can see that he offers the following principle: Affirm commonalities and acknowledge differences within a trinitarian process of theological reflection. Three brief points should be noted.

God the Father: Common Humanness, Diverse Cultures

Having made his case that Jews and Gentiles alike are "not justified by observing the law, but by faith in Jesus Christ" (Gal. 2:16), Paul proceeds to offer a trinitarian viewpoint that holds in tension twin truths: one gospel (1:6–9) and many perspectives. The first stone in this trinitarian foundation has to do with God the Father.

Paul harkens back to Genesis and speaks of God's choosing of Abraham and his descendants, who are chosen precisely so that in them all the Gentiles will be blessed (Gal. 3:6–9; cf. Gen. 10:32; 12:3). Paul draws our attention to the first twelve chapters of Genesis, where it is emphasized that God created *all* humans. Paul also reminds us that Abraham is specially chosen so that in him and his descendants all the *ethne*, all the "nations," will be blessed. This same God who created all humans is the one who in judgment and mercy by divine intervention confused the languages at Babel and thus created the multiplicity of cultures in the world (Gen. 11). The phenomenal diversity of languages and cultures around the world is also attributed to the direct work of this same God of all who wishes to bless all the nations through the instrumentality of Abraham. Thus, following Paul's logic, on the basis of creation, we can simultaneously affirm commonalities and acknowledge differences.

God the Son: Common Faith, Diverse Faith Stories

Paul then takes the second step in developing his trinitarian viewpoint, which holds in tension the twin truths of one gospel and many perspectives. This second stone in Paul's trinitarian foundation has to do with God the Son, Jesus Christ.

> But now that faith has come, we are no longer subject to a disciplinarian, for in Christ Jesus you are all children of God through faith. As many of you as were baptized into Christ have clothed yourselves with Christ. There is no longer Jew or Greek, there is no longer slave or free, there is no longer male and female; for all of you are one in Christ Jesus. And if you belong to Christ, then you are Abraham's offspring, heirs according to the promise.
>
> Galatians 3:25–29 NRSV

Paul proclaims that in Christ the dividing wall is broken, a new humanity has been created, and all peoples of all cultures are brought together to become members of the same family (cf. Eph. 2:11–3:19). In Christ, even the Gentiles become offspring of Abraham! Yet in the midst of asserting this almost unbelievable truth, Paul also makes reference to the ways in which Paul's hearers and their society subdivided and separated humans in terms of culture, socioeconomics, and gender. So Paul recognizes that there are differences between Jew and Greek, slave and free, male and female. But in spite of such differences, all are brought together and created into a new family, the offspring of Abraham. Thus, on the basis of salvation in Jesus Christ, we can simultaneously affirm commonalities and acknowledge differences.

God the Holy Spirit: Common Fruit, Diverse Gifts

The third and final step in Paul's trinitarian viewpoint has to do with God the Holy Spirit.

> The fruit of the Spirit is love, joy, peace, patience, kindness, generosity, faithfulness, gentleness, and self-control. There is no law against such things. And those who belong to Christ Jesus have crucified the flesh with its passions and desires. If we live by the Spirit, let us also be guided by the Spirit. Let us not become conceited, competing against one another, envying one another.
>
> Galatians 5:22–26 NRSV

The Holy Spirit comes to all believers in Jesus Christ without any distinction, and the fruit of the Holy Spirit is given to all equally. In Ephesians, Paul says, "There is one body and one Spirit—just as you were called to one hope . . . one Lord, one faith" (4:4–5). Thus, in Acts 2, at Pentecost, the many tongues of flame come from one fire. All together receive the same fruit of the Holy Spirit and are one family of faith.

Yet even here, while affirming the unity of the church in the one Holy Spirit, Paul interjects the concept of multiplicity and diversity. "All must test their own work. . . . All must carry their own loads. . . . Let us [each] work for the good of all" (Gal. 6:4–5, 10 NRSV). Paul wants his readers to recognize the differences that exist between believers.

So how do we manage to hold in dialectical tension the twin truths of one theology and many perspectives? I believe Paul would answer by pointing to Jesus Christ. In the final analysis, the glocal church of the twenty-first century must be centered in the cross and the resurrection of our Lord. Only there is it possible to have a new creation in which we learn simultaneously to acknowledge differences and affirm commonalities.

Conclusion

A healthy congregation of disciples of Jesus lives out its catholicity by intentionally and actively participating in Christ's mission in a glocal fashion. It is active simultaneously in global and local mission, dynamically fostering the glocal interaction between the global and the local. This means that the glocal church's task of critical theologizing involves a dialectical tension: The gospel can be known only within cultural frameworks, yet the gospel is always distinct from—sometimes affirming of and often prophetically critical of—all human cultures.

In doing theology in a globalizing world, we might begin from the following presuppositions:

1. *All* cultures are sinful and fallen and cloud *all* human understanding of God's revelation.
2. *All* cultures have some degree of general revelation or prevenient grace whereby certain aspects of God's revelation in Jesus Christ may be clearly understood.
3. *All* Christian revelation must necessarily be incarnated into a culture in order for it to be understood (it is to be "infinitely translatable" [Lamin Sanneh]).
4. *All* understanding of the gospel in *all* cultures is partial (we see as through a glass darkly [1 Cor. 13:12]).
5. *No one* Christian understanding of the gospel has a complete grasp of the essence of God's revelation in Jesus Christ; contextualization or inculturation is not a goal but rather an epistemological process of seeking to know God in context.

This means that a truly catholic local group of believers is in fact the local manifestation of the universal glocal church. It implies that, like my desktop PC, which is an integral part of the Internet, a local group of disciples of Jesus, by its very nature, is a part of the global church. These glocal believers—no matter where they are in the world—are therefore commissioned to be "witnesses in Jerusalem, *and* in all Judea *and* Samaria, *and* to the ends of the earth" (Acts 1:8) simultaneously. Thus, a healthy glocal group of believers in this new century must be involved, at the same time, in God's mission locally *and* globally, that is, glocally. This has implications even for how we think of church planting. Church planting becomes an invitation to those who do not yet know Jesus Christ to become disciples of Jesus, ambassadors of the kingdom of God, and members of the glocal church—brothers and sisters with one and a half billion others who profess a similar faith. May we all learn to become in practice who we are: one glocal church of Jesus Christ.

8

"Experience-Near Theologizing" in Diverse Human Contexts

ROBERT J. PRIEST

Nearly all the wisdom we possess, that is to say, true and sound wisdom, consists of two parts: the knowledge of God and of ourselves. And although they are closely connected, it is difficult to say which comes first.

John Calvin

Wisdom in Two Parts

The Christian gospel contains specific understandings of God (theology) and specific understandings of humans (anthropology). The call to repentance and faith involves a call to specific self-understandings undergirded and informed by specific understandings of God. Theological wisdom, if we are to follow Calvin's lead in the above quotation, ought to involve deep knowledge both of God and of humans. Furthermore, the link between the two must be understood as organic. True knowledge of humans potentially feeds into and serves knowledge of God. And true knowledge of God, and of what God tells us about ourselves, ought to directly shape and inform our knowledge of self. They mutually constitute each other.

180

It is when I know myself through actual personal experience as a sinner, for example, that a knowledgeable fear of a holy God comes into clear focus. But it is also as I learn about the God revealed in Scripture that I come to sense and experience myself as a sinner (Priest 2003). It is indeed often difficult to say which comes first.

If we broaden our use of the term *theology* to include more than an understanding of God, to also include God-given understandings of humans, then theologians must be concerned to think and speak both about God and about humans. Because of the organic link between these two parts of wisdom, an inability to speak knowledgeably and truthfully about humans actually hampers one's ability to communicate knowledge of God. But while what we can know about God is directly dependent on and limited to what God has chosen to *reveal* of himself, what we can know about humans is only partially given through divine revelation. That is, we can know ourselves directly through our own experiences. Other humans can also reveal themselves to us; they can tell us their experiences, thoughts, secrets, fears, hopes, and dreams. Furthermore, we can actively observe other humans, interrogate them in interviews, read their diaries, ask them to fill out questionnaires about themselves, film them, and so on. In other words, the entire enterprise of the human sciences is built on the assumption that we can take disciplined steps to grow in our knowledge of human realities beyond knowledge of our individual self. Women can acquire understandings of men. An American can acquire understandings of the moral lives of recent converts to Christianity in New Guinea (Robbins 2004). And those who have never shoplifted can acquire deep understandings of the subjective experience of those who have (Katz 1988, 52–79).

If the Bible tells us truth about humans, then people's actual lived experiences will reflect such truths, and a wise minister will be able to help people recognize those truths about themselves—recognize them simultaneously in their own experience and in a word that comes from God (see Stromberg 1985; Priest 2003). Such ministerial wisdom requires both biblically given knowledge of human realities and knowledge of human realities acquired on other grounds.

Theologians necessarily speak both about God and about humans. But their understandings of humans derive from multiple sources: from what Scripture reveals but also from personal experience, what others have told them, stories their society tells about humans, and what they have read. For many theologians, historically, these other sources have not received conscious attention and have not formally been a part of an academic theological process of careful attention to method, data, and epistemology. Nor have they received significant attention in the pastoral training curriculum of many evangelical seminaries.

If theologians or pastors existed in a relatively unchanging and homogeneous society (where everyone else could be presumed to be socially and culturally very much like the theologian or pastor), and if such ministers had a reasonably good understanding of themselves and were reasonably competent members of their stable and homogeneous culture, then the improvisational discourses they produced relating biblical teaching and human experience might be fairly effective. But in fact ministers and theologians exist in a rapidly changing world and a culturally and socially diverse world. Global flows (of people, ideas, media, things) bring all of us into relations with people who are socially and culturally "other." In such a world, purely intuitive and improvisational efforts by ministers and theologians to extrapolate from what they understand about themselves to audiences of diverse social "others" will simply not work. A more responsible and formal process must underpin the wisdom we seek as it relates to diverse human selves.

If we assess contemporary evangelical theologians in terms of Calvin's understanding of wisdom in two parts, in my own view, evangelicals generally have been stronger in their theological discourses about God than they have in their theological discourses pertaining to humans—particularly as they relate to actual lived experience. This chapter takes one biblical concept directly relevant to how we understand humans, that of sin, and invites readers to consider the sorts of contextual and experiential knowledge that are needed if one is to communicate biblical understandings of sin to diverse human audiences.

Theology and Human Experience

Ministers, even when they have studied hamartiology, frequently find themselves unable to speak of sin effectively or persuasively. This may be felt even more keenly when attempting to speak of sin in diverse cultural contexts around the world. It was not uncommon historically to hear missionary refrains such as, "These people don't even feel guilt for doing wrong, only shame if they are caught." "These people don't even have a word for sin." Some missionaries suggest that sin need not be a part of the gospel message. Others stress that years of instruction are necessary before sin is understood, which only then makes true conversion possible. What all such responses attest to is the difficulty of speaking persuasively and effectively of sin in many cultural settings. Yet the concept of sin is not optional or peripheral to Christian understandings. The concept of sin is foundational to the biblical narrative, the cross, the gospel, salvation, repentance, confession, forgiveness, justification, reconciliation, sanctification, and the final judgment. Without the concept of sin, many of these other ideas fail to make sense. An inability to speak persuasively about sin adversely affects one's ability to speak plausibly about all the rest. An inability to speak plausibly about sin undercuts our ability to speak persuasively of God and of what human relationship with God entails.

Tite Tiénou and Paul Hiebert (2002) have suggested that while systematic theology is important for helping us understand such things as sin, another kind of theology, missional theology, is also needed. Missional theologizing, as they conceive it, is context-sensitive theologizing oriented toward formulations of the Christian message not only for Christians but also for non-Christians in diverse cultural settings. Systematic theologians historically have treated sin in relatively abstract and acontextual terms. Missional theologians, as Hiebert and Tiénou conceive them, ought to focus on producing context-sensitive theological discourses (on such theological concepts as sin) in specific cultural contexts around the globe.

As I have wrestled with this proposed contrast between systematic and missional theology, I have found a distinction made by Clifford Geertz to be helpful. Geertz (1977) has distinguished between what he calls "experience-near" and "experience-distant" concepts. An experience-near concept is one that an individual might use naturally, effortlessly, and colloquially to describe what he or others of his community see, think, imagine, and experience. Indeed, so intuitive and unself-conscious is the use of experience-near concepts that users often do not recognize that there are any concepts at all. "That is what experience-near means—that ideas and the realities they disclose are naturally and indissolubly bound up together" (Geertz 1977, 482). An experience-distant concept is one that a specialist or scholar might use, a concept that is often more abstract or theory dependent. Love is more experience-near than object cathexis or the categorical imperative; fear is more experience-near than phobia; snobbery is more experience-near than social stratification; and shoplifting is more experience-near than hamartiology.

While some academic disciplines, such as philosophy or physics, have historically privileged experience-distant concepts, Geertz (1977, 491) says that anthropologists aspire to work with both—dialectically tacking "between the most local of local detail and the most global of global structure . . . between exotic minutiae and sweeping generalization," attempting to bring both experience-near and experience-distant concepts into view at one and the same time. The anthropologist strives "to grasp concepts which, for other people, are experience-near, and to do so well enough to place them in illuminating connection with those experience-distant concepts that theorists have fashioned to capture the general features of social life" (Geertz 1977, 482).

Theology and Its Conversation Partners

As I understand Hiebert and Tiénou, systematic theology historically employed the assumptions, categories, questions, and methods of the discipline of philosophy—a discipline that, according to Geertz, historically strove for abstract and experience-distant understandings stripped of contingency, distinctiveness, and particularity. Philosophers achieved ostensibly universal understandings in the study and the armchair. Immanuel Kant, for example, without traveling fifty miles from where he was born, convinced fellow philosophers that he had plumbed the depths of morality through abstract ratiocination and had articulated what was universally at the core. Even when philosophers have stressed the centrality of experience, such an emphasis historically has not coincided with philosophers' elaborating and practicing a methodology that systematically brings them into close relation with the full range of human experience. The human sciences, rather, have developed methodologies (fieldwork, interviews, observational studies, ethnographic film, etc.) systematically designed to bring the scholar into contact with diverse textures of human life. And it is anthropology more specifically that has made the full range of human experience around the globe and through time its central project.

Anthropology as a discipline, like philosophy, strives for encompassing understandings but from the bottom up, so to speak. Leaving the library, the office, or the armchair, an anthropologist goes into very specific places around the globe and through long-term "obsessively fine-comb field study in confined contexts" (Geertz 1973, 23) studies human realities. Mega-concepts that philosophers treat in capital letters—authority, power, beauty, love, pain, pleasure, good, and evil—are also studied by anthropologists but in humble settings: in village, barrio, suburban neighborhood, or mental institution. As Geertz notes, anthropologists study such things with the capital letters removed and with a concrete specificity and "sensible actuality that makes it possible to think not only realistically and concretely *about* them, but, what is more important, creatively and integratively *with* them" (1973, 23). Furthermore, anthropologists do not merely bring concepts to the field with them; they discover and map new concepts of the people they are with: Japanese *amae*, Filipino *pakikisama*, Korean *han*, Tahitian *tabu*. These concepts are understandable only through understanding the everyday human realities to which they relate.

Neither philosophy nor anthropology, as intellectual enterprises, is more or less God ordained than the other. Each is equally a human project fraught with all the limitations, biases, and problems of any intellectual project carried out by sinful humans. Each is equally available as a constructive conversation partner for those interested in building on special revelation.

But as conversation partners, each pushes the theologian in different directions. Philosophy pushes the theologian toward logical entailments, formal consistency, and abstract rationality. Scripture itself has a wide range of genres, some of which nicely lend themselves to formal analyses enhanced by conversation with philosophy. But Scripture itself is also filled with such things as genealogies, blood rituals, experiences of nakedness and shame, contrasts between clean and unclean foods, and the cutting of human genitalia. These are not the natural subject matters of philosophy, and the study of such realities historically has not been the philosopher's preferred route to knowledge of humans. On the other hand, these are precisely the sorts of things that anthropologists focus on to achieve understandings of humans. But while biblical scholars have, on occasion, found anthropology a helpful conversation partner when examining such matters in the biblical text, systematic theologians have been less inclined to embrace anthropology as a conversation partner.

As a conversation partner, anthropology would push theology to acquire experience-near understandings of contemporary human realities around the globe and to generate theological discourses reflective of such understandings. But while there are good reasons to commend the value of anthropology, systematic theologians historically have chosen philosophy and not anthropology[1] as their conversation partner—even when addressing subject matters that might naturally benefit from such a conversation (such as theological anthropology or hamartiology). Some, such as John Milbank (1990), actively campaign against valuing the human sciences as helpful conversation partners for theologians. More commonly, systematic theologians have simply failed to pursue and cultivate such a dialogue. The results, in either case, are the same. Interestingly, this is in marked contrast to many contemporary moral philosophers (such as Alasdair McIntyre or Martha Nussbaum) who are actively drawing from and cultivating a conversation with the human sciences.

Hiebert and Tiénou call for theology to be carried out in dialogue with anthropology and the human sciences, not only with philosophy. If we follow Geertz's line of thought, it is not primarily the grand theories of anthropology that we need. Rather, we need anthropology's ability to help us develop experience-near understandings of diverse people, bringing experience-near understandings into meaningful relationship

1. A few theologians (Tanner 1997; Hughes 2000; Taylor 2000; Davies 2002) are beginning a dialogue with anthropology. I am not aware of any evangelical theologians cultivating such a dialogue.

with experience-distant ones, both anthropological and theological. This is what missional theologizing involves.

The Limits of Experience-Distant Discourse

Let's imagine Dave, a seminary graduate, going as a missionary to the thirty-five thousand Aguaruna of northern Peru. Dave's message is not only about God. He also wants his hearers to understand themselves in terms of understandings given in Scripture by God—including an understanding of themselves as sinners in need of forgiveness, salvation, and personal transformation. That is, Dave wants to tell the Aguaruna about themselves, despite knowing virtually nothing about the Aguaruna in experience-near terms. In systematic theology classes, Dave has sharpened his understanding of the nature of sin, its origins, its transmission, its extent, and its effects. Such theological understandings will underpin what he communicates. But since Dave lacks any corresponding understanding of Aguaruna moral discourses and sensibilities, any understanding of how envy, lust, avarice, gluttony, or pride, for example, work themselves out in the intimacies of Aguaruna daily life, his efforts to communicate understandings of sin will inevitably be abstract and experience-distant.

Dave will immediately begin to sense that his discourses on sin are failing to hit the mark, and he will improvisationally strive to make his discourses experience-near. One way he will do so, like biblical prophets and evangelists, is to speak of sins, not just of sin. He will look around for visible evidence of specific sins. While the Aguaruna have clear ideas of right and wrong, like people around the world, they hide their transgressions, making them less easily observable to cultural outsiders. On the other hand, Dave will see plenty of easily observable public behaviors not thought of as morally wrong (why else would they be done in public?) but which in Dave's mind are sinful. If Dave is anything like many missionaries before him, he will make these behaviors the center of his effort to speak of sin in experience-near terms.

He will notice Pujupat's two wives and will immediately think he has found a sin to which he can point. He assumes the second marriage resulted from excessive and sinful sexual desire. He does not realize that when Pujupat's brother died, leaving a rather unattractive wife and three sickly children, Pujupat was pushed to marry her, despite his reluctance, and that rather than feeling guilty for wanting too much sex, Pujupat feels virtuous for having overcome his temptation not to care for her and her children in the morally prescribed way. Dave will observe that *nijamanch*, the staple Aguaruna drink that is consumed in large amounts, is alcoholic and may again conclude that he has found another sin to be pointed out. And so it goes.

At the same time, Dave knows that the persuasiveness of his message depends on the messenger exemplifying a morally virtuous life. Dave believes his monogamous marriage and his refusal to drink *nijamanch* provide a powerful witness. What he may not understand is that his audience will not see these as virtues and may instead judge him morally deficient on other grounds—grounds he simply fails to understand.

Dave comes from a society where gluttony is a sin against the self, its sinfulness explained as a matter of doing harm to the temple of God, the body. He enters a society where food, or rather protein, is available in limited and irregular amounts. Dave will be invited to eat with the Aguaruna whenever he visits and will be pleased that he is able to accommodate their "uncultured" pattern of crouching in a circle around a single large serving of food, while reaching with fingers to break off pieces of meat and manioc. He will be oblivious to the moral dimensions of this event. Everyone else may have gone two days without meat or protein of any kind, and now they have killed a small game animal. But since Dave has arrived on a visit, his hosts will do the morally virtuous thing and share their limited supply with him, giving him no clue that they are anything but thrilled for him to join them. He will notice that others eat large amounts of manioc, a starch he finds tasteless (but assumes they must love), while they eat only small pieces of meat. He will eat his meat in larger amounts and his manioc in smaller amounts than his hosts. If he were a small Aguaruna child, his parents would scold him: *"Ushu aipa!"* ("Don't be a glutton!") or *"Etsemjau aipa!"* ("Don't be a meat glutton!"). Every child would have learned a rich and diverse vocabulary for speaking about the moral evils of gluttony, would have heard dozens of myths in which the evils of gluttony were stressed, would have repeatedly been made to fast as a means of learning to control appetite on behalf of others, and would through experience have recognized the pain of having someone else eat more than his or her share while one goes hungry. No Aguaruna would think of gluttony as a sin against the self but as a sin against others. Every child would have learned specific codes for how to eat—a small piece of meat, followed by a large piece of manioc, never two pieces of meat in a row. If their own child ate like Dave, parents would have yelled, *"Apatua yuata!"* ("Eat it joined together!") or *"Apatuata!"* ("Join it together!"). But one does not correct an adult visitor with such scolding. Other visitors would know to quickly insist that they have had enough (*maaka*), but not Dave. In short, Dave is likely to be seen as the worst kind of glutton, an *etsemjau*, a "meat glutton."

The Aguaruna tend to read oral and socially aggressive impulses as parallel, with myths constantly demonizing gluttony, especially meat gluttony as cannibal gluttony. Furthermore, the Aguaruna tend to read oral and sexual appetites as parallel, with a failure of oral control (which is evident in public space) thought to disclose one's sexual proclivities (which occur in private space). Common words for gluttony (*yawetchau* and *mijamchau*) are equally used for sexual desire not under personal restraint. In fact, people will tend to read the two as a single characteristic worked out in both arenas. Dave will have learned American ways of interacting across gender lines, which in Aguaruna culture will be decoded as expressing sexual interest, thus lending further evidence to the suspicion of sexual appetites not under social control. Furthermore, Dave will have learned in America that mealtime is private family time. He will not have grown up in a home where parents exhorted adolescents preparing for marriage on how to run a household: "*Tsagka ataya!*" ("Be generous/hospitable!") or "*Suji aipa!*" ("Don't be stingy!"). He will be less likely than any Aguaruna to invite visitors to share his food. That is, he will be seen as *suji* (stingy) and not *tsagka* (generous/hospitable).

If Dave had read his New Testament missionally, he would have understood that conscience is God given and thus present among all peoples (Rom. 2:1–15; 2 Cor. 4:2), although variable and fallible (see Rom. 14; 1 Cor. 4:4; 8:1–13; 10:27–32), and that even those who have not been socialized by the written law of God nonetheless already embrace and promote moral understandings. The Aguaruna emphases on generosity and on restraining appetite on behalf of others and the Aguaruna condemnation of adultery are good. That they constantly emphasize moral virtues in their discourses does not mean that they live up to their ideals. Indeed, the very intensity of their moral rhetoric reflects the depth of their feeling that there is a major moral problem here, that these moral virtues are not being adequately lived out. Scripture suggests that God does not convict individuals of sin by criteria they have never heard of but by criteria they already recognize and use to judge one another, criteria evident in the moral discourses they themselves produce (Matt. 7:2; Rom. 2:1–15; James 4:17). The apostle Paul was attentive to conscience. He understood that the consciences of Jews and Greeks were likely to differ at points, and he adjusted his message based on his understandings of conscience. He recognized that his own conscience was fallible (1 Cor. 4:4) and that he needed to be responsive to the consciences of his audiences. He attempted to commend himself to everyone's conscience (2 Cor. 4:2), to exemplify in his own life virtue as understood by those he wished to reach. He would not have wanted the Aguaruna to judge him morally defective in terms of their own deepest moral sensibilities. He would have wanted to exemplify virtues that they could recognize as virtues. (For a fuller discussion of culture and conscience, see Priest 1994.)

Missional theology, unlike systematic theology as historically prac-ticed, must generate discourses that are context sensitive, that explicitly take into account the consciences and moral discourses of those whom one is engaging. Missional theology does not attempt to tell people about themselves purely through experience-distant understandings—to tell the Aguaruna about themselves with complete ignorance of the Agua-runa moral world in experience-near terms. Rather, it seeks to acquire experience-near understandings and vocabulary as a critical component feeding into the missional discourses being produced. It capitalizes on conscience as a God-given experience-near ally in the missional task. It recognizes that discourses about humans, discourses that actually capture and correspond to lived experience, are key components in the ability to generate discourses about God that have subjective plausibility. The person who hears a discourse about sin and a God who punishes in hell but who receives no help in linking discourses of sin to his own lived experience and to his deepest moral sensibilities may quite naturally find that the message is uncompelling. The Aguaruna would call such a message *sakam* (tasteless), by which they mean not that they know the message is false but simply that the message fails subjectively to move them, to touch them.

The Value of Experience-Near Christian Discourse

As Dave becomes increasingly knowledgeable about Aguaruna moral realities and sensibilities, he may find it easier to speak of moral failings in ways that are ratified by Aguaruna consciences. But he may still face many challenges in relating those moral failings to transcendent Christian understandings. He may easily find words for theft, adultery, gluttony, pride, incest, and many words that do not easily translate into English, like *etsemjau* (meat glutton) (experience-near kinds of words), but he may find it harder to find vocabulary for sin generically. That is, many of the theological points Dave wishes to communicate require speaking of sin in the singular, not only the plural. Like many missionaries, he may quickly come to the conclusion that the Aguaruna language is defective, that the Aguaruna have no word for sin. One by one he rejects possible Aguaruna terms as not faithfully catching the full meaning of the word *sin*.

He will often hear people say, for example, that others are *pegkegchau*. Thieves, the incestuous, slanderers, liars, and those who are stingy, glut-tonous, or lazy are all *pegkegchau*. But so is anything ugly, deformed, dirty, damaged, bad tasting, or worthless. *Pegkegchau* is not an exclusively moral term and is close to the English word *bad*. Dave will likely reject this as the term for sin.

Again, Dave will hear *katsek* used of adultery, theft, lies, homicide, fighting, and most disapproved behaviors. *Katsek* is typically used with strong affect, frequently accompanied by exclamations of dismay, alarm, or indignation. But it is also used when one accidentally breaks a pot or burns down a house or when a chicken or a dog threatens to contaminate one's food. The underlying idea is that of harm, ruin, damage, destruction—an idea extended into the arena of moral relationships but not restricted to the moral.

Perpetual liars, thieves, disobedient children, women who actively pursue affairs, and men who continually approach women's beds under cover of dark may be condemned as *detse*. But an animal born with an extra leg, a baby chicken with two beaks, two bananas in one banana peel, and someone with a clubbed foot, six toes on a foot, one eye, a deformed ear, or a harelip is also characterized as *detse*—a word speaking of a failure to conform to some ideal form, whether physical or moral.

Tudau is another term of moral disapproval, used exclusively in contexts of moral judgment—used to characterize anyone engaged in active transgressions such as incest, bestiality, sexual exhibitionism, wife beating, adultery, theft, and, above all, complaining of the food one's wife or mother has prepared. But it is never used of less active character traits such as stinginess, gluttony, pride, or laziness, although these are condemned.

To be *yajau* is to be cruel, brutish, malicious, lacking interpersonal empathy, and without normal moral scruples. Anyone who beats his own mother, wife, child, or dog from anger is *yajau*. One who is *yajau* maliciously kills his neighbors' animals, offers his sister to a passing stranger, molests women at night, and draws or carves images of female genitals on earth or tree. A woman who kills her own infant in anger, who beats her children, or who is constantly pursuing sexual affairs is *yajau*.

Antuchu literally means "doesn't listen," but it is used to characterize anyone who is disobedient and refuses to attend to moral correction and instruction. Anyone who habitually violates right moral order, as articulated by parents and ancestors, is *antuchu*. A sexually promiscuous woman may be characterized as *kugkatan antuchu*. *Kugkatan* is a compound word joining the word for enticing smell (*kug*) with the word for penis (*katan*). Sexual desire, in Aguaruna culture, is consistently symbolized in terms of attraction to an enticing odor. Thus, a sexually promiscuous woman is characterized as *kugkatan antuchu*, as one who "doesn't listen because of the enticing smell of the penis." (One cannot get much more experience-near than this.)

Tsuwat literally means "filthy" or "something filthy" but is continuously invoked as a term for moral evil. Slander is referred to as *tsuwat chicham* (dirty speech) and the slanderer as *tsuwat wenintin* (one with a dirty mouth). *Tsuwat anentaintin* (the dirty-hearted one) is one who, to outward appearances, has correct moral sentiments but is inwardly malevolent, planning evil. One who commits adultery or steals is said to be one who "works filth" (*tsuwat takaamu*).

Tsumain means "disgusting" and is typically used of foul smells, of decaying corpses and feces, and of any creature that comes in contact with such items—notably vultures, opossums, maggots, flies, and dung beetles. But *tsumain* is also used of any reprehensible moral act, particularly of a sexual nature. Incest and bestiality are stigmatized as *tsumain*, but so is any man who is overly desirous of sex, even with his own wife.

A person whose life is a mess, who constantly fights with his neighbors or commits incest, for example, is said to be *pachimkamu*. But so is a house with items strewn all over or a fishing line or thread that is tangled. The underlying metaphor is of order versus disorder, immorality being one kind of disorder, among others.

Space does not permit further exploration of terms, but several observations may be made. First, even people without the written law of God will have an extensive and rich vocabulary speaking to moral failure (cf. Evans-Pritchard 1956; Burkhart 1989; Strand 2000; Schlatter 2002). Second, such vocabulary, even when applied broadly to many kinds of moral failure, is an experience-near kind of vocabulary. It is experience-near both in the sense that it draws metaphorically from everyday human experience (of attractive smells, disgusting foods, listening to one's parents, broken things, deformed things, filthy things, things tangled up and out of place, etc.) and in the sense that these words are used in everyday life in relation to all sorts of lived situations. It is experience-near in the sense that the words were learned in lived settings of moral failure and judgment. The very usage of the terms draws on associations with prior experiences of moral failure and evokes memories of moral shame, guilt for the pain one's transgression inflicted on others, and so on. These are not words reserved for religious settings and are not the preserve of academic or religious specialists. An evangelist who effectively uses such vocabulary when speaking of failures before God speaks in experience-near terms.

If Dave is like many missionaries, he will look for one word he can use for sin—a word filled with all the meaning of the English word *sin*. One by one he will eliminate Aguaruna words because of their failure to fully coincide with the word *sin*. None, for example, is intrinsically theocentric in the way *sin* is. Most Aguaruna words can be applied to objects or actions that are not sinful, such as the accidental breaking of a clay pot. Dave may eventually end up unhappily using one Aguaruna word (perhaps *katsek* or *tudau*) and then attempt to fill that word with all the meaning of the English word *sin*. If Dave went to a seminary that did not require Greek or Hebrew, this might be excusable. But if he studied Greek and Hebrew, he should understand that neither the Old nor the New Testament limits itself to one word for sin, and none of the words they use have the same range of meaning as the English word *sin*. None, for example, is exclusively religious, intrinsically theocentric. Each was used in everyday contexts that were not religious and did not entail the idea of God. *Hattah'*, for example, although frequently translated in English as sin, was used of slingshots missing a mark by mistake, as well as of human acts violative of interpersonal relationship. *'Avar* was used for the act of crossing the Jordan River and for the act of disobeying one's king or God—the image involving that of a moral prohibition as a kind of line or moral boundary that must not be crossed. *'Awah* was used of bent or twisted physical objects as well as of twisted moral character. Altogether more than twenty Hebrew and Greek words are translated into English as sin. None of these was an exclusively religious word. Each was more experience-near than is our own use of the word *sin*. Yet such words were also fully adequate to the task of speaking of our moral failures before God and of pointing us to the salvation God provides.

The word *sin* has been influenced by two thousand years of theological discourse, discourse designed to construct a theologically sophisticated intrinsically theocentric word. In the process, we have acquired clearer rational formulations of Christian truth, but we have done so in part by creating special religious speech and a vocabulary discontinuous from usage in normal everyday life, that is, by making them more experience-distant.

Dave would do well to emulate the biblical writers' refusal to limit themselves to a single word, instead drawing from a wide range of everyday vocabulary to speak to their audiences in experience-near terms. If Dave would stop fixating over the fact that no word quite matches the English word *sin* and would seek to master the full range of Aguaruna moral vocabulary, he would discover he has powerful resources with which to communicate everything he wishes to say—just not through a single word. Furthermore, he would discover that people are more responsive to words that are experience-near than to those that are abstract and experience-distant. He would find that Aguaruna words can be used to tell the biblical story of salvation, that Aguaruna words can help people rework self-understandings into forms that serve the knowledge of God.

In the name of God, Dave can speak of *tudau*, the "crimes" and active transgressions committed by many, crimes that deserve punishment. But he can also speak of our moral characters. He can tell how God made us in his image, wanting us to be like him in our moral characters, but that we are all *detse*—failing to conform to the perfect ideal God intended. He can speak of moral failures in terms of *katsek*, highlighting the harm that our transgressions cause. He can stress that all of us, on occasion, are *yajau*. That is, we all harbor envy, resentment, and malice toward others, failing at interpersonal empathy and love. He can speak of the wonderful harmony and order that come when we listen to God and to what is right. He can stress that we are all *antuchu*, willfully refusing to listen to, attend to, and obey messages that call us to live rightly. As a result, our lives are *pachimkamu*, a disordered mess. He can stress that when we kill, commit adultery, commit incest, or steal we are *tsuwat takaamu* (working filth), that when we slander others we have filthy mouths (*tsuwat wenintin*), that when we smile and act like we love others but harbor envy, hatred, and grudges toward them we have dirty hearts (*tsuwat anentaintin*)—hearts hidden from others but visible to God. He can speak of the disgust (*tsumain*) God feels for our dirty acts. That is, Dave can convey a message from God (taught in Scripture) that speaks to human realities in experience-near forms that are immediately recognized and perceived as a subjectively plausible description of our human condition. He can speak of deserved punishment for our *tudau*, of the *diwi* (debt) we owe, not only to others but also to God, as well as of Christ's suffering for our *tudau* and God's offer of forgiveness of the *diwi* we cannot pay. He can speak of the shame of our filthy acts and of the cleansing from *tsuwat* Christ provides. He can hold out an offer of hope: Despite our *detse* character and *pachimkamu* lives, those who enter into a relationship with Christ are reborn and commence a transformation into the image we were originally designed to be. Our lives become characterized by moral integrity and order.

Historically, it has not been uncommon for secular anthropologists to claim that a sense of sin is absent from cultures that have no historic connection with the Christian faith, such as the Aguaruna, and thus that genuine conversion to Christianity is not possible for such people (see Kroeber 1948, 612; Mead 1949, 126, 164, 277; Sahlins 1996, 425). But, in fact, the biblical message about sinfulness is empirically accurate, ratified through conscience and through the moral discourses already present in such societies even without the written law of God. Furthermore, when Christian discourses of sin are framed in experience-near terms, large numbers of Aguaruna have been quick to discover their sin (Priest 2003) and to respond to a gospel of grace.

When Christian discourses about humans are both derived from God's Word and connected to lived experience, these discourses are an essential element in communicating the broader message of the gospel. They are essential in the sense that self-understandings of the right sort actually serve and feed into knowledge of God.

Implications for Theology

As I understand my colleagues Tiénou and Hiebert, theology must be done from different social contexts. Western theologians are doing important work but must help to validate and create space for non-Western theologians to join the theological conversation (see Tiénou in this volume). In addition, Western systematic theologians ought to recognize the potential value of a theological process that works with anthropology and the human sciences. Those who study and teach hamartiology, for example, would do well to read works on sin and human evil by psychologists (Capps 1989; Menninger 1973; Schimmel 1992), sociologists (Katz 1988; Lyman 1989; Schoeck 1969), and, in comparative global context, anthropologists (Burkhart 1989; Edgerton 1992; Fürer-Haimendorf 1967; 1974; Foster 1972; Hallowell 1939; Hertz 1922; Parkin 1985; 1996; Priest 2003; Robbins 1998; 2004; Shweder, Marapatra, and Miller 1990).

On the other hand, the primary concern of Tiénou and Hiebert is not that theologians in systematic theology departments become experts at what they call missional theology but rather that they recognize that others, with other disciplinary strengths, are already doing missional theology. Missiologists, for example, have long worked to help others speak appropriately of sin in diverse human contexts (Adeney 1995; Ayabe 1992; Dye 1976; Grayston 1953a; 1953b; Grimes 1966; Harrison 1985; Hesselgrave 1983; Loewen 1975; Noble 1975; Pike 1979; Priest 1993; 1994; 1997; 2003; Schlatter 2002; Steenbergen 1991; Strand 2000). Tiénou and Hiebert, then, are contesting what they perceive as a common tendency to treat certain disciplines (such as pastoral counseling or missiology) as marginal "applied" disciplines. They argue instead that, done rightly, missiology (and doubtless pastoral psychology) is in itself a kind of theological subdiscipline with partially overlapping, and yet also distinct, methods, theories, and data. A missiologist does not merely apply hard intellectual work done by systematic theologians. Rather, a missiologist engages the same biblical text that a theologian engages but in the context of a dialogue with anthropology and diverse human experience rather than in the context of a dialogue with philosophy. This engagement is not simply "applied." It involves rigorous scholarship and intellectual work that attend to a different sort of data—experience-near data in culturally diverse settings around the world. Not only does one exegete Scripture, but one also learns to exegete human realities—realities that missiologists were forced to think about simply because missionaries struggled to articulate meaningfully the Christian faith in radically different human settings. Exegeting human realities (such as the Aguaruna realities referred to in this chapter) involves discipline-specific skills—skills every bit as demanding as those involved in exegeting

Scripture or in articulating biblical truth in forms refined by systematic theologians. Missiology, as missional theology, contributes strategically to the larger task of theologizing in a global world.

Christians need systematic theology, but they also need missional theologizing, theologizing that is context sensitive, experience-near. Missional theologizing takes into account Christian communities around the world and the contexts of their witness as the audiences for which the message is intended. Missional theologizing speaks within each and every language, to each and every human community. Missional theologizing aims to engage persons fully (including their consciences) on behalf of the message, calling for personal responses of repentance, confession, faith, love, and obedience. Missional theologizing requires understandings of Scripture and builds on understandings of systematic theology, but it goes one step further to require experience-near understandings of human realities—understandings that are best acquired through methodologies pioneered by the human sciences. Missional theologizing finally requires that these different sorts of understanding be brought together in a discursive form that commends the gospel of Jesus Christ to culturally specific others.[2]

2. I would like to thank the following individuals for reading an earlier version of this chapter and providing helpful feedback and critique: David Hesselgrave, David Pao, Harold Netland, Douglas Sweeney, Eckhard Schnabel, Kevin Vanhoozer, Robert Yarbrough, Lawson Younger, Richard Averbeck, Thomas McCall, Stephen Greggo, and Bryan Maier.

Part 3

Implications
of Globalizing Theology

9

The Challenge of Economic Globalization for Theology

From Latin America to a Hermeneutics of Responsibility

M. Daniel Carroll R.

Globalization is a difficult term to define with precision and comprehensiveness. Depending on their particular interests, theorists focus on different contemporary trends that are connecting and transforming the planet in innumerable and novel ways. In his important work *The Next Christendom* (2002), Philip Jenkins offers an account of the increasing globalization of Christianity, by which he means its explosive growth in Asia, Africa, and Latin America. This demographic shift toward the Southern Hemisphere has already begun to impact the nature of Christian worship and practice worldwide, to encourage the relocation of the centers of denominational politics to outside the United States and Western Europe, and to set a fresh theological agenda for the coming decades.

As Jenkins points out, most Christians today come from, and in the foreseeable future will continue to come from, the ranks of the poor. This fact requires that an awareness of Christianity's geographical and numerical expansion be informed in multiple ways by economics. Indeed, one of the most salient facets of contemporary globalization is the inescapable reality and far-reaching impact of a hegemonic global capitalism (or neoliberalism). The question that naturally arises, therefore, is whether the theologizing that is being done by those in Jenkins's "next Christendom" is grappling with economic issues. If so, what shape are these efforts taking? Can they offer lessons for the theological enterprise to evangelicals in other parts of the world?

The context for the reflections in this chapter is Latin America. The discussion is divided into three principal parts. The first section summarizes some of the more visible characteristics of the global economy and then notes its mixed reception in Latin America. The second part explains how economic globalization is being analyzed and evaluated theologically there. Naturally, liberation theology plays an important role in that narrative, but evangelicals are also contemplating the meaning of Christian identity and mission in the midst of the new economic realities. The third and final section posits some fundamental considerations for forging a theology for Christian mission that can appropriately respond to the challenges of the twenty-first century.

The purpose of this chapter is a modest one, even though the discussion ranges widely. What follows is more suggestive than evaluative; the goal is hortatory, if you will. It lies beyond our purview to assess the theological or the methodological correctness of all that is surveyed or to identify and develop a specific set of themes for a full-fledged contextual hermeneutics and theology. Rather, the hope is that the discussion will serve to underscore the significance of economics and thereby encourage fresh thinking in how better to incarnate the truth of the gospel in a rapidly changing world.

The Potential and Threats of the Global Economy: A Latin American Perspective

The last several decades have witnessed the demise of socialism and the undisputed rise of international capitalism. The end of the decades-long era of conflict between these two competing ideologies was symbolized dramatically by the fall of the Berlin Wall in 1989, but multiple cracks in the social, political, and economic practices and institutions of the former Soviet Union, Eastern Europe, and Latin America had begun to appear before then. The domino effect was swift; it was, to borrow a phrase from Francis Fukuyama, "the end of history" (Fukuyama 1992). Capitalism reigned supreme. No other economic system, along with its attendant sociopolitical arrangements, remained to contest its preeminence.

The form of capitalism that has been developing since the 1980s has moved away from the more state interventionist model of John Maynard Keynes to the ideals of Joseph Schumpeter, which champion the stricter separation of government and economic activity, wealth creation, and free trade. Jagdish Bhagwati, professor at Columbia University and former special advisor to the United Nations on globalization, offers a succinct description of the global free-market system:

> Economic globalization constitutes integration of national economies into the international economy through trade, direct foreign investment (by corporations and multinationals), short-term capital flows, international flow of workers and humanity more generally, and flows of technology. (2004, 3)

The key term here is *integration*. Projects, transactions, decisions, and investments are no longer bound as tightly to national, even regional, boundaries. Economic innovations and the ongoing movement of funds and expertise are due in large measure to what Thomas Friedman calls a threefold democratization, that is, those conditions that permit access and participation to more and more people in the global economic network: the democratization of technology, finance, and information (2000, 43–70). This situation has generated opportunities for communities and individuals around the world to compete in marketing, technology development, and services, all of which contribute to "flatten" the economic playing field (Friedman 2005). For some countries in the majority world, these economic outcomes have necessitated (sometimes severe) structural adjustments to solve a host of difficult problems that are the fruit of protectionism, obsolete business procedures, bureaucratic inefficiency, political cronyism, and corruption. Ideally, these adjustments are to be accompanied by (and in many ways require) the positive advancement of democratic initiatives. In Latin America, in addition to the implementation of these kinds of policies by several nations (whether on their own or imposed externally by, for example, the International Monetary Fund [IMF] or the World Bank), important agreements have been reached to facilitate trade in the hemisphere. The year 1994 witnessed the launching of the North American Free Trade Agreement (NAFTA) between the United States, Canada, and Mexico, and in May 2004, the Central American Free Trade Agreement (CAFTA) between the United States, the five Central American nations (Guatemala, El Salvador, Honduras, Nicaragua, and Costa Rica), and the Dominican Republic was signed.

While the potential benefits seem impressive, the actual results in Latin America have been varied. Economists and social scientists argue over the efficacy and justice of what has transpired. In some cases, the sociopolitical and economic modifications have led to the pauperization of the masses, cuts in social spending, heavier foreign debt, higher inflation, a worrisome upsurge in unemployment, and greater political unrest. Of course, there have been the huge economic meltdowns in Mexico in 1994–95 and more recently in Argentina. Accordingly, some analysts give a negative assessment of these neoliberal efforts (Huber and Solt 2004). Others, while agreeing with some aspects of this appraisal, assign more blame to institutional shortcomings and are more optimistic for the long term (Walton 2004). Still others advocate for stronger safety nets for the disadvantaged and for the involvement of more constituencies in the decision-making process in the move toward assimilation into the global economic system (Korzeniewicz and Smith 2000).

Book-length studies hypothesize a variety of causes for the recent economic and political failings of Latin America. Lawrence Harrison, for example, suggests that the cause ultimately rests on cultural attitudes toward work, education, frugality, and justice. These values can be traced back, he believes, to the Ibero-Catholic traditions brought by the Spanish hundreds of years ago. Though the situation is due to a number of factors, Harrison argues that only constructive cultural change can bring the kind of prosperity and peace that the continent longs for (Harrison 1997; cf. Martin 1990; Novak 2004, 103–7). Hernando de Soto points instead to the choking effects of endless legal regulations and the lack of proper documentation for property rights (which would allow these assets to be used for collateral, investing, etc.). The issue for him, in other words, is procedural and concerns the liabilities inherent in national infrastructures, not cultural shortcomings (de Soto 2000).[1] On a broader scale, former White House cabinet member and senior vice president of the World Bank Joseph Stiglitz blames the intransigencies of the IMF for causing much unnecessary suffering and economic chaos; their stubborn refusal to abandon a one-size-fits-all strategy and the unreasonable emphasis on lowering inflation have pushed several majority world countries to the edge of disaster (Stiglitz 2002). With Bolivia as one of his case studies, Jeffrey Sachs considers an expansive matrix of multiple causes of world poverty and offers an equally multileveled proposal for its amelioration (2005).

Clearly, the situation is complex, and no facile solutions exist. Meanwhile, frustration and discontent grow. For many, the desperate economic conditions and uncertain political future of Latin America vis-à-vis the wealthier nations of the North/West (and also now of the Asian Pacific rim) are simply a continuation of a pattern of exploitation that has per-

1. These studies by Harrison and de Soto build on earlier work. See Harrison (1985) and de Soto (1989).

meated national life and international relations for over five hundred years. The opening words of the classic work by the Uruguayan author Eduardo Galeano, *Open Veins of Latin America: Five Centuries of Pillage of a Continent,* eloquently express these feelings:

> The division of labor among nations is that some specialize in winning and others in losing. Our part of the world, known today as Latin America, was precocious: it has specialized in losing ever since those remote times when Renaissance Europeans ventured across the ocean and buried their teeth in the throats of the Indian civilizations. Centuries passed, and Latin America perfected its role. We are no longer in the era of marvels when fact surpassed fable and imagination was shamed by the trophies of conquest—the lodes of gold, the mountains of silver. But our region still works as a menial. It continues to exist at the service of others' needs, as a source and reserve of oil and iron, of copper and meat, of fruit and coffee, the raw materials and foods destined for rich countries which profit more from consuming them than Latin America does from producing them. (1997, 1)

Clearly, the trajectory of capitalism in Latin America is not the success story that had been hoped for. Even avid promoters of neoliberal policies recognize that capitalist strategies must work better to accomplish the goals of combating poverty, raising labor standards, and achieving healthier democracies. While Bhagwati contends that much of contemporary anticapitalism rhetoric is misinformed and misplaced, at the same time he feels that economic globalization needs a more human face (2004). Friedman, in his typically witty way, warns countries of contracting MIDS (Microchip Immune Deficiency Syndrome: the inability to respond effectively to the information revolution) and of the consequences of failing to put on the "Golden Straitjacket" (which is the set of economic structures that allows for vigorous economic globalization), but he too knows that programs should be put in place to provide a measure of security for the unfortunate and excluded in the new global economy (Friedman 2000, 389–447; 2005, 371–413).

Michael Novak weaves an appeal to the virtues within his proposal for a more politically democratic and economically prosperous world that can move beyond the ominous, self-destructive threat of the clash of civilizations (2004). His is a vision self-consciously (and critically) grounded in his Catholic tradition. For Novak, religion provides the indispensable moral substratum for nurturing the proper values for political liberty and economic relations in a globalized world.[2]

---

2. His theological defense of capitalism appears in Novak (1982). Friedman briefly mentions his Jewish background and views of God as his source for moral values in the marketplace (2000, 447–53).

Here economics is acknowledged to be a topic worthy of theological reflection, and the compatibility of Christian doctrine and values with certain economic theories and sets of practices is debated. This appreciation that religious faith is fundamental to the globalization debate serves as a transition to the next section. In Latin America, where economic issues are central to national politics and society in general and constantly impinge on daily living, how is global capitalism being processed theologically? This is the question to which we now turn.

The Global Economy and Theologizing in Latin America

Liberation Theology

It is well established that the commitment to do theology in light of socioeconomic realities is fundamental to Latin American liberation theology, and it is here that we begin. That the commitment to relate the nature and duties of Christianity to the context is not limited to these circles, however, is less well known. For over a century, Catholic social teaching officially has addressed issues related to capitalism, from *Rerum Novarum* (1889) to *Centesimus Annus* (1989) and beyond. In addition to papal encyclicals and more general statements, the General Conference of Latin American Bishops has spoken to the precarious situation of the continent, most famously at their meeting in Medellín (1968) but also at Puebla (1979) and Santo Domingo (1992). At more local levels, the Catholic Church also has offered reflections on economic trends in both scholarly and lay formats. In Guatemala, for example, the archbishop's Human Rights Office has published *Los Cristianos Frente al Neoliberalismo,* an illustrated presentation and (negative) evaluation of neoliberalism (Bermúdez 1996). This sort of effort is noteworthy. If globalization extends its impact as far as the lives of the peasant population, then even the simplest of people need to have made available to them some sort of theological and pastoral orientation that they can comprehend. In other words, liberation theology does not arise within a theological-ethical vacuum. Still less understood has been how evangelicals in Latin America have dealt with these problematic issues. This is the topic of the second part of this section.

The methodology of liberation theology has been explained in detail elsewhere and does not need to be rehearsed in this chapter (e.g., Boff 1987; 2000; cf. Carroll R. 1992, 91–122, 312–19; 2001). For our purposes, it is enough to remember that, for liberation theology, theology is a "second act" that identifies the option for the poor as its starting point. That is, theology cannot be a neutral or an abstract science. To know and to serve God require grasping the reality of the Latin American situation, from which can flow appropriate pastoral and political action. This theology-praxis dynamic demands socioeconomic analysis. To this end, liberationists have utilized Marxist theory. Theirs, however, has not been an uncritical acceptance of Marxism. Liberation theology has demonstrated a sophisticated understanding of Marxist history and its various streams, and it has been steadfast in its refusal to follow some aspects of Marxist thought (Dussel 1993a; 1993b).

With the collapse of the socialist option, liberationists, as did the Latin American left in general, entered into a time of crisis (Castañeda 1993).[3] Socialism had seemed to offer the most humane future for the masses, and Nicaragua, which witnessed the direct involvement of a number of clergy, had been the grand experiment of trying to wed that system with liberationist principles. With the defeat of the Sandinistas in 1990, these hopes were dashed. The continent was thrust into a cauldron of economic activity for which it seemed ill prepared. Globalization proponents championed the theme of *integration* into the new world order, but instead the outcome seemed to be more like the double *exclusion* of Latin America—exclusion of these countries as a block from the socioeconomic gains of the global system, and exclusion of the popular classes within each nation from any possibility of truly benefiting from these new arrangements. How could one comprehend the hand of God in the triumph of global capitalism? What might be the theological evaluation and, in light of their commitments, a proper engagement with this state of affairs? What follows briefly refers to the views of two key figures who have dedicated much of their work to the interface of economics and theology: Enrique Dussel and Franz Hinkelammert.[4]

To begin with, for many, the older paradigm of dependency theory, which defined the world as organized into a center-periphery dichotomy, had proven inadequate. Dependency theory held that a core group of countries (Western Europe, Japan, and especially the United States) dominated the less-developed world, exploiting those nations for raw materials and cheap labor to maintain their own profit margins and prosperity, even as they used them as a market for their exports through the machinations of multinational corporations (Dussel 1988, 135–57).

3. The amount of self-reflection within liberation theology published since 1990 is quite large, but much of it is not available in English. Not only have liberationists themselves considered how their theology needs to be reconfigured, but others who are critically sympathetic to the movement also have argued for the importance of preserving and redirecting some of its foundational elements, even if a new direction is needed. See, for example, Bell (2001) and Petrella (2004).

4. Another important source is Hugo Assmann, but I will not deal with his work due to the constraints of this chapter.

Yet the economic landscape within each individual country and in the interconnected global system no longer neatly fit (if it ever did) this pattern.[5] Nevertheless, Hinkelammert is not willing to abandon the dependency paradigm. He believes that the material conditions of the poor are actually worse today than when the theory was in vogue, thereby confirming its essential tenets (1997, 29–30). For his part, Dussel has developed a lengthy ethics developed around the theme of the victimization of the masses under hegemonic capitalism (1998).

This is not the time then to forsake completely the insights provided by the Marxist tradition. Dussel comments:

> The relevance of Marx will grow in the future, since he appears as the great critic of capital, even more if it pretends to be the triumphant Power of the end of the twentieth century. Its contemporary fetish character, without any rival, makes it more monstruous and the direct cause of the misery of a large part of humanity, in the "South" (the so-called third world). (1993b, 5)

In fact, for liberation theology, the orientation provided by Marx's discussion of fetishism powerfully illumines a crucial theological category: idolatry (Dussel 1998, 17–20; 1993b; Hinkelammert 1986; cf. 1992). From this perspective, the concept of God and the Christian faith itself have been perverted. God is identified as the protector of the global economic system and the guarantor of its providential and immutable market laws, and correct religious devotion is defined as living according to the ideals of capitalism. Commodities assume the value of persons, while actual persons lose their true worth. Humans are now perceived as *homo oeconomicus*—either they are the providers of the system's goods or its consumers. This pernicious religious construct, liberationists say, holds the power of life and death over the world's poor masses, who slave to maintain what they can neither control nor enjoy. At one level, then, atheism is not the central theological problem of our time; rather, the battle is to be waged over a false view of God. On the other hand, atheism is redefined as believing in what is not truly God; in that sense, atheism is rampant. What is needed within Latin America, Dussel and Hinkelammert believe, is a fresh vision of the God of life—life in all of its social, material, and spiritual fullness.

Liberation theology tries to grasp the meaning of Christian faith in a world of injustice and inequality. Economics, therefore, is a central category of theology. It affects many theological themes, such as, as we

5. In the introduction to the anniversary edition of his foundational book, Gustavo Gutiérrez notes his change in perspective concerning the applicability of dependency theory. See Gutiérrez (1988, xxiii–xxv). For his initial view, see 49–57. Cf. Petrella (2004, 69–92).

have just seen, idolatry. The social sciences, then, are a necessary instrument in the hands of liberation theologians in order to give reflection and pastoral action substance and relevance. Again, our purpose is not to evaluate the liberationist viewpoint; the goal is methodological. We are concerned with how economic realities affect the doing of theology. For liberation theology, its importance is patent. What can be said of evangelical thinking on Latin America? Are these issues important in those circles as well?

The Evangelical Movement

There are several possible avenues to explore in the study of the relationship between evangelicalism (and its impressive growth) and economics in Latin America. Interestingly, whatever might be the level of theologizing that actually is being done in evangelical churches and training centers, discussion of the connection to economics is fundamental to all sorts of research on evangelicalism. In his recent study of religious trends in Latin America, Andrew Chestnut (2003) even utilizes macroeconomic theory to describe how the religious scene there works. He explains that, unlike what was the case in the traditional socioreligious environment shaped by the historic monopoly enjoyed for centuries by the Roman Catholic Church, the contemporary arena is a religious free market. On the one hand, consumers pick and choose their religious affiliation according to what best fits their personal needs; on the other hand, Protestant denominations and the Catholic Church must work at making themselves attractive to prospective devotees and at advertising the multiple advantages that joining their flock can have.

One way of envisioning the evangelical-economics correlation is to define it along the lines of some sort of conspiracy theory. Those who defend this view tend to come from elements of the religious and political left and from several sectors of the Roman Catholic Church hierarchy (e.g., Galindo 1993).[6] Evangelicals, especially those of certain Pentecostal varieties, are said to represent the vanguard of the intrusion of capitalistic values into the continent and to be intimately linked monetarily and ideologically to the New Religious Right, if not to the United States government itself. The goal of this nefarious religio-political plot is to change Latin culture and society so that they mirror North American life and to bring these countries into the neoliberal web. At the same time, they say, Pentecostals are too otherworldly in

6. This attitude is evident at local levels. For example, for Guatemala, see Barrio (1989).

their beliefs and ecstatic practices, and the escapism that these things engender neglects the pressing problems of society and is counterproductive to social change.

Recent sociological studies have increasingly brought these conspiracy theories under question. In his groundbreaking *Tongues of Fire*, David Martin says that at best there exists an affinity or mutual reinforcement between Latin American Pentecostalism and aspects of capitalism, and the possibilities of formal ties to United States interests are even more remote. The voluntarism and activism of these movements, the empowerment of followers through leadership training and broad lay participation, and their moral ethos can create a people more equipped to make the adaptations that can help a homegrown form of capitalistic economy take hold and flourish (Martin 1990). Others have shown that conversion to evangelicalism and adherence to its strict ethical code regularly bring greater stability to families, especially among the poor (Garrard-Burnett and Stoll 1993; Cleary and Stewart-Gambino 1997). The end of alcohol consumption, increased sexual fidelity, greater respect for women as wives and as leaders in local congregations, better treatment of children, and the encouragement to be wise stewards of family funds all have had a positive economic impact. All of these behavioral changes, though, are in many ways strategies of survival; they are not oriented by any extensive theological or defined ideological framework other than the simple conviction that this is what the Bible teaches. Any ethical impulse to reach out to the wider society is likely to be an expression of Christian charity at the local level; rarely would it result in involvement in structural debates and social movements. The poverty in theological thinking is also evident in the political arena, where evangelicals have begun to have a voice, in large part due to their demographic growth. All too often in their brief political experience, evangelicals have lacked a formal political philosophy (let alone one that is consciously and substantially informed by Christian belief and tradition), and the record of instances of manipulation and corruption has been disheartening (Freston 2001, 9–58, 191–280).

In addition to these multiple sociological approaches, it is also possible to trace the ebb and flow of evangelical thinking on social and economic issues from a historical perspective (Núñez and Taylor 1996, 372–436; Míguez Bonino 1997). This account is inseparable from the chronicle of European and North American missions in Latin America, which have tended to import the religious debates taking place in their home countries and constituencies to the field. The fundamentalist-modernist controversy in the United States, for example, generated a stance adverse to social involvement and to the consideration of contextual issues, like economics, among Latin American evangelicals for a generation and still exerts a powerful influence among many today.

Still another approach focuses on formal reflection on the relationship between theology and economics. What does the current evangelical theological landscape vis-à-vis the economic realities of the continent look like? Not surprisingly, the breadth of perspectives and the depth of reflection among evangelicals are as diverse as the ecclesiastical options. Such diversity in assessing capitalism, of course, is not limited to Latin America (note Gay 1991). It is a fact, though, in the Latin American context that this variety stands in stark contradistinction to the more coherent and consistent stances of the Roman Catholic Church, which are based on official pronouncements and a long legacy of socioeconomic and political involvement, and of liberation theology, which is defined by its particular ideological commitments. Two evangelical options are succinctly described here. This categorization, obviously, is overly simplistic, but it serves our methodological purpose and marks the ample range of opinion.[7]

We begin with those of the health and wealth orbit. These teachers and pastors are acquiring an increasingly prominent place in the public square, especially since this perspective is popular among the burgeoning Neo-Pentecostal megachurches. This group enthusiastically proclaims capitalistic ideals, such as wealth creation and savings, and interprets positive financial results as clear manifestations of divine favor. Evangelistic campaigns promising eternal life, healing from physical disease and the demonic, and material blessings are not uncommon. This kind of sensationalistic ministry obviously displays a certain kind of theology and ideology of economics, both in a systemic sense and as a way of life before God. The involvement of God in the economic realm is more of the laissez-faire type, limited to special moments of granting material help and blessings to the saved and faithful, and his demands on economic life are circumscribed primarily to a morality of honesty and hard work on the job and to consistent, sacrificial tithing in the local church. Little attention is given, theologically or in any fashion, to global economic affairs, except perhaps where these are thought to signal events of eschatological significance.

A second and more profound voice comes from *La Fraternidad Teológica Latinoamericana* (FTL; the Latin American Theological Fraternity). The FTL was born in 1970 at a gathering in Cochabamba, Bolivia, to respond to the felt need of doing theology from an expressly evangelical and Latin American perspective (especially at that his-

7. One example of someone who falls outside our classification is Amy Sherman, who champions neoliberal strategies (1992).

torical moment as an alternative to liberation theology). It is not an association of churches or theological institutions; rather, the FTL is an international and interdenominational association of like-minded men and women committed to doing theological reflection on pressing contextual issues in light of the Word of God. Numbered among the founders and earliest leaders of the FTL are the foremost Latin American theologians of our time—such as Emilio Antonio Núñez, René Padilla, Samuel Escobar, and Orlando Costas—all of whom have produced significant works on the mission of the church. Escobar recently has articulated a comprehensive christological missiology that takes into account the history of Christianity in Latin America, theological trends on the continent and around the world, the contribution of the social sciences to theology, and an assortment of practical issues for the new mission movement that is arising from within Latin America (Escobar 2002).[8]

The FTL has organized a series of continent-wide congresses (Lima 1979; Quito 1992; Quito 2000) to process how best to be and grow the evangelical church. It has chapters in most countries so that area theologians, pastors, laypeople, and students can gather and interact theologically. The FTL's publishing arm, Ediciones Kairós, which is located in Buenos Aires, produces an assortment of quality literature, some of which in the last few years has grappled with the topic of the global economy and its significance for Latin America. For example, Fernando Bullón (2000) engages economic globalization in a well-informed manner with other concerns that cannot be separated from discussions of the economy in Latin America, such as the environment, the life of indigenous peoples, the role of nongovernment organizations, and education. His thoughts on necessary economic change, which ideally would be congruent with the natural resources and sociocultural identity of Latin America, is incorporated into a holistic and hopeful vision of the mission of the evangelical church.

On a continent that in all kinds of ways lies at the margins of the world economy or at least has yet to enjoy to any large extent its much publicized benefits, globalization is at the center of much theologizing. This theologizing is not homogeneous in its orientation or uniform in its depth. But what is clear is that the present effects and the future implications of economic globalization loom over every imaginable level of daily existence and that theologically it cannot be ignored. Are there any lessons to be drawn from this situation for the theological enterprise within that "green continent" (to steal a phrase from Germán Arciniegas) and beyond?

8. In addition to Escobar, also note Núñez (1997) and Padilla (1998).

Toward a Hermeneutics of Responsibility

In light of the preceding, at least two important points need to be made. The first is the most obvious but bears emphasizing: In a world so profoundly interconnected, for good or ill, by globalization, economics matters for theology. We discount it at our peril. The majority world has grasped this theological imperative, even if there is not agreement on how the issues need to be analyzed or evaluated and on where the best solutions might be found. The hegemonic capitalism that largely defines our lives must be processed theologically, even as our theologies themselves need to be examined for any possible ideological captivity and/or potential to nurture alternative biblical perspectives and values. This chapter does not venture to specify a method, theological topics, or biblical texts for this crucial task. This is, quite frankly and very modestly, a clarion call to all to scrutinize theological agendas, content, and purposes in light of global reality.

The second point builds on the first. The worldwide church needs Latin America and other troubled regions for its own theological health and faithfulness. Philip Jenkins begins one of his chapters with a powerful quote from Archbishop Desmond Tutu of South Africa: "Be nice to whites, they need you to rediscover their humanity" (2002, 191). Such a profound statement and so true. The more privileged part of the world, which lives at an incredible advantage in the global economy, comfortable with its democracies, secure in its history of peaceful politics, energized by economic stability and growth, confident in high levels of education and physical health, and blessed with cutting-edge technology (and the list could go on), needs to come face-to-face with those who live on the underside of this historical and economic development, with those who for innumerable reasons have experienced its dark side. There is a need to see and move close to that greater part of the world's population, its unfortunate masses, as human beings and as theologians. Their plight prods us to seek how globalization might acquire a kinder face as well as to expose its capacity for evil; they remind us that globalization is a finite creation by fallen creatures in a fallen world and that our ultimate hope lies beyond and above this economic system, in the kingdom of God's Son.

This global reality of opportunity and poverty is inescapable; it is not only "over there" in faraway lands. The demographic shifts, which Jenkins documents, also include the migration of millions from the majority world to the North/West, from where they send remittances back to their countries to sustain their families and their homeland's economy. This new context is where they now try to negotiate their cultural and religious identities (Peterson, Vásquez, and Williams 2001). The demographic, economic, and theological, in other words, continue to move together into unforeseen and more intricate configurations.

In a word, then, globalization requires a hermeneutics of responsibility. Elsewhere I have explained in greater detail some of the commitments that must undergird an evangelical contextual hermeneutics (Carroll R. 1992; 2004). Here I assume the authority of Scripture, the leading of the Spirit, and sound textual study. I move from those solid foundations to a plea to incorporate the complexity of human existence into theological considerations and missiological obligations. We stand as responsible before God, his Word, his people, and the world. May we embrace the challenge.

10

Globalization, Nationalism, and Religious Resurgence

Vinoth Ramachandra

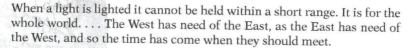

When a light is lighted it cannot be held within a short range. It is for the whole world. . . . The West has need of the East, as the East has need of the West, and so the time has come when they should meet.

Rabindranath Tagore, Nobel Prize acceptance speech, 1913

Borderless History and Lateral Thinking

There is a growing awareness among educated people worldwide, largely as a result of media coverage of environmental catastrophes and international wars (including in recent years international terrorism), that we belong to *one* world. Moreover, an increasing number of individuals and organizations act across national borders. The German sociologist Ulrich Beck writes of a new "globality," which means "that from now on nothing which happens on our planet is only a limited local event; all inventions, victories and catastrophes affect the whole world, and we must reorient and reorganize our lives and actions, our organizations and institutions, along a local-global axis" (1997, 11).

However, the novelty of this phenomenon should not be exaggerated. While the intensity and pace of globalization have increased in recent decades, nations, empires, and cultures have always interacted and influenced one another through the movement of commodities, peoples, and ideas. A. G. Hopkins reminds us that globalization has taken different historical forms, from seaborne and land-based globalizing expeditions of the Byzantine and Tang Dynasty periods; to the Islamic and Christian expansionisms of the 1500s; to the spice trade of the East India companies and imperialistic colonization; to the opening of the Suez Canal; to the dispersion of the Jews, the Chinese, and other diasporas. Lipton tea was the first global drink, predating Coca-Cola and Starbucks. Hopkins adds, "Today, as in the past, globalization remains an incomplete process; it promotes fragmentation as well as uniformity; it may recede as well as advance; its geographical scope may exhibit a strong regional bias; its future direction and speed cannot be predicted with confidence and certainly not by presuming that it has an inner logic of its own" (2002, 3).

Christopher Bayly has argued in his recent work, *The Birth of the Modern World, 1780–1914,* that we should see the unfolding saga of modernity as a multicentered enterprise, involving the active participation of many societies around the globe. Cultures did not—and do not—merely stand by as passive recipients or bemused observers (Bayly 2003). In the eighteenth-century age of "archaic globalization," societies were already becoming interconnected, not least by dynamic networks of trade. The late eighteenth and the early nineteenth century saw a profound unsettling of the old agrarian regimes, with pressures for change being strongly evident in China, India, Persia, and Arabia. But they erupted explosively in the American and French revolutions, unleashing a truly global struggle for power. Viewed in this wider context, the future of nineteenth-century Europe was decided as much by events in Egypt, India, and the West Indies as by the Peninsular Wars or Napoleon's defeat at Waterloo. The Taiping Rebellion in China, the so-called Indian Mutiny, and the American Civil War were all global events (though triggered by local causes) that reflected and further propelled the forces of ideological, economic, and political change.

Thus, the conventional geographical compartmentalizing of history, embodied in the writing of national histories, is as distorting of reality as is the geographical compartmentalizing of theology. Recent historians of the British empire such as Linda Colley and Peter Van der Veer have pointed out that it is impossible to understand nineteenth- and early twentieth-century British society apart from the wider context of its global empire (Colley 2002; Van der Veer 2001). It was not simply a matter of recognizing how British national identity came to be defined over and against the threatening "other" (increasingly Hindu India rather than Catholic France) but how profound transformations in the concepts of religion, race, and secularism all occurred in the interaction between the periphery and the margins. If India today cannot be understood apart from British history, no less can Britain be understood apart from Indian history.

Eighty-four percent of the world's land mass was under colonial rule as late as the 1930s, and the same area is now postcolonial. Colonialism was the midwife to European capitalism and now stands accused, in the mushrooming discipline of postcolonial literature, of all the ills of contemporary non-Western societies. Ever since Edward Said[1] transformed the word *Orientalist* into a term of academic abuse, it has been taken for granted that every attempt by Western scholars to understand the non-Western world had as its aim the imperialist subjugation of the other. It is often forgotten that the goal of the traditional Hindu king was universal empire and that the bulk of Orientalist writing in the nineteenth century (the heyday of empire) had a German, not a British, provenance. Britain exploited India and did some terrible things there, but, as David Smith reminds us, "Orientalism in its original meaning was not oppression of the East, but the colonization of the Western mind by the East. It is the strength of Indian ideas and Indian texts that overpowers the Western scholar, and forces him to spend his life in willing servitude to them" (2003, 101).[2]

Moreover, to see the conflicts of the present world as a clash of Western rationalist ideals and oriental religious zeal is profoundly misleading. If European powers justified their imperial conquests with claims of progress and enlightenment, Asian rulers translated those same Promethean claims into brutal nationalist projects, murdering millions of their own countrymen in doing so. In the twentieth century, these projects resulted in the mass graves of the Gulag and the killing fields of China, Indonesia, and Cambodia. The Taliban's destruction of the unique Buddhist rock-carved statues in Afghanistan in 2000 was foreshadowed by the Meiji samurai who, in their modernist reformation of the Japanese state in 1867, changed their kimonos for tailcoats and top hats and set about smashing Buddhist temples and transforming their country in the name of progress, science, and enlightenment. Most revolts against Western imperialism, and its local offshoots, borrowed heavily from Western ideas.

1. There is an extensive literature dealing with Said's thesis. See, for example, Sprinker (1992) and King (1999).
2. See also Kejariwal (1988, 226): "The world of scholarship and the world of administration . . . were worlds apart" during this period.

This is why it is such a "misfortune," as Ian Buruma and Avishai Margalit observe, for the Middle East to have encountered the modern West for the first time through echoes of the French Revolution. "Robespierre and the Jacobins were inspiring heroes for Arab radicals: progressive, egalitarian, and opposed to the Christian church. Later models for Arab progress—Mussolini's Italy, Nazi Germany, and the Soviet Union—were even more disastrous" (2004, 12). Can we understand the radicalized Islamist movements that take up so much attention in the Western mass media today without reference to the harsh secularisms of Kemal Ataturk and Reza Shah or the failed state socialist experiments in Egypt, Syria, and Algeria? Or can we ignore the influence of European fascism and nationalism on the Ba'athism of Syria and the recent regime in Iraq?

Bayly and others observe that the modernity of the nineteenth century was a period not of widespread religious skepticism but of multicentered religious ferment. Religion, secularism, and nationalism interpenetrated one another all over the world, creating permutations and hybrids of dizzying variety. Seizing on the novel possibilities of printing and mass communication, but also responding to Christian evangelism, Islam, Hinduism, and Buddhism began to reconfigure themselves as world religions, competing for converts, borrowing extensively from the Christian West, but also drawing deeply on their own theological and cultural traditions. Hindu religious texts could now be standardized, printed, and disseminated on an unprecedented scale. The advent of modern communications meant that pilgrimage to Mecca became more practicable and affordable than before, stimulating a greater sense of global Islamic brotherhood. The epidemic of nineteenth-century church building in Britain was matched by the construction of temples, mosques, and other places of non-Christian worship across Africa and Asia. And goaded by the vigorous assertion and renewal of non-European religions, Christianity was in turn forced to rethink its own identity.

The Construction of Spirituality

In 1893, a passionate young Bengali known as Swami Vivekananda electrified the World Parliament of Religions in Chicago.[3] Vivekananda represented Hinduism at the parliament and in his speech declared his pride in "belonging to a religion which had taught the world both toler-

3. This was attached to the Columbian Exhibition, celebrating the four-hundredth anniversary of Columbus's voyage to the New World and also Chicago's recovery from the great fire of 1871. The driving force behind the parliament was the Congregational clergyman John Henry Barrows (1847–1902), later president of Oberlin College, an untiring advocate of world brotherhood through religious tolerance and understanding.

ance and universal acceptance" (Mullick 1993, 221). Both in his speech and throughout his writings in English, he contrasts the spirituality of the East, embodied supremely in Hindu Vedanta, and the materialism of the West. The East had to receive science and technology from the West, but the West learned wisdom and spirituality from the East. Vivekananda's message resonated widely with American audiences. His lecture tours in the United States and Europe following the parliament led to the founding of Vedanta Societies in many Western cities.

Before he became Swami Vivekananda, a name he assumed when he took his ascetic vows, Narendranath Datta had been educated in Western philosophy and had been exposed to both Christian missionary influence and the Hindu reform movement, the Brahmo Samaj. But the deepest transformation in his life he owed to an encounter with Ramakrishna, a priest in the Kali temple of Calcutta who had become something of a cult figure among the Bengali literati of Calcutta. Ramakrishna was a medium, not of ancestral spirits, which would have put him on the rank of low-caste groups that associate with the world of the dead, but of the Mother Goddess Kali. His frequent trances were interpreted as divine possession. The young Datta was mesmerized by the charismatic Ramakrishna and became an ardent disciple. The rest of his relatively brief life was devoted to "sanitizing" the highly eroticized Tantric practices and beliefs of Ramakrishna into a modernizing discourse of anticolonial, anti-Christian spirituality for the middle classes of Calcutta. Chicago gave him a wider audience among those in the United States and Europe who found congenial his disdain for Christian talk of sin and redemption and who sought to wrest spirituality away from the controlling discourse of an ecclesiastical establishment.

Though his campaign was polemical, Vivekananda's strategy was subtle. Even as he universalized Hindu Vedanta and depicted it as authentic *sanatana dharma* (eternal religion), capable of contesting an inauthentic, colonial Christianity, he insisted that it embraced all spiritual experiences and recognized a variety of religious paths as valid at different levels and appropriate to a devotee's spiritual temperament. But attachment to "personal founders" and the unreliable particularities of history cannot be a basis for universal truth. Real religion is an individual's own experience, a private affair between a human and God. "We Hindus do not tolerate, we invite ourselves with every religion, praying in the mosque of the Mohammedan, worshiping before the fire of the Zoroastrian, and kneeling to the cross of the Christian. We know that all religions alike, from the lowest fetishism to the highest absolutism, are but so many attempts of the human soul to grasp and realize the Infinite. So we gather all these flowers, and binding them together with the cord of love, make them into a wonderful bouquet of worship" (cited in Thomas 1976, 121).

Thus, Vivekananda homogenized the multiple Hindu discursive traditions into a totalizing Hindu spirituality and wielded the latter as an ideological tool in the emergent nationalism of India. This proved a remarkably influential move. It left its mark on men like Mohandas Gandhi and Sarvepalli Radhakrishnan and also shaped the Hindutva discourse of current Hindu nationalist politics. *Spirituality* became a militant, polemical term with which to oppose colonial Christianity. The Hindu spirituality sought to outdo Christian missions in social reform and active involvement in education (the ample funds that Vivekananda brought back from the United States enabled him to set up an ascetic order, the Ramakrishna Mission, in 1897 that combined disciplined meditation with social service projects and that has subsequently spread to other cities around the world), and Ramakrishna's selfless devotion to the Mother Goddess Kali is now translated into selfless devotion to Mother India. One could be a "renouncer" in the authentic Hindu manner and yet be committed to social and political causes. There was no dichotomy between an individual's spiritual awakening and the political emancipation of the Indian nation.

Within this discourse, even scientific knowledge no longer remains the exclusive preserve of the modern West but can be discovered in the ancient Indian scriptures. Writers such as Peter Van der Veer have drawn attention to the continuing significance of Vivekananda's creation of yoga as the Indian science of "supraconsciousness." *Yoga* is a Sanskrit word that can be translated as "discipline." It has a complex history with a number of divergent traditions, but the classical text is Patanjali's *Yogasutra*, which was probably composed around the fifth century. Under Vivekananda's influence, yoga became the unifying sign of the Indian nation and central to what Van der Veer calls the "relentless marketing of India's spirituality" (2001, 74)[4] in the contemporary Western world:

> This is a new doctrine, although Vivekananda emphasized that it was ancient "wisdom." Especially the body exercises of hatha yoga, underpinned by a metaphysics of mind-body unity, continues to be a major entity in the health industry, especially in the United States. What I find important in Vivekananda's construction of yoga as the core of Hindu "spirituality" is that it is devoid of any specific devotional content that would involve, for example, temple worship and thus a theological and ritual position in sectarian debates. Vivekananda is, first and foremost, interested in Hindu unity. (Van der Veer 2001, 73)

4. Much of this section is stimulated by Van der Veer's work.

The irony, of course, is that Vivekananda, Gandhi, modern Hindutva ideologues, and New Age gurus in the Western world all borrow this construction of Hindu spirituality (and its essential otherness) from the Orientalist scholarship[5] of the late eighteenth and the nineteenth century. It was the advent of Orientalist scholarship that led to the creation of Hinduism and its identification with a corpus of Sanskrit texts (Vedas, Upanishads, etc.)[6] painstakingly edited and translated into Western and modern Indian languages and now bestowed with canonical authority over Hindu practices in a manner similar to the semitic faiths, and to the periodization of Indian history into Hindu, Muslim, and British stages, with Indian civilization identified with the earliest stage and the Muslim presence effectively occluded.

Moreover, it was an Orientalist history that attributed the modern concept of tolerance to Hinduism, even though as a doctrinal notion it had no specific place in Hindu discursive traditions. Modern Hindu thinkers have come to interpret hierarchical relativism in Hindu discourse in Orientalist terms as tolerance. Wilhelm Halbfass argues convincingly that the step to reconcile all religious and philosophical traditions was not taken prior to the colonial period.[7] The characteristic manner in which it was done was by relativizing truth claims and including all religious traditions within the Vedanta, the spiritual essence of "pure" philosophical Hinduism, as in the famous saying of Sarvepalli Radhakrishnan, the first president of India and professor of Eastern religion and ethics at Oxford: "The Vedanta is not a religion, but religion itself in its most universal and deepest significance" (cited in Halbfass 1988, 409).

Orientalist writing on Indian texts was largely done in Germany, where university chairs in philology and Sanskrit mushroomed almost overnight.[8] Johann Gottfried Herder's emphasis on language and culture as the key to the *Geist*, or spirit, of the German nation and the linguistic philosophy of Humboldt, Hegel, and Grimm became central to German ethnic nationalism. For Herder, "There is a plurality of incommensu-

5. I use "Orientalist" in the pre-Said sense to refer to Western scholars whose scholarship of the Orient was motivated by the love of learning.

6. The Vedas were transmitted orally and were only transcribed into written texts by the nineteenth-century Orientalists, starting with Max Müller's six-volume edition of the Rg-Veda.

7. Cf. Halbfass (1988, 403–18).

8. Buddhism was discovered for the West mainly by British missionaries and civil servants in Ceylon in the nineteenth century. The works of a Methodist minister, Rev. Robert Spence Hardy, were important sources for Western knowledge of Buddhism, and excerpts were often used by encyclopedias of religion. One of the earliest works on Buddhism to appear in the English language (by a British Buddhist scholar, Rhys Davids) was published by the Society for the Propagation of Christian Knowledge in 1877. Cf. Gombrich (1971) and Allen (2002).

rable cultures. To belong to a given community, to be connected with its members by indissoluble and impalpable ties of common language, historical memory, habit, tradition and feeling, is a basic human need, no less natural than that for food or drink or security or procreation" (Berlin 1979, 12).

This worldview not only influenced the early Max Müller, a German scholar who devoted his entire life to the study of ancient Indian texts from his library in Oxford, but also had a lasting effect on American anthropology in the twentieth century, thanks to its German founder, Franz Boas. Müller was critical of pretensions of racial superiority in the British nationalism of his time, and his work was enthusiastically embraced in India to support a Hindu nationalism built on the racial superiority of the Hindu Aryans. "They used philology in the way the Germans used it in their own country. Sanskrit philology provided them with the tools to dig up the origin and essence of the nation, that is, the Hindu nation. It also gave them a scientific language to exclude 'latecomers' such as Muslims, as outsiders to the story of the nation" (Van der Veer 2001, 132). A significant number of modern-day Hindus, quite understandably, want to construct their religion as historically ancient, cohesive, and centered, as a viable "world religion" able to compete with Islam and Christianity in global society.

No discussion of modern Hindu and Buddhist resurgence can sidestep the strange phenomenon of the theosophical movement of the late nineteenth century. One of the two representatives of the Theosophical Society at the Chicago Parliament of Religions was a remarkable British woman, Annie Besant (1847–1933), who traveled to India later that year and made that nation her home for the rest of her life. Besant became in 1917 the leader of the Indian National Congress, the highpoint of a career fraught with controversy and contradiction. Married at twenty, she separated from her children and husband, an Anglican clergyman, rejecting both his Christian faith and his bourgeois values, and threw herself into secularist, socialist, and educational causes. She was a close friend and coworker of Charles Bradlaugh, the militant atheist and first president of the National Secular Society (set up in 1866),[9] and helped to edit his journal, the *National Reformer*. The first woman to enroll for a science degree at London University, Besant was active in Britain throughout the 1870s for women's rights, trade unionism, contraception, socialism, and secularism. There was strong interest in spiritualist

9. George Holyoake (1817–1906), whom Bradlaugh ousted as the president of the London Secular Society in 1858, adopted the word *secularism* in 1851 to mean a positive alternative to atheism and to delineate "the province of the real, the known, the useful, and the affirmative." Secularist groups were to become active in a campaign for the rights of atheists and in ridiculing the church and the Bible. See Herrick (1985, 156–69).

seances and Eastern religions in the radical circles in which she moved. She found in theosophy the anti-Christian religion she craved, and this became her grand enthusiasm for the rest of her life.

Spiritualism in the second half of the nineteenth century in Britain was a kind of home-based, do-it-yourself religion. It did not involve theological doctrines or ethical codes, was considered part of rational, experimental science (secularist meetings at the London Hall of Science invited many spiritualist speakers), circumvented the authority of church and chapel, and cut across class divisions in a way that no Christian denomination did. Alternative healing, crystal ball gazing, mesmerism, and other forms of parapsychology united London's elite society with working-class households. Interest in contacting the dead through spiritualist seances understandably reached a peak in the years following the First World War, even as they did in the United States after the Civil War. The theosophy that became Besant's passion shared the anti-Christian, anticolonial radicalism of British working-class spiritualism. Although Bradlaugh had little time for spiritualism, he took an interest in Indian affairs and was very popular with Indian students in Britain for his anti-imperialist stance. Despite winning the Northampton elections in 1880, he spent the next six years fighting legal battles to enable him to take his seat in the House of Commons because he had refused to take his parliamentary oath on the Bible. Among the many mourners at his funeral was a twenty-one-year-old student by the name of Mohandas Gandhi.

Following Bradlaugh's death, Besant made India her home. She joined the theosophists in India and befriended many of the Indian nationalist elites. Motilal Nehru and his son, Jawaharlal (later to become the first prime minister of independent India), were involved for a brief while in the Theosophical Society. She initiated the Hindu response to the founding of a Muslim university at Aligarh by setting up Benares Hindu University in 1911. Recent scholarship has shown that Besant and other theosophists were arch-supporters of the myths of racial evolution popular among both British imperialists and Hindu nationalists.[10] Ironically, they all believed (and appropriated for their differing purposes) the Orientalist theory that India was a Hindu nation with a golden Aryan past that had subsequently declined. As race replaced religion as the dominant element in British nationalism in the late nineteenth century, such ideas flourished. Ideas of superior and inferior races, coupled with mythologies of racial origins, were employed by a host of writers to argue that conquest by stronger races could lead to cultural regeneration in the weaker. It was what also allowed great liberals such as John Stuart

10. Cf. Viswanathan (1998, 187–223).

Mill to advocate freedom at home and champion colonialism abroad.[11] Besant herself was strongly influenced by the writings of Matthew Arnold and Ernst Renan. The theosophists, moreover, dreamed of the evolution of humanity through spiritual miscegenation to a universal brotherhood ruled by a spiritual hierarchy. The highest spirituality was possessed by the Aryan race. It is no accident that the swastika, an ancient Sanskrit symbol of auspiciousness, was embraced as an identifying emblem both by the theosophists and by the Nazi Party in the 1930s.

Theosophy did not make much headway in India, and it was soon left behind as Hindu reform and the Indian nationalist movement, in all its multiple factions, gathered momentum. The initial fascination among the Indian elites was in the discovery of Westerners who considered Hinduism and Buddhism far superior to Christianity and who supported self-rule for India. But once Indian nationalists found in Gandhi a leader who brought his own brand of universal spirituality, theosophy lost its political role. In Ceylon (Sri Lanka), however, the influence of theosophy on the development of Buddhist nationalism was immense.[12]

The Ironies of Modernity

What this historical discussion has shown is that the binary polarizations of spiritual and secular, Eastern and Western, national and foreign are far more problematic than is suggested by their customary usage. Christianity, Hinduism, Buddhism, and other religious traditions were transformed, under the conditions of nineteenth-century nation building, into powerful nationalist discourses. Evangelicals, Utilitarians, theosophists, and Hindu and Muslim reformers debated social change and the notions of progress, freedom, religion, and so on from within their varying social locations in the wider project of global empire. An Indian scholar has noted that "the first and only community of followers of [Auguste] Comte's Religion of Humanity with its full paraphernalia of man-oriented rituals was established in the city of Calcutta" (Raychaudhuri 1995, 60). Then and now, Western-style rationalism and nativist revolt exist within the same institutions and in the minds of the same people.

In Europe, the flow of information about India and other Eastern countries had been steadily increasing from the Middle Ages onward. The flow intensified with the Jesuit missions and the remarkable influx

11. Mill, like his father before him, was employed by the East India Company and, toward the end of his career, was appointed to that company's highest administrative position.
12. Cf. Gombrich and Obeysekera (1988).

and circulation throughout Europe of Jesuit letterbooks and histories.[13] But it was only in the period of the European Enlightenment that the significance of this new knowledge began to be utilized by intellectuals. The discovery of supposedly ancient Hindu thought coincided with the revival of Stoic and Greco-Roman paganism among the European elites of the seventeenth and eighteenth centuries.[14] One of the most widely read texts of the Enlightenment was the Frenchman Raynal's (1713–96) treatise on colonialism, *The Philosophical History of the Two Indies,* which surveyed the entire range of European colonization and drew heavily on the observations of explorers to the East.

Much of the "othering" that goes on in European thought has to do not so much with contrasts between the "enlightened West" and the "despotic East" (whether China, India, or Persia) but rather with the critique of European (specifically Christian) institutions and practices as intolerant, violent, or backward. The comparison of Christianity with other religions and civilizations is an important feature in the works of Voltaire, Montesquieu, and Diderot in the French Enlightenment. Voltaire used Indian religion to attack Christianity, ironically using as proof of Hindu wisdom the *Ezour Veda,* a Sanskrit text faked by Jesuits in support of their own beliefs. By locating in ancient Hinduism everything that the West had claimed as its own unique spiritual insights, Voltaire challenged the exceptionalism of Christianity and argued for a universal, natural monotheism. What was deeply distasteful about Christianity to the *philosophes* of the Enlightenment was not its religious character but the doctrines of a unique historical revelation, human depravity, and the necessity for divine atonement.[15] Far from doing away with religion in Europe, the Enlightenment was built on (what was then assumed to be) the unshakeable foundations of rational, universal religion, and natural science, rational religion, and a secular state were presumed to form one seamless web.

Therefore, the origins of modernity lie not exclusively in the Western Enlightenment, superficially understood as an atheistic project, but in the complex, historical interplay of European and non-European civilizations beginning in the eighteenth century.

Modernity has a global history. This does not imply a single origin of concepts and blueprints that are developed in the Enlightenment (both American and French) and exported, resisted, and adopted, elsewhere. Nor does it imply the dialectic between an already finished idiom of modernity that confronts an already existing idiom of tradition, out of which a syn-

13. Cf. Lach and Van Kley (1993).
14. Cf. Reventlow (1984, 14, 71ff.) and Oestreich (1983).
15. Cf. Williams (1995).

thesis emerges. Rather, it manifests a history of interactions out of which modernity, with its new historical problematic, arose, offering creative tensions, not solutions. (Van der Veer 2001, 160)

Several ironies in this story of the interaction of modernizing civilizations and the blurring of conventional academic boundaries need to be highlighted.

First, contemporary "secular" culture represents the spurning of Christianity on the basis of Christian social and cultural achievements. Henrikus Berkhof noted that "secularization is a child of the gospel, but a child who sooner or later rises against his mother" (cited in Runia, 1993, 2). The very notion of the secular, it has often been pointed out, originated in Christendom. The opposite of the secular is not the spiritual or the sacred but the eternal. The secular denotes the temporal order that, while incapable in itself of delivering the kingdom of God, is hallowed by creation and incarnation and called to anticipate God's reign in the ordering of human life. The constellation of social and political ideas that flowered in the fifteenth and sixteenth centuries, and eventually limited the authority of popes and bishops, was nourished in the womb of Christendom.

Oliver O'Donovan has reminded us that the essence of Christendom's legacy to the late-modern world is the legal-constitutional conception of government, namely, of governmental responsibility and accountability to international law. Moreover, O'Donovan argues:

The flowering of an idea comes when it assumes a structural role that determines what else may be thought. Its origin is never contemporary with its flowering, nor are its organisational implications apparent to the minds that first conceived it. And so, as historians may point out with perfect justice, the eighteenth century was actually formed far less by the "Enlightenment" ideas that we associate with it than by the older tradition of religious ideas common to Christendom. Modernity-criticism is less history of ideas than "genealogy." It is we who find the Enlightenment ideas particularly important, because it is we who have seen them grow to form a matrix within which everything that is to be thought must be thought. (1996, 272)

Second, Christian missions had a powerful *secularizing* thrust insofar as Christian attitudes to local language and culture (paradoxically denying their intrinsic sacrality while elevating them to vehicles of divine communication) stood in marked contradiction to Muslim and Hindu notions of eternal, divine tongues (Arabic and Sanskrit respectively) and of a religious homeland. However, the modernizing project of the secular, colonial state in fact gave religion a new impulse and salience.

In the South Asian context, the British East India Company had sought to distance itself from Christianity and was, for a long time, hostile to any attempt at religious conversion, which it feared would offend local sensibilities and interfere with local commerce. The company officials continued the traditional practice of Asian rulers of maintaining and supporting Hindu, Muslim, and Buddhist temples and religious rituals. Pressure from evangelicals in Britain changed all that. Once India officially became a colony of the British government, a new policy of religious "noninterference" was established. The administration and maintenance of Hindu temples and rituals were handed over to new, rising elites who had their own reformist agenda concerning religious education and ritual action. They used the British legal apparatus to create a new "corporate Hinduism" whose reverberations still echo throughout the Indian political and social landscape.

Thus, Indian religions were transformed in opposition both to Christian mission and to the colonizing state, and religion became crucially important in the emerging public sphere. Denied participation in the political institutions of their modernizing nation, a significant body of Indians—Hindu and then Muslim—began to develop alternative institutions of a jointly political and religious nature. Ironically, the demand by Christian churches and missionary agencies for the secularity of the colonial state (however hypocritical in practice) led to the formation of a public sphere in which religious movements produced an anticolonial Hindu spirituality that was fully modern. Indigenous cultural and religious renewal, the transmission of scientific and secular political ideals from Europe to the rest of the world via Christian schools and universities, and the arrogant posture of cultural superiority conveyed by some of the later European missionaries and administrators served, in the long term, to undermine the plausibility of Christian preaching. For now, there were viable alternatives to the Christianity of the West.

"It was religion," writes Linda Colley in her brilliant study of the formation of Great Britain from 1707 onward, "that first converted peasants into patriots, long before the onset of modernisation in the shape of railroads, mass education, advanced press networks and democracy" (1992, 369). This was also the case for many European countries and the United States. The impact of Protestant Christianity on the development of British national identity, however, tends to be ignored in contemporary political theory. Liberal theorists take it for granted that religious discourse is antithetical to both liberty and the rationality of the public square. On the contrary, religious conviction was a major source of the moral indignation and political debate that surrounded the abolitionist movements and the national soul-searching over the operations of the British East

India Company (climaxing in Edmund Burke's searing indictment of Warren Hastings in the parliamentary debates of 1787). The agitations for and against Catholic emancipation, the evangelical antislavery petitions and campaigns, and the emergence of Bible societies and voluntary missionary associations were crucial to the creation of a public sphere and a national identity. Their counterparts in nineteenth-century India were the anti-*sati* Hindu reform movements, the Ramakrishna missions, and the cow protection campaigns of the Arya Samaj.

Andrew Walls has drawn our attention to the influence of missionary newsletters and magazines on the creation of an informed, socially sensitized core of Christian citizens:

> The missionary magazine went to many people who had never previously been periodical readers at all. The magazines helped to form opinion, they developed images and mental pictures, they built up attitudes. Their effect on popular reference books in the nineteenth century was considerable. The average reader of the *Missionary Register* or the other missionary magazines knew exactly what he thought the British government should do about the temple tax in Bengal, or about the *sati* of Hindu widows, or the opium trade, or slave running. And a mass readership was produced, a readership concerned and informed about the world outside their own country as perhaps no other group in the nation. (1996, 252)

Fourth, in being co-opted into a nationalist, and later imperial, discourse, Protestantism was profoundly changed. For many Victorian Christians, British gunboats were agents of the divine will. Massive blind spots paralyzed an evangelical challenge to the evils committed by colonial governments. For example, consider the system of indentured labor (usually Indian migrants) introduced in many British colonies to work on the traditional plantations. While slavery was abolished in theory, the superstructure of slavery remained. Writing in the context of Ceylon's coffee and (later) tea plantations, where general mortality and maternal and infant mortality rates were higher than in the rest of the country, Kumari Jayewardena notes that the plantation system was a strictly "authoritarian, hierarchical form of organization" in which "labour was dragooned and subjected to a military type of discipline and housed in primitive barracks on the estate itself." She continues: The usual concomitants of free labor—namely, money wages in full, freedom of movement after work, and freedom of association—were absent, and there was a total denial of any civil rights. The plantation was essentially a "total institution" where all aspects of the lives of those working there were controlled (2000, 98).

It was a grim tale of neglect by the colonial government and harsh treatment by the British planters. The narrowness of the missionaries' vision in matters of social policy is shown in their indifference toward this problem.[16] The scathing words of an eminent historian of Sri Lanka have a kernel of truth, however biased may be the understanding of missionary motives: "The Baptists and the Anglicans had missions to the migrant Indians, but they were interested in the immigrants only as potential converts, or as Christians to be kept within the fold. They kept silent, although they could hardly have been ignorant of the abuses of the immigration system; no missionary voice was raised against the planters or in urging upon the Government the adoption of protective or welfare measures" (De Silva 1965, 287–88).

The contemporary relevance of this example from the nineteenth century is reflected in Hugh Tinker's study of the system of indentured migrant labor in the heyday of global capitalism:

> Perhaps the British opponents of slavery did not understand so clearly that legal servitude and economic servitude were identical upon the plantation. . . . Everybody in a sugar colony from the Governor and the wealthiest merchant . . . down to the meanest field hand was involved in the production of sugar for a distant market. The laws, the revenues, the communications were all created for a single purpose; and unless the economic base was transformed everything would continue to serve that purpose under a system of slavery and also under a nominal system of free labour. (1974, 2–3)

Religion and the Global Order Today

We have seen that religion has been and continues to be an important resource for nationalist, modernizing movements. Globalizing processes both corrode inherited cultural and personal identities and at the same time stimulate the creation and revitalization of particular identities as a way of gaining more power or influence in this new global order. What was true of Protestant Christianity in the world of Victorian Britain also applies to the nationalist transformations of Hindu Neo-Vedanta, Theravada Buddhism, Shintoism, and Shi'ite Islam in the non-Western world. Religions are not unchanging, ahistorical "essences," and we cannot understand them or their adherents apart from their historical, political, and social contexts.

16. One outstanding (though belated) exception was the Anglican missionary Charlie Andrews, a close friend of Tagore and Gandhi, who campaigned successfully for the abolition of indentured labor in the British Empire as well as full independence for India. Andrews enjoyed a unique standing among ordinary Indians, being hailed as *Deenabhandu*, "Friend of the Poor." Cf. Tinker (1979).

In many Muslim-majority nations today, Islamists have created much of the organizational and ideological framework for middle- and lower-middle-class Muslims to enter the workings of the modern economy and state. They support bureaucratization and promotion by merit, the use of the ballot box, the rule of law, and the codification of that law, *sharia*, into forms that may be applied by modern judiciaries. Their schools, clinics, hospitals, and neighborhood meeting places have often grown up because the state has failed to provide the infrastructure to support the tens of millions who have moved in recent times from the countryside to the cities. These institutions contribute substantially to the structure of civil society. However, the Western schedule of human rights, especially equality for religious minorities and for women, is vigorously opposed by all Islamists (though in some nations women have made considerable progress in education and employment).

The spread of global communications, the radicalization of some Islamist groups, and the rise of a free-floating transnational army of fighters (*jihadis*), drawing their support from Pakistan, the Arab world, Southeast Asia, and Chechnya, have meant that conflict in one part of the Muslim world, with its specific local causes and character, is immediately presented and utilized as part of conflict in another region. The globalization of local conflict serves powerful propaganda purposes.

The Indian and Chinese diasporas today are significant carriers of cultural and religious globalization, especially as professionals and business entrepreneurs have replaced the cheap migrant labor of the nineteenth and the early twentieth century. The 200,000 strong Punjabi Sikh communities in British Colombia in Canada, the Gujarati Patels in Kenya, the Malayalis in the Gulf countries, and the Tamils in Singapore and Malaysia are some of the well-known diaspora Indians. It is reported that 38 percent of doctors, 12 percent of scientists, 36 percent of those in NASA, 34 percent in Microsoft, 28 percent in IBM, 17 percent in INTEL, and 13 percent of Xerox employees in the United States are Indians. Over 400 Hindu temples have been built by Indians in the United States. An increasing number of Indian students go overseas for higher studies. In the year 2001, the figures were as follows: United States, 42,337; United Kingdom, 5,000; Australia, 11,280; Germany, 846; and France 1,100 (*New Indian Express* 2001, 9).

Moreover, the movement of forms of Hinduism and Buddhism around the world through the efforts of traveling gurus and monks is an important event in modern times that has taken place alongside the emigration of South Asians and South Asian culture. The relaunching of Hindu Vedanta, first by Vivekananda and then by the innumerable gurus who have followed in his wake, as a "global spirituality" (in contrast to what is taken to be the narrow historical particularism of the Christian faith) continues to resonate among the affluent classes of the postmodern world. Vedanta's central notion of spiritual hierarchy and levels of truth enables it to encompass all religions without leaving any doubt as to its own superiority. Also, the individualist spiritual techniques of Hindu and Buddhist traditions (shorn of their temple rituals and social practices) make them more attractive to cultures of individualist consumerism. They leave the political and economic status quo largely unchallenged.

The great majority of the readers of this chapter will be North American evangelical Christians. The entrepreneurship of the modern guru has its Christian counterpart in the largely U.S.-exported management missiologies and church growth strategies that threaten to subvert the integrity of the church's mission. The obsession with sociology and statistics to the near exclusion of historical and theological reflection, and its complicity with global capitalism, has meant that evangelical churches have largely been shorn of their prophetic voice in global civil society.

Such blind spots, similar to those of earlier generations of British missionaries, need to be confronted. The double standards practiced by the U.S. and the British government when it comes to human rights, democracy, free trade, weapons of mass destruction, and so on have rarely been publicly challenged by evangelical Christian leaders, least of all by missionaries and mission agencies that proclaim so loudly the globalization of the church. Even before 9/11, the United States was ripping up the international rule book and was trying to bend the world to suit its military and economic interests. Several international treaties (from the Kyoto Protocol to the restriction of trade in small arms) were sabotaged and international institutions such as the International Criminal Court and the WTO undermined. The unconcealed scorn that U.S. administrations have shown toward international conventions, treaties, and organizations leaves a deep sense of foreboding among all who care for global justice and international cooperation.

Moreover, "the parochialism of Western public opinion is striking," notes Philip Jenkins. "When a single racial or religiously motivated murder takes place in Europe or North America, the event occasions widespread soul-searching, but when thousands are massacred on the grounds of their faith in Nigeria, Indonesia, or the Sudan, the story rarely registers. Some lives are worth more than others" (2002, 163). The silence of the church in the face of both U.S. hegemony and a hypocritical, biased media undermines the credibility of American evangelical missions in the early twenty-first century, just as the co-option of large swathes of British Christianity into the imperialist project has had dire consequences for the credibility of the gospel among sensitive non-Christians both in the West and in the postcolonial world.

Another way of stating this is by invoking Paul Hiebert's celebrated principle of critical contextualization. What I am suggesting is that the greatest missiological challenge the American church faces is not, say, the Islamic world but rather the lack of critical contextualization of the gospel in much of American cultural and political life. Mission begins in our own backyard and with an eye to the greater body of Christ in the world to which we belong and from which we receive.

In the words of Jonathan Sacks, the chief rabbi of the United Kingdom, "The scope of our interconnectedness defines the radius of responsibility and concern" (2002, 121).

11

Bearing Witness in Rome with Theology from the Whole Church

Globalization, Theology, and Nationalism

ELOISE HIEBERT MENESES

If, as Christians, we are to engage in truly global theologizing, it is critical that we take full and explicit account of the political realities within which we are functioning. Christians in the United States have been somewhat loath to do this. Here, politics has been treated as external to the church, except where the legislation of morality is concerned. Yet ironically, the rejection, or the purported ignorance, of political realities makes the church vulnerable to syncretism with ethnic- and state-based pseudo-religions. By failing to engage directly in a discussion of the loyalties we feel to our people and our country or, worse, by giving them divine sanction, we leave ourselves open to the idolatry of nationalism, thereby dividing ourselves from the church elsewhere.

This chapter analyzes the fundamental nature of nationalism for two purposes: first, to provide the widest possible framework for understanding the world's present political circumstance, a circumstance in which global theologizing must of necessity be done, and second, to demonstrate the impact of that circumstance on the lay theologizing being done at the current center of world power, the United States. At issue is the two-millennia-old question of how Christians are to relate to the state. I acknowledge that there has been a range of views on this matter in the history of the church. But I would suggest that the church universal has always acknowledged the *tension* between loyalty to the state and loyalty to God, ever reserving the right to listen to God rather than to human authorities (Acts 4:19). Nowhere is listening to God more critical than at the center of political power. Hence, in the current world circumstance, it is especially incumbent upon Americans to discern carefully what they should give to Caesar and what they should give to God.

Church and State

The Christian church is composed of the disciples of Jesus Christ. As his followers, we of the church declare Jesus to be the true Lord, not just of our personal lives but of the entire earth, including all humanly constructed social, economic, and political systems (Col. 1:16). It is true that the ruler of this world has not yet been fully banished. As a result, the principalities and powers that rule us sometimes institute God's good governance (Rom. 13:1–7; 1 Pet. 2:13–17) and sometimes try to usurp his authority, an abuse for which they will be paraded through the streets in public disgrace at the end of time (Col. 2:15; cf. 1 Cor. 15:24; Rev. 6:15).[1] Furthermore, rulers and governments, on the whole, do not acknowledge the fact that their own power is contingent upon God's. They imagine that they are able to establish and maintain power in their own right. And from their position of power, they expect from their citizens ultimate allegiance.

In reality, no caesar, no humanly constructed political system, has ever been willing to permit its subjects freely to choose allegiance to God over allegiance to itself in matters that pertain to political order. In some cases, rulers have attempted to resolve the tension between loyalty to God and loyalty to the state by appropriating God's power and declaring themselves divine, or divinely appointed, as with ancient Egypt, State Shinto Japan, or Buddhist Tibet. In other cases, they have tried to evict God entirely, as with the Soviet Union or Maoist China. In most cases, however, they have maintained an uneasy truce with God by permitting religious freedom in arenas without political significance and insisting on a civil religion in those that are politically important.

1. I am grateful to David Fraser for assisting me in coming to this understanding of the theology of the state.

The church, for its part, has wavered significantly in its ability to hold firm in battles between rebellious caesars and God. In 1994, for instance, the caesars defeated the church in Rwanda. Despite their common faith in Christ (74 percent of the country is Christian), ethnic Hutus and Tutsis fell on one another murderously in a struggle for control of the central government. The genocide was not the result of mass hysteria—at least not in the sense of a chaotic outbreak of violence. There had been a long history of political machinations on both sides, designed to construct ethnicity as much as to build antagonisms around it.[2] In the immediate months previous, a highly planned and organized campaign of vilifying the Tutsis had been conducted by President Habyarimana and a select core of Hutu leaders. As with Nazi Germany, a youth militia had been trained in the propaganda of ethnic and national pride and had been sent into towns and villages across the country to promote "Hutu Power." On April 6, when the president was assassinated, the signal was given, Hutus rose up against Tutsis, and Tutsis responded in like manner. The result was that an estimated eight hundred thousand men, women, and children were slaughtered. So perhaps it was hysteria after all—the calculated and cultivated hysteria of ethnic nationalist loyalty.

Christians, both inside and outside Rwanda, have now had ten years to contemplate what happened to the unity of the church in that instance. Brothers and sisters in Christ in Rwanda killed one another. Sisters and brothers elsewhere failed to intervene effectively or even to be adequately concerned about what was happening because of the perceived differences between "them," the Africans, and "us," the Americans, Europeans, or Asians. Inside Rwanda, church grounds became convenient places for systematic exterminations (Kritzinger 1996). Outside Rwanda, churchgoing people shook their heads and clucked in mild dismay as they continued about their business, imagining themselves to be immune from such sin. Allegiances to the caesars divided Christians from Christians, both nationally and internationally, such that the body of Christ was quite literally severed into pieces.

Understanding Nationalism

We live in the era of nation-states. The demise of colonialism has put notions of multiethnic world empires based on high order civilizations to

2. The following information was obtained from Human Rights Watch (http://www.hrw.org), World Vision International (http://www.worldvision.org), and the United Nations Children's Fund (http://www.unicefusa.org).

rest—at least for a time. Following in the wake of the empires have been the agonized struggles of nation building based on territory, citizenship, and ethnicity. The *ethnos*, the peoples, of various places are valued for their distinctive histories and cultures, and the postcolonial expectation is that the boundaries of states are to be demarcated by them. Each people is to rule their own. The colonial caesars were foreign rulers, but the caesars of our time are from among us and therefore represent us—they are, in fact, we ourselves. Hence, in nation-states, especially in those that are democracies, there is understood to be no excuse for a lack of allegiance to the government.

Yet nations are complex entities, and the nature of the loyalty they demand is complex as well. This complexity can be revealed with the help of analysis from the social sciences. In anthropology, nation-states are so called because they are states (i.e., sovereign political orders) built on nations (i.e., ethnic groups, as defined by a common culture). In ideal form, they are a people ruling themselves. But in reality, they are always a compromise between different peoples and between the principle of ethnic self-government and the principles of a modern political system. We can begin to understand the complexity of the nation-state by examining early postcolonial political history.

Writing in the late 1960s, the anthropologist Clifford Geertz (1973) described the disappointments of the early nationalist leaders who were attempting to construct new states. These leaders, Nehru, Nasar, Sukarno, and others, discovered quickly that imagining a new nation was a good deal easier than constructing one (Geertz 1973, 235). Difficulties included the internal struggles between new elite and old, the failure to deal effectively with social problems, the discovery that political freedom had not bought economic freedom from the West, and, most significantly, a chronic difficulty with "the definition, creation, and solidification of a viable collective identity" (Geertz 1973, 238).

As long as oppressive colonial rulers were in place, national unity was a splendid and seemingly achievable goal. But as soon as freedom was obtained, the intractable problem of precisely *who* was meant by "we, the people" raised its ugly head. Regional, ethnic, tribal, caste, and class loyalties needed to be superceded with a national identity:

> The first, formative stage of nationalism consisted essentially of confronting the dense assemblage of cultural, racial, local, and linguistic categories of self-identification and social loyalty that centuries of uninstructed history had produced with a simple, abstract, deliberately constructed, and almost painfully self-conscious concept of political ethnicity—a proper "nationality" in the modern manner. (Geertz 1973, 239)

By elevating unities and subjugating differences and by portraying themselves as representatives of one corporate identity, nationalist leaders tried to remain in power and to integrate their new nations at the same time. The backward notion was that "the nationalist would make the state, and the state would make the nation" (Geertz 1973, 240).

Geertz notes that the nationalist project was doomed from the start. Its philosophical base consisted of two opposing ideas or themes:[3] (1) that the new states were legitimized by the purported common roots of their citizens in a primordial past, a notion that Geertz describes as "the indigenous way of life," or *essentialism*, and (2) that the new states were the product of a bright new era of modern political principles, a notion that he describes as "the spirit of the age," or *epochalism* (1973, 243). "There is no new state," said Geertz, "in which both these themes . . . are not present; few in which they are not thoroughly entangled with one another; and only a small, incompletely decolonized minority in which the tension between them is not invading every aspect of national life from language choice to foreign policy" (1973, 241).

Essentialism: Essentialism, also called primordialism, refers to a conflation of cultural, geographic, and racial features done to construct a defined sense of ethnicity. The history of the Hindutva movement in India illustrates an attempt to build a nation on essentialist principles. In 1923, V. D. Savarkar, while in a British prison for political insurgency, wrote a book titled *Hindutva* (Hindu-ness), which captured the imagination of the incipient, radical nationalist fringe. In the book, Savarkar used the method and tone of historical scholarship to establish a perfect equation among the Hindu religion, the Sanskrit-descended languages, the Aryan-descended peoples, and the territory of India. India is the primordial holy land of the Hindus:

> We Hindus are bound together not only by the tie of the love we bear to a common fatherland and by the common blood that courses through our veins and keeps our hearts throbbing and our affections warm, but also by the tie of the common homage we pay to our great civilization—our Hindu culture, which could not be better rendered than by the word Sanskriti suggestive as it is of that language, Sanskrit, which has been the chosen means of expression and preservation of that culture, of all that was best and worth-preserving in the history of our race. We are one because we are a nation, a race and own a common Sanskriti (civilization). (1999, 57)

3. Geertz (1973, 243ff.) makes it clear that these "themes" are not merely opposing ideologies but conflicting social processes that, taken together, constitute the world's current historical circumstance. Social and political structures are formed, altered, and destroyed with ideological change as "a dimension of that process itself" (1973, 244).

Savarkar draws lines around the *ethnos* very explicitly. The Jains, the Sikhs, and even the Buddhists are incorporated as "Hindus" and therefore patriots. The Christians and the Muslims are excluded because their holy lands are elsewhere—in Arabia and Palestine. They cannot be considered fully Indian (the true gloss for Savakar's *Hindu*) because "their love is divided" (Savarkar 1999, 70), despite the fact that they have "Hindu blood in their veins" (Savarkar 1999, 57). Therefore, those Aryan-descended, Sanskritic-language-speaking peoples of the country who are Christian or Muslim have betrayed their own past and their own people. Only Hindus are true Indians, and Indians must be Hindus.[4]

In his lifetime, Savarkar was a member of a movement so radical that even the nationalists considered it criminal. Mahatma Gandhi's assassin had been a friend and disciple of Savarkar. Hence, Savarkar and others like him were repeatedly imprisoned, not only by the British but later by the postindependence government. For nearly half a century, Nehru's vision of a secular, socialist country prevailed in the central government of India. But beneath the political surface, extreme Hindu nationalism continued to grow at the popular level, especially among the middle and high castes. By now, Savarkar has become the patron saint of a movement whose stated motto is "Hindustan (India) is for the Hindus." His book is widely read, and his portrait appears on posters, pamphlets, and in household picture frames across the country. Funds from wealthy expatriate Hindus are flowing in, and many respectable educated people have joined at one level of involvement or another. In 1998, the Bharatiya Janata Party, which espouses a somewhat moderated Hindutva, won election to central government to the surprise and dismay of many observers. It narrowly lost the election of 2004 but continues as the primary opposition party, popular with an increasingly vast majority of middle-class Hindus both inside and outside the country.[5]

Essentialism has tremendous power to motivate people to political action. Such power can be harnessed in the creation of a nation-state but can just as easily thereafter threaten to destroy it. Geertz states:

> Economic or class or intellectual disaffection threatens revolution, but disaffection based on race, language, or culture threatens partition, irredentism, or merger, a redrawing of the very limits of the state, a new definition of its domain. Civil discontent finds its natural outlet in the

4. Savarkar establishes the equation between Hindu and India at the outset by tracing the roots of both words back to the Sanskrit *Sindhu*, or "river," referring to the Indus River, where the earliest Aryans encountered an existing civilization, conquered it, and established themselves on the subcontinent.
5. For an encyclopedic account of the rise of Hindu nationalism, see Jaffrelot (1996).

seizing, legally or illegally, of the state apparatus. Primordial discontent strives more deeply and is satisfied less easily. If severe enough, it wants not just Sukarno's or Nehru's or Moulay Hasan's head, it wants Indonesia's or India's or Morocco's. (1973, 261)

It is the sense of firstness, of being fundamental and therefore un-changeable, that gives primordialism its power to produce the cultivated mass hysteria of Hindu nationalism in India, of Hutu or Tutsi Power in Rwanda, or, for that matter, of Nazi pride in Germany.

Yet the features that identify primordial attachments—race, language, culture, and territory—are far from immutable: Race has been shown to be socially constructed;[6] languages exist in a constant state of flux, lending and borrowing terms and changing to accommodate linguistic needs; cultural traditions are sometimes invented on the spot for clear purpose; and territorial lines, of course, are subject to shifts resulting from annexation and war. Furthermore, the boundaries of one primordial feature do not coincide with the others: Languages cross state bound-aries, the purported races are divided by cultures, territories contain a multiplicity of languages, and so forth. It is virtually impossible to match up racial, linguistic, and cultural boundaries with those of a state's territorial lines.

In truth, the lines of the modern nation-states are hardly the result of primordial developments. Throughout Africa, Latin America, and Asia, territorial boundaries are still in existence that were once the compro-mises of Europeans whose primary rivalry was not with the rest of the world but with one another. Indigenous ethnic groups were variously split and lumped together to form the empires of England, Germany, France, Belgium, Spain, and Portugal. Political structures and forms of leadership, both within and between ethnic groups, were altered as the Europeans endeavored to administer their territories cheaply and productively. Furthermore, developments in political ideology in Europe, transmitted to the colonies through the educational system, provided the basic framework of government for the new nations. Few early national-ists were interested in returning to their own feudal pasts or in redrawing the lines of states to match ethnic realities. Most were captivated by the high ideals of freedom and democracy, which they hoped to make full realities in their own contexts. Dadabhai Naoroji, for instance, remem-bered as "the architect of Indian nationalism" (Hay 1988, 87), credited the British with having provided for India:

6. Geneticists report that there are no clear boundary lines between populations of human beings such as might identify races, nor have there ever been in the past (Cavalli-Sforza, Menozzi, and Piazza 1994; Gould 1996; Templeton 1999).

Peace and Order. Freedom of speech and liberty of the press. Higher
political knowledge and aspirations. Improvement of government in the
native States. Security of life and property. Freedom from oppression
caused by the caprice or avarice of despotic rulers, and from devastation
by war. Equal justice between man and man (sometimes vitiated by partial-
ity to Europeans). Services of highly educated administrators, who have
achieved the above-mentioned good results. (1988, 89)

So when the Europeans departed, two things remained as a legacy to
the new nations: their territorial lines and their conceptions of good
government.

Epochalism: Geertz defines *epochalism* as "the general outlines of
the history of our time, and in particular to what one takes to be the
overall direction and significance of that history" (1973, 240). He does
not give further specifics, but we may infer that he means the modern
conception of the nation-state, which is characterized by self-rule (vs.
foreign rule), religious freedom, democracy, egalitarian justice, territori-
ally based citizenship, and ethnic pluralism. Epochalism, then, derives
from a worldwide consensus on what constitutes good government, and,
as such, it comes to any one nation from the outside. Democracy, for
instance, carries such legitimacy that even dictators have to hold peri-
odic pseudo-elections. The Islamic marriage of religion with the state is
disapproved of in most corners of the globe, even by many Muslims. In
general, human progress and the future, rather than tradition or the past,
are valued. Hence, though epochalism is a principle in the construction
of the nation-state, it represents a set of universal values.

Perhaps Marxism best illustrates the epochalist theme. Marxism projects a future utopia that, in addition to being completely equitable, will
be culture-free, or homogenous. The primordial pasts of incorporated
peoples are obstacles to the establishment of that utopia. Parochialism
divides. Class consciousness unites across primordial boundaries and
even across state lines to the global level. So Marxism declares that it
will usher in the true worldwide democracy, as the proletariat rules in
everyone's interest. "All previous historical movements were movements
of minorities, or in the interests of minorities," declares the *Communist
Manifesto.* "The proletarian movement is the self-conscious, independent movement of the immense majority, in the interests of the immense
majority" (Marx 1988, 76). The reference here is to class, not ethnic,
minorities. But the principle holds that whatever divides working people
from one another plays into the hands of the elite, and whatever unites
them will bring the greater good of all. Hence, cultural differences have
no place in the communist vision of the good society.

Yet for all its powerful visions of the future, epochalism is a far weaker motivator to political action than is essentialism. Geertz notes that essentialism is "psychologically immediate but socially isolating," while epochalism is "socially deprovincializing but psychologically forced" (1973, 243). Hence, it has only been by the use of significant coercion, from massive propaganda campaigns to violent revolutions, that Marxist regimes have been able to create states at all. The primordial attachments within these states have had to be labeled "counter-revolutionary" and heavily repressed. In the end, the project has failed in the most prominent places, with states such as the Soviet Union disintegrating into primordial chunks.

Much scholarly work has been done on nationalism since Geertz first wrote on the subject. Benedict Anderson has identified a nation as an "imagined political community" (1991, 6), constructed in part by a process of highly selective remembering and forgetting (and even both at once!) (1991, 199ff.). Arjun Appadurai (1997) has led an entire movement in anthropology in the study of transnationalism, the maintenance of nationalist "communities of sentiment" across state boundaries. Still, identifying the interplay between the themes of essentialism and epochalism can yet be useful in the diagnosis of the national and international ills that afflict our time.

The Role of the Global Economy

On the face of it, it would appear that essentialism, in the form of ethnic nationalism, has won out over epochalism, in the form of Marxism and other utopian ideals, in the global political arena. But this view fails to take into account the significance of developments in the economic arena. The political breakup of colonialism and the rise of the new nation-states were not accompanied by a breakup of the economic order that colonialism had established. Under colonialism, raw materials and natural resources from Africa, Asia, and Latin America were being exchanged for the industrial products of Europe under terms of trade that were significantly advantageous to the latter. Europe was being enriched and its colonies impoverished, despite the much touted gains of infrastructure and "good" government in the colonies. After independence, new nation-states faced the difficult decision of whether to continue the international exchange dominated by the West or to attempt to protect themselves from it with policies of socialism and isolationism. The Marxist experiment was the grandest of the self-protection schemes. But it failed, as have most other attempts to isolate from the world capitalist order. So that order has been successful in progressively permeating the economic systems of the nations for over four hundred years and certainly shows no signs of abating now (Wallerstein 1979). It is characterized by an increasing flow of market-based trade; the elimination of local, regional, and national barriers to that trade; and, in general, the predominance of business concerns in the establishment and maintenance of international relations.

Despite its aura of pragmatism, the global capitalist order has a utopian vision of its own. That vision promises a time when poverty, oppression, and other social ills will be eliminated by the production of increasing amounts of wealth and by the provision of freedom from traditional constraints. Such constraints include everything from the social obligations of tradition-based societies to the political controls of communism, socialism, or even the regulated market economy. In the place of constraints, capitalism offers the market itself as the means to an ordered society. The market is an arena in which people may pursue their own interests. Freedom to act in one's own interest, it is said, will bring the common good.[7] Why should this seemingly illogical notion be the case? Because people who are free to pursue their own interests will be willing to work for their gains. That work will then benefit others through the production of commodities that are generally desired. If everyone has what he or she needs materially, then the real purpose of society is accomplished.

So deeply held is this depiction of reality that most people in market-based societies do not believe that a vision guiding the construction of the global economic order exists at all. They assume that the order is simply evolving, the natural course of human development, not an alternatively, or perhaps even arbitrarily, chosen direction. Ironically, then, the people who feel they are most free to choose as individuals do not believe they are choosing collectively among alternative futures at all. What is happening, and will happen, in the course of economic globalization is inevitable. Resistance is futile.[8]

7. This popularly held view is a gross simplification of Adam Smith's argument. In *The Theory of Moral Sentiments,* Smith makes it clear that he expects actors in the market to be constrained by a strong sense of conscience based on a natural concern for others. "How selfish soever man may be supposed," he writes, "there are evidently some principles in his nature, which interest him in the fortune of others, and render their happiness necessary to him, though he derives nothing from it, except the pleasure of seeing it. Of this kind is pity or compassion, the emotion which we feel for the misery of others, when we either see it, or are made to conceive it in a very lively manner. . . . The greatest ruffian, the most hardened violator of the laws of society, is not altogether without it" (1966, 3).

8. This last phrase is the watchword of the Borg in the science fiction series Star Trek. The Borg is a collectivity of formerly human automatons serving society with such mindless self-sacrifice that they together become a violent machine, assimilating other species and cultures. No doubt, the writers' depiction was originally intended to critique

Yet surely such a view ought to concern us greatly wherever it is found and for whatever purpose. Complete fatalism in the populace is always a dangerous state of affairs. The political theorist Yaron Ezrahi reminds us that "the most arbitrary powers in history always hid under the claims of some impersonal logic—God, the laws of nature, the laws of the market" (cited in Friedman 1999, 161). A vision that claims its own version of the future to be the inevitable outcome of an impersonal logic encourages people to collaborate with or capitulate to "arbitrary powers." No vision is more powerful to manipulate, in fact, than the one that claims simply to *be* reality.

In addition to a vision, market capitalism proposes certain values: private ownership of property as a motivator to work (and to invest); honesty and transparency in business practice as a matter of fair play; instrumental rationality making for decisions that promote efficiency; a competitive arena that permits newcomers to enter and benefits consumers with lower prices; noninterference of government authorities; segregation of private from public life lest families be overly influenced by market-style thought or business decisions be made to accommodate families; and above all else, an individualism that keeps the laboring population mobile for shifts in the employment needs of business and industry and that allows people to consume by personal choice.[9] Other values are not espoused that might mitigate the unchecked power of these, such as the communal sharing of wealth that has held together social units from families to villages to chiefdoms in traditional societies (Acheson 1989); constraints on consumption that remind people of the spiritual life and of their dependence on God; and leisure as rest, not laziness, giving opportunity to enjoy all that God has provided for us rather than that we have worked to attain.

In the matter of market values, we can see another way in which true freedom is absent in the global capitalist order. The values espoused by capitalism are not optional for people who wish to remain employed. Worldwide, few laborers can choose to work part-time or with flexible hours in the interest of being available to their families. Business owners with a propensity to rest are likely to lose out to the competition. And the slightest downturn in consumption threatens someone's (or some country's) livelihood. Market capitalism demands, in fact, a commitment to prioritize according to its own values: work over family, efficiency

---

communism, but I see a similar danger in the collective commitment to the capitalist enterprise.

9. In the film series *Millennium: Tribal Wisdom and the Modern World*, the anthropologist David Maybury-Lewis remarks, "Nothing else will produce a more stupefied boredom than talking about the consumer society. And nothing else will produce a more vicious anger than suggesting we change it."

over generosity, one's own business over one's neighbor's, and so forth. Failure to prioritize accordingly can result in consequences that threaten a viable life.

A depiction of reality (what is), a set of values (what ought to be), and a demand for commitment constitute a religion (Geertz 1973, 87ff.). And, in fact, like Marxism, market capitalism can be espoused with religious fervor. Roger Friedland and A. F. Robertson have suggested that capitalism has become "a modern secular religion" (1990, 4), and David Korten remarks that it is "a fundamentalist religious faith. . . . To question its doctrine has become virtual heresy" (1995, 69). Market capitalism is the epochalist faith of our time.

Nationalism and the United States

In the United States, market capitalism approaches being a state religion. This is in no small part due to the role capitalism has played in the history of the country. By importing a population from Europe, annexing the natural resources of a vast land, establishing its own industry, and rejecting the colonial excise taxes early, the United States eventually produced not only enormous wealth but also the most powerful capitalist system in the world. In part, this was due to religious and cultural developments that provided a work-and-save ethic and promoted creativity and investment (Weber 1976). In part, it was due to the nation's commitment to political democracy, which promoted cooperative effort for common gain. The French sociologist Alexis de Tocqueville, who studied Anglo-Americans in the middle of the nineteenth century, wrote:

> The United States of America have only been emancipated for half a century from the state of colonial dependence in which they stood to Great Britain; the number of large fortunes there is small, and capital is still scarce. Yet no people in the world has made such rapid progress in trade and manufactures as the Americans. . . . In the United States the greatest undertakings and speculations are executed without difficulty, because the whole population is engaged in productive industry, and because the poorest as well as the most opulent members of the commonwealth are ready to combine their efforts for these purposes. (2000, 687)

Anglo-Americans had cut their primordial ties to Europe and were captivated by their own vision of the future. Generations of immigrants traded in their ethnicities and set themselves to work hard to attain the bright material future promised by democratic capitalism. Essentialism was abandoned, and a nation was built on the epochalist vision of the American Dream.

Yet not all Americans joined the project freely. It is in the nature of epochalism to coerce those who will not relinquish their primordial roots. Anglo-American expansion first necessitated the removal of the Native American peoples. According to one estimate, only 5 percent of the original population of the Americas survived the onslaught of guns and diseases (especially the latter) brought by the Europeans (Diamond 2003, 145). Those Native Americans who remained alive were first forced into reeducation programs and then corralled into reservations, separate microeconomies without sufficient resources. African Americans were forcibly imported to the country for clear economic purpose. Slave labor was thought so vital to the system that disagreement nearly split the country when the international antislavery movement reached it from Europe. Post-slavery, African Americans were first segregated out and then reluctantly admitted to the larger society, conditional upon their acceptance of the culture and the values of the American Dream and the abandonment of their own ruined pasts.

On the international front, the country oscillated between policies of military intervention and isolation. In good times, it refrained from military solutions and spread abroad instead the economic development that Americans so optimistically felt would bring the American Dream to the rest of the world. In bad times, it intervened freely and coercively, such as in Latin America, to secure political alignment and beneficial terms of trade. The Cold War produced the greatest threat to the country. It also produced the most vigorous response, as the United States made loans, sold arms, and intervened directly to defend capitalism against communism around the world. In the end, one epochalist vision was defeated, and the other, rooted deeply in the American nation, claimed victory. The United States withdrew its money and its military support from dozens of countries around the world and lapsed back into international complacency.

The United States is the Rome of our time. It is a wealthy and powerful nation built on enlightened principles of government and civil society. And as with the Roman Empire (or the colonial empires, for that matter), the United States has been content to refrain from the use of direct force when trade relations with other countries were strong and beneficial. It is always cost effective to allow indigenous political systems to administer their own people, as long as they are cooperative. But now, with the strange admixture of heightened fear, new global awareness, and enhanced curiosity about others that ordinary Americans are experiencing since the events of September 11, 2001, it is doubtful that the United States will continue its policy of international laissez-faire. The invasion of Afghanistan and then Iraq has been followed with threats to invade yet other countries that harbor terrorists. Countries that do not agree with U.S. policy are abandoned as friends, even vilified. Countries that do agree can expect political and material support. Globally, a new international order is being established, with every nation being defined by its relationship to the center, the United States.

Within the country, an emerging cultivated mass hysteria (based as always on a sense of external threat) is being combined dangerously with militarism. The United States currently has the largest military in the world by sixfold.[10] As the nation gears up for war upon war, the American people are divided between those who see divine purpose in the country's preeminent role in history and those who fear the misuse of such tremendous power. Disagreements such as these are not new at the global center. Roman citizens must surely have had them. Colonialists most certainly did.

Rendering unto Caesar

The church of Jesus Christ has outlasted every state and empire of the last two millennia, and it will outlast those present now.[11] If Christ does not return soon, the United States will rise and fall into historical oblivion, while the church will continue its advance toward the culmination of the kingdom. How are we, the disciples of Jesus Christ, to witness to that reality in "Rome"? How are we to avoid syncretizing the gospel at the very place in which it is the most dangerous—the center of global power? Surely this will be possible only with the witness of Christian people from other places. It will be possible to remain truly faithful to Christ in America only by listening carefully to sisters and brothers from elsewhere and by receiving with humble acceptance a theology from the whole church.

Paul Hiebert, an early member of the postcolonial wave of culturally sensitized missionaries, has played a major role as an anthropologist

10. According to the Central Intelligence Agency's World Factbook (http://www.cia .gov), the U.S. military budget for 2004 (actual spending) was an estimated $370.7 billion. That is six times as high as the budget for the next largest military in the world, which is China's at $60 billion. Anup Shah of Global Issues (http://www.globalissues.org) reports that the U.S. military requested a budget for 2005 of over $420 billion, or eight times as much as that of the next highest military.

11. Lesslie Newbigin states, "The Church is an entity which has outlasted many states, nations, and empires, and it will outlast those that exist today. . . . The Church can never settle down to being a voluntary society concerned merely with private and domestic affairs. It is bound to challenge in the name of the one Lord all the powers, ideologies, myths, assumptions, and worldviews which do not acknowledge him as Lord. If that involves conflict, trouble, and rejection, then we have the example of Jesus before us and his reminder that a servant is not greater than his master" (1989, 221).

and a missiologist in paving the way to a truly global church. Drawing on the insights of Henry Venn, who recognized even in the nineteenth century the need for autonomy in the churches away from the centers of power, Hiebert has highlighted the importance of valuing the voice of the indigenous church. To Venn's three selves of the mature local church—self-propagating, self-supporting, and self-governing—he has added self-theologizing (Hiebert 1985, 194).

> Most mission movements have led to theological crises. Three or four generations after a church is planted in a new culture, local theologians arise and struggle with the question of how the gospel relates to their cultural traditions. How can they express the Good News in terms the people understand, and yet retain its prophetic message? In answer to these questions they develop new theologies. Today, for instance, we hear of Latin American theology, African theology, and Indian theology. . . . This proliferation of theologies in different historical and cultural settings raises important issues about the nature of theology. (Hiebert 1985, 196)

The theologies of different times and places emerge from different circumstances and are valuable for the penetrating and practical solutions they offer to Christians attempting to faithfully follow their Lord.

Hiebert reminds us that local theologies are never the full equivalent of the truthfulness of the Bible (1985, 197). All theologies are flawed by human sinfulness. Yet in their very diversity, we can see the various aspects of God's truth. This is not to say that there is no core to the Christian faith. Hiebert distinguishes between Theology (with a capital letter)—that which holds true for all Christians, such as the doctrines of creation, sin, and redemption—and theology (with a small letter), that which is contextualized (1985, 198). The best contextualization, as Hiebert describes in a later work, is based on a philosophy of critical realism, which relates text (the Bible) to context (culture) through the use of symbols and models of reality that are relevant to the particular place and time (1999, 99).

The first value of a critically contextualized theology is to the people who formulate it. Indigenous theologies allow the gospel to become real to people, just as vernacular translations of the Bible "warm the heart." The focus is at home. The second value, though, is to those in the church elsewhere. The critically contextualized theology of one place can be a benefit to those in other places because of the witness it provides from outside. Such a witness is often a challenging one. And especially when churches from elsewhere witness to the center of power, the warning against syncretism with that power is most valuable. Unfortunately, historically, the churches at the center have found it difficult to shed the false sense of confidence they receive from their cultures and to really listen to their Christian brothers and sisters from less powerful places. Yet such critique can almost literally be the saving grace of a church at the center. Hence, in the present time, it is the American church that needs most to listen to the theological critique coming to it from the church worldwide.

One such critique comes from the Scottish missiologist Andrew Walls. Walls describes American self-theologizing as having produced

> vigorous expansionism; readiness of invention; a willingness to make the fullest use of contemporary technology; finance, organization, and business methods; a mental separation of the spiritual and the political realms combined with a conviction of the superlative excellence, if not the universal relevance, of the historic constitution and values of the nation; and an approach to theology, evangelism, and church life in terms of addressing problems and finding solutions. (1996, 234)

American theological thinking is pervaded by the expansionist business values that come to it from the history of the nation. Walls reminds us that such a theology (small *t*) does not prevent God from working through Americans to bear witness to the gospel of the risen Christ. Americans have sent out many good missionaries, and American theology has revitalized theologies elsewhere by its enthusiasm (Walls 1996, 236). But it is important that the peculiar characteristics of American theology not be universalized or, in Hiebert's terms, be made part of the Theology of the church rather than a theology from America. Put simply, American Christians must not fail to be Christians first and Americans second.

Litmus tests are not hard to find. In March 2003, the United States ignored the recommendation of the United Nations and invaded Iraq. A Gallup poll done just before the invasion revealed that 63 percent of American Christians, defined by those who attend church weekly, supported the invasion—a *greater* percentage than the general populace (59 percent).[12] This was no doubt in part the result of a general resurgence of civil religion that occurred after September 11, 2001. Over 80 percent of Americans report that they are Christians. Many nonchurchgoing Americans believe that God has specially blessed the United States, that the country is a chosen nation, destined to be a light to the rest of the world, and that patriotism is a sacred duty. The American characteristic of expansionism, when combined with civil religion, becomes a call to salvific intervention, purportedly on the side of justice but frequently with covert self-protective and economic purpose. And in the face of a

12. All statistics in this paragraph are from Gallup surveys (http://www.gallup .com).

perceived external threat, such civil religion can very quickly produce a cultivated mass hysteria that results in violent action.

How might things have been different if the American church had listened first to the rest of the body of Christ, the global church, and only secondarily to its own government? C. René Padilla and Lindy Scott have published a detailed account of the reaction of the Latin American church to the U.S. invasion of Iraq. The authors state that "the overwhelming majority of Latin American churches that took a public position regarding the war strongly denounced it, and they based their denunciations primarily on moral grounds" (2004, 12–13). This included the Council of Latin American Churches (of the World Council of Churches), the Venezuelan Evangelical Pentecostal Union, the Latin American Theological Fraternity, the Baptist World Alliance, and many other Christian organizations from across the theological and denominational spectrums. The war was variously termed illegal, immoral, and inhumane and a great sin. There was no lack of a prophetic voice calling American Christians to an allegiance higher than that of their government at the time.

Rendering unto God

Most Christians affirm that the government is an institution ordained by God. Certainly the church has always acknowledged the role of the state in protecting people, both internally and externally, from the effects of rampant sinfulness. Yet no sector of the church has ever suggested that an *uncritical* allegiance be given to any government. Luis Lugo, himself a Reformed theologian, demonstrates this by returning to the passage of Scripture most commonly cited in support of obedience to government, Jesus' statement that we should "render to Caesar the things that are Caesar's, and to God the things that are God's" (Mark 12:17 RSV).

Lugo begins by reminding us that Jesus made this statement under circumstances of threat. The Pharisees were trying to trap him between the claims of the Roman government to divine authority and the claims of the Zealots to anarchic freedom. Hence, Jesus' answer was subtle, paradoxical, and "elliptical, almost to the point of being evasive" (Lugo 1996, 2). Far from presenting a magnum opus on the subject of church and state, Jesus was eluding his enemies at the time. Readers of the passage who forget this political context will take the statement at face value and may be inclined to think that a separation of spheres, political and religious, is indicated. And we may remember here that Walls identifies this separation as a core element in the expression of American Christianity (1996, 232, 234). Hence, American Christians are uniquely inclined to think that the passage frees them to keep the government out of the church and to relinquish the church's authority when it is time to serve the government.

But, says Lugo, a separation of spheres is not what Jesus was indicating. To make his point, Jesus requested a coin, pointed to the image on it, and suggested it be given back to its owner. Coins, in the image of Caesar, belong to Caesar. But people, in the image of God, belong to God. There is no separation of spheres. There is a priority of ownership:

> The purpose of Jesus' "rather cryptic answer" is: to negate Caesar's claims to absolute authority, not to mention divinity, as *pontifex maximus,* and to undercut the essentially anarchist logic of the Zealots' argument that since God has exclusive rights over his people, the claims of human government are illegitimate. . . . While Jesus clearly intends to affirm his followers' obligations to the state, even a pagan state, the main thrust of his statement is to underscore the fact that these obligations are rooted not in the presumed ultimacy or autonomy of human political institutions but in the absolute sovereignty of God, the creator and sustainer of all things. (Lugo 1996, 4–5)

The state may own its purposes, then, but it is itself owned by God. Hence, Christian people may obey the state insofar as it is functioning as it should as a human institution under God's authority. But the state has no claim to a Christian's ultimate allegiance, which belongs to God alone.

As I have already mentioned, states are rarely if ever willing to abide by this limitation. The history of the church shows that even Jesus' balanced approach is threatening to governments. The church was persecuted in the early centuries because it had introduced "a competing sovereignty credo ('Jesus is Lord'), one that placed it in radical opposition to the claims of absolute state sovereignty ('Augustus the Divine'), the core principle of Caesarism" (Lugo 1996, 5). Even under Christendom, the rivalry between king and pope was never settled. Now, nation-states will tolerate religious affiliation only as long as it remains subordinated to citizenship. Under the influence of its fallen condition, the state is simply not willing to remain truly "under God."

Hence, the American church is going to have to choose. Will it follow Caesar to victory or Jesus to martyrdom? But it must not make this decision alone. The churches from elsewhere must assist by providing theological critique from the outside. This will not be easy for either party. With the United States at the center of global power, Americans are given a false sense of confidence in their own perspective, and Christians from elsewhere have an equally false hesitancy to challenge that confidence. How are we to circumvent this penetration of the world's ways of thinking into our consciousnesses? Surely, it is by remembering our common redemption in Christ. Those with worldly power must remember their spiritual and moral powerlessness apart from Christ, and those without worldly power must remember the spiritual and moral power they are given by Christ. Christians from elsewhere must take a compassionate interest in whether their American brothers and sisters go astray. Such international Christians must be willing to face resistance and conflict in their encounter with Americans, remembering always that evil influence can blind the minds and hearts of any of God's people. Yet when the warning comes, the onus will be on Americans themselves to turn back to God and not to rely on their own strength, as Israel was invited to do by the prophets.

Political realities are not external to the church's concerns. It is important that we as Christians understand them. Such understanding is valuable in assisting us in subordinating our political structures, ideologies, and motivations to our allegiance to Christ. The church is incarnated into the political world as Jesus was into flesh. Yet true and lasting power resides not in the state but in the body of Christ and in its ability to transform individuals, groups, and societies as part of God's kingdom work. Global theologizing must be grounded in this simple fact.

12

Theological Implications of Globalizing Missions

JAMES E. PLUEDDEMANN

While globalization has had both negative and positive influences on the church, one of the blessings has been the worldwide expansion of missionary activity. We live in a most exciting era of mission history. Not only has the church of Jesus Christ expanded throughout the world, but many of the emerging churches have caught the vision for sending cross-cultural missionaries. The Pakistani missiologist Michael Nazir-Ali wrote a book in 1991 called *From Everywhere to Everywhere* (cf. Escobar 2003, 18). His thesis fifteen years ago was that the gospel no longer disseminates from only a few sending countries; it is crossing cultures from almost every country in the world. As the Lausanne Covenant suggests, "Missionaries should flow ever more freely from and to all six continents in a spirit of humble service" (par. 10).

This chapter reviews trends in emerging missions, looks at theological insights to be learned from emerging missions, and explores biblical insights on future structures for sending missionaries from everywhere to everywhere.[1]

1. Many attempts have been made to identify the church with roots in the West to distinguish it from the growing church in the rest of the world. I use the terms *established church* and *established mission agencies* to represent missions that grew out of the influence of Northern Europe and North America and the terms *emerging church* and *emerging*

Developments in Emerging Missions:
From Everywhere to Everywhere

About 95 percent of the world's people have a Bible or a New Testament, 99 percent can understand the *Jesus* film, and 99 percent can hear the gospel through radio in a language they can understand (Johnstone and Mandryk 2001). As peoples from every corner of the world hear and respond to God's plan of salvation, they are also hearing and responding to Christ's admonition, "As the Father has sent me, I am sending you" (John 20:21). Each of the five hundred Bible translations contains Christ's command to make disciples in all nations and to be witnesses in their own Jerusalem, Judea, Samaria, and the ends of the earth. It is no surprise that as the church emerges around the world, missionary activity also emerges. When emerging churches are taught to obey everything Jesus commanded, they also obey his command to make disciples in all nations. Mission activity should naturally emerge from obedient, emerging churches.

Africa

Worldwide missionary activity is expanding through informal migration and also through intentional mission agencies. Some of the largest churches in Europe have been planted and pastored by Africans. Mission agencies are rapidly expanding in Africa. Cross-cultural missionary zeal is especially notable in some of the poorer countries of the world such as the Congo and Ethiopia. Nigeria is an outstanding example of missionary fervor, with the Evangelical Missionary Society (EMS) of the Evangelical Churches of West Africa (ECWA) sending over twelve hundred cross-cultural missionaries. It is interesting to note that the mission agency, EMS, was founded in 1954, while the denomination, ECWA, was not legally registered until 1956. The Sudan Interior Mission (SIM), now known as Serving In Mission, helped to plant a mission agency before it helped to organize the denomination ECWA. Panya Baba is an influential Nigerian missionary statesman who directed EMS, Africa's largest indigenous mission society. He

---

mission agencies for the churches growing out of Asia, Africa, and Latin America. Such a distinction is not altogether accurate but is probably better than the terms *first world* and *third world* or *less-developed* and *more-developed* countries. While the term *majority world* is understood by missiologists, it is confusing to the general reader. The average person on the street wonders if *majority world* refers to wealth, population, or some other indicator. I am also aware that people seeking worship renewal for the church in the United States use the term *emerging church*, but the term is not clearly defined and so far is not descriptive of a worship style that is emerging worldwide.

helped to pioneer mission training in the interdenominational Nigeria
Evangelical Missions Association (NEMA) and helped to found the
Evangel Fellowship International Mission Association (EFIMA) made
up of all the mission agencies that grew out of the denominations that
SIM helped to plant (Calenberg 2000). Another pioneer in Nigerian
missions was the late Byang Kato. He fostered cross-cultural missions
in the Association of Evangelicals of Africa and gave a plenary address
at the Lausanne Congress on World Evangelization. His major work,
Theological Pitfalls in Africa (1975), provides a powerful theology of
missions (Bowers 2000).

Asia

Mission agencies have grown rapidly in Asia. India, Korea, Japan, and
the Philippines have been the most active cross-cultural mission-send-
ing nations. Many Asian mission agencies tend to focus on the 10/40
window[2] or may work cross-culturally within their own country. Most
are primarily funded from within Asia (Lee 2000). Korea is a powerful
example of how missionary passion grows out of spiritual awakening.
Two years after the first great awakening in Korea in 1907, the Presbyterian Church of Korea sent seven cross-cultural missionaries (Park
2000). The church in South Korea is a missionary church, sending more
missionaries today than any country other than the United States. The
explosive growth of Korean missions has led to the growth of missionary training schools.

Thousands of Indian missionaries are serving in over two hundred
indigenous mission agencies, and many partner with international mission organizations (Hedlund 2000). India has a long history in sending
missionaries. The Mar Thoma Syrian Evangelistic Association was organized in 1888, the Indian Missionary Society in 1903, and the National
Missionary Society in 1906. The India Evangelical Team and Friends
Missionary Prayer Band are significant mission agencies. India is sending
missionaries through denominational and interdenominational mission
agencies and is partnering with international agencies to send missionaries outside India (Athyal 2000). The Evangelical Church of Maraland in
India worked with the India Evangelical Mission to send a missionary
to Sudan with SIM (Serving In Mission). This missionary is now the
SIM director in Sudan. Asian missionaries are leaders not only in Asian
missions but also in international missions.

2. The 10/40 window represents the area of the world with the greatest need for
evangelism. The window forms a box 10 degrees north to 40 degrees north of the equator,
beginning off the coast of West Africa and moving eastward to the other side of Japan.

Latin America

The growth of evangelicalism in Latin America is having a powerful effect on world missions (Palomino 2005). As an outcome of revival in Chile, the Methodist Pentecostals sent missionaries to Argentina in 1919, and the Argentinean Baptists sent missionaries to Paraguay in 1925 (Escobar 2000). For many years, international mission agencies such as Wycliffe Bible Translators, Operation Mobilization, Youth With A Mission, and Latin America Mission have included Latin Americans in their agencies. Organizations such as the International Fellowship of Evangelical Students have encouraged missionary vision and have been influential in stimulating missions. The Ibero-American Missionary Co-operation (COMIBAM) has been a significant movement for promoting cross-cultural missions. The purpose of COMIBAM is "to glorify God in awakening and developing the missionary vision and action to all the nations in the local churches of Ibero-America, and to serve as a link of cooperation between the different missionary efforts" (Deiros 2000, 211). COMIBAM has influenced churches in Ibero-America through international congresses and through branches in Spanish- and Portuguese-speaking countries. COMIBAM has also been most helpful in advising international mission agencies on how to partner with indigenous Latin agencies.

Brazil has been a leader in emerging missions, being one of the first Latin countries to see itself not only as a mission field but also as a sending country. Antonio Barro and Ted Limpic (2000) suggest that when local pastors or evangelists are paid with foreign funds, these pastors see themselves as missionary-receiving churches and are slow to become missionary-sending churches. Indigenous missions must grow out of indigenous churches. In Brazil, indigenous missionary efforts began as early as 1907 with the Presbyterians sending a missionary to Portugal and the Baptists sending missionaries to Chile and Portugal. Faith missions began to grow rapidly in the 1960s as local churches began to host missions conferences. COMIBAM has played a significant role in stimulating missions in Brazil. Seventy-five percent of Brazilian missionaries are sent by mission agencies, with 25 percent sent by local churches. Brazil sends missionaries not only to neighboring and Portuguese-speaking countries but also to distant resistant people groups as well.

Stages of Emerging Missionary Activity

Emerging churches do not immediately or automatically begin to send missionaries to the ends of the earth. A study of Scripture and church history suggests that the typical response of local churches is to look inward and to neglect God's call to be a light to the nations.

Acts 1:8 can be seen as a possible model for stage development in missionary activity. Using this model, *Jerusalem* evangelism might entail sharing the gospel with family and friends. *Judea* evangelism might include witnessing to people of the same culture and language in nearby towns. *Samaria* missions might expand outreach to people of near but different cultures and languages. *Ends of the earth* missions take place outside a country's boundaries where missionaries learn another language and culture.

Stage 0: Receiving the Gospel

When the gospel is first introduced to a people group, people may struggle to understand the message, and when it is accepted, believers are often like newborn babes dependent on outside nurture. Newborn Christians are naturally dependent on those who brought them the gospel. There is nothing abnormal about newborn believers seeing themselves primarily as recipients of the gospel. A problem arises when they fail to grow in the faith and neglect the commission Christ gave. In spite of the growing emphasis on missions from everywhere to everywhere, it is quite possible that the dominant attitude of many emerging churches is an unhealthy dependency and lack of missionary vision. Joel Simbitti, a missiologist in Tanzania, writes that "the greatest missionary problem of the church in Africa . . . is lack of mission-mindedness in response to the Great Commission" (2003). Could it be that the cutting edge of mission strategy should be to challenge and assist emerging churches around the world to catch God's vision for the world?

Stage 1: Sharing the Gospel Locally (Jerusalem Evangelism)

When a people group comes to Christ, there should normally be a healthy response of wanting to share the good news with family and friends. Often entire families are so eager about their newfound faith that they cannot help but tell aunts, uncles, classmates, and neighbors. For example, the Ethiopian Kale Heywet Church has grown to over five thousand churches, not primarily through missionary influence but through new believers enthusiastically sharing the good news locally.

Stage 2: Evangelizing Near People Groups (Judea Evangelism)

When the gospel is enthusiastically accepted by people in a town or village, the natural response is to share the good news within the people group. In rural areas, families from neighboring towns walk a long distance to attend church. Eventually, people decide they do not need to walk so far to attend church, and they begin a church in their own town. Stories of exploding church growth in Nigeria and Ethiopia show that the gospel spreads from witness to near neighbors, to the multi-village markets, and through contacts with relatives in nearby towns. Such growth is usually spontaneous and seldom results from long-term planning.

Stage 3: Sending Missionaries to Cross-cultural People Groups (Samaria Missions)

A church that is grounded in the Bible and is obedient to the commands of Christ will have a passion to take the gospel to neighbors who might have traditionally been enemies. For example, the Gourma church in Burkina Faso caught the vision of Christ's commission and took the gospel to the Fulani people, traditional rivals of the Gourma. The church in Ethiopia began sending "barefoot evangelists" to neighboring people groups who had been hostile to their people group. At times, these missionaries were persecuted and even killed for their witness. But the Word of the Lord continued to spread through well-taught believers obedient to Scripture.

Stage 4: Sending Missionaries to Distant People Groups (Ends of the Earth Missions)

Possibly the most dramatic development in missions since Acts 2 is the expansion of worldwide, cross-cultural missions. No longer do Africans, Latins, and Asians reach out only to people who speak their own language. The enlarged vision for cross-cultural ministry is a healthy and hopeful sign for worldwide missions.

Every mature believer needs to be involved in some way in all four of these spheres of ministry. If we are called to serve within our own culture, we need to be prayerfully involved in supporting cross-cultural ministries. A healthy church in any people group will have some level of ministry in Jerusalem, Judea, Samaria, and the ends of the earth.

Theological Insights from Emerging Missions

The development of missions from emerging churches can provide valuable insights for established churches and missions. A fresh global perspective could bring renewal to worldwide missions.

1. *Modified models:* The expansion of mission activity in the emerging world does not seem to be the result of Western models for
   goal setting, long-range planning, and efficiency. Differences in
   approach may be related to culturally different ways of organizing
   reality. Much of the world is made up of "high-context" cultures,
   where communication is deeply embedded in present relationships
   and situations. The Western management paradigm more often
   involves "low-context" activity, where communication involves
   abstract principles, long-range planning, and written contracts
   (Hall 1976; Plueddemann 1991). While we should be thankful
   for the way God has used missionaries with a mind-set for long-
   range planning and objective goals, some missiologists from the
   emerging churches object to what they see as the Western management model and the cult of quantification (Escobar 2003, 79;
   Araujo 2000, 62–63). Western missiologists are also challenging a
   paradigm of control, predictability, and efficiency (Engel and Dyrness 2000; Plueddemann 1995; 2000). The growth of the emerging
   church is not so much the result of goal setting with logarithmic
   graph paper but instead comes from Bible teaching, discipleship,
   and the movement of the Holy Spirit. At the same time, many of
   the practical problems missionaries from emerging churches face
   result from a lack of planning and management. Both models are
   needed for ongoing growth and longevity.
2. *Money:* The emerging missions movement did not result from
   a massive infusion of funds from wealthy countries. There are
   stories of barefoot Ethiopian evangelists sent out by their local
   churches to neighboring people groups with astounding results.
   The Evangelical Churches of West Africa in Nigeria has sent out
   hundreds of farming evangelists to reach their Muslim neighbors
   to the north. House churches in China are sending missionaries as
   traders back along the Silk Road. In fact, it is possible that outside
   funding might hinder emerging missions by creating a receiving
   mentality rather than a vision of outreach. Barro and Limpic suggest that when emerging churches see themselves as objects of
   funding from more wealthy countries, they are slow to become
   involved in cross-cultural missions (2000). Several indigenous
   mission agencies in Asia have a policy of not accepting foreign
   funds for fear that hostile governments will look on their groups
   as an arm of Western imperialism. While healthy ways exist for
   established churches to assist emerging missions financially, a
   spirit of dependency will likely stifle missionary vision and make
   it difficult to form interdependent partnerships with international
   agencies.

3. *The Holy Spirit:* The dynamic movement of emerging missions com-
   pels us to affirm the work of the Holy Spirit in missions. Emerging
   missions are reminding established missions of the importance of
   spiritual warfare and spiritual gifts. The Holy Spirit is not tied to a
   five-year plan, and revival cannot be predicted. Close cooperation
   between charismatic and noncharismatic missions is needed, as
   charismatic missions stay true to Scripture and noncharismatic
   missionaries rediscover the power of the Holy Spirit and the unseen
   world.
4. *Bible translation:* One of the most significant factors in promoting
   world missions has been the translation of the Bible into hundreds
   of local languages. A crucial reason why the gospel is at home in
   every culture is because all people can discover God's revelation for
   themselves in their own cultural setting (Sanneh 2003). Because
   of Bible translation, the gospel is not a foreign implant. Emerging
   churches study the Bible in their own language and discover that
   Christ's commission is not just for foreign missionaries from the
   West but for all people. Yet just as false teaching has squelched
   a passion for missions in many Western churches, false teaching
   could kill a passion for making disciples among emerging missions.
   Both established and emerging missions must place a strong emphasis on the solid foundation of Scripture and radical obedience
   to its teaching.
5. *Wholistic ministry:* Both emerging and established missions have
   a strong record of wholistic ministries, but many of the emerging missions have a firsthand understanding of poverty, sickness,
   persecution, and injustice. Missionaries from emerging agencies
   may have a greater ability to approach missions from a wholistic
   rather than a dichotomistic perspective. Dichotomistic (or low-context) agencies tend to emphasize predetermined goals and preset
   job descriptions, while wholistic (high-context) agencies tend to
   place a greater emphasis on the present situation and unfolding
   opportunities. While most established mission agencies have a solid
   history of wholistic ministry, some dichotomistic relief and development agencies do almost no evangelism, and some dichotomistic
   church planting missions do little to meet physical needs. Such a
   distinction would not make sense to a wholistic missionary from
   an emerging mission agency. It is possible that emerging missions
   can remind us of the wholistic compassion of Jesus for the soul
   and the body, while established missions can make a contribution
   to the planning process.
6. *Sacrifice:* Emerging missions have often been birthed in suffering and sacrifice. They understand that doing missions involves a

high cost. Sudanese missionaries humble us with their vision for reaching people groups who have persecuted them. Evangelists in Bangladesh inspire us by their willingness to share the gospel under threat of death. Missionaries from South Korea serve around the world, knowing it will be almost impossible to integrate their children back into the Korean school system. Missionaries from Ghana to Muslim countries know that they will not have a system for evacuation if they become sick or if they need to flee political instability. Many missionaries from the emerging church come from countries with little political influence, which would become an issue should their missionaries get in trouble. Few missionaries from the West have had the experience of starting new churches while in prison, yet missionaries from Ethiopia to India have had these experiences.

7. *Prayer:* Though established mission agencies place a high priority on prayer, there is much more to be learned about prayer from emerging agencies. The Korean church is well known for its early morning prayer gatherings, which have become foundational to local and world outreach. When missionaries have almost no money, little political influence, and limited access to health care, prayer may well be a higher priority than for missionaries from wealthy countries with medical care and political influence. This may be why Ethiopian missionaries on a short-term mission to Pakistan spent the night in fasting and prayer while lying prostrate on the floor, weeping for the souls of Muslims.

8. *Organizational structures:* Missionaries sent from the emerging church tend to have multiple structures for missions. Migration with the explicit aim of sharing the gospel is becoming a more intentional strategy. Guest workers from such countries as the Philippines often have opportunities for spreading the gospel in Islamic countries (Pantoja, Tira, and Wan 2004). Political and economic refugees are having a significant impact on Europe. But one of the most interesting developments is the explosion of missionary-sending agencies from the emerging church. *Operation World* reports that over 50 percent of the world's mission agencies originate in Africa, Asia, and Latin America (Johnstone and Mandryk 2001).

While the number of mission agencies is growing in the emerging church, established agencies are facing criticism by some churches in North America. Some claim that mission agencies are a relic from ancient history that should be discarded as the world moves into a postmodern era. Is the idea of a mission agency biblical, or are mission agencies an indication that the local church is not fulfilling its missionary mandate? Are mission agencies integral to the task of globalizing missions, or are they scaffolding to be torn down as soon as possible?

In an email discussion, a missions pastor from a large American church described three approaches to missions. He identified the approaches as paradigm shifts. The first is the paradigm of sending missionaries for long-term, cross-cultural service, the second is sending money to nationals, and the third is church-to-church partnerships. He critiques the first paradigm of sending long-term missionaries as being expensive and ineffective. The second paradigm of sending money to nationals is less expensive and more effective, he says, but tends to deaden missions interest in the sending church. The third paradigm involves a longer-term commitment to mission field churches and involves sending project funds and regular short-term missionaries from the United States. He sees this third paradigm as the wave of the future. According to this missions pastor, sending long-term missionaries through agencies is not a paradigm for the future. His particular church feels that its primary missions obligation is to sponsor seminars that help churches in other cultures learn from this church's principles of success.

It is interesting to note that all three of the above approaches assume that the sending church is wealthy. Church-to-church partnerships work only if the initiating church is wealthy. It would be difficult for the church in Ethiopia to send hundreds of short-term missionaries to India or for the church in Bolivia to create church-to-church partnerships in Bangladesh. The globalization of world missions calls for sending structures that make it possible for the church anywhere in the world to play a vital role in fulfilling Christ's commission anywhere else in the world.

Theology of Mission Agencies

The church, the worldwide body of Christ, has two components, the local church and the apostolic team or mission agency. Both depend on each other and have complementary functions within the same body, and both are ordained by God. This chapter builds on what others have written about the relationship between church and mission (Chaplin 1998; Wilson 1989; Winter 1971).

The family of God, the entire community of saints, is God's agency of worldwide reconciliation. We are given authority to act on behalf of God to carry out his task in the world or to be his agency of reconciliation. Just as Israel was to be a priest to the nations (Exod. 19:4–6), so through Christ we are "a chosen people, a royal priesthood, a holy nation, a people belonging to God, that you may declare the praises of him who called you out of darkness into his wonderful light" (1 Pet. 2:9). The concept of agency is at the heart of the gospel and is seen in all of Scripture. In an important sense, all followers of Jesus are called to be members of his mission agency. All the people of God are called to be his agents, to be a light to the Gentiles, to make disciples in all nations, to be ambassadors of Christ to the world. Missions is not relegated to a few people with a special calling; it is for all who have been reconciled by Christ. But in a practical sense, the majority of Christians are called to stay in their own country and minister among their own people. When the Holy Spirit called Barnabas and Saul for an itinerant ministry, he did not call Simeon, Lucius, or Manaen (Acts 13:1–2). Most spiritually gifted persons were to have a local ministry even as they supported and encouraged the itinerant ministry. The Holy Spirit sent an apostolic team away from the local church at Antioch to have an itinerant cross-cultural ministry. This apostolic team was the mission agency used of the Holy Spirit to spread the message of reconciliation to the nations (Murphy 1976, 103–17; Severn 2000, 320–26).

While the entire body of Christ is given the task of world missions, it appears that the Holy Spirit made a distinction between the role of the local church and the role of the apostolic team. He called Barnabas and Saul to an itinerant cross-cultural mission. The apostolic team was the agency used of the Holy Spirit to carry out his nonlocal mission. The local church at Antioch had a primary role of ministering locally, while the apostolic team was given a complementary but distinct itinerant task within the body of Christ. The apostolic team was not called to administer local churches or to become one with the churches they planted. The team evangelized, taught, appointed elders, and moved on. At the same time, neither was the church in Antioch responsible for administering the apostolic team. Scripture seems to teach two distinct organizational functions within the church, local and itinerant. While there is overlap and interdependence between the two, the distinction between the apostolic team and the local church is real and important.

The Old Testament

Leadership roles in the Old Testament included the functions of prophet, priest, and king. The priests had the local function of taking care of the temple and the sacrifices. Together with their Levite tribe, they were assigned special cities and special duties. Kings were responsible for ruling the nation. Prophets had the dual function of speaking the Word of the Lord both locally and nonlocally. While kings had national boundaries and priests were to live in special cities, the prophets often roamed around Israel and traveled cross-culturally. Their prophetic words were not only for Israel but also for the nations. Amos traveled from Judea to Samaria. Jonah was a prophet to Nineveh. Elijah traveled to visit the schools of the prophets and had a ministry in Zarephath of Sidon. Elisha traveled with the company of the prophets and ministered to Naaman of Aram. Daniel ministered as a cross-cultural prophet while in exile in Babylon.

Prophets were called to speak both to Israel and to the nations. The prophets were given oracles for Babylon, Assyria, Moab, Damascus, Cush, Egypt, Edom, and Arabia. Isaiah prophesied, "Come near, you nations, and listen; pay attention, you peoples! Let the earth hear, and all that is in it, the world and all that comes out of it" (34:1). The entire book of Obadiah is a prophesy to Edom, and Nahum is a prophesy for Nineveh.

While prophets were God's messengers or agents to Israel, prophets were also assigned a ministry to the nations. Jeremiah was given a task: "See, today I appoint you over nations and kingdoms to uproot and tear down, to destroy and overthrow, to build and to plant" (1:10). Isaiah was given the dual job of ministering to Israel and to the nations: "It is too small a thing for you to be my servant to restore the tribes of Jacob and bring back those of Israel I have kept. I will also make you a light for the Gentiles, that you may bring my salvation to the ends of the earth" (49:6). Ezekiel, a prophet to the exiles, prophesied to the nations so that "they will know that I am the LORD their God" (28:26).

The tasks of the prophets included both to bring revival to Israel and to extend the kingdom of God beyond the borders of Israel, to be a light to the Gentiles. This does not mean that the role of the prophets was more important than that of the priests and kings, but one role was clearly local and the other included an itinerant extension of the rule of God.

The New Testament

A similar distinction is found in the New Testament. Deacons, elders, bishops, and overseers were responsible for ministry in a specific location, while apostles were the "sent ones," the messengers, with the primary task of traveling to extend the church in areas where there was no church. Apostles were responsible for planting and nurturing churches, but as soon as a church was begun, it was turned over to local elders and deacons. Apostles did not administer local churches but were sent from local churches to establish new churches. The functions of elder and apostle were complementary but distinct.

The word *apostle* is used in several ways in the New Testament. It is used for the twelve disciples or apostles. The twelve apostles had special authority in the early church with the tasks of prayer and teaching the Word. The Twelve were not given the task of the administration of local churches (Richards 1985, 60). But in a more generic sense, the word *apostle* is used in the New Testament for someone sent by one party to negotiate with another party. The word means "envoy, ambassador or messenger commissioned to carry out the instructions of the commissioning agent" (Rightmire 1996, 33–35). While Luke most often used the term *apostle* to mean the Twelve, Paul used the word *apostle* to include others who were sent with authority to be messengers of the risen Christ. Paul includes himself as an apostle along with Barnabas, Andronicus, and Junias. Apostles were itinerant messengers doing evangelism and teaching where the church had not yet been planted.

When the administration of the local church became too heavy, the apostles chose seven deacons who were full of the Holy Spirit and wisdom. The task of administration was turned over to the seven (Acts 6:1–6). Paul gave Timothy the qualifications for overseers and deacons (1 Tim. 3:1–16), who minister in "God's household, which is the church of the living God" (1 Tim. 3:15). Paul commanded Titus to appoint elders in every town and outlined the qualifications for being an elder (Titus 1:5–9). Elders had a responsibility to minister locally. Apostles were not responsible for local church administration but kept moving in an itinerant ministry. Deacons and elders were not responsible for administering these itinerant apostolic teams.

The book of Acts describes the expansion of the church from Jerusalem to Judea to Samaria and to the ends of the earth. There are suggestions in Acts that Jesus' final words before the ascension were not taken seriously by the apostles. The first seven chapters describe the early formation of the church, the need for administration, and the beginning of persecution. Luke reports that there were "God-fearing Jews from every nation under heaven" listening to Peter's sermon at Pentecost (Acts 2:5). But there are few indications of an intentional planned expansion into Samaria and beyond until persecution broke out in Jerusalem, scattering all except the apostles. It is interesting that, while the apostles remained in Jerusalem, the deacon Philip did the work of an apostle or sent one to Samaria and to the Ethiopian (Johnstone 1998, 46). Persecution and visions, not spontaneous outreach or intentional planning, were stimuli for cross-cultural missions. A crucial turning point comes in Acts 11:19–21:

> Now those who had been scattered by the persecution in connection with Stephen traveled as far as Phoenicia, Cyprus and Antioch, telling the message only to Jews. Some of them however, men from Cyprus and Cyrene, went to Antioch and began to speak to Greeks also, telling them the good

news about the Lord Jesus. The Lord's hand was with them, and a great number of people believed and turned to the Lord.

Spontaneous outreach to non-Jews began in a low-key manner, seemingly by accident and because of persecution. We do not even know the names of the first intentional missionaries to the Gentiles, but these sent ones began a chain reaction that changed the world. These men from Cyprus and Cyrene were the agents used of the Lord to intentionally take the good news to non-Jews.

While the New Testament contains other hints of missionary activity in the early church, we have little recorded information about other outreach. Tradition suggests that after Peter's miraculous escape from prison, he and the other eleven apostles left Jerusalem and became actively involved in reaching out to the ends of the earth. Eckhard Schnabel writes, "If this reconstruction is correct, then the striking fact emerges that the Twelve understood themselves not primarily as organizers or coordinators of the work of the church but rather as missionaries" (2004, 913).

Insights from Church History

For the first five hundred years, the church wrestled with heresy and sporadic persecution. It struggled to define the doctrine of the person of Christ and the relationship between church and state. While the established church became occupied with political concerns, a quiet revolution took place, at first without the permission of official leaders. Patrick founded missionary monasteries to establish the Celtic church in Ireland, and Nestorius gathered a missionary band that spread the gospel through Syria and Iran and to China and India. The church spread not through conquest but through apostolic teams or religious orders. Mark Noll writes, "The rise of monasticism was, after Christ's commission to his disciples, the most important—and in many ways the most beneficial—institutional event in the history of Christianity" (1997, 84). The early expansion of the church was pioneered by the monks of Patrick, Boniface, Cyril, Methodius, and Lull. "The missionary expansion of Christianity was unthinkable apart from the activity of monks" (Noll 1997, 99).

As the Western world discovered the rest of the world, missionary activity expanded rapidly through the religious orders of the Jesuits, the Franciscans, and the Capuchins. By the time of the death of Francis Xavier, Catholic Christianity had spread to India, Malaysia, Indonesia, and Japan. It is interesting to note that the age of discovery coincided with the Reformation and with the rapid expansion of the worldwide church. Yet it took 150 years for Protestant missions and 250 years for English-speaking Protestants to become involved systematically in world missions. Why did it take so long for the Protestant church to catch the vision for worldwide evangelism? Patrick Johnstone argues that a primary reason the Reformers did not become involved in world missions was because they dismantled the religious orders, the mission agencies (1998, 77). Could it be that when the Reformers dismantled the religious orders they dismantled the agency used of God for the task of world missions? Possibly the Protestant church lost its vision for world missions because it lost the agency used of God to fulfill Christ's commission. "In abolishing rather than reforming the monasteries and orders, the Reformers destroyed the only contemporary model for engaging in mission beyond the frontiers" (Dowsett 2001, 112). They did not understand the complementary roles of the local church and the mission agency.

As a result of revival, the Moravians established a mission movement and began intentionally to send missionaries to unreached people groups in 1727. Later, William Carey challenged the church with the Christian's obligation to use means to reach the heathen. He established a voluntary society to send missionaries, which became a model for hundreds of mission agencies. These mission agencies, both denominational and interdenominational, took on many of the characteristics of religious orders.

God has chosen both the local church and the mission agency to be interdependent partners in fulfilling Christ's commission to make disciples in Jerusalem and to the ends of the earth. Mission agencies build on the tradition of the prophets and apostles and follow the historical pattern of religious orders. When the distinction is confused, prophets and apostles take the role of priests and elders, or elders and priests seek to become apostles and elders. World missions will suffer if the local church loses a vision for missions, and the outreach of the local church will be stifled without the itinerant function of mission agencies.

Implications for the Future of Mission Agencies in a Globalizing World

We live in a most amazing era of missions. For the first time in two thousand years, cross-cultural missionaries have the potential of being sent from every country in the world. Most mission agencies are not ready for such a massive shift in focus and must change to become key players in a globalizing world. Traditional mission agencies need to make sure they do not get bogged down with the administration of churches they helped to plant, nor should they merge with these churches. Mission agencies will need to expand their focus from evangelism and church planting to mission-agency planting. Mission agencies must change organizational structures so they can partner with the mission agencies that grow out of the churches they helped to plant. The study of Scripture and church history would suggest that mission societies have the potential to adapt and move into a world of rapidly changing Christianity to become a dynamic structure that unites national mission agencies into a powerful international force for the kingdom of God.

There will be many economic, cultural, and psychological challenges for mission agencies as they move beyond their national limitations and become truly global. Since the church of Jesus Christ is made up of people from every language, people, and nation, shouldn't mission agencies also reflect that worldwide body of Christ?

Conclusion

- Our globalizing world has been influenced by technology and by economic and political systems, but it has also been greatly influenced by the worldwide growth of the church.
- As the church around the world continues to grow, so does the missionary impact of the emerging churches. Christian missionaries are now coming from everywhere and going to every country of the world.
- The gospel of the kingdom is being preached in the entire world, and new believers are catching the vision of fulfilling Christ's command to make disciples in all nations.
- Emerging missions teach us in new ways of the importance of the Holy Spirit, spiritual warfare, prayer, sacrifice, organizational models, Bible translation, and wholistic ministry.
- While short-term missions and church-to-church partnerships can do much to enhance the cause of Christ around the world, it is likely that apostolic teams or mission agencies will continue to be a crucial model for emerging missions.
- Churches and mission agencies must work together in harmony, with a deep appreciation for each other and a realization of the crucial significance of both.
- When a mission agency fuses with a church it helped to plant, it loses its distinctive prophetic and apostolic function.
- Mission agencies cannot exist without local churches. Mission agencies have a dual function: to plant churches where they do not yet exist and to be a blessing and a stimulus to sending churches.

- Local churches should not seek to administer apostolic teams but should partner with mission agencies as ambassadors to the world. It is difficult for missionaries to become a part of an apostolic team with members from many nations if they are administered only by a local sending church.
- For emerging and established missions to work together in true international partnership, both must be willing to change. As emerging missions move beyond nationalistic boundaries, established missions must be willing to modify their financial and administrative systems to become truly international.
- The distinction between established church and emerging church will eventually disappear. We look forward to the day when the entire body of Christ will overcome nationalistic boundaries, reaching out in unity to the entire world.
- We long for the day when "the earth will be filled with the knowledge of the glory of the LORD, as the waters cover the sea" (Hab. 2:14). Even so, come Lord Jesus.

13

Globalizing Theology and Theological Education

Lois McKinney Douglas

Not long ago, I turned in a grade for a supervised research project. This is an everyday event in the life of a professor; it would not usually provide an attention-raising lead for a chapter in a book. But this tutorial was different. I sent Tonica van der Meer's grade for a project she had completed in Brazil by email from the United States to the director of the Doctor of Missiology program of the Asia Graduate School of Theology (AGST) in the Philippines. Tonica is a Brazilian with cultural roots in the Netherlands. She completed a diploma in missions at All Nations Christian College in England and a master's degree in theology at the Baptist Theological Faculty in São Paulo and currently serves as director of a well-established missions training center in the state of Minas Gerais. While we were working together on her project, Tonica made several overnight bus trips to my home in the neighboring state of São Paulo. We also got together at professional meetings or during my visits to her campus. Email and telephone calls kept us connected during the intervals between these personal contacts.

The structure of the AGST program requires that students work with an in-country team of tutors who are responsible for various aspects of their dissertation preparation. I worked with Tonica on her literature review, which focused on missionaries in situations of crisis and suffering. This topic was far more than an abstract, academic concern for her. She had lived and served as a missionary alongside Angolan believers in the midst of the chaos and tragedy of a seemingly never-ending civil war. Our cognitive research tasks were intermingled with tears of pain and sorrow as we focused on the realities of a nation in turmoil.

The experience Tonica and I shared provides a microcosmic glimpse of global theological education. Africa, Asia, Europe, North America, and South America are all represented. Alternative modes of theological education are employed. Technology plays an important role. Most importantly, theological reflection extends beyond traditional categories to encompass global and contextual concerns—in this case, those related to crises and suffering.

The Globalization of Theological Education

To move beyond our microcosms toward a truly global view of theological education, a good starting place is to let our imaginations soar and to envision each of our planet's leadership development efforts as a light beaming up to an orbiting satellite and reflecting back to earth. Thousands upon thousands of focal points would be seen. Some would appear to be glowing by themselves, but if we examined them more closely, we would recognize a global interconnectedness among them. They have become linked through expatriate missionaries and national leaders who have studied abroad. Faculty and student exchange programs and other short-term and longer-term intercultural experiences have had an impact. The explosion of information technology and the exponential increase in literature publication and distribution have also played their part. We must include the international networking that occurs through congresses, consultations, and professional associations. With all of these factors interacting among one another, the globalization of theological education is no surprise.

A descent from outer space to cyberspace confirms our observations. Among the many expressions of globalized theological education, the most visible are the two international agencies that provide communication and coordination among regional and national accrediting agencies. The World Conference of Associations of Theological Institutions, which has conciliar roots, serves twenty-two regional and national associations, including the Association of Theological Schools in the United States and Canada (ATS). The other international body, the International Council for Evangelical Theological Education (ICETE), helps eight regional associations, representing 852 theological institutions in 101 countries, to communicate and interconnect with one another. Their link to North America is the Association for Biblical Higher Education (ABHE) (see Ferris 2000a, 33; ICETE 2005).

The Quest for Institutional Renewal

From its inception, ICETE has seen its mission as extending beyond the coordination of regional agencies. The council has had an ongoing commitment to the renewal of theological education. In 1983, it adopted a *Manifesto on the Renewal of Evangelical Theological Education*, giving a united voice "to our longing and prayer for the renewal of evangelical theological education today—for a renewal in form and in substance, a renewal in vision and in power, and a renewal in commitment and in direction" (ICETE 1990, 1). The document affirmed twelve crucial components of worldwide theological education: contextualization, churchward orientation, strategic flexibility, theological grounding, continuous assessment, community life, integrated programs, servant molding, instructional variety, a Christian mind, equipping for growth, and cooperation among programs (ICETE 1990, 2–4).

Robert Ferris rightly points out that even though

the stirring rhetoric of the [ICETE] "Manifesto" has been grist for faculty discussion in many theological schools . . . educators must tap their own creativity to discern how advocated commitments can be implemented. As a result, in most nations theological schools and churches continue to await a renewal of ministry training that will yield an adequate supply of leaders equipped for effective ministry in church and society. (2000b, 945–46)

Two examples of creative regional efforts toward renewal in ministry training (one in Russia and the Ukraine and the other in the West) are described below (Charter 1997; Banks 1999).

In Russia and the Ukraine. Miriam Charter (1997) has examined issues related to the educational initiatives of three theological institutions developed through Western efforts among new Protestant churches in Russia and the Ukraine. Five concerns were identified by a panel of educators and explored through ethnographic interviews with faculties and students from these institutions. The first was a lack of long-term planning (Charter 1997, 122–23). Programs were being developed too hastily. There was competition for Western funds and students. Territoriality and intolerance were evidenced. A nucleus of clergy and laypersons who grasped the importance of time-consuming, in-depth reflection on spiritual formation, theological competence, and ministry skills was missing.

The second issue addressed by the study was the lack of literature (Charter 1997, 136). Theological education was seen as heavily dependent on Western-based texts. The theological content and vocabulary had been influenced by Western teachers and missionaries, some of whom were still learning the language. Concerns were raised that, if the situation continued over time, the development of truly indigenous theologies and churches would be threatened.

Third, the panel identified a lack of national theologians and faculty as an issue of concern (Charter 1997, 150–51). Even though students preferred to be taught by national professors, they recognized that the quality of instruction needed to be improved. Dependence on Western professors or national professors trained in the West had perpetuated noncontextual forms of theological education. Few of the national professors had both academic credentials and experience in ministry. Opportunities were needed for ministers to pursue academic programs without having to leave their country.

An issue was also raised in relation to the impact of Western influence on the curriculum (Charter 1997, 205–7). Russians, throughout their history, had experienced a succession of forcibly imposed, nonindigenous educational systems. Now a love-hate relationship with the West had developed that included a fascination with Western education. The positive and negative impacts of these cultural importations on the nature and processes of educating and theologizing within these institutional contexts needed to be assessed.

The last issue raised regarded the lack of ownership by the church of institutional theological education (Charter 1997, 221–23). Westerners were the initiating force behind the development of the theological schools in this study, and from their inception, they had been largely supported with Western funds. Now the Westerners were withdrawing and saying that it was time for the Russian churches to take over. Understandably, the churches were unhappy.

In Western Seminaries. Robert Banks (1999) addresses similar concerns within Western seminaries. He observes that the current discussions in theological education revolve around two sets of issues. The first of these looks at means-and-ends questions: Does the institution have the resources it needs? Is it being well administered? Are faculty, staff, and students involved in decision-making processes? Are faculty and students able to give priority to their main responsibilities? Are faculty, staff, and trustee development programs in place? (1999, 10–11).

Banks's second set of issues, which he sees being addressed only intermittently, are related to the goals, contexts, ethos, and curricula of seminaries: How well is the seminary balancing spiritual formation, professional development, and academic excellence? Is it relating well to churches within its immediate and broader contexts? Has an atmosphere for intellectual and communal sharing been created? Does it extend to minorities? How well is the curriculum integrating theory, practice, and theology with contemporary issues? (1999, 10–11).

The second set of questions Banks raises above suggests the need for a missional alternative to traditional theological education. He points out that since the 1980s the debates in theological education—across mainline, evangelical, and Catholic traditions—have been shifting from largely operational issues toward theological discussions focused on the contextual realities of theological schools. Third world voices have entered this debate. They see Western models as fundamentally flawed and plead for more indigenous, culturally sensitive, and biblically oriented models of theological education. Banks listens to these voices and draws on their issues in these debates as he examines four current models of theological education and explores a missional alternative (1999, 10–11).

Banks first considers the *classical* model represented by Edward Farley, the Richard Neuhaus symposium, and two groups of feminist theologians. The model emphasizes theological formation that shapes theological thinking, moral and spiritual formation, and the conduct of ministry. Its primary concern is intellectual and moral processing of the Christian faith, and its focus is on cognitive wisdom (Banks 1999, 17–33, 142–44).

The second model, developed by Joseph Hough Jr., John Cobb Jr., and Max Stackhouse, is *vocational.* A focus on theological interpretation attempts to develop skills in relating the Christian tradition to contemporary issues, to influence personal identity and values, and to shape and define the practice of ministry. Its concern involves the reflective and practical goals of the Christian story, and its focus is on cognitive discernment (Banks 1999, 34–45, 142–44).

The *dialectical* model, developed by Charles Wood, David Kelsey, and Rebecca Chopp, is the third model. It stresses theological vision or practice that not only focuses on God but also affects vocational and social life. Its concern is Christian ethos, both mental and behavioral, and its focus is on cognitive insight (Banks 1999, 46–64, 142–44).

The fourth model, presented by George Schner and Richard Muller, is *confessional.* It emphasizes theological information that provides systematic shape to Christian beliefs and direction for personal growth and the practice of ministry. Its concern is the cognitive and ethical content of Christian revelation, and its focus is on acquiring cognitive knowledge (Banks 1999, 64–68, 142–44).

After comparing and contrasting these alternative models, Banks proposes a *missional* model of theological education. The focus here is on theological mission, with a unique emphasis on experiential partnership in ministry combined with interpretation of tradition, reflection on practice, and a strong spiritual and communal dimension. Its concern is informed and transforming service of the kingdom. The focus is on obedience in all its cognitive, practical, moral, and spiritual dimensions (1999, 144).

Banks goes on to identify some of the limitations of other models that the missional model attempts to correct. The classical model focuses on a disposition to act rather than on engaging in the action itself. The vocational model often provides reflection *on* ministry rather than reflective practice *within* ministry. Sometimes an emphasis on spiritual formation within theological education can create a close relationship with God and the seminary community but allow people to remain alongside rather than move within the painful and joyful realities of daily life (1999, 144–47).

Through his missional model, Banks attempts to overcome some of the limitations of the other models. He pleads for a more immediate connection between action and reflection and a more complex relationship between theory and practice (1999, 157–68). This is followed by a reconception of teaching that makes a strong case for theological education within the marketplace (1999, 169–86).

Theological Education by Extension. Banks's emphasis on theological education within the marketplace opens the door to a broader discussion of alternatives to traditional educational models. Among these is theological education by extension (TEE). The movement began in the early 1960s, when three Presbyterian missionaries in Guatemala, Ralph Winter, James Emery, and Ross Kinsler, made what was then a radical and innovative break with traditional theological education. Instead of bringing church leaders to a residential seminary to study, they took theological education to them in the context of their ministry. The timing was right; felt needs were met. The Guatemala experiment was heavily publicized throughout the missions world, and within a decade it had expanded into a global movement. I was personally involved in TEE during most of the 1970s and early 1980s, first as the executive secretary of the Brazilian TEE association (AETTE) and later as executive director of the EFMA/IFMA Committee to Assist Ministry Education Overseas (CAMEO).

In spite of inevitable mistakes and shortcomings, the TEE model was basically sound. Students reflected on self-instructional texts and other educational materials in the midst of their active ministries. During regular encounters, their reflection and action were integrated as professors and students shared their experiences. Regional and national gatherings were also held from time to time.

Today, over forty years later, often under other names and with many adaptations and mutations, TEE is still with us. In the 1970s, I accompanied and encouraged an Assemblies of God TEE program in Brazil during its founding and early growth stages. When I returned for a visit in 2004, this initial TEE effort had evolved into two distance education programs. The first is called EETAD (Escola de Educação Teológica das Assembléias de Deus) or BEST (Brazil Extension School of Theology). The second is FAETAD (Faculdade de Educação Teológica das Assembléias de Deus) or BAST (Brazil Advanced School of Theology).

EETAD currently has 18,300 Portuguese-speaking students throughout Brazil, Portugal, the United States, England, and Japan. Their curriculum is also used by extension schools in Angola and Mozambique. It is a Bible institute–level program. FAETAD has 1,000 students throughout Brazil and a handful in Portugal and the United States. It offers a bachelor in theology degree through extension. The programs serve students involved in both lay and professional ministry. Local extension campuses or study centers in churches enable students to interact with center leaders. Each extension campus is provided a small library that includes 110 reference books. Extension staffs, tutors, and students have access to a website where they are able to keep in touch with administrators and professors at the headquarters. Even though distance education continues to move ahead, EETAD and FAETAD are also facing a demand for residential programs. An eight-building campus has been developed, and on-site opportunities are now underway.

President Terry Johnson sees positive trends emerging in Brazilian distance education, such as growing numbers of computer literate persons and increasing global partnerships. He is concerned about the quality of many of the distance education programs that are proliferating. Some unfortunately have become "diploma factories." Many times the teaching materials are not written by educators, and their quality is very low (Johnson 2005).

Distance Education. Linda Cannell (1999) has provided a comprehensive literature review and critical evaluation of distance education (DE). She is encouraged by DE's emphases on interactivity, learning communities, and cognitive processing. Even though she is concerned about technology's strong link to distance education, she recognizes its value, especially in enabling international collaboration. She raises a series of questions that need to be addressed as we face the future:

What understandings of education will embrace both formal and nontraditional modes as a part of the whole enterprise?

How do we provide theological education for the whole people of God?

How do we serve the continuing professional development needs of our alumni and other ministry professionals?

What are the implications of conceiving of education not as preparation for some future ministry, but as continuing development in ministry?

How do we address issues of authority, power and elitism in higher education? (1999, 59–60)

Cannell concludes her discussion by emphasizing several important perspectives: Education is an art as well as a science. Students need to become increasingly responsible for their own learning; faculties are not the sole providers of knowledge. Education is a lifelong process; it does not consist of an abundance of degrees. Educational environments are flexible and negotiable; we must not allow ourselves to be locked into any one model (1999, 60).

Cannell's last point is especially relevant to global theological education. Efforts to educate for ministry require culturally and theologically appropriate models that are as diverse as the contexts in which they occur.

The Quest for a Globalized Theology for Theological Education

If theological education around the world is to experience renewal, focusing on operational issues will not be enough. Commitments must be reexamined in the light of fundamental beliefs and values. My own attempts at this kind of reflection have caused me to conclude that globalized theological education is rooted in *missio Dei*, celebrates spiritual formation, affirms the missional nature of the church, and emerges from hermeneutical communities. The discussion that follows expands on these affirmations.

Globalized Theological Education Is Rooted in Missio Dei

Since the early decades of the twentieth century, there has been a gradual shift toward an understanding of mission as *missio Dei* (God's mission). David Bosch (1991, 389–93) provides a historical perspective on this movement. Theologies of mission during the Enlightenment tended to create a triumphalistic blend of concerns with saving the heathen, bringing them the civilizing influences of the West, crusading for the expansion of the church, and transforming the world politically and socially into the kingdom of God (Bosch 1991, 389).

In 1931, at the Brandenburg Missionary Conference, a paper was read by Karl Barth in which he challenged the Enlightenment-influenced mission thinking of the day, reminding the participants that mission is the activity of God himself. The thoughts of Barth and others simmered for two decades until finally the full-blown concept of *missio Dei* surfaced at the International Missionary Council meeting in Willingen in 1952: Mission is derived from the nature of God; God sends the Son; the Son sends the Spirit; the Father, Son, and Spirit send the church into the world, not triumphalistically but in solidarity with the incarnate, crucified Christ (Bosch 1991, 389–90).

Affirming the mission of the Triune God as the foundation for a global theology will have a profound impact on our efforts to educate theologically and missiologically. Worship will no longer be just an add-on activity, such as a routine chapel service or a quick prayer at the beginning of a class. In the words of Kate Wilkinson's hymn, our desire will be that the mind of Christ will live in us (Phil. 2:5), the Word of God will dwell in our hearts (Col. 3:16), and his peace will rule our lives (Phil. 4:7) as we become worshiping theological communities (Brown and Norton 1995).

When *missio Dei* becomes the organizing principle for our curriculum, worship and scholarly reflection will be brought together. Old Testament studies will focus on the Triune God, who is calling out a people for himself, drawing the nations to himself, and preparing the world for the Messiah. In the New Testament, we will see God the Father sending his Son into the world and the Father and the Son sending the Holy Spirit, who empowers the church to be Christ's global witnesses. Church history will be seen as the history of God's mission through his church. The concept of *missio Dei* will help ministry-oriented courses to see teaching, preaching, evangelism, church planting, counseling, discipling, leadership development, and social action as *penultimate* activities through which we are participating in what God is doing in the world. His *ultimate* purpose through these missional efforts is to call out a people for himself so that someday voices from all nations, tribes, languages, and cultures will be joined in praise to him before the throne (Rev. 7:9–17).

Globalized Theological Education Celebrates Spiritual Formation

It is easy to miss the full impact of the global celebration before the throne (Rev. 7:9–17) if we see only the multitude and fail to focus on the spiritual transformation of the individual persons who are wearing robes washed white in the blood of the Lamb (vv. 9, 14) and waving palm branches (v. 9). Their voices are celebrating God's salvation (v. 10). They are serving him day and night in his temple. They are sheltered in his tent (v. 15). Their hunger, thirst, and tears are gone (vv. 16–17). Their earthly anguish and suffering in the midst of great tribulation were God's instruments for spiritual formation, which has prepared them to worship and enjoy him forever. Spiritual formation grows out of *missio Dei*, what God is doing in the world *and in the lives of individuals* through his church.

Dangers and Opportunities

When Richard Foster began writing on the topic in the late 1970s, the concept of spiritual formation was virtually unknown outside Roman Catholic circles. Today, few evangelical leaders have not heard the term. Conferences, seminars, and literature on spirituality abound. Foster observes that courses on spiritual formation within theological institutions have "proliferated like baby rabbits" (2003). They have crossed theological traditions and spread around the world.

In spite of its widespread acceptance, Foster is concerned that many individuals, churches, and theological institutions do not yet seem to understand what spiritual formation is all about. A pure focus on the spiritual growth of seminary students has often been clouded by the advantages these programs create in funding and accreditation efforts or by a kind of pride or arrogance related to what their schools are doing. He sees much of what is going on as faddish and derived from formulae (2003).

Dallas Willard voices his concern that, even within "Christian" spiritual formation, efforts can be lost or misdirected by the subtle influences of New Age or secular worldviews. Perhaps just as dangerously, spiritual formation can lose its transforming potential and become merely a new label for the old activities: "worship, hearing the word, community, quiet time, plus a new twist or two, such as spiritual direction" (n.d.).

Happily, in the midst of critiques, there is still much room for encouragement. Foster reminds us that

> the blazing light and life of Christian faithfulness overcame and supplanted all the "spiritualities" of Rome in the early centuries of the Christian era. The same can happen today . . . if we will 1) understand the absolute necessity of Spiritual Formation (no more optional discipleship), 2) make a firm intention to pursue it at all costs, 3) learn something of its means, and 4) faithfully practice it in daily life. (2003)

Foster goes on to identify three essential foci as we move forward: focusing on Jesus, focusing on Scripture, and focusing on spiritual disciplines. Renovaré, an organization growing out of the efforts and influence of Foster and others, is committed to implementing this kind of a balanced vision of the spiritual life and to developing spiritual formation groups in which the vision can be implemented (2003).

Other spiritual formation efforts have also emerged. One of these is the Spiritual Formation Forum (SFF), which has been seeking to

> [increase] collaboration among leaders in Christian ministries worldwide who are committed to biblically defined and Holy Spirit energized spiritual formation within and through their ministries. This ministry stimulates genuine spiritual formation in the various ministry arms of the church as a means of helping Christians fulfill their calling to be salt and light in the world through living a Christ-like life. The SFF sponsors spiritual formation discussion forums, articulates models of spiritual formation, provides training opportunities for ministry leaders, and encourages them to implement appropriate models in their spheres of ministry (e.g., in local churches, denominations, Christian colleges and seminaries, international ministries, soul care, campus ministry groups, and other para-church ministry organizations). (Spiritual Formation Forum 2003)

My personal spiritual journey has been encouraged through these efforts. I read Richard Foster's *Celebration of Discipline* shortly after it was published in 1978. Even though it rang true, I was too absorbed in my activistic, ministry-controlled lifestyle to allow God to change me. Later, in the early 1990s, both my missiological and spiritual journeys were transformed as I immersed myself simultaneously in David Bosch's *Transforming Mission* (1991) and readings in spiritual formation. Over the next several years, my love for God and my desire to worship him deepened. My husband, Ross Alan Douglas, and I attended the first Spiritual Formation Forum at Trinity Evangelical Divinity School in 1999. I was able to participate in the SFF in Dallas in 2001, and Ross and I were together again at the 2004 forum in Los Angeles, just three months before he went home to be with Jesus. While we lived in Brazil, we were part of an ongoing spirituality group led by Pastor Osmar Ludovico da Silva that focused on *lectio divina*. This shared journey is a precious memory of our marriage.

Common Threads

The literature on spiritual formation has identified common threads that need to be woven into our perspectives and practices of theological education.

In the first place, spiritual formation must be *defined by Scripture*. David Larsen (2001) has affirmed and expanded this theme by demonstrating that truly Christian spirituality is rooted in basic biblical doctrines related to God, the Trinity, Jesus, salvation, the church, and eschatological hope. Both within and beyond evangelical circles, there are tendencies toward subjectivity and an excessive focus on experience. A solid biblical base is sorely needed.

Dallas Willard emphasizes a second common thread of spiritual formation: It must be *transformed by Jesus Christ*. He defines spiritual formation as

> the process of transformation of the inmost dimension of the human being, the heart, which is the same as the spirit or will. It is being formed (really, transformed) in such a way that its natural expression comes to be the deeds of Christ done in the power of Christ. . . . [It] is the process through which the embodied/reflective will takes on the character of Christ's will. (n.d.)

Willard reminds us that the New Testament passages that outline progression in spiritual growth (Rom. 5:3–5; Col. 3:12–14; 2 Pet. 1:4–7) always conclude with *agape* (Willard n.d.). Seeing *agape* as the end point of spiritual formation lines up squarely with Jesus' emphasis on the Great Commandment (Mark 12:28–34). It moves us beyond our preoccupation with ourselves and our own spirituality toward a communal and global commitment to *agape*.

A third thread of concern in spiritual formation is that the process be *led by the Spirit*. The New Testament makes the crucial role of the Holy Spirit in individual lives, Christian communities, and global outreach abundantly clear. For many of our institutions, this affirmation will mean engaging in interdisciplinary scholarship across traditions and around the globe. In Brazil, spiritism is widespread in Roman Catholic popular religion and persists as a syncretistic practice within some evangelical circles. Many Asian believers continue to struggle with familial relationships and ancestor veneration. In North America and other parts of the world, issues related to spiritual gifts and spiritual warfare have become divisive. Even these kinds of debates and disagreements can become a part of our corporate spiritual formation when they are intermingled with *agape* and the worship of God. Martin Luther's magnificent hymn "A Mighty Fortress Is Our God," which grew out of suffering and persecution during the early Reformation movement, will keep reminding us that the battle belongs to Jesus Christ. One little word—his name—will fell the prince of darkness and a world full of devils. Our role is radical obedience—leaving family and possessions and even accepting martyrdom. Why? Because he must win the battle! His kingdom is forever!

Throughout this discussion, we have been assuming a fourth thread of concern related to spiritual formation: It must be *practiced in community*. The faculty of the Lutheran Theological Southern Seminary (Columbia,

South Carolina) has been especially incisive at this point. They define spiritual formation as the "intentional practice of the Christian faith, both corporate and individual, insofar as it seeks to build up Christian identity and nurture 'life in the Spirit' in the multiple dimensions of personal existence" (Reisz 2003, 30–31). The seminary's suggestions for fostering intentionality in the communal practice of spiritual formation include observing corporate times of prayer, quiet, and contemplation; integrating spiritual disciplines into courses (for example, *lectio divina* as a part of biblical courses); and the involvement of faculty, staff members, and students in spiritual direction (Reisz 2003, 37).

These kinds of emphases are in tune with what God wants to do through global theological communities. As people listen to God and respond to what he is doing in the world, they will break out of their ingrown preoccupation with themselves and their own needs. They will leave their parochialism, ethnocentrism, and isolationism behind them. Their love for God the Father, who sent his Son into the world, their commitment to Jesus Christ, who died for the sins of the world, and their confidence in the continuing work of the Holy Spirit will overflow into a global proclamation of the gospel and practice of Christian presence.

Relationships within communities committed to spiritual formation will grow out of interdependence. This concept is in sharp contrast with the radical independence I internalized during my Bible school days in the early 1950s. I was warned more than once that, when I was on the mission field, I would have to be my own pastor and be able to care for my own spiritual needs. Other missionaries would be too busy in ministry to take care of me; national Christians would expect me to take care of them. These expectations of self-sufficiency and going it alone were very much a part of the individualistic, modern, Western mission paradigm. Today, in stark contrast, agencies and churches that are responsible for member care are discovering exaggerated expectations of dependence and spiritual support on the part of some of the postmodern young people who find their way into missions. Either extreme can be unhealthy. The challenge theological education faces is to develop an interdependence in which individual spirituality is fostered through the practice of personal disciplines (solitude, silence, private prayer, meditation, and listening to God) within the context of caring, loving, nurturing communities.

Globalized Theological Education Affirms the Missional Nature of the Church

The inextricable link between a global theology and the missional nature of the church leaps out of the greetings and doxology that introduce the book of Revelation. Jesus Christ, who loves us, shed his own blood for our sins, rose from the dead, and rules over the kings of the earth, has made us (his church) a kingdom and priests to serve his Father. "To him be glory and power for ever and ever!" (Rev. 1:6). Jesus' reign is global. Eternal glory and power are ascribed to him. We are his people with a mission. We are his priests and servants, locally (e.g., in the seven churches) and globally (among the multitudes from every tribe and nation), both in historical situations (Rev. 2–3) and in the eschatological future (before the heavenly throne).

The relationship between missiology and ecclesiology has been recognized by both theologians and missiologists. Jürgen Moltmann sees the theology of mission as one of the strongest impulses toward the renewal of the theology of the church (Bosch 1991, 369). Lesslie Newbigin concurs. For him, the church's missionary dimension is manifested through the life of local churches that have become pliable, innovative, equipping, worshiping communities with intentional "points of concentration" on evangelism and work for justice and peace (Bosch 1991, 373).

David Bosch (1991) identifies several elements in a missional ecclesiology. The church is a pilgrim people, temporary residents who, in the here and now, are fleshing out God's future reign. The church is salt, light, and yeast; its focus is on helping and serving. As the people of God in the world, it is seeking truth, justice, and mercy in anticipation of Christ's kingdom. In the midst of its mission, the church lives with the creative tension of being *in* the world, integrally a part of the human community, and yet *different from* the world, maintaining a distinct identity as God's people for the sake of ministry (Bosch 1991, 372–78).

The implications of this "in" and "different from" tension in which the church is living are elaborated on in Bosch's definition of evangelism:

> Evangelism [is] that dimension and activity of the church's mission which, by word and deed and in the light of particular conditions and a particular context, offers every person and community, everywhere, a valid opportunity to be directly challenged to a radical reorientation of their lives . . . embracing Christ as Savior and Lord; becoming a living member of his community, the church; being enlisted into his service of reconciliation, peace, and justice on earth; and being committed to God's purpose of placing all things under the rule of Christ. (1991, 420)

When these profoundly theological concerns that Moltmann, Newbigin, Bosch, and others emphasize are integrated into the vision and mission of churches and theological schools, they have a transforming impact on their ministries.

This transformation is badly needed. Seminaries want to serve churches, denominations, mission agencies, and other national and global organizations through specialized academic and professional programs. But as Robert Banks has reminded us, the structures and curricula of theological education too often focus on a disposition to act rather than on engaging in action itself, or reflection *on* ministry rather than reflective action *within* ministry (1999, 142–48). At the same time, an increasing number of churches are deciding to go it alone. They are focusing on operational and pragmatic approaches, such as sending teams abroad for short-term ministries, often with little reflection on the meaning of their activities in relation to God's ultimate purposes for his church in the world. Within both theological schools and churches, there is a desperate need for a global and missiological ecclesiology that will transform and undergird their mission.

I love the church. For fifty years, I have been committed to developing lay leaders, pastors, theological educators, and missionaries for the church. There have been triumphs and disappointments. Sometimes the triumphs have made me ecstatic. I remember the tears of joy in the 1970s when I saw Brazilian theological education by extension becoming nationalized. My tears flowed again at the first Ibero-American Missionary Congress (COMIBAM) in 1987 where, in keeping with the conference theme, Latin American and Iberian countries celebrated their transformation "From a Mission Field to a Mission Force."

There have also been moments of deep despair. My husband and I were members of a church in Brazil when, over an eighteen-month period, the pastor divided and almost destroyed the congregation and scandalized the community through his top-down leadership style, mismanagement of funds, spousal abuse, and adultery.

One of the questions I want to ask God when I get to heaven is why he chose the church as his instrument for world evangelization. The only answer I have from my earthbound perspective is that he chose the church so that *all* the glory will belong to him! Similarly, Bosch states:

> The church is both a theological and a sociological entity, an inseparable union of the divine and the dusty. Looking at itself through the eyes of the world, the church realizes that it is disreputable and shabby, susceptible to all human frailties; looking at itself through the eyes of the believers, it perceives itself as a mystery, as the incorruptible body of Christ on earth. We can be utterly disgusted, at times, with the earthliness of the church, yet we can also be transformed, at times, with the awareness of the divine in the church. It is *this* church, ambiguous in the extreme which is missionary by its very nature, the pilgrim people of God. (1991, 389)

Globalized Theological Education Emerges
from Hermeneutical Communities

Before two world wars and the sociopolitical shifts of the mid-twentieth century, thoughts about global theologizing seldom occurred. I vividly remember a chapel service during my first semester as a student at Biola in 1949. A large world map covered the front of the auditorium, virtually from the ceiling to the floor and from wall to wall. On it were hundreds of lights, representing locations around the world where Biola graduates were serving. On this occasion, we were remembering the missionaries who had been forced to withdraw from China during the ascension of the People's Republic. Our eyes were glued to the map while, one by one, the lights in China were turned off. I heard quiet sobs throughout the auditorium and found myself crying as well. The missionaries were gone. The churches would die.

A decade later, when I became a missionary appointee with CBInternational, I completed a required list of readings on the indigenous church. I came to realize how wrong that "funeral service" had been. The churches in China were not only surviving without missionaries but thriving! What was dying was an era of colonialism and paternalism.

Along with thousands of other missionaries during the 1960s and 1970s, I internalized and passionately supported indigenous church principles. Our goal was to work ourselves out of a job by establishing self-governing, self-supporting, and self-propagating churches. Yet without minimizing the significance of the concept, we recognize retrospectively that indigenization still fell short of contextualization. The "three selfs" did not extend to self-theologizing (Hiebert 1994a, 96–97). Sending churches widely assumed that the practices, patterns, and beliefs that they had exported were universal and would be perpetuated under national leadership.

This theological hegemony of the North and the West was soon challenged by voices from the South and the East. Among the earliest and most vocal of these was Latin American liberation theology, which was developed from the "underside" as the poor began to speak and act for themselves out of their contexts of poverty, oppression, and injustice. These expressions took on many forms and shapes. I am most familiar with its manifestation through base ecclesial communities. Their values and methodologies are often an expression of adult educator Paulo Freire's "pedagogy of the oppressed" (1993). Freire believed that the poor allow themselves to be oppressed because of their fatalism. They must learn to be subjects rather than objects, recognizing the factors that are exploiting them and oppressing them, taking control of their own world, and saying their own word as they work toward social change.

To illustrate how Freire's pedagogy may look in practice, let us visit a storefront building in a *favela* (slum) in the city of São Paulo where members of a base ecclesial community have gathered. The nun who is facilitating the meeting begins with Scripture to remind the group that Jesus has a preferential option for the poor. He will be with them and empower them as they work for change in their community. Then she asks a leading question: What are we most concerned about in our community? Several persons blurt out the same answer, almost at the same time: "We need to get rid of the garbage dump! It has a nauseating stench, and it's a breeding ground for rats and disease." The nun continues to ask consciousness-raising questions: Do all communities have open garbage dumps? Why do some communities have them while others do not? Does Jesus want us to live by a garbage dump? What can we do to get rid of it? Together, they develop a strategy to get the dump filled in. They will invite a TV station to film a protest in front of the dump and a march to the city hall, making sure they have prepared chants and a petition to deliver to the authorities. In this situation, we may assume that the community's social action will be successful. It will be only a matter of months before the dump is filled in.

What does a garbage dump have to do with theology? Liberationists would say, "Everything!" A local context has been exegeted. Social action has reflected Jesus' love for the poor and oppressed and has resulted in liberating social change. Yet there are some legitimate concerns here as well. Bosch warns of the dangers of extreme relativism as an infinite number of local theologies emerge (1991, 427–28). Paul Hiebert raises issues related to the lack of interaction with other theologies and communities, along with the tendency to ignore history; to view human society, organization, and culture as good; and to open the door to syncretism (1994a, 88–91). Craig Blomberg sees a need for balance that goes beyond most liberation theology and most evangelical theology (1993, 217). A traditional gospel that offers only spiritual salvation and a vertical relationship with God lacks credibility in situations of oppression, poverty, and physical suffering. Focusing only on social needs leaves people without hope for eternal fellowship with God, which more than compensates for even the greatest suffering of this life.

Since its founding in 1970, the Latin American Theological Fraternity (LATF) has been exemplary in its commitment to the kind of balance Blomberg describes. Through their strong emphases on both biblical truth and social transformation, the writings of LATF scholars such as Orlando Costas, Samuel Escobar, and René Padilla have succeeded in avoiding the extremes of liberation theology on the one hand and fundamentalist expressions of evangelicalism on the other.

The scholarship, passion, and social concern that have characterized the LATF bridge nicely into the discussion of another characteristic of hermeneutical communities: They hold *theoria, praxis,* and *poiesis* together in creative tension (Bosch 1991, 431). For Aristotle, *praxis* was reflective action within the sociopolitical context. *Poiesis* was knowledge expressed in poetry, art, architecture, skilled craftsmanship, and other creative activities. *Theoria* described knowledge that came through reflection on ideas within a philosophical/conceptual framework.

The reflection of *theoria* and the action of *praxis* are the fundamental and well-known elements in the hermeneutical circle or spiral. Active reflection and reflective action are colliding with each other and changing each other in dynamic "twin moments" of interaction. Within evangelical theological institutions and churches, the concept of critical contextualization has modified this hermeneutical process. The reflection and action are between the unchanging Word and a changing world, between the deep roots of the biblical text and the shifting soils of the cultural contexts, and between the absolute truth of Scripture and the incomplete and partial understandings reflected in our attempts to interpret it.

The important role of *poiesis* within the hermeneutical process is less understood and less often applied. I became aware of it early in 1992 as I was interacting with David Bosch's *Transforming Mission* in preparation for my presidential address at the American Society of Missiology annual meeting in June of that year. Bosch quoted Samuel Rayan's extension of traditional hermeneutical methodology by going beyond practice and theory to include "discussion and prayer, social analysis and religious hermeneutics, involvement and contemplation in a single process" (Bosch 1991, 425). Similarly, Bosch affirms Max Stackhouse's warning regarding the dangers in reducing contextual hermeneutics to being only a problem between *praxis* and theory. "People do not need only truth (theory) and justice (praxis); they also need [the] beauty [of *poiesis*], the rich resources of symbol, piety, worship, love, awe, and mystery" (Bosch 1991, 431).

In my 1993 American Society of Missiology presidential address, I attempted to combine Stackhouse's insights related to *poiesis* with a conceptual model for the preparation of twenty-first-century missionaries that sees

> *praxis* and *poiesis,* theological contextualization and spiritual formation, being brought together in listening and responding movements of missions.
> . . . Missionaries will be best prepared for missions in the new century through emphases upon (1) nurture for *praxis* as they learn to exegete the Word, exegete the world, and bring these together in local theologies, and (2) nurture for *poiesis* as their worship and witness become expres-

sive craftsmanship and spiritual service within Christian communities. (McKinney 1993, 55)

I ended with a turn-of-the-century critique and challenge:

> My guess is that as historians write the history of late twentieth century missions, they will have at least one severe indictment: these were the decades of activism and pragmatism . . . when we became so absorbed in our strategies and methodologies that we all but lost sight of what God is doing in the world . . . when we allowed the theological base for missions to erode and replaced it with a shallow reliance on the social sciences . . . when the spiritual preparation of missionaries was subordinated to demands for academic excellence. May God help us as we enter the twenty-first century to restore listening and responding to missions. May . . . our missions activity grow out of a theological and spiritual response to what [he] is doing in the world. (McKinney 1993, 63)

Conclusion

The above discussion has been a thinly disguised appeal for institutional transformation on a global scale. In spite of many encouraging experiences over the last forty years, I continue to be frustrated by how little has changed. Theological education has globalized not only its healthy innovations but also its dysfunctions. Far too many programs are being driven by pragmatic concerns related to accreditation, funding, recruiting, and the expectations of constituencies. If we are ever to break out of this pattern of business as usual, creativity and intentionality are needed.

Happily, there are many creative efforts at regional and global levels. Let me share three examples. In his contribution to the work of the Association of Theological School's Task Force on Globalization, Craig Blomberg (1993) describes a "process of globalization for biblical understanding." One's earlier interpretation of the text is allowed to be altered through interaction with a fresh set of questions based on the agenda of religious and secular communities worldwide. To illustrate this process, he discusses five items that are consistently included in the agenda of globalization: liberation theology, feminism, pluralism, economics, and contextualization. (His processing of liberation theology was summarized above in this chapter.)

In July 1991, theological educators from around the world gathered at the London Bible College for a forum sponsored by the International Council for Evangelical Theological Education (ICETE, then ICAA). The theme was "From Text to Context in Theological Education." Three layers or strands of material were explored. Donald Carson presented exegetical studies of selected Scripture passages. These were followed by theological and contextual reflection by the participants. This international and intercultural dialogue enabled global understandings to emerge (Kemp 1994).

An example of a different kind comes from the Congo. John Gration, professor at Wheaton College Graduate School and former AIM missionary/executive, engaged French- and Swahili-speaking pastors in theologizing across tribal cultures and between Africa and the West. The seminar process was guided by four reflective questions: (1) What is the gospel? (2) What is culture? (3) How and where has the gospel touched or transformed your culture? (4) How and where has the gospel not yet transformed your culture? The last question generated an agenda of topics for discussion. Both local and global elements emerged through this process (Gration 1984). My hope is that the diversity of approaches and contexts represented through these examples will continue to multiply and remultiply across traditions and cultures in efforts to flesh out and enrich the globalization of theology.

In spite of these and many other encouraging examples, more (much more!) intentionality is needed if the pattern of globalizing superficial and dysfunctional programs is to be broken. We can go a long way toward this kind of transformation by intentional efforts within our own spheres of influence. The starting place is to mobilize a core group of persons who are willing to put time and energy into working toward change. Their job is not to tell their colleagues and cohorts what needs to be done. They need to develop a process that will enable institutions and their stakeholders, such as trustee boards and churches, to dream and plan together.

A long enough time frame is needed. The process is likely to take months or even years. Face-to-face groups will need to be organized. Some of these groups should enable persons to work with those who are most like themselves, and others should encourage dialogue among those with disparate views.

The group process could utilize some of the elements developed in this chapter by beginning with theological foundations. Do the suggested commitments to *missio Dei*, spiritual formation, the missional nature of the church, and hermeneutical communities reflect our institution's values? What needs to be modified? What will our schools, associations, denominations, and global networks look like when our commitments are internalized? This kind of reflection could be followed by interaction with the elements of the ICETE *Manifesto*. How can we provide for contextualization, churchward orientation, strategic flexibility, theological grounding, continuous assessment, community life, servant molding, instructional variety, a Christian mind, equipping for growth, and cooperation among the programs of our institution? Throughout the process, we should try to work within a *praxis/poiesis* framework, bringing the Word, the world, worship, and witness together in integrative, dynamic spirals. Above all, we must keep listening to what God is saying to us, allowing him to raise our sights and attune our hearts to his plans and purposes. This is his mission. The sending God has sent us into the world to worship him and to serve him as we participate in his plans and purposes. One day his people from all cultures and nations will worship him and enjoy him forever before his throne.

14

The Missionary as Mediator of Global Theologizing

PAUL G. HIEBERT

To say that we live in a time of rapid change is to state the obvious. Peter Drucker writes:

> Every few hundred years in Western history there occurs a sharp transformation. We cross what some . . . have called a "divide." Within a few short decades, society rearranges itself: its worldview; its basic values; its social and political structure; its arts, its key institutions. Fifty years later, there is a new world. And the people born then cannot even imagine the world in which their grandparents lived and into which their own parents were born. . . . We are currently living through just such a transformation. (cited in Van Engen 1997, 437)

I grew up at the end of the old missionary era when missionaries went abroad for life, returned on furlough every seven years, retired "at home," or, preferably, died and were buried abroad. Now missions is changing rapidly, and we need a vision of what the new paradigm for missions should be for the twenty-first century. What are the changes taking place, and what implications do these have for Christian missions?

In recent years, scholars have turned their attention to the emergence of world systems, but studies show that most people still live in local and regional settings, even though they may venture from home from time to time. Out of these discussions have emerged theories of a "glocal" world in which different kinds of globalization interact in complex ways at global, regional, and local levels (Berger and Huntington 2002; Lewellen 2002; Inda and Rosaldo 2002). It is important to remember that the missionary movement was itself one of the earliest forces creating global networks and new media of communication no less powerful than those established by the markets and information technology of the twentieth century. This was true of Catholic missions in the sixteenth and seventeenth centuries and even more so of Protestant missions in the eighteenth, nineteenth, and twentieth centuries.

The glocalization of the world and the church has profound implications for missions in the twenty-first century, implications we have only begun to explore under the topics of truth, dialogue, religious pluralism, relativism, contextualization, ecumenism, partnership, and local and global theologies. How should churches around the world relate to one another when there are great social, cultural, and theological differences but when there is a desperate need to live together in peace? How do we respond to religious differences when we are committed to the truth of the gospel and the priesthood of all believers? What does globalization mean when it comes to evangelism and missions?

Globalization

In the last decades, the world has rapidly become interconnected through travel, trade, communications, immigrations, and political interactions. At a fundamental level, this globalization has led to people meeting others who are different from themselves, raising questions of how they view and relate to others and otherness. Specifically, how should Christians respond to the impact of globalization on the church, and how should they deal with the theological pluralism that is emerging as young churches begin to read and interpret Scripture for themselves?

People have always had stereotypes of their "others." In 1527, Henry Agrippa declared, "In singing also the Italians Bleat, the Spaniards Whine, the Germans Howl, and the French Quaver" (Harris 1968, 399–400). During the High Middle Ages, educated Europeans saw foreigners as monsters or infidels. The invading Muslims were clearly humans, but they had heard the gospel and had rejected it. Therefore, they had to be driven back and killed.

European perceptions of the world changed radically at the end of the fifteenth century. Explorers discovered unknown lands and strange people not found on their maps, raising profound questions. Who were these others? Were they humans? Did they need salvation? The Western commercial world saw the newly discovered others as a source of goods and labor, of gold and slaves. Some argued that they were like children. Therefore, Europeans were justified in their colonial expansion, in which they acted as parents, educating and managing the natives' wealth for the natives' own good (McGrane 1989). Scientists saw these others as barbarians and savages who could be compared with Europeans and animals. Christians saw them as humans in need of salvation. The result was the birth of the modern mission movement.

The Modern Era

The definition of others in the West changed with the coming of the Enlightenment and an intellectual environment dominated by social Darwinism. All humans were incorporated into one cosmic story of progress from simple to complex, from primitive to civilized, from prelogical to logical. The superiority of Western science and technology was self-evident. These enabled the West to conquer and rule the world. Now others were no longer savages but "unenlightened," and evil was no longer sin but "ignorance." The earlier distinction between refined Christian versus idolatrous savage was replaced by *civilized* European versus superstitious, ignorant *primitive*. Others were also "aboriginals." They represented humans who had not evolved as those who lived in the West. They still lived in the stone age. But if these others were now like European ancestors once were, they helped modern people understand their own story. The people of the world reveal *their* history, and they knew how the story ends; they *were* how the story ends (McGrane 1989).

The Enlightenment deeply influenced Western Christians. Christians led the fight against slavery and human exploitation, and many died to bring the gospel around the world. Many missionaries, such as John Williams, Lorimer Fison, and George Turner in Melanesia (Hitchen 2002) and W. H. and C. V. Wiser in India, played key roles in the development of ethnology, working closely with anthropologists and publishing penetrating studies on non-Western cultures. R. H. Codrington, one of the early great missionaries and ethnographers, wrote, "When a European has been living for two or three years among strangers, he is sure to be fully convinced that he knows all about them; when he has been ten years or so amongst them, if he is an observant man, he finds that he knows very little about them, and so begins to learn" (1891, vii).

After the early nineteenth century and the introduction of secular evolution as the dominant anthropological paradigm, tensions arose between missionaries and anthropologists. But missionaries were also people of their times, part of the modern *zeitgeist,* which they absorbed in the air they breathed. Charles Taber notes:

> The superiority of Western civilization as the culmination of human development, the attribution of that superiority to the prolonged dominance of Christianity, the duty of Christians to share civilization and the gospel with the benighted heathen—these were the chief intellectual currency of their lives. (1991, 71)

All this must be said, but as Lamin Sanneh (1993) points out, many of the missionaries were concerned with communicating the gospel to other peoples. To do so, they lived with the people, learned their languages, studied their cultures, and often defended them against oppression by governments and business. Moreover, by translating the Bible into native languages, communicating to the people a universal gospel, and baptizing the converts into the global church, missionaries dignified the people and helped them more than other Westerners to preserve their cultural identities.

Two schools of thought emerged in anthropology, which studied humans around the world and their differences. Social anthropology compared social systems around the world, such as families, clans, tribes, and peasant societies, and helped us see that social systems are real and powerful. It showed us that humans organize their societies in radically different ways, and it gave us ways to compare different social systems.

Social theories have had a great impact on Western missions. In the West, we expect individuals to make personal decisions to follow Christ, but in many parts of the world, important decisions are made by the significant groups to which people belong—their families or lineages. In missions, this led to a great deal of discussion of "mass" or "multi-individual" movements to Christ. Early mission strategies were largely based on geography, but missionaries found deep social divisions in the same geographic area, divisions that shaped responsiveness to the gospel. This led to a focus on people groups, social dynamics, and the church growth movement. It led to discussion of the "three selves" and questions of indigenizing the church in local social systems. Traditionally, missionaries exported their ecclesiologies. Anglicans ordained bishops, Presbyterians appointed presbyteries and synods, and free churches held elections, even if these forms of leadership caused confusion in societies where they were foreign.

Social theories also have limitations and distortions. They are often reductionist and use linear causality, explaining most human realities in terms of social dynamics. Religions are seen as important to keep groups together but not "true" in any ontological sense. There is no place for God and spiritual realities. Initially, social anthropology focused its attention on small societies and examined them as closed systems. Consequently, it had difficulties in understanding larger, complex societies, such as cities, and the global systems emerging today. Social anthropology also saw societies as harmonious organic wholes and change as bad. There was no place for oppression, injustice, and human sinfulness. Missionaries were often castigated for changing societies.

Cultural anthropology emerged in North America, where anthropologists studied the Native Americans who had been overrun by white settlers and placed on reservations. They could not understand the Native Americans without taking history, outside forces, and change into account. Moreover, while the social systems of the Native Americans had been radically altered, the Native Americans maintained a sense of cultural identity, even in the most difficult and oppressive situations. American anthropologists focused their attention on cultural systems, such as languages, beliefs, myths, rituals, and worldviews. They rejected the word *civilization* and replaced it with *culture*. Bernard McGrane writes, "The emergence of the concept 'culture' has made possible the democratization of differences. . . . The twentieth-century concept of 'culture' has rescued the non-European Other from the depths of the past and prehistory and reasserted him in the present: he is, once again, contemporary with us" (1989, 114).

Cultural anthropologists saw cultures as good but did not see change as always evil. Consequently, anthropology was used to study change and to support programs advocating the rights of Native Americans and human development.

Early anthropologists saw themselves as scientists analyzing humans as objects, using scientific categories, methods, and logic. As they studied local peoples for long periods of time, they learned to know them as real persons. They began to see others no longer as primitives. These others were fully rational beings having their own autonomous cultures that made sense to them. They were "natives." Cultures were seen as unique and autonomous. Each was seen as discrete, bounded, and self-contained and functioned to maintain a harmonious society. Cultures were also seen as morally neutral. People in one culture should not judge other cultures. To do so was ethnocentric and imperialistic.

Now it became important for anthropologists to learn how the people they studied saw the world around them. This *emic* approach challenged the idea that human studies are hard sciences. The key methods shifted from observation to participation and from observable empirical "facts" to hermeneutics—to seeking to understand what is in the minds of the people by examining speech, acts, music, and dance as "texts." Out of this emerged interpretative anthropology championed by Clifford Geertz and others. Geertz (1988) argues that anthropology is the study of humans and that humans cannot be reduced to purely objective scientific observations. Anthropology is more a humanity than a science. This was a move away from positivism and objective materialism to instrumentalism and the communication of lived-through experiences.

Cultural anthropology, too, has its limitations. It tends to reduce everything to cultural explanations. Moreover, those who use Saussurian semiotics see signs, such as words, as referring to subjective images in the mind, not to objective realities, and cultures as essentially arbitrary creations of human societies (Barnard 2000, 120–38). Consequently, all cultures are seen as relative. None can stand in judgment of another. According to this view, there is no external objective truth, and even if there is, it can only be known subjectively. Moreover, secular cultural anthropology has no place for God or spiritual realities. Consequently, it does not take the ontological claims of religions seriously. It claims a privileged stance as a science, as an objective, outside assessment of reality.

Cultural anthropology has helped missionaries understand the reality and power of cultural systems (including languages), patterns of behavior, rituals, myths, beliefs, and worldviews. Missionaries do not come as scientists but often as outsiders seeking not only to convert people but also to teach them modern medicine and education, in which science is central. As they live among people over long periods of time, they too come to recognize that people do not live in the same world with different labels attached to it but in radically different conceptual worlds. Descriptive linguistics helped missionaries to learn and analyze new languages, and the use of Saussurian semiotics led to dynamic equivalence Bible translations that stress the accurate communication of the meanings of the text by allowing changes in the literal referential signs. Symbolic anthropology has helped missionaries and national leaders seeking to contextualize worship and rituals in particular cultures. Cognitive anthropology contributes to an understanding of the local belief systems and worldviews of the people missionaries serve.

In missions, this move to understand cultures in their own terms has led to attempts at radical, often uncritical, contextualization of the gospel. However, without external objective criteria to determine whether accurate communication has taken place, the gospel becomes whatever people believe it to be. Moreover, this view denies the importance of our common humanity and history and of a divine cosmic story. It reduces everything to momentary personal experiences that, in the end, are transient and meaningless.

The Postmodern Era

At the end of the twentieth century, anthropologists, such as Peter Harries-Jones (1985, 224–48), challenged the very assumptions of the mid-twentieth-century approach to the study of humans, provided a rationale for anthropology, and pointed to the direction it should take in the twenty-first century. Harries-Jones noted that anthropological research is based on the assumption of an exchange of communication between human equals of two cultures. In reality, anthropologists saw the local people mainly as informants and objects to be studied, "as a mine whose product was extracted for export to the Western academic community" (1985, 227). This was true even in *emic* studies that sought to understand how other people think. Rarely was there a genuine two-way exchange of information and beliefs to discover reality and truth. Moreover, ethnographic studies carry no commitment of responsibility on the part of an anthropologist to the community in which he or she lived and studied.

Harries-Jones (1985), David Harvey (1990), and others point out that the day of moral neutrality is over. Anthropology can no longer be taught as an objective, morally neutral description of culture. Knowledge is used by participants in the social, economic, and political arenas of life. It carries with it responsibilities to facilitate mutually beneficial interaction among different social and cultural groups. In the past, anthropologists studied others from the viewpoint of Western culture. Now they must also interpret the views of local peoples. Moreover, anthropologists must help minority communities cope with the impact of majority cultures in a rapidly changing world.

Jacob Loewen notes that on the whole missionaries have been less guilty than anthropologists of exploiting the societies they studied (1992, 48). They stayed and sought to serve the people they learned to know, while many anthropologists, often funded by colonial governments, tried to help their colonial governments rule the people more effectively and humanely (Kuper 1973, 123–49). Adam Kuper writes:

> Social anthropology has a bad name through its association with colonialism, and the anthropologist has an even harder time than most of his social science colleagues even getting permission to do fieldwork in the newly-independent states. And once there he is no longer able to rely upon the privileged status of a white man crossing a detested racial barrier; he is now an outsider of a different kind, a foreigner, less secure and perhaps less welcome. (1973, 233–34)

Some missionaries also collaborated with colonial governments—at least in the eyes of the local people—and even now many see ethnographic knowledge not as a way of building deep mutual relationships but as a useful tool for carrying out missions more efficiently.

A recent school to emerge out of this self-analysis is radical postmodern anthropology. This is a reaction to the arrogance of modern positivism, colonialism, and a concern for the subaltern and oppressed. It critiques the creation by anthropologists of the other (and consequently the definition of the self) as the driving force of all previous theories in the human sciences. It argues that all grand narratives and definitions of others are set up by an elite and are oppressive, not true.

Postmodernity is also based on the principle of reflexivity. When anthropologists returned home, they began to study their own cultures using the theories and methods they used to study others abroad. Radical postmodern anthropologists go further. They claim that no true statement can be made about another culture. There are only the anthropologists' perceptions and interpretations of parts of a culture or, in the extreme case, what anthropologists say happened to themselves when they were in another culture. As Alan Barnard notes, "Radical reflexivists are happy to write more about themselves doing ethnography than about the ethnographees, their subjects" (2000, 174). The result is a radical epistemological relativism that denies any possibility of knowing or making known the truth.

This post-Enlightenment view of others is an important corrective to the arrogance and oppressions of the past, but it leaves others as simply others. There is still an insurmountable wall between us and them. In a global world with all its diversity, the question is how people of different communities can seek the truth together and build a world of harmony, justice, and love. Edward Said asks:

> Can one divide human reality, as human reality seems to be genuinely divided, into clearly different cultures, histories, traditions, societies, even races, and survive the consequences humanly? By surviving the consequences humanly, I mean to ask whether there is any way of avoiding the hostility expressed by the division, say, of men into "us" . . . and "they." (1995, 45)

The Global Era

Macro-analysis shows the spread of global forces around the world, including languages, intelligentsia, popular culture, and religious movements (Berger and Huntington 2002). People no longer can live in their own little worlds; they increasingly must relate to those of other societies and cultures. To do so, they must develop global systems that enable them to live together.

There are many levels of cultural encounter today that are leading to a post-postmodern or glocal world (Smith 1982; Laudin 1996; Hiebert 1999). On the global level, cultures and nations around the world increasingly confront one another as travel, trade, global networks, and transnational organizations emerge. Within nations we are becoming increasingly aware of deep cultural differences as powerless communities increasingly find their voices in the public arena. Immigrant communities find social and cultural assimilation in their adopted lands full of tensions and misunderstandings. Generational differences also engender conflicts and misunderstandings between the older, more modern parents and the younger, often postmodern children, and between them and their post-postmodern children.

In a glocal world full of tensions and conflicts, how can we work toward the unity of the church and theology? One way is to develop global systems from the top down—from centralized institutions built around specialists who define theology and organized missions. Another is to work toward global networks that begin at the local level and develop mid-level and global dialogues, partnerships, and networks of fellowship and ministry. From a free church perspective, the latter is explored here. The questions are: How can we start with the many local and regional churches around the world and build a global fellowship? How do we start with local theologies and work toward a global understanding of theology as universal truth by doing theology together, without silencing the weak but drawing on the wisdom of those who are mature in faith?

Global mediation must begin with how we view others and otherness. In a church made up of people from many ethnic groups, cultures, and classes, there is always the tendency to break up into parties that seek to control the church. As long as there is a division between us and them in the church, worshiping, living, and working together become a contest of power. To move toward the unity of the church, for which Christ prayed (John 17:20–21), Christians must show how humans of different kinds can live together in peace and justice. Otherwise the gospel becomes good news only for a few—the powerful. Christians must address the sin of divisions in the church: racism, culturalism, genderism, classism, and ageism. They must not see others as primitives, backward, or irreconcilably other. In a global world, they must view others not as others but as us. They must meet one another in their common humanity and their common sinfulness. In the church, they must meet one another as members of one family in Christ.

How can we build these bridges between churches and, in particular, theologians? Not everyone can go around the world to learn to know others, nor can global conclaves hear the voices of all. We must build relationships between communities and begin the long and difficult task of developing mutual understandings and affirmations of the unity of the church and the gospel, which transcends social and cultural differences. But this process requires global mediators who break down the walls that divide humans and build bridges of understanding and fellowship.

Missionaries as Mediators

What is the shape of the new mission paradigms emerging in the twenty-first century? A consensus has not yet emerged, but several elements are increasingly clear. One is that missions to new and unreached peoples must continue. The number of people who have not heard the gospel meaningfully enough to make an intelligent response is greater now than when Ziegenbalg and Plütschau left for India in 1706. The task of pioneer missions is not finished. It is greater than ever.

A second fact is that a growing number of missionaries are "inbetweeners," standing between different worlds, seeking to build bridges of understanding, mediating relationships, and negotiating partnerships in ministry. In the past, missionaries went from the "Christian" West to the uttermost parts of the world. Today, there are large churches and mission movements in many non-Western countries, and the West is now also a mission field. Increasingly, missionaries are bridge persons, culture mediators, who stand between different human worlds.

Missionaries are mediators in a number of ways. All Christians are called to be mediators between the gospel and the world in which they live. In the past, the world was defined as the non-West. It was assumed that the West had heard the gospel and was essentially Christian. The rest of the world was pagan and heathen. Today, the church is global. The most vital churches are found in the non-West, and the West is itself a mission field. This has profoundly changed the way we perceive missions. The globalization of the church has made us much more aware of the need to contextualize the message in our local cultures and the messenger and the church in local social systems.

Globalization raises profound questions regarding the need for and limits to contextualization. It is here that missionaries can first add much to the dialogue on the mediation between gospel and human cultures because, through their encounters with other cultures, they are deeply aware of cultures and their differences and of ways to study cultures. The dangers are to undercontextualize and to overcontextualize the gospel and the church. Global discussions on contextualization need missionaries and global leaders who understand both the gospel and human cultures well and who can bridge between them. In this, missionaries must not speak only to the world from the church but also for the world to the church. Most churches know little about their own neighborhoods, let alone people in other parts of the world. Missionaries must help their sending churches understand, identify with, and love people around them, and around the world. For example, they need to help Western churches understand the great ethnic, cultural, and religious diversity that is increasingly found in their own communities.

Second, missionaries are mediators between Christianity and non-Christian religions. The question of religious pluralism is one of the critical issues in the twenty-first century. In the past, missionaries faced this question as they encountered other religions abroad. Now churches in the West face the same question. Most have given little thought to the deep issues involved and are unprepared to defend the uniqueness of Christ in a multicultural and multireligious world. Missionaries can help Christians in the West understand the issues involved in interreligious dialogue and ways to present the gospel winsomely, speaking the truth in love.

Third, missionaries are mediators in global church-to-church relationships. In the past, mission churches were often supervised by sending churches. Today, they are increasingly mature, independent churches. Moreover, there has been a rapid growth in locally initiated denominations with few official ties to those in other lands. The globalization of the church raises questions of power and control. How can the church in all its diversity show the world that it is indeed one? In much of the world, the dividedness of the church has been one of the great obstacles to its message. How can churches in different parts of the world work in partnership in mission? How can the gospel be presented so that it is seen as belonging to the world, not one part of it? How can cultural differences in multicultural teams be worked out so that they enhance, not undermine, the work? Missionaries and other transcultural Christian leaders should be the mediators among diverse Christian communities, seeking to build bridges of understanding of the gospel and partnership in mission.

Fourth, missionaries are mediators in the academy between theology and human studies. Missions is communicating the gospel to humans. It therefore requires an understanding of both the gospel and humans. The first draws on theologies, the second on human studies. For the most part, missionaries are well trained in exegeting Scripture. Most have little or no training in exegeting human societies. Eloise Meneses, Vinoth Ramachandra, Darrell Whiteman, and Robert Priest, in this volume, show us that we need a far deeper understanding of the sociocultural contexts in which we minister. Too often missionaries have been afraid of using the human sciences lest they become captive to disciplines such as anthropology and sociology, but they have not stopped to reflect on the danger of becoming captive to Greek philosophy and modern history. In a rapidly changing world, we can no longer minister effectively without knowing and identifying with the people we serve. We can no longer settle for stereotypes and secondhand reports of peoples and their cultures. An intimate knowledge of them is needed that includes understanding them as they see themselves and as they see us.

Fifth, missionaries must be mediators between missions as a movement and missiology as an academic discipline. Too often those involved in missions do not take time for deep research and reflection on their ministries, and those in the academy lose touch with the realities of ministries in the field. We need careful research and reflection on the Word and on the world. Missions requires the best research and theoretical reflections to help guide us in an increasingly complex and confusing world. As such, it must draw on the best that the academy can offer.

The missiological academy itself must become global. Too often it has been dominated by the West (Tiénou 1993). The voices of scholars around the world have been largely ignored, often because Western scholars have not taken the time to learn other languages. Here missionaries and national scholars need to counter the hegemony of the Western academy, give voice to the theologies emerging in the young churches, and help to build bridges of understanding and consensus among scholars around the world.

Finally, missionaries as mediators are central to global theologizing. If, as we in the free churches affirm, all Christians and Christian communities should do their own theological reflection, then we must begin with a great deal of theological diversity arising in part out of the fact that these reflections are done in different human contexts. How can we, given such diversity, seek together to understand the deeper truths of the gospel, truths that are learned from different theological traditions?

The Ministry of Mediation

How can missionaries and other global leaders live and minister as mediators? Our model is Jesus, who in his incarnation was fully God and fully human. He was equally at home as King of the universe on the throne in the palaces of heaven and as an infant in a manger in a cattle shed on earth. We can never begin to emulate him, but he provides us with a way of understanding our role in bridging between different worlds.

Essential to developing global understandings and networks between churches and theologians is the process of intercultural mediation. Simply living between cultures does not make one a good mediator. What are some of the essentials for such a ministry?

Transcultural Identities

D. J. Bachner and U. Zeutschel note that persons and parties involved in intercultural mediation must develop a transcultural frame of reference and identity whose norms transcend national and monocultural boundaries (1994, 39). Modernity claimed privileged truth, which had to be taught to others. No mediation was required—only accurate translation. In the postmodern world, science has lost its privileged position, and all belief systems have equal place. But there is only dialogue, no mediation. We cannot be sure that we truly understand others, so we focus on ourselves. There can be no real concern for others because they are others and inscrutable. In our day, we need people who can mediate between different worlds—whether these differences are based on culture, ethnicity, generation, or theological conviction.

In one sense, missionaries belong to two or more worlds. They begin by leaving their home cultures, where they are insiders. There they are known as missionaries, a role recognized and respected. They enter another culture as outsiders. There they cannot be missionaries because it is not a role in that society. The people fit them into their local inventory of roles as best they can. Often the missionaries are seen as rich landlords, patrons, colonial rulers, or foreign spies.

As missionaries live in the new society, they learn its ways and identify with it more deeply. They learn the language and begin to see the world as the people do, emically. In so doing, they become, to some extent, insiders. But they never fully become one with the people. They are *outsiders*-insiders.

When missionaries return to their home societies, they find that they do not fully fit in. They now begin to see their cultures as outsiders do. Here too they are outsider-insiders. In a sense, they belong to two cultures; in a sense, they do not belong fully to either. Increasingly, wherever they go, they are outsiders-insiders.

This inner dividedness creates an identity crisis. One way to resolve this tension of identities is to affirm one "home" cultural identity and to go to other worlds as outsiders and visitors, but in doing this, they will never effectively communicate the gospel to the people or speak for them to their home churches. A second answer is to seek to "go native." This is impossible in one lifetime, and those who seek to identify fully with another community are seen as frauds and rivals (Howard 2004). Moreover, this destroys their ability to be bridges between different cultures. A third answer is to be cultural chameleons, to take on the trappings of the culture in which they find themselves. But then they become cultural schizophrenics with no true identity of their own. A fourth answer is to develop transcultural identities. P. S. Adler notes that such a person is

> a person whose essential identity is inclusive of life patterns different from his own and who has psychologically and socially come to grips with a multiplicity of realities. Multicultural man is the person who is intellectually and emotionally committed to the fundamental unity of all human beings while at the same time he recognizes, legitimatizes, accepts, and appreciates the fundamental differences that lie between people of different cultures. This new kind of man cannot be defined by the languages he speaks, the countries he has visited, or the number of international contacts he has made. Nor is he defined by his profession, his place of residence, or his cognitive sophistication. Instead, multicultural man is recognized by the configuration of his outlooks and worldview, by the way he incorporates the universe as a dynamically moving process, by the way he reflects on the interconnectedness of life in his thoughts and his actions, and by the way he remains open to the imminence of experience. (1977, 25)

Global mediators must be bicultural or transcultural people who are able to live in different worlds and are not fully at home in any one of them. Transcultural mediators need to know both communities well and speak to each for the other. Being insiders, they build trust in each community. Being outsiders enables them to bridge the groups. They must also live with the fact that both communities are sometimes suspicious of them because the communities do not know what they are doing when they are with the others.

Good mediators are inbetweeners who often feel they have no home or identity because they live in two or more worlds and must constantly change their identities as they move from one to another. What keeps them from being schizophrenic? Here a metaphor may help. Eagles are not going from one place to another. Their home is in the sky, in flight. Perhaps flight is their way of being in the world, in an era of globalization.

Transcultural Analytical Frameworks

Transcultural people need to develop transcultural analytical frameworks that enable them to live in different cultures and translate, compare, and evaluate them by means of a metacultural grid that is outside any one of them. This frame emerges as they live in more than one world and seek to understand each of them deeply from its own perspective while also comparing and evaluating them. Such a framework is not itself a culture. It is a framework that enables people to understand, translate, compare, and evaluate different cultures. In a sense, it is like a computer program that takes documents written in one format and translates them into another format.

There is no single metacultural framework. Anthropology has been working on such a grid from its inception. The early metacultural frameworks were essentially Western cultural grids. Taxonomies of different social, economic, political, and cultural systems were created using modern scientific categories. As the views of other peoples were taken seriously, those frameworks were rejected, and newer ones developed. The current comparative frameworks are not fully accurate, but they are better than the earlier classifications and theories, just as modern translation theories are better than the old ones based on literal or Saussurian semiotics. It is important that all parties involved in mediation participate in the formation of such a grid.

In doing global theologizing, it is important for committed Christian theologians from around the world to develop a metatheological framework that enables them to understand, compare, and evaluate local theologies, the questions each is seeking to answer, and the sociocultural contexts in which each must define the gospel (see fig. 1).

Figure 1

Metatheological Frames

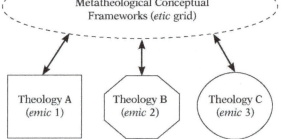

Once such understandings are formed, the hard process of developing a global theology that is true for everyone can begin. Theologies must not only seek to communicate the gospel in local contexts but also affirm the oneness of the gospel for all humans, because at the deepest level, they and the gospel are one. Dialogue regarding a global theology will continue as the world and we change, but for those committed to the authority of Scripture as divine revelation, not simply human reflections, there is a common basis from which to begin. Moreover, theology is more than affirming a set of propositions about truth; it involves living that truth by being committed followers of Jesus Christ as Lord. Globally, we need to discuss what that means in each of our local contexts.

In developing a metatheological framework, we must deal with the question of semiotics. Modernity was built on the view that signs referred directly to objective realities. The word *tree* referred to a real tree, the word *rose* to a real rose. According to this view, people in different cultures live in the same world but give different labels to the same realities. Consequently, translation meant finding equivalent words and formulating sentences the way others did. This produced literal translations.

As anthropologists began to see the world through the eyes of other peoples, they discovered that people in different cultures do not see the same world with different labels attached to it; they live in conceptually different worlds. They organize their world using different categories, logics, and worldview assumptions. Ferdinand de Saussure argued that signs do not refer to external realities. They refer to categories and images in the mind. They are mentally constructed, culturally shaped, and subjective. Translation, therefore, involved communicating mental meanings, not literal forms, because the latter often have radically different meanings in different cultures. The result was dynamic equivalence translations in which forms were changed to preserve meanings. According to this view, however, accurate communication becomes impossible, because there are no external reference points against which two subjective perceptions can be compared. The result was postmodern anthropology in which an anthropologist can speak only of what happened to himself or herself in a cross-cultural setting.

Charles Peirce (1940) argued that signs are triadic. They have (1) a form—the symbol, word (such as *tree*), or other sign that can be communicated to others, (2) the realities to which the sign refers—real trees, and (3) the mental images they create in the minds of people. Forms and meanings are linked to realities, and meaning lies in our understandings of these realities. Communication, therefore, is possible and is not measured merely by what the sender means or the receptor comprehends but by the correspondence between what the sender and the receptor experience and understand about reality. This correspondence can be tested by the use of realities external to the minds of those involved in communication.

A second essential in developing a metatheological framework is its epistemology (Laudin 1996; Hiebert 1999). Positivism, the epistemological foundation for modernity, assumed that human knowledge, particularly the sciences, had a photographic or one-to-one correspondence view of reality. Therefore, it was objective truth—true for everyone everywhere and unaffected by the scientist, who was outside the picture. Instrumentalism holds that knowledge is created in the mind, and we cannot show that it corresponds to reality. We use it because it is useful. Critical realism holds that knowledge is like maps of reality. Maps must be true to reality. They must correspond to reality in the areas in which they claim truth. Road maps must map roads accurately, and weather maps show the weather. In critical realism, knowledge is focused, approximate, and complementary.

Transcultural Mediation Skills

A number of characteristics mark the effective transcultural person (Corbitt 1998; Hammer, Bennett, and Wiseman 2003; Vulpe, Protheroe, and MacDonald 2001). At minimum, a transcultural person should be able "to communicate interpersonally; to adjust to various cultures; to develop interpersonal relationships; to deal with diverse societal systems; to understand another; and to manage psychological (intercultural) stress" (Cook 2005, 22).

One central task of cultural mediators is to help participants in the process understand one another deeply—to see others as they see themselves and to see themselves as others see them. Mediators cannot side fully with either party, and they must honestly and positively represent each side to the other, helping each to see the other's perspective. For example, missionaries must not only present Christ to Hindus and Muslims but also help churches see how Muslims and Hindus see themselves and Christians and Christ. In doing so, they must not deny or hide their commitment to him as the only way to salvation, but they and other Christians must understand how others see Christ if they want to present him to them in love.

One particularly difficult task missionaries face is to mediate disagreements and conflicts and to bring about reconciliation where there are deep hatreds and memories of oppression. Often they must help members of communities divided by long histories of suspicion and hostility to love one another (Volf 1996). At the heart of mediation is love. Missionaries must truly love the people and identify with them in their common humanity. Only then can they bear bold witness to the gospel without arrogance and control.

Transcultural Community

Global mediation also requires a transcultural forum. Mediators themselves need a community in which they can learn from one another.

Theologically, they affirm the "universal cosmopolitan composition of the Church" (Kane 1986, 141; Acts 17:24–28; Eph. 3:15).

Where do missionaries find such communities? In one sense, they find fellowship with members of the various communities in which they participate and mediate among these churches. They realize that in the church believers are members of one new people (*ethnos*). For Paul, unity and living as fellow citizens in the new kingdom are the ways the church demonstrates that it is indeed the church. John Stott writes, "For the sake of the glory of God and the evangelization of the world, nothing is more important than that the church should be, and should be seen to be, God's new society" (1979, 10). Missionaries as global mediators begin to understand that this world is indeed not their home—that home for Christians is heaven and that in this world they are resident aliens.

But missionaries who no longer belong fully to any one local church need others who understand them and can help them understand themselves and their ministries. They often find their closest relationships with other missionaries and other transcultural people who understand the outside-inside nature of their identity. They belong to a global fellowship with friends around the world. They become models for other Christians. Herbert Kane writes:

> As a child of the kingdom the believer then becomes a World Christian. By calling he belongs to a universal fellowship—the Christian church. By conviction he claims a universal message—the Christian gospel. By commitment he owes his allegiance to a universal king—Jesus Christ. By vocation, he is a part of a universal movement—the Christian mission. (1986, 137–38)

Mediating Global Theologizing

One area of great importance in the glocal church is mediation among churches doing local theologies and theology as truth for everyone. Young churches around the world are now doing their own theologizing. This raises difficult questions about the relationship between these theologies as habitus, dynamic, and context sensitive (Tiénou 1993, 247) and theology as an understanding of the gospel as universal truth. It raises questions about the relationship of systematic (philosophical), biblical (historical), and missional theologies (Hiebert and Tiénou 2002a). And it raises questions about the use of different categories and logics in the formulation of systematic theologies. These are difficult questions to address because they deal with the very heart of missions, bearing witness to the gospel in all human cultures, and the building of a new family that transcends all societies. The answer we give to this question of the relationship between theologies and theology depends in large measure on our semiotic, epistemological, and hermeneutical frameworks.

To move from local theologies to an understanding of transcultural truths revealed in Scripture, we need a metatheology, a theological reflection on how local theologies should be done and how to mediate the dialogue among them. For evangelicals, the first requisite of such a metatheology is the affirmation that Scripture is divine revelation and the final authority in all matters it addresses. If we affirm the priesthood of all believers and encourage everyone to study Scripture for themselves, our common ground becomes the Bible and its objective truthfulness.

The second requisite in a metatheology is to differentiate between God's revelation as recorded in Scripture and human understandings expressed in theologies. Today, as young churches develop their own theological formulations, they face a theological crisis. They must deal not only with new theological issues but also with the theological fact itself—with African, Latin American, Indian, Chinese, and other theologies. If theological unity is based on specific theological formulations, how are they to deal with this diversity?

Many evangelicals answered this question by requiring churches abroad to hold the doctrinal systems of the older church in the West, but already in the eighteenth century, there was a growing awareness that young churches have the rights and responsibilities not only for self-governance, self-support, and self-propagation but also for self-theologizing. If they are to make the gospel relevant to their own people, they must contextualize it within their cultural settings.

If churches do local theologies, where are theological absolutes? How can we preserve universal truth and avoid relativism if we allow all believers to read and interpret Scripture in their own cultural settings? Peircean semiotics and a critical realist epistemology help us to avoid total subjectivism, relativism, and solipsism. They help us to affirm that there are universal, objective realities and truths but that these must be subjectively understood by humans in their contexts. This does not give priority to subjective perceptions. Rather, it calls for us constantly to test our understandings against reality. The authority of Scripture means that we must constantly go to the Bible to test our beliefs and behavior. To the extent that our theologies are rooted in Scripture, they contain objective truth, even though as human understandings in particular human contexts they are partial and colored by personal and cultural biases. We may see truth through a glass darkly, but we do see enough to hear and respond to God's Word to us.

To recognize that theologies are done by humans in their contexts means that we must study human contexts deeply to know how they shape our thinking and to seek the biblical message not through the eyes of our culture but as it was understood by those who recorded it. We need to study human cultures to build understanding among them and to communicate the gospel in them in ways that transform them in the light of God's truth, beauty, and righteousness.

Yet another essential element in metatheology is the church as a hermeneutical community. This raises difficult questions regarding hermeneutics in a multicultural community. Different cultures raise different theological questions that need to be answered through the study of Scripture. But the questions go deeper. Different cultures use different categories and create categories using different principles (intrinsic and extrinsic, digital and analogical, or fuzzy) (Zimmerman 1985; Hiebert 1994b) and different logics (abstract algorithmic analytical versus concrete functional versus tropological) (cf. Wilson 1970), which they bring to the study of the Bible. How do we deal with these fundamental worldview differences? Robert Priest shows that Western theological categories cannot simply be translated into other languages (2000, 59–75; see also his chapter in this volume). Theological reflection in different cultures must be done initially in their conceptual categories. Then metatheological frameworks are needed to help theologians from different theologies understand, compare, and evaluate their understandings of Scripture. Priest notes also that theological reflections must link abstract, experience-distant concepts, which are often reductionist, with concrete, experience-near manifestations in everyday life, which are rich and intertwined.

Andrew Walls points out in this volume that the hermeneutical community involves not only churches in different cultures and theological traditions but also the church today and the history and legacies of the church through history. He laments the fact that Western Christian scholars are often little aware of or concerned with what is going on in the church and Christian scholarship around the world and take little time to learn other languages.

Missionaries and transnational church leaders from around the world are called on to be mediators in doing global theologizing. They must help theologians from different cultures understand one another deeply and become more self-aware of their own cultural perspectives. They are also called to mediate between formal theologies and the lives of ordinary Christians in the churches.

The final requisite for an evangelical metatheology is the guidance of the Holy Spirit. Too often we depend primarily on human reason to discern the truth. As Christians, we must be humble about the limitations of our knowledge and learn to discern the understanding that comes through the Spirit.

Missionaries and transnational church leaders are critical in mediating the growing encounters between cultures and churches in the emergence of a glocal world and a glocal church. Nowhere is this more important than in doing theology, for theological reflections lie at the very heart of our being as Christians.

Conclusion

Globalizing Theology

CRAIG OTT

> Christianity is not a garment made to specifications of a bygone golden age, nor is it an add-on whimsical patchwork rigged up without regard to the overall design. Rather, Christianity is a multicoloured fabric where each new thread, chosen and refined at the Designer's hand, adds luster and strength to the whole. In this pattern of faith affirmation we should stress the importance of interwoven solidarity with fellow believers, past, present, and future.
>
> Lamin Sanneh (2003, 56)

We are living in a day when realization of the vision of Revelation 7:9–10—a church composed of people from every nation, tribe, people, and language worshiping the Lamb of God—appears not far off. Not only has the church of Jesus Christ become a truly global church, but that global church reflects theologically and expresses itself in fresh and creative ways. In our age of global communication and travel, theological exchange and dialogue among members of the global church are possible in ways never dreamt of previously.

This development holds both promise and peril. Western Christianity could attempt to utilize such developments to further its ecclesial and theological dominance. Various forms of civil religion, nationalism, and ethnocentrism—in both Western and non-Western settings—might increase as a backlash to the seemingly irresistible forces of globalization. The negative effects of economic globalization could threaten the unity, integrity, and witness of the church. On the other hand, globalization offers the church unprecedented opportunities to spread the gospel and to interact as a global church. The church of the global South and East is not only growing numerically but also fully participating in missionary sending, and it has brought forth significant theologians.

The emergence of world Christianity also presents the church with not merely the opportunity but indeed the *obligation* to listen to and learn from one another. As has been pointed out throughout this volume, as Christians of a global church, we can no longer afford to ignore one another. This is no longer an option. The challenges are too great to be mastered alone and the opportunities too precious to be squandered. Our unity as the global body of Christ, the urgency of our global mission, and our witness before a watching world demand it. The rewards that await us as a global church are enormous if we will but face the challenge and take advantage of the opportunities.

The call for global theological dialogue is not new. Over thirty years ago, John Mbiti (1974) argued that the church had become "kerygmatically universal" while remaining "theologically provincial." He decried the one-sided dominance of Western theology, which he found impotent in addressing the needs of the emerging church.[1] William Dyrness wrote in 1994, "The interrelated nature of the Christian community and the demands placed on the church at the end of this millennium make genuine exchange in the theological arena not only possible, but indispensable" (1994, 10). The church of the global South and East is not without theologians of stature. Some of them have come to occupy significant positions in Western academic institutions. But as Robert Schreiter observes, we must "examine how fully participative Christian communities around the globe have become in the totality of the church, and to what extent a colonial mentality still remains" (2002, 15). A further call for globalizing missiology was sounded by William Taylor (2000a) and the World Evangelical Alliance.

Vinoth Ramachandra eloquently demonstrated in this volume that religious influence has long moved in both directions between East and

---

1. "Theology should strain its neck to see beyond the horizons of our traditional structures, beyond the comforts of our ready-made methodologies of theologizing; it should be with the church where it is, rubbing shoulders with human beings whose condition, outlook, concerns, and world views are not those with which we are familiar" (Mbiti 1974, 253). This article is still worth reading. Later he pointedly opines, "It is utterly scandalous for so many Christian scholars in older Christendom to know so much about heretical movements in the second and third centuries, when so few of them know so little about Christian movements in areas of the younger churches. We feel deeply affronted and wonder whether it is more meaningful theologically to have academic fellowship with heretics long dead than with the living brethren of the Church today in the so-called Third World" (1974, 259).

West. The conciliar movement preceded evangelicals in the endeavor to promote international theological dialogue. Its commitment has been admirable but the results often disconcerting to evangelicals.[2] The World Evangelical Alliance (WEA) and the Lausanne Committee for World Evangelization (LCWE) have through their various conferences, working groups, and consultations been the pioneers of genuine intercultural theological dialogue among evangelical Christians. Though progress has been made, as Tite Tiénou pointed out in his chapter, apart from the mission community, that progress has in fact been minimal.[3] Andrew Walls also noted in this volume that whereas the secular academy generally acknowledges the importance of understanding Christianity to understand Africa, "In the theological academy, . . . there appears much less recognition that, if one wishes to study modern Christianity, it is necessary to know something about Africa."

The global spread of Christianity and its attendant theological reflection open up unexplored territories and new horizons, offering expansive vistas to theologians everywhere. But will we pause to take them in? Can these multiple perspectives lead to greater understanding and deeper faithfulness for all?

That has been the plea of this book. The contributors have attempted to pursue the vision of Paul Hiebert (1988; 1991; and here) and others to consider the implications of the global expansion of Christianity and its "self-theologizing" for theology in the church as a whole. The day of Western Christianity's numerical dominance has past. Though the theological dominance of the West may continue due to its long theological heritage and its advantage in resources, if it is to serve the global church well, its theology must be globalized in the sense that it surrenders its position of privilege and enters genuine dialogue with theologians from non-Western traditions. This development need not denigrate the value

2. Not only have leaders from the non-Western world played significant roles in the ecumenical movement in general, but the Ecumenical Association of Third World Theologians, established in 1986, has also provided a forum to promote such theologizing. The recurrent and predominant themes have been social justice, feminism, ecology, and similar concerns.

3. While books have been written by Western evangelicals examining and evaluating the contribution of non-Western theology, relatively few titles by non-Western theologians are taken seriously by Western theologians. Positive examples include Dyrness (1990; 1992; 1994), the series of theological works by Kärkkäinen (2002a; 2002b; 2003; 2004), and InterVarsity's series Christian Doctrine in Global Perspective. The *Dictionary of Historical Theology* (Hart 2000) has numerous entries and references to non-Western theologies and theologians, but a perusal of the indices of the systematic theologies released by evangelical authors over the past twenty years reveals that most make no reference to non-Western theologians whatsoever. The few exceptions cite only Latin American liberation theologians. On the other hand, reference to Hegel, Heidegger, and even Hitler are common. Gandhi is the most frequently referenced non-Westerner of modern times.

of the Western theological tradition and its rich insights. Globalization of theology not only must include dialogue partners from the broad diversity of world Christianity that exists *today* but also must remain in continuity and discussion with the church and its theology of the *past*. We would be fools not to stand on the shoulders of those who have gone before. But then the reason for standing on someone's shoulders is to gain *new* perspectives and to see *further*.

M. Daniel Carroll R. has drawn attention to the fact that rapidly accelerating globalization greatly affects people's lives economically. He calls evangelicals to responsible theological reflection on such developments. Globalization has also drawn Christians around the world together in new ways. Annually, over one million Americans serve on international short-term mission trips (Peterson, Aeschliman, and Sneed 2003, 241ff.). A congregation in rural Atlantic, Iowa, partners with a congregation in Kazan, Tatarstan, Russia. Not only can the consumer habits, investment strategies, and political sympathies of citizens of Atlantic affect the economy and well-being of citizens of Kazan, but through personal contact, values, beliefs, and religious expressions are being mutually influenced. These and other global developments demand biblical, theologically reasoned responses.

The contributors to this volume have taken us over diverse and at times challenging terrain. The way forward has not always been clear, and even the tentative conclusions were sometimes uncomfortable. We are left wanting more. This is but a small step on a long journey that did not begin with us and will not end with us. This concluding chapter attempts to project a path for the next steps forward into this still relatively uncharted territory.

Globalizing Theology and the Place of Local, Contextual Theologies

In the name of contextualization, various local theologies have been developed, often addressing local concerns. Such local theologizing is necessary as an act of faithfulness in living out the gospel in a people's unique cultural context. Specific application of biblical truth to local issues evidences the ongoing and universal relevance of the gospel. Biblical contextualization also transforms and sanctifies traditions, speaks to specific worldviews, and employs vernacular expressions and modes of argumentation. Contextual theologies should by no means be replaced by global theologies. On the contrary, in the face of globalization and pressures toward cultural homogenization, the need is greater than ever to continue to develop local theologies that appreciate diversity and respond to ever-changing challenges.[4] Insofar as contextual theologies reflect universal human experiences and biblical values, they also contribute to the theology of the global church and can shed light on broader issues.

At the same time, the danger of contextual theologies emphasizing the local over the universal must be recognized. They remain only partial. As Laurent Magesa states it, "As such local churches in the South could run the danger of becoming simply the opposite expression of the universal claims they denounced in the North, and entertaining extreme parochialism in their systems" (2001, 205).[5] Lesslie Newbigin (1989, 144) warned of a "domestication" of the gospel in non-Western as well as Western cultures. Globalizing theology can help alleviate such imbalances.

Furthermore, political, technological, and economic globalization is making local cultures increasingly interconnected and interdependent. A locality is rarely monocultural and may even reflect an amalgam of premodern, modern, and postmodern worldviews. This means that even specific local theologies have much more in common with one another. Issues that concern local Christians in Sri Lanka are increasingly likely to overlap with concerns of Christians in Liberia, Honduras, or Serbia. Globalizing theology can bring local theologies into conversation with one another on mutual concerns.

Systematic theology has often sought to formulate biblical truth in an encyclopedic manner, cataloging and summarizing the teaching of Scripture on overarching themes that are universally true and relevant for all people in every culture. Such theology is of course influenced (often unconsciously) by contextual and historical factors and is in danger of imposing philosophical systems on the biblical text.[6] But this need not undermine altogether the attempt to reach common biblical understandings about questions of universal interest.[7]

4. E. G. Singgih writes, "In an era of globalization theologians of Asia should not put contextualization in antithesis to globalization" (2000, 366). Robert Schreiter states concisely, "*Globalization is inevitable; hence contextualization becomes essential*" (1993, 63, italics in original). Contextualization becomes "a means to help hold up what is noble and immensely human and humane in a local culture against the onslaughts of forces—both historical and contemporary—that seek to undermine the dignity of the local culture" (1993, 68). See also Koyama (1998).

5. Hiebert stated it in this way: "If we now speak of 'theologies' rather than of 'theology,' have we not reduced Christian faith to subjective human agreements and thereby opened the door for a theological relativism that destroys the meaning of truth?" (1994a, 94).

6. "There is a temptation for every generation of theologians to bring a cluster of inherited metaphysical commitments as self-evident, requiring no further justification, to the task of theology" (McGrath 1990, 5).

7. See the discussion by Hesselgrave and Rommen (1988) with a response from Vanhoozer.

The globalizing of theology seeks to expand theology's horizons through the use of new forms of argumentation, alternate cognitive styles, and new idiomatic expressions. It may help theologians become more aware of unreflected presuppositions that they have taken for granted but that are not shared by Christians everywhere. William Dyrness argues that non-Western theologians can fill gaps in the theological encyclopedia[8] and claims even more boldly that "any renewal that will come to Western theology will come by interaction with voices from alternative traditions" (1994, 13). On the other hand, Western theology, with its often individualistic and rationalistic orientation, has not always served the non-Western church well.[9] The point is, however, to move beyond an East versus West critique, which often employs gross generalizations while failing to point the way forward.

Globalizing Theology: A Many-Colored Tapestry

Our concern is to expand the discipline of theological inquiry beyond local-contextual theologies, on the one hand, and rigidly defined systematic theology, on the other, to theological inquiry that is truly global in nature and scope. As stated in the introduction to this volume, by globalizing theology, we mean theological reflection rooted in God's self-revelation in Scripture and informed by the historical legacy of the Christian community through the ages, the current realities in the world, and the diverse perspectives of Christian communities throughout the world, with a view to greater holiness in living and faithfulness in fulfilling God's mission in all the world through the church.

To return to Sanneh's metaphor cited above and to apply it to theology, the theology of the church needs to move from conformity to specifications of a bygone age (the narrow parameters of the Western or other

8. Hiebert's landmark article "The Flaw of the Excluded Middle" (1982) is an example of how the worldview of Western theologians led to a blind spot regarding the biblical teaching on unseen powers, a teaching desperately needed especially in animistic contexts.

9. Non-Western theologians, for example, stated their dissatisfaction with Western forms of theologizing in the Seoul Declaration: "We have recognized that if Evangelical theology is to fulfill its task in the third World it must be released from captivity to individualism and rationalism of Western theology in order to allow the Word of God to work with full power. Many of the problems of our churches are, in part, the result of this type of theology. Consequently, we insist on the need for critical reflection and theological renewal. We urgently need an Evangelical theology which is faithful to Scripture and relevant to the varied situations in the third World" (Seoul Declaration 1982). Hwa Yung lists the following reasons for dissatisfaction with Western theology: different histories and realities are presupposed, a different worldview is presupposed, the negative impact of Enlightenment thought, and an "unengaged" theology (1997, 1–9).

theological traditions) and beyond being a patchwork (of local theologies) without regard to the overall design (fragmentation) to become a genuinely multicolored fabric with various threads (from diverse perspectives) chosen and refined by the Designer adding to the luster and strength of the whole (a truly global theology). In advocating the globalizing of theology, we are suggesting neither a homogenization nor an attempt to formulate a one-size-fits-all universal dogma. The goal is more that of a harmonizing effort of common inquiry from multiple perspectives and in mutual respect in the quest for greater faithfulness to Christ and his purposes for the church. The desired result is an interweaving of diverse perspectives on issues of belief and practice that concern the global church as well as local churches from a perspective of biblical authority. The tapestry that emerges will be more revealing and profound than one composed of monotone shades or patchwork chaos.

But what is the place of the traditional Christian creeds, confessions, and doctrinal statements? Are these to be cast off as products of Western Christian culture? Have they no enduring place in the globalizing of Christian theology? These questions must be openly discussed as a part of a global dialogue. Andrew Walls notes in his chapter how some early creedal formulations were the result of reflection in Greek categories. This process nevertheless yielded a richer understanding of Christology that nearly all Christians can appreciate. The contribution by Steve Strauss in this volume also points out that even classic Christian confessions and creeds must be understood in light of language, history, and other contextual factors. Theological reflection, including creeds and confessions, remain human attempts to summarize and clarify biblical teaching. They are often brilliant, but they are not Scripture and are subject to human limitations. Creeds and other doctrinal formulations were forged in specific historical, cultural, and ecclesial contexts, often with the very purpose of creating boundaries or "social demarcation" (McGrath 1990, 37–52). When properly understood, such boundaries have a legitimate place in the church. But if improperly understood and applied, they can actually impede fuller and richer theological understandings.

One way of approaching this question is to affirm that theological formulations in the Western tradition are no less true in Africa or Asia than they are in Europe or America. However, they are not necessarily equally relevant, understandable, or adequate in all contexts. Nor are such formulations exhaustive. Here is where theological insights from non-Western perspectives hold so much promise. They open the door not necessarily for *alternative* but rather for *fuller* theological understanding.

But let us be clear. We are not advocating theological innovation or creativity as ends in themselves. It would be foolhardy to cast off lightly creeds or doctrinal formulations that have united Christians and served the church for nearly two thousand years. Nor are we suggesting theological speculation or "subjective impressionism" (see Bromiley 1979). As Timothy George has stated, "Theologians are not freelance scholars of religion, but trustees of the deposit of faith that they, like pastors, are charged with passing on intact to the rising generation" (1998, 49). But there remains always the need for fresh perspectives on biblical truth, new light shed on cherished doctrines, and relevant application to contemporary challenges. Globalizing theology can help us in this effort.

Out of the House of Mirrors: Criteria for an Evangelical Globalizing of Theology

We cannot check our cultural, linguistic, or historical garb at the door of theological inquiry. But does this condemn us to captivity to our garb? Do these clothes become fetters to progress? Radical approaches to theology that give primacy to a theologian's cultural situatedness and claim the equal legitimacy of any and every contextual approach lead us—to change metaphors—into a house of mirrors where we grope in circles but never move forward. We could see only Feuerbachian images of ourselves in our theologies. As noted already, this splinters theology into innumerable fragments that have little to say to one another.

On the other hand, in global dialogue, we can become in a positive sense mirrors for one another, helping us to see ourselves in new ways and to find our way out of the maze, doing together what we could not do alone. We stand to learn from one another just how our situatedness affects our theology and actions—and especially in our globalizing world, how they affect others. We may not want to return to the "one rule" (to use Vanhoozer's term) for theological method, but we must nevertheless seek some consensus in the method and goals of theology if there is to be any common ground for progress. This raises the thorny question of criteria.[10]

By criteria, I am not speaking primarily of a standard for evangelical identity or of a rigid methodology on which all must agree, though criteria will have much to do with how those matters are ultimately

---

10. Langdon Gilkey has identified the problem of theological method as a problem of "sources, content and criteria of theology as a form of thought" (cited in Kelsey 1999, 5). Many contemporary theologians reject altogether the attempt to arrive at universally acceptable criteria for justifying belief. This complex discussion cannot be entered here. Suffice it to say that evangelicals need not share such skepticism. On the other hand, as Carl Braaten writes from an even broader conciliar perspective, "If we are clear about the sources and norms of theology, it should be possible to do theology in an ecumenical age on a collaborative model" (1996, 143).

addressed. Rather, I am speaking of broad criteria that serve to identify the starting point, source, and center of theology and something
about the process of theological inquiry so as to provide a basis for
evangelical dialogue and constructive advancement of theological
understanding.

Much of evangelical theology has been reactive (i.e., a response to
teaching or doctrine felt to be inconsistent with orthodoxy or the teaching of Scripture). Though there is certainly a place for boundaries, a
centered-set approach will be more helpful than a bounded-set approach
in advancing a constructive, positive, and forward-looking evangelical
theology.[11] To quote Carl Braaten, "To be clear about the dogmatic center makes it possible to explore the wider circumference without losing
one's way" (1996, 147).

There exists among evangelicals a considerable diversity of opinion
about theological method.[12] This is further complicated as the globalizing of theology brings additional perspectives, logics, and experiences
to the discussion. We cannot attempt to untangle these knots in these
few pages. Nevertheless, questions of criteria and method must be can-
didly approached, for this is the problem that "dogs theology in this
new ecumene" (Schreiter 1993, 119). As Paul Hiebert and Tite Tiénou
assert, "Theology is a research tradition not because it has arrived at
one universally agreed upon answer, but because those in the field are
seeking to answer the same questions by using accepted methods of
inquiry and examining the same data" (2002a, 30).

For evangelicals, basic agreement on the ultimate authority of Scripture is a necessary starting point. Kevin Vanhoozer in these pages called
this the canonical principle. Scripture as God's revealed Word to humanity is the primary source for theology. As this Word is brought into
interface with the experience of the church in specific cultural and historical settings (a second source of "data" for theologizing), Scripture
must remain authoritative and normative. Scripture is to be the judge

11. The bounded- and centered-set approaches to understanding theological method
can be traced back to Hiebert's thinking (1978a, 1983). The bounded-set approach has
come to be associated with "traditionalist" and the centered-set approach with "reformist"
approaches to evangelical theology (Johnston 1997; Olson 1998). This polarized use of
centered- and bounded-set theory is both unfortunate and unnecessary. For purposes of
ecumenical cooperation, church polity, doctrinal clarity, ordination, etc., a bounded-set
approach is warranted. However, for the purposes of deeper theological understanding
and intercultural theological dialogue, a centered-set approach is more appropriate. These
two approaches should not be played against each other. One must first be clear about the
center before attempting to identify the boundaries. Emphasizing the center, on the other
hand, should not be construed as a license to ignore or take lightly the historic doctrinal
convictions of the church regarding the boundaries of legitimate Christian belief.

12. See, for example, Stackhouse (2000).

and arbiter of *all* theology and practice.[13] The goal must be a biblically rooted theology that may at times affirm but will certainly at other times challenge the values, practices, and worldview assumptions of any given culture. If we are to escape the house of mirrors, then this much we must agree on: Theology is first and foremost about God as he has revealed himself and his ways in Scripture.

This leads naturally to the second criterion on which consensus must be reached: biblical hermeneutics. Few subjects today are more hotly debated and greatly influenced by culture than hermeneutics. Vanhoozer also sketched some of these challenges in this volume. But if Scripture is our guide out of the labyrinth, then we must help one another in interpreting its message. Evangelicals generally affirm that the message of the biblical text is to be taken seriously in its natural sense while respecting its genre, historical setting, and place in the biblical canon. An interpreter is not free to import meaning into the biblical text but seeks to be informed by the text.[14] Though no interpreter is entirely free from his or her cultural biases and presuppositions, a critical realist approach affirms that, though we do not understand Scripture perfectly, we can understand it adequately. Or to quote Hiebert, "We see through a glass darkly, but we do see. We are not totally blind" (1994a, 67). It is precisely through global dialogue that hopes for seeing more clearly are not threatened but rather rise. D. A. Carson (1996, 121–22) uses the mathematical example of the asymptote: As a curved line approaches an asymptote but never quite touches it, so our interpretations may never reach perfect or exhaustive understanding, but they can come ever closer to that goal. Such interpretations (as calculations) are accurate enough for practical usefulness and reliability, even if imperfect.

Grant Osborne (1991) speaks of a hermeneutical spiral whereby an interpreter's presuppositions are continually challenged and corrected in dialogue with Scripture. By globalizing theology, the hermeneutical spiral is expanded beyond an isolated interpreter to include a multicultural hermeneutic community. Here we have not so much an "epistemological privilege" of the poor or a "theological hegemony" of the West but an intercultural hermeneutical dialogue whereby each voice can contribute. The Holy Spirit is active in this interpretive process. When the historic

13. North American evangelicals, however, must realize that certain formulations regarding the nature of Scripture that have emerged in their historical context will not necessarily be equally valued in other contexts of the global church.

14. Lest one suspect that this is a Western approach to hermeneutics, a 1998 confession of faith formulated by four major house church groups in China states, "We are opposed to interpreting Scripture by one's own will or by subjective spiritualization" (cited in Lambert 1999, 61).

Christian community is included in the spiral, we have something akin to Vanhoozer's catholic principle.

Agreement on the christological center of theology is a criterion on which evangelicals must also maintain consensus. This includes affirmation of the uniqueness of Christ as incarnate Word, risen Savior, and returning Lord. A tendency in much conciliar theology is to advocate the validity of non-Christian religions and to relativize the uniqueness of Christ and the Christian faith. Some attempts at producing a global or universal theology have moved strongly in this direction, for example, emphasizing the common elements of all human religious experience.[15] A hallmark of evangelicalism is, however, unflinching affirmation of the unique revelation of God in Christ and his centrality to faith and life. In the words of Vanhoozer (in this volume), "All other truths must be engrafted into and encompassed by the drama of Jesus Christ." The gospel must be preached to every people with a view to conversion. The precise nature of non-Christian religions and their relationship to Christianity may remain topics for further inquiry and discussion, but the person and work of Christ must remain central to global evangelical theological dialogue.[16]

A further criterion for evangelical globalizing of theology is that of right practice. Theology must ensue in more faithful living according to the gospel.[17] Wilbert Shenk, as quoted by Tiénou above, is worthy of repeating here: *"Only theology that motivates and sustains the church in witness and service in the world deserves to be accredited"* (Shenk 2001, 105, italics in original). This criterion may strike some Western theologians as strange and difficult to assess, a reaction that betrays strains in Western theology, disconnecting right thinking from right living, and a tendency to abstraction. But it is consistent with Vanhoozer's (here and 2000, 81) call to move theology from *theoria* (good conceptual logic) to *phronesis*

15. See, for example, Smith (1981), Balasuriya (1984), Ambler (1990), Krieger (1991), Smart and Konstantine (1991), Reat and Perry (1991), Bracken (1995), and Nessan (2001). Carl Braaten protests even from a more conciliar standpoint: "Some theologians from different schools are clamoring for theocentricity . . . , but they propose to achieve this at the expense of christology. This is a false move; it contradicts the ecumenical center of the faith: the revelation of God in Jesus Christ" (1996, 144; cf. also 150).

16. "A global theology is an impossibility—if by that we mean a theology set in static propositions and affirmations that all Christians throughout the world can embrace and confess without any adaptation or exception. On the other hand, there is a golden thread—a universal given in God's revelatory and redemptive act in history—that must lie at the heart of all contextual theologies" (Cunningham 1997, 358).

17. Richard Cunningham defines theology in this way: "Theology is not an abstract static set of ideas but a dynamic living process in which the ancient faith becomes contemporary in every generation in ways that make it relevant to the living of authentic Christian life and to being and doing the work of the church in the world" (1997, 351).

(practical reasoning resulting in right action, wisdom) and with David Wells's (1993, 100) third element of theology as cultivation of virtue and wisdom. Non-Western theologians have generally been more concerned with theological issues that affect daily life and witness and are more likely to question the validity of a theology that is disconnected from life. This is of course entirely biblical.[18] Suffice it to say that a global theological discussion will have little patience for ivory-tower theology and armchair theologians aloof from the realities facing ordinary Christians.

David and Cynthia Strong described in these pages how the early church resolved theological controversy at the Jerusalem Council described in Acts 15. The above criteria can be observed in those deliberations. Various parties representing diverse theological convictions and ethnic interests were given a fair hearing. Yet ultimately it was the appeal to Scripture and recognition of the confirming work of the Holy Spirit in the lives of Gentile believers that led the council to consensus on the mind of God in the matter. With this landmark decision regarding the relationship of law and gospel, the fully sufficient salvific work of Christ was affirmed, unity in the church was maintained, and the believers were strengthened. The gospel was also set free from the confines of Judaism and could find diverse expression among Gentile peoples. Such an approach and such attitudes can serve as a model for the process of globalizing theology today.

D. A. Carson summarizes the nature of a globalizing of theology based on such criteria in this way:

> Listening to diverse cultures today can be an entirely salutary experience, when it is coupled with a profound desire to understand and obey what God has disclosed of himself in Scripture and supremely in Jesus Christ. . . . Instead of appealing to principles of contextualization to justify the assumption that every interpretation is as good as every other interpretation, we will recognize that not all of God's truth is vouchsafed to one particular interpretive community—and the result will be that we will be eager to learn from one another, to correct and to be corrected by one another, provided only that there is a principled submission to God's gracious self-disclosure in Christ and in the Scriptures. The truth may be one, but it sounds less like a single wavering note than like a symphony. (1996, 552)

Modes of Theologizing

A multiplicity of modes for theologizing is possible on the basis of these criteria. Robert Schreiter (1985) has noted at least four approaches

18. A plethora of biblical references could be cited; see for starters Prov. 1:7; Matt. 7:16–27; James 2:14–26.

to theology: theology as commentary on sacred text, theology as wisdom, theology as critical knowledge, and theology as praxis. Paul Hiebert and Tite Tiénou (2002a; 2002b) have described various modes and logics of doing theology. These include philosophical theology, Western systematic theology, non-Western philosophical theology, biblical theology, and tropological theology. They then propose a missional theology that "seeks to build the bridge between Biblical revelation and human context" (2002a, 38). Their model uses the logic of modern common law as developed in England and the United States[19] and nonlinear logic similar to that of case law.

Kevin Vanhoozer in this volume and elsewhere (2000; 2005b) proposes a method that is suitable to the subject matter of theology: the drama of redemption, the words and acts of God that culminate in Jesus Christ. "The form of theology is 'dramatic' inasmuch as it concerns a word addressed by God to man and a response from man to God. . . . The task of theology, therefore, is to enable hearers and doers of the gospel to respond and to correspond to the prior Word and Act of God" (2000, 69). The script of Scripture is played out on various contextual stages by the church as directed by the Holy Spirit. There is room for improvisation from context to context, yet the basic plot remains the same. Theodrama is Vanhoozer's way of making theology missional as doctrine provides direction for the church's participation in the ongoing triune mission. Such an approach holds considerable promise for globalizing theology because drama (though sometimes differently understood) is familiar in nearly every culture. It furthermore allows for a diversity of local creativity and expression while retaining an overall unity in the story line of the divine playwright's intent.

Anthropology has long been valued by missiologists for its value in understanding people and their cultures. Anthropological models for contextualization have been proposed by conciliar theologians (Bevans 2002), but anthropology has seldom been a serious discussion partner in evangelical theology. Robert Priest's contribution in this volume illustrates how linguistic and social scientific insights can help theologians overcome blind spots, uncover presuppositions, discover deeper insights of the human experience, and perhaps shed new light on the gospel itself. Making anthropology a discussion partner with theology, in addition to philosophy and history, is a challenging proposal yet to be fully

19. "Systematic theology plays the role of constitutional law. . . . Biblical theology and church creeds and confessions play the role of statutory law. . . . Missional theology plays the role of modern case law. It seeks to apply these in the infinitely diverse and particular situations of human life" (Hiebert and Tiénou 2002a, 38–39).

realized by evangelicals.[20] Andrew Walls concurs (in these pages) that, given the cross-cultural transmission of Christianity through history, a good historian needs the qualities needed for cross-cultural encounter. In this volume, Darrell Whiteman builds on Hiebert's insights (a pioneer in the integration of anthropology, theology, and missiology). Whiteman then describes various ways in which anthropology can help advance missiological and theological understanding, providing tools not only for better human understanding but also for better self-understanding of the theologian.

Our plea for globalizing theology is that such various modes of theologizing be mutually appreciated and explored. They can meet in global dialogue in a complementary manner, triangulating and enhancing understanding in new and exciting ways.

> Just as an architect makes different blueprints for the same building—structural, electrical, plumbing and so on, and as planners use different maps to map a city—roads, population density, zoning and so on, so we as humans need to look at reality from different perspectives and through different lenses. Different theologies throw different light on the nature of God and his works and revelation. (Hiebert and Tiénou 2002a, 40)

In his contribution to this volume, Hiebert calls for a further step: "Committed Christian theologians from around the world must be involved not only in examining and comparing local theologies but also in constructing the metatheological grid by which these are translated, compared, and evaluated."

Theological Triangulation

Many of us learned the principle of triangulation in a high school mathematics or physics class. By triangulation one can determine the height of tall buildings, navigate the seas, or survey a landscape. The unknown location of a point is determined by formation of a triangle with several known points or measures and the use of trigonometry. One fixed point or measure alone is not adequate. Triangulation is used analogously in reporting, social science research, and other forms of

20. See Conn (1984), Priest (2000), and Dyrness (1992, 23–29). For broader approaches, see Adams and Salamone (2000) and van der Jagt (2002). It should be kept in mind that making the social sciences the primary framework for theologizing makes theology susceptible to becoming captive to particular social or political ideologies (as has often been criticized of liberation theologies), just as systematic theology has at times been made captive to Western philosophy.

inquiry. By using a single method or perspective, a one-dimensional picture emerges lacking depth and accuracy. However, triangulation by using multiple methods and modes of inquiry can not only better validate findings but also achieve innovation in conceptual frameworks (Olson 2004).

Is not something analogous to triangulation also desirable and necessary in theology? Would not multiple perspectives bring us to deeper, more accurate understandings of a given theological question and its implications for faith and practice? The subject being explored remains the message of Scripture and its implications for life: how to live and serve as Christians in a complex and changing world. But the perspectives brought to the task can be diversified through the globalization of the theologizing process.

Multiple methodologies and multiple perspectives could bring greater validity, but innovative conceptual frameworks for theology could also emerge. These would not necessarily contradict insights of theology as understood historically but could shed new light, raise new questions, have more globally valid conclusions, and increase relevance for new generations and ever-changing contexts. "Complementarity" of various theological viewpoints combine so that a clearer picture emerges (Hiebert 1994a, 68–69).

Text and Context in Globalizing Theology

There are various ways to conceptualize the relationship of Scripture and culture in the theological task. These have profound implications not only for local theology and practice but also for the possibility of globalizing theology. One approach is to assume that culture is basically fallen and has nothing to contribute to Christian expression (see fig. 2). In effect, this naively assumes that there is only one correct, universally valid way to think and theologize and one biblically Christian culture that should emerge. It also overlooks that all theology is influenced by cultural and philosophical presuppositions that are not necessarily universally valid or understood. Scripture is pitted against culture. There is little or no room allowed for individual, local expressions of the faith. The goal is a more or less homogenous, universalized theology and practice, generally presumed to be of the Western variety.

Figure 2
Revelation and Culture in Opposition

Revelation ———▶ ◀——— Culture

Another approach is to value and affirm indigenous culture. Culture and Scripture are viewed as equals in determining theology and practice, with culture at times taking priority. This could be compared to an ellipse with the double foci of text (revelation) and context (culture), with text and context in creative tension (see fig. 3). This approach often sees God as already present in any given culture—apart from or prior to the entrance of the Christian message. One of the tasks of the theologian is then to discover in what ways God is already present or at work in the culture and to reflect on this in light of the gospel. But such an approach tends to deny the priority and prophetic power of Scripture to challenge and transform culture as part of the contextualization process. It can also result in a fragmentation of Christian theology into multiple, at times contradictory, local theologies emerging from various cultural contexts. These theologies are self-contained, have little to say to one another, and recognize no common criteria for dialogue or mutual correction.

Figure 3

Revelation and Culture as Equals

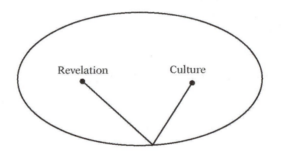

I propose another approach to conceptualizing the relationship between text and context that retains scriptural authority and priority while allowing for local diversity. This conceptualization for globalizing theology can be compared to a parabolic lamp, as familiar to us in a flashlight or automobile headlight. Light emanates from a single focal point and is reflected from a parabolic surface so as to project the light in a single direction. In this analogy, God's revelation provides the single focal point from which the "light" of theologizing emanates. It is singularly determinative and authoritative. This is the unifying element and primary criteria for global and local theology.

Yet the truth of Scripture is reflected in various ways at differing angles in each cultural context (in fig. 4, culture A and culture B). These reflection points represent various cultures into which the gospel has entered. This aspect would allow for diversity in local expressions of faith and practice. Because every culture is fallen, the light of God's revelation is initially distorted or reflected at the wrong "angle." Each local culture must therefore be transformed by the truth of Scripture so as to conform to the appropriate "parabolic curve" at its point and thus reflect the glory and mission of God in its unique way (i.e., at the appropriate "angle of reflection"). Local realities, be they social, political, intellectual, or otherwise, affect both the concerns and the manner of theologizing locally. Cognitive style may influence the mode and logic of theologizing.[21] Similarly, local manners of expression, communication, socialization, and so on shape the forms of Christian life and ministry. This is the diversifying element in the globalizing of theology.

Figure 4

**Revelation as Determinative
Culture as Reflective**

In this process, ideally, all will reflect together the glory of God and realize the mission of God in ways greater, clearer, and brighter than possible from merely a single cultural reference point. Globalizing theology in this sense is not a homogenizing but a *harmonizing* of local expressions and an amplification of the overarching concern. The entire process is empowered by the Holy Spirit. Through mutual dialogue and correction, the surface of the lamp (i.e., the faith and practice of the church in various contexts) is brought into a more perfect parabolic form so as to reflect the light of revelation more faithfully in that same direction: God's mission and glory.[22] This would necessitate the transformation of culture locally and uniquely so as to harmonize with the common vision and mission of the global church. This gives globalizing of theology both a doxological and a missional purpose.

21. For just two interesting discussions of this, see Chang (1984) and Bowen (1991).
22. Lamin Sanneh notes a similar understanding as missionaries translated the gospel into various languages, and a diversity of linguistic expressions for God were legitimized: "Languages were seen as the *many* refractions in which believers testified to the *one* God, so that particular cultural descriptions of God might convey in concrete terms the truth of God without in any way excluding other cultural descriptions" (1995, 56).

Emerging Agendas for Global Theologizing

Determining the unified direction of faith and practice (i.e., what it means to glorify God and to carry out the mission of God in the world today) should shape the agenda for global theologizing. As William Barr states, "As in all theological inquiry, the primary aim is to seek a clearer, deeper understanding of God in relation to the world and human life for the sake of more faithful and responsible participation in God's mission in and for the world" (1997, 4).

Just how this is specifically understood is a complex question. Robert Schreiter, in his book *The New Catholicity: Theology between the Global and the Local*, speaks of "global theological flows." These "are theological discourses that, while not uniform or systemic, represent a series of linked, mutually intelligible discourses that address the contradictions or failures of global systems" (1997, 16). He names four such flows: liberation, feminism, ecology, and human rights. These reflect relatively recent trends that have been the focus of much conciliar theology and are indeed concerns affecting the global church. Evangelicals have perhaps given too little attention to these issues. Nevertheless, as isolated themes they fail to align with the historic themes of theology. They have often become self-justifying and determinative paradigms for theology as a whole, overriding other more central themes of Scripture. The globalizing of theology must address these issues but integrate them into a larger biblical picture.

Stephen Bevans and Roger Schroeder in *Constants in Context: A Theology of Mission for Today* (2004) identify six recurring questions that provide continuity amid the great diversity of church and mission throughout the ages. The first two themes, drawn from Andrew Walls (1996), are Christology and ecclesiology. To these they add eschatology, salvation, anthropology, and culture.

> We propose, therefore, six *constants* in Christianity, six questions that Christianity constantly needs to answer, six questions that shape the way the church will preach, serve and witness to God's reign: (1) Who is Jesus Christ and what is his meaning? (2) What is the nature of the Christian church? (3) How does the church regard its eschatological future? (4) What is the nature of the salvation it preaches? (5) How does the church value the human? and (6) What is the value of human culture as the context in which the gospel is preached? (Bevans and Schroeder 2004, 34)

These are largely consistent with the issues with which theology has historically concerned itself. They must clearly remain central to any agenda for globalizing theology today. According to Bevans and Schroeder, it is not the content of how these questions are answered that provides continuity in Christian history but rather the fact that these issues are consistently urgent and central.[23] However, on the basis of the criteria described above, evangelicals in global dialogue can hope to reach not only greater consensus in answering these questions but also greater depth and breadth in how they are answered.

Given the global reality of world Christianity today, in addition to traditional theological questions, a long list of issues could be included in an agenda for the globalizing of theology. Particularly, evangelicals must overcome a tendency to focus merely on local concerns and personal piety, on the one hand, and grand theological abstractions, on the other. As M. Daniel Carroll R. and others have reminded us, they must expand their theological horizon to include a global perspective on pressing theological and practical questions. Here are just a few:

Missiologically

- What are the nature and implications of the *missio Dei* in our time?[24]
- How should a sequel to David Bosch's *Transforming Mission* (1991) be written, defining a biblical paradigm mission for the twenty-first century?[25]
- What are the implications of the current state of world Christianity for our mandate to fulfill the Great Commission and make disciples of all nations?
- What can we as a global church learn from one another regarding the encounter of Christianity and non-Christian religions and various worldviews?

Ecclesiologically

- What are the ecclesiological constants amid the diversity of forms and expressions of the church? How should the reality of a truly

23. "Answers to these questions . . . have certainly varied through the two millennia of Christianity's existence, as the church has lived out its missionary nature in various contexts. As *questions*, however, they remain ever present and ever urgent, because how they are answered is how Christianity finds its concrete identity as it constitutes itself in fidelity to Jesus' mission" (Bevans and Schroeder 2004, 34).

24. The term *missio Dei* has been so variously interpreted that its usefulness has rightly been questioned, being called a "container" term, into which and out of which one can put and take whatever one wants (Günther 1998, 56), or even a Trojan horse in the theology of mission (cited in Bosch 1991, 392). Nevertheless, the concept of the church's mission as participation in God's mission is a powerful one worthy of further study and reflection.

25. David Bosch's (1991) masterful work surveys the historical development of six paradigms for mission theology and practice but concludes with only a tentative and broad proposal.

global Christianity affect our understanding and experience of the diversity and beauty in the body of Christ?[26] Charles Van Engen in his chapter pointed the way forward in this discussion.

- How might an understanding of the Trinity provide insight into questions of unity and diversity in the church?
- In what ways should the vision of a new humanity in Christ according to Ephesians 2 and other biblical texts be realized in the local and global church today?
- How can the experience of the persecuted or suffering church enrich and fill gaps in our ecclesiology?

Historically

- As Andrew Walls reminded us in these pages, "The study of the past is always a cross-cultural exercise." What are the implications of this for the writing of church history today given the multiethnic nature of world Christianity?
- In what ways must our understanding of the spread and growth of Christianity be expanded or corrected?[27] Walls noted for us great gaps in the study of Western as well as non-Western Christianity.
- How must historical theology be rewritten in light of the way culture has affected theology—particularly in the non-Western world? To quote Walls again, "A culture-sensitive reading of the history of Christian doctrine might note how the crossing of cultural frontiers extends and enlarges theology."

Ethically

- How must we as a global church respond to the great pressing social issues of our day, such as poverty, injustice, war, racism, the AIDS crisis, bioethical questions, use of technology, materialism, sexual and family ethics, women's rights, stewardship of the environment, etc.?
- What can the church do to promote racial and ethnic reconciliation?
- What are the theological and ethical implications of globalization? Carroll has sounded a call to evangelicals in his chapter to address this topic more seriously with a "hermeneutics of responsibility."
- How can theological dialogue in the global church lead us to better understandings of civil religion, nationalism, ethnic identity, and church-state relations? Eloise Hiebert Meneses in these pages indicated the urgency of such dialogue.

26. See, for example, Leonard (2004).
27. See, for example, González (1993) and Hofmeyr (1998).

The agenda for global theologizing will continue to evolve as new issues arise and discussions proceed. Various international writing projects, consultations, working groups, and forums have already been at work on many of these issues. We can continue to anticipate creative and challenging answers if we have the will to pursue more intentionally such dialogue and to make it happen.

Making It Happen

Though much is already happening, much more needs to be done to promote more intentionally this process and to overcome obstacles. Here are just a few practical suggestions.

Creating a Round Table

The famous legend of King Arthur's round table might serve as a lesson for the church today. Arthur's round table was supposedly the key to overcoming quarrels in his court over seating precedence and rank. A round table has no head, and all seated at it are equals. According to legend, the round table was so effective in promoting solidarity that Arthur went on to defeat the Roman emperor Lucius and become emperor himself.[28]

What would a global round table of theologians look like?[29] For one, there would be no head of the table where Western theologians are seated making the rules and guiding the discussion. There would be no protests or complaints rising from non-Western theologians suffering under a sense of inferiority or motivated by ethnic pride. Privilege, rank, and ethnicity would fade into the background altogether. In fact, the bipolar distinction between Western and non-Western theologians would no longer be useful or necessary. Each participant would have an equal voice and a fair hearing to express his or her own unique perspective as part of the larger conversation. The encounter would focus on the contribution that each brings, and there would be freedom to question,

28. From http://www.kingarthursknights.com/arthur/legendary.asp, citing the *Illustrated Encyclopedia of Arthurian Legends* (accessed November 29, 2004). According to David Nash Ford, the origin of the concept of a round table has been variously traced back to a tradition that Christ and the apostles sat at a round table during the Last Supper or to Celtic tradition (cited at http://www.earlybritishkingdoms.com/arthur/rtable.html [accessed November 29, 2004]).

29. William Barr (1997, 6) suggests the idea of a round table discussion for theologians representing various cultures and backgrounds. His book is an attempt in written form to model such a round table discussion.

critique, learn, and discover in every direction around the table while respecting diversity.

Practically speaking, greater intentionality must be given to inclusion of international theologians and spokespersons in conferences, journals, publications, and teaching. Grassroots theologians must also be given a voice, even though that voice may lack some of the expected academic sophistication.[30] International denominational and ecumenical events should recognize and celebrate the diversity that the global church now has to offer. All this must be more than a tokenism or a faddism but rather a genuine sign of respect and a desire to learn and be mutually enriched.

Submitting to Peer Review

The *Chicago Tribune* recently reported that "a panel of forensic experts convened to explain the highest profile mistake in the history of modern fingerprint comparison." An Oregon lawyer had been falsely linked to the terrorist bombing of a train in Madrid that killed 191 people. The report went on to identify the reason for the mistake as "human error, defensiveness and a failure to follow some fundamental scientific practices, such as *proper peer review*."[31]

Peer review has become a standard procedure for various professional undertakings of importance, including forensic investigation. Perhaps it is time for theologians and Christian leaders to consider more seriously the necessity of *international* peer review in their writings, teaching, and praxis.

> Just as believers in a local church must test their interpretations of Scrip-
> tures with their community of believers, so the churches in different cultural
> and historical contexts must test their theologies with the international
> community of churches and the church down through the ages. (Hiebert
> 1994a, 103)

Craig Blomberg sees the need for "every interpreter to subject his or her views to the scrutiny of persons from very different backgrounds to see what additional truths may have been missed or distorted and to assess what may have been put forward as biblical which is in fact merely cultural" (1993, 226).

30. As John Mbiti stated it, "Indeed there is a great deal of spontaneous theologizing going on in the Church in Africa. It is informal, quiet, unwritten, unpolished theology, but nevertheless theology in its own way, and a theology which must be allowed a place in the Church universal" (1974, 258).

31. Emphasis added. "Report Blasts FBI Lab," *Chicago Tribune*, November 14, 2004, front page.

Historically, Western theologians have considered themselves to be the judges entitled to assess the validity of non-Western theologies. But how many theologically "justified" evils and aberrations in the Western church might have been avoided if Western theologians had been willing to submit to something like global theological peer review?[32] Vinoth Ramachandra, Eloise Hiebert Meneses, and M. Daniel Carroll R. have drawn our attention to how differently issues of global importance are perceived by Christians around the world. The consequences of such differences have far-reaching implications for global witness and unity today.

Tite Tiénou in these pages argued convincingly that theology should be a community task and a collaborative effort. But this is seldom practiced in any significant manner locally, much less in any kind of global theological community.[33] What is being proposed here is certainly nothing like an international expert panel of theologians who would sit in judgment over others. This is rather a call for theological community, the informal submission of ideas to others representing the global church for dialogue and critique, with a sense of mutual accountability. While even a theological community can err, as Robert Johnston puts it, "One is more likely to get the truth right in community, for here are present other Christians illuminated by the same Word and Spirit" (1997, 29). Positively viewed, such peer review could potentially expand theological horizons and be greatly affirming, encouraging further development in a given direction.

It should also be noted that peer review can be expressed in indirect forms of critique or disagreement rather than in direct or public confrontation. Many cultures value harmony, respect, and restraint of face-to-face critique over direct forms of negative communication. Dialogue, indirect communication, consensus building, and other forms of social interaction need to be explored to achieve similar corrective or affirming results of peer review as it is known in the more direct Western forms.

Several conditions are necessary for peer review to function meaningfully: humility, trust, consensus on criteria, and valuing community. Not only will the results of a theology forged in global dialogue be potentially richer, but the community of believers is likely to be better served by such a theology. David and Cynthia Strong pointed out the remarkable commitment to community present at the Jerusalem Council as a biblical example of theologizing in community.

32. Consider, for example, the theological justification of slavery, racism, colonialism, and civil religion, to mention only a few.
33. Professional societies sometimes provide such peer feedback. Occasionally, journals provide written responses to feature articles. There is, however, generally little sense of mutual accountability in such peer reviews.

Leveling the Playing Field

One of the greatest hindrances to the globalizing of theology as it is being advocated here is that the playing field is not level for Western and non-Western theologians. Actually, there are various playing fields. First, there is the financial playing field. Non-Western theologians rarely have the financial resources to participate in international conferences, take sabbatical leaves, fund publications, promote research, afford research assistants, and the like. Because of this, non-Western theologians generally have less opportunity to reflect, research, write, consult, and participate in theological dialogue. Already creative ways are being sought to level this field through grants, faculty exchanges, and other ways of sharing financial resources in the global theological community.

Fortunately, new technologies have opened up greater possibilities for non-Western theologians to publish: reduced production costs, funding grants, e-books, and Internet publication. Western book publishers and journals increasingly include non-Western authors. Still, the reality is that most Western theologians are relatively unaware of the writings of non-Western theologians.

Second, there is the uneven "equal access" playing field. Non-Western theologians generally have less access to libraries, formal education, communication technologies, and information in general. These are not necessary conditions for producing biblically profound theology. In fact, the lack thereof may well have contributed in many cases to the development of truly indigenous theology (Sanneh 2003, 109ff.). But a lack of access to such resources does inhibit participation in global dialogue and the international cross-pollination of ideas. Andrew Walls ironically notes, "Every year important books on Africa are published at prices no African institution can afford and that would swallow any African professor's salary for months ahead." He therefore rightly admonishes us, "Perhaps the test of real sharing within the body of Christ could be whether new heartlands could get greater access to the stockpiled scholarly resources of the West, not just the leftovers but the substance."

Third, there is the linguistic playing field. For all practical purposes, Western languages—particularly English—have become the mode of communication for the global church. Many of the most important resources for theological study are available only in European languages. Theology is of course not alone on this count. English has become the lingua franca of global science, technology, and economics. However, language clearly has a greater influence on how we talk about God than how it affects talk about DNA, RAM, or GDP.

Tite Tiénou pointed out above the limitations of this situation for formal theology. Robert Priest illustrated the practical importance of language in the understanding of basic theological concepts such as sin, whereby vernacular terms may well be better suited to express biblical concepts than English terms. John Parratt has noted that "the coining of categories of theological methodology from non-Western languages is as yet fairly undeveloped, but will need to develop if Third World theologians are fully to break out of First World parameters of doing theology" (2004, 9). Kwame Bediako (1998, 2002), Lamin Sanneh (1989, 1995), and others explain the profound impact that the use of vernacular languages has on not only the transmission of the Christian faith but also theological expression and understanding. When theologians are forced to dialogue exclusively in European languages, not only nuances of meaning but entire insights may lose their impact or be lost altogether. Yet the miracle of Pentecost in Acts 2 demonstrated the validity and adequacy of all human languages as an instrument of the Holy Spirit in communicating the gospel (González and González 1993, 13).

This is also an admittedly difficult field to level. A common language normally must be determined for conferences and dialogues, and English or French still tend to be the most widely spoken languages among Christians. The Western academy has long expected doctoral students in theology to acquire a reading knowledge of English, German, and/or French. While it is unrealistic to expect theologians to learn numerous African, Asian, or other languages, perhaps such languages could be substituted for a traditional research language in Western institutions.

Key Bridge Builders

In the effort to promote the globalizing of theology, at least four major bridge builders are in a position to facilitate the process: ecumenical organizations, the academy, missionaries and mission agencies, and churches and denominations. Organizations such as the WEA and the LCWE will no doubt remain at the forefront of advancing evangelical international dialogue on theological issues. Other similar regional organizations will also play major roles through various consultations, forums, and academic meetings.

The academy has in many ways also promoted the effort, but with a more mixed commitment. The subject of internationalizing theological education has been a topic of broad discussion for some time and need not be rehearsed again here.[34] Lois McKinney Douglas has addressed

34. See, for example, Stackhouse (1988), Evans, Evans, and Roozen (1993), and Tiénou's reference in this volume to discussions in the Association of Theological Schools in the United States and Canada. The spring 1993 issue of *Theological Education* (29, no. 2) features articles on teaching classical theological disciplines from a global perspective.

the topic in these pages. The exchange of *both* theologians and students, in *both* directions, from East to West and from West to East, must be more vigorously pursued.

The curriculum of Western seminaries should be expanded to include significant developments in the history of the non-Western church, and not only courses on third world theology and contextualization. Non-Western theologies should also be included in standard theology courses and readings. Vinoth Ramachandra insightfully describes the transgenerational and multiethnic nature of the new adopted family to which every Christian belongs:

> What this means is that, for me as an Asian Christian, Augustine and Irenaeus, Teresa of Avila and Mary Slessor, Calvin and Bonhoeffer all become my ancestors, part of my personal family tree. And, for Western Christians, their family tree now includes John of Damascus, Panditha Rambai, Sadu Sundar Singh, Kagawa and a host of outstanding Asian Christian men and women. I often wonder what a revolution this simple gospel concept would cause in Western theological education if grasped and applied in the curriculum! (1999, 136–37)

Non-Western theology is often considered exotic or presumed to deal with quaint issues of only local interest. Such theologies appeal perhaps to "intellectual or spiritual tourism" (Stackhouse 1991, 250) but are in effect sidelined as irrelevant to mainstream theologizing. Non-Western theologies may at times lack the academic sophistication expected in Western academic contexts, but profundity is not to be equated with scholarly erudition. As John Pobee has put it, intellectual pursuit "may not be the only criterion of excellence in theology in a context of globalization" (1997, 25).[35] Such resistance in the Western academy must be overcome if mutual respect, dialogue, and a genuine globalization of theology are to be advanced.

Missionaries and mission agencies have long been the bridge builders between cultures, as Paul Hiebert pointed out in this volume. Missionaries have normally learned the local languages, appreciated the culture and issues, and are the link to international relationships. They have provided scholarships, funded theological education, and published literature in their places of ministry. Missionaries have unfortunately often failed to encourage self-theologizing, and the patronizing attitudes of missionaries and the complexities of dependency need not be recalled here. But for all practical purposes, in many parts of the world, missionaries and

35. Indeed, the language of Jesus is that of the common person in contrast to the often hallowed, obtuse, and intimidating language of theologians (Sanneh 2003, 100–102).

mission agencies remain the primary links between local churches and the broader body of Christ. As Hiebert in this volume notes:

> Missionaries and transnational church leaders from around the world are called on to be mediators in doing global theologizing. They must help theologians from different cultures understand one another deeply and become more self-aware of their own cultural perspectives. They are also called to mediate between formal theologies and the lives of ordinary Christians in the churches.

Today, the movement of missionaries is no longer limited to West to East or North to South directions. Missionaries are from everywhere and go everywhere. In this regard, missionaries will all the more be key bridge builders in linking the global church. The missionary movement has not only been an agent of globalization but has itself become internationalized and globalized. This has profound implications not only for mission but also for theology, as James Plueddemann pointed out in these pages.

Churches and denominations have also long been promoters of bringing the global church together. As church-mission relations evolved in the later twentieth century into church-church relations, new possibilities opened up. As noted above, perhaps the most dramatic development in this regard is that local congregations in the West are now taking a more direct initiative to build relations with other local congregations internationally. This means that local churches are agents of mission and internationalization. No longer are denominational leaders and mission agencies the major players. Unfortunately, many local churches involved in direct partnerships are uninformed of the complexities of intercultural encounters, church-mission relations, and contextualization. Yet in many cases, they are having the most direct influence at the grassroots level of mission and ministry.

Thus, the globalizing of theology must include local pastors and laypersons. While professors, pastors, and laypersons are increasingly traveling internationally, as Hiebert pointed out in these pages, mere travel is not enough to become true learners and mediators. International sojourners must truly dialogue with ordinary people of host countries and overcome the temptation of "theological tourism" (Thistelwaite 1994). They must go as learners and not merely as experts. As much as possible, they should seek to encounter the life and Christian experience of the local people, attempting to understand their questions, challenges, joys, and spirituality, which are likely to be much different from their own. This will contribute more powerfully to intercultural understanding and a genuine globalization of theology.

Indeed, in our rapidly shrinking and globalizing world, informal personal relationships,[36] congregation-to-congregation partnerships, Internet messaging, and other alternative and grassroots initiatives will likely be the leading factors in globalizing theology. They are likely to overshadow the role of the more formal institutions listed above in the process of global theological exchange and creativity. This process will not necessarily be guided by traditional centers of theological influence or ecclesial power.

Conclusion

Returning to the eschatological vision of Revelation 5:9–10 and 7:9–10, we are reminded of the multiethnic worship of God by those who have been redeemed by the Lamb from every nation, tribe, people, and tongue on earth. In the eschatological kingdom, these distinctions will not be obliterated but harmonized to the glory and honor of God. The vision is ultimately one of a new humanity (not ethnic pride), a new city (not a locality), a new citizenship (not nationalism), and a new creation (not a fallen one).

Until Christ's return, the realization of this vision will only be partial as a sign of what is yet to come in fullness. However, that vision is to be no less passionately pursued now. If theology is understood as a part of worship, then our theology should no less reflect the manifold richness of human diversity and expression present in the heavenly vision. This is the purpose of globalizing theology.

The path we travel as global theologians is more one of faith than of sight. It is not one of perfected theological clarity that might lead to pride or false confidence. We confess with the apostle Paul, "Now we see but a poor reflection as in a mirror; then we shall see face to face. Now I know in part; but then I shall know fully, even as I am fully known" (1 Cor. 13:12). Obtaining perfect understanding will no doubt occupy us for all eternity! Our path today is one of faith leading to deeper worship and service of the living God, whom we seek to love and understand more fully. Or to continue quoting Paul, "And now these three remain: faith, hope and love. But the greatest of these is love" (1 Cor. 13:13). What could demand greater love, deeper humility, and more childlike faith than the human endeavor to understand and serve the eternal, living God? To do this more faithfully, we must live and think more as a global church, interconnected and interrelated, not merely by new technologies of a globalizing world but by our common bond with our heavenly Father.

36. "The task of Christian expatriates is . . . an important one, for they are on the front lines in the convergence of cultures, religious traditions, social issues, theologies, and—most importantly—people. In the final analysis, in theology it is people who are the most precious, and it is people for whom Christ lived, died, and lives today" (Adams 1987, 110).

Reference List

Acheson, James M. 1989. "Management of Common-Property Resources." In *Economic Anthropology*, ed. Stuart Plattner, 351–78. Stanford: Stanford University Press.

Adams, Daniel J. 1987. *Cross-cultural Theology: Western Reflections in Asia*. Atlanta: John Knox.

Adams, Walter Randolph, and Frank A. Salamone, eds. 2000. *Anthropology and Theology*. Lanham, MD: University Press of America.

Adeney, Bernard. 1995. *Strange Virtues: Ethics in a Multicultural World*. Downers Grove, IL: InterVarsity.

Adler, P. S. 1977. "Beyond Cultural Identity: Reflections upon Cultural and Multicultural Man." In *Culture Learning: Concepts, Applications, and Research*, ed. R. Brislin, 24–41. Honolulu: East-West Center.

Ådna, Jostein. 2000. "James' Position at the Summit Meeting of the Apostles and the Elders in Jerusalem (Acts 15)." In *The Mission of the Early Church to Jews and Gentiles*, ed. Jostein Ådna and Hans Kvalbein, 125–61. Wissenschaftliche Untersuchungen zum Neuen Testament, 127. Tübingen: Mohr Siebeck.

Alemayehu, Moges. 1995. Interview by Steve Strauss, July 25, Addis Ababa.

Allen, Charles. 2002. *The Buddha and the Sahibs*. London: John Murray.

Allen, Diogenes. 1985. *Philosophy for Understanding Theology*. Atlanta: John Knox.

Ambler, Rex. 1990. *Global Theology: The Meaning of Faith in the Present World Crisis*. Philadelphia: Trinity Press International.

Andersen, Wilhelm. 1961. "Further toward a Theology of Mission." In *The Theology of Christian Mission*, ed. G. H. Anderson, 300–313. Nashville: Abingdon.

Anderson, Benedict. 1991. *Imagined Communities: Reflections on the Origin and Spread of Nationalism*. New York: Verso.

Anderson, Walter Truett, ed. 1995. *The Truth about the Truth: De-confusing and Re-constructing the Postmodern World*. New York: Tarcher/Putnam.

Appadurai, Arjun. 1997. *Modernity at Large: Cultural Dimensions of Globalization*. Minneapolis: University of Minnesota Press.

Appiah-Kubi, Kofi, and Sergio Torres, eds. 1979. *African Theology En Route: Papers from the Pan-African Conference of Third World Theologians, December 17–23, 1977, Accra, Ghana*. Maryknoll, NY: Orbis.

Araujo, Alex. 2000. "Globalization and World Evangelism." In *Global Missiology for the Twenty-first Century*, ed. William David Taylor, 57–70. Grand Rapids: Baker.

Arrington, French L. 1988. "Hermeneutics." In *Dictionary of Pentecostal and Charismatic Movements*, ed. Stanley M. Burgess and Gary B. McGee, 376–89. Grand Rapids: Zondervan.

Association of Theological Schools in the United States and Canada. 1999. In Section 7, "Guidelines for Evaluating Globalization in ATS Schools." *Handbook on Accreditation*. Pittsburgh: Association of Theological Schools in the United States and Canada.

———. 2002. *Bulletin 45*, part 1. Pittsburgh: Association of Theological Schools in the United States and Canada.

Athyal, Saphir. 1980. "Toward an Asian Christian Theology." In *Asian Christian Theology: Emerging Themes*, ed. Douglas J. Elwood, 67–80. Philadelphia: Westminster.

———. 2000. "India." In *Evangelical Dictionary of World Missions*, ed. A. Scott Moreau, 478–80. Grand Rapids: Baker.

Avram, Wes, ed. 2004. *Anxious about Empire: Theological Essays on the New Global Realities*. Grand Rapids: Brazos.

Ayabe, Henry. 1992. "'Tsumi' in the Context of Preaching the Gospel." In *Step inside Japan: Language, Culture, Mission*, ed. Henry Ayabe, 119–24. Tokyo: Japan Evangelical Missionary Association.

Ayala, Takla Haymanot. 1981. *The Ethiopian Church and Its Christological Doctrine*. Addis Ababa: Graphic Printers.

Aymro, Wondemagegnehu, and Joachim Motovu. 1970. *The Ethiopian Orthodox Church*. Addis Ababa: Ethiopian Orthodox Mission.

Bachner, D. J., and U. Zeutschel. 1994. *Utilizing the Effects of Youth Exchange: A Study of the Subsequent Lives of German and American High School Exchange Participants.* New York: Council on International Educational Exchange.

Bakhtin, Mikhail M. 1986. *Speech Genres and Other Late Essays.* Austin: University of Texas Press.

Balasuriya, Tissa. 1984. *Planetary Theology.* Maryknoll, NY: Orbis.

———. 2000. "Globalization." In *Dictionary of Third World Theologies,* ed. Virginia Fabella and R. S. Sugirtharajah, 91–94. Maryknoll, NY: Orbis.

Banks, Robert. 1999. *Reenvisioning Theological Education: Exploring a Missional Alternative to Current Models.* Grand Rapids: Eerdmans.

Barber, Benjamin R. 1996. *Jihad vs. McWorld: How Globalism and Tribalism Are Reshaping the World.* New York: Random House.

Barclay, John M. G. 1996. "Christianity and Ethnicity in the Gospel of Matthew." In *Ethnicity and the Bible,* ed. Mark Brett, 171–95. Leiden: Brill.

Barnard, Alan. 2000. *History and Theory in Anthropology.* Cambridge: Cambridge University Press.

Barr, William R. 1997. "Re-forming Theology in the Global Conversation." In *Constructive Christian Theology in the Worldwide Church,* ed. William R. Barr, 1–9. Grand Rapids: Eerdmans.

Barrett, C. K. 1998. *A Critical and Exegetical Commentary on the Acts of the Apostles.* 2 vols. International Critical Commentary. London: T & T Clark.

Barrett, David B., George Kurian, and Todd M. Johnson, eds. 2001. *World Christian Encyclopedia: A Comparative Survey of Churches and Religions in the Modern World.* 2nd ed. New York: Oxford University Press.

Barrington-Ward, Simon. 1988. "Christianity Today." In *The World's Religions,* ed. Stewart Sutherland, Leslie Houlden, Peter Clarke, and Friedhelm Hardy, 287–304. Boston: G. K. Hall.

Barrio, Monseñor Próspero Penados del. 1989. *La Iglesia Católica en Guatemala: Signo de Verdad y Esperanza,* pastoral letter of Monseñor Próspero Penados del Barrio, Archbishop of Guatemala. Guatemala: Nuestra Imprenta.

Barro, Antonio C., and Ted Limpic. 2000. "Brazilian Mission Boards and Societies." In *Evangelical Dictionary of World Missions,* ed. A. Scott Moreau, 143–44. Grand Rapids: Baker.

Barth, Karl. 1958. *Church Dogmatics.* Vol. 4. Trans. G. T. Thomson. Edinburgh: T & T Clark.

Bauckham, Richard. 1995. "James and the Jerusalem Church." In *The Book of Acts in Its First-Century Setting*. Vol. 4, *The Book of Acts in Its Palestinian Setting*, ed. Richard Bauckham, 415–80. Grand Rapids: Eerdmans.

———. 1996. "James and the Gentiles (Acts 15:13–21)." In *History, Literature, and Society in the Book of Acts*, ed. Ben Witherington III, 154–84. Cambridge: Cambridge University Press.

Bavinck, Herman. 1956. *Our Reasonable Faith: A Survey of Christian Doctrine*. Grand Rapids: Baker.

Bayly, Christopher. 2003. *The Birth of the Modern World, 1780–1914*. Oxford: Blackwell.

Beck, Ulrich. 1997. *What Is Globalization?* Cambridge, UK: Polity Press.

Bediako, Kwame. 1995. *Christianity in Africa: The Renewal of a Non-Western Religion*. Maryknoll, NY: Orbis.

———. 1998. "The Doctrine of Christ and the Significance of Vernacular Terminology." *International Bulletin of Missionary Research* 22, no. 3 (July): 110–11.

———. 2002. "The Challenge of Mother Tongue for African Christian Thought." *Journal of African Christian Thought* 5, no. 1 (June): 1–60.

———. 2004. *Jesus and the Gospel in Africa: History and Experience*. Maryknoll, NY: Orbis.

———. N.d. *Urgent Questions Concerning Christianity in Africa: Some Reflections on a Manifesto*. Unpublished paper.

Bell, Daniel M., Jr. 2001. *Liberation Theology after the End of History: The Refusal to Cease Suffering*. London: Routledge.

Berger, Peter. 1997. "Four Faces of Global Culture." *National Interest* 49 (Fall): 23–29.

Berger, Peter L., and Samuel P. Huntington. 2002. *Many Globalizations: Cultural Diversity in the Contemporary World*. Oxford: Oxford University Press.

Berhanu, Gobena. 1993 (1985 Ethiopian Calendar). *Amde Haimanot (Pillar of Faith)*. Addis Ababa: privately printed.

Berkouwer, G. C. 1976. *The Church*. Grand Rapids: Eerdmans.

Berlin, Isaiah. 1979. "The Counter-Enlightenment." In *Against the Current: Essays in the History of Ideas*, ed. Henry Hardy, 1–24. London: Hogarth.

Bermúdez, Fernando. 1996. *Los Cristianos Frente al Neoliberalismo*. Colección Nueva Presencia 3. Guatemala City: Oficina de Derechos Humanos, Arzobispado de Guatemala.

Best, Ernest. 1955. *One Body in Christ*. London: SPCK.

Bettenson, Henry. 1947. *Documents of the Christian Church*. New York: Oxford University Press.

———. 1956. *The Early Christian Fathers*. London: Oxford University Press.

———. 1963. *Documents of the Christian Church*. New York: Oxford University Press.

Bevans, Stephen B. 1992. *Models of Contextual Theology*. Maryknoll, NY: Orbis.

———. 2002. *Models of Contextual Theology*. Rev. ed. Maryknoll, NY: Orbis.

———, and Roger P. Schroeder. 2004. *Constants in Context: A Theology of Mission for Today*. Maryknoll, NY: Orbis.

Bhagwati, Jagdish. 2004. *In Defense of Globalization*. New York: Oxford University Press.

Bietenhard, Hans. 1976. "People, Nation, Gentiles, Crowd, City." In *The New International Dictionary of New Testament Theology*, ed. Colin Brown, 788–805. Grand Rapids: Zondervan.

Bilezikian, Gilbert. 1993. *Christianity 101: Your Guide to Eight Basic Christian Beliefs*. Grand Rapids: Zondervan.

Blauw, Johannes. 1962. *The Missionary Nature of the Church*. Grand Rapids: Eerdmans.

Blomberg, Craig L. 1993. "Implications of Globalization for Biblical Understanding." In *The Globalization of Theological Education*, ed. Alice Frazer Evans, Robert A. Evans, and David A. Roozen, 213–28. Maryknoll, NY: Orbis.

Blyth, E. M. E. 1935. "The Church of Ethiopia." *Hibbert Journal* 34 (October): 80–91.

Boff, Clodovis. 1987. *Theology and Praxis: Epistemological Foundations*. Maryknoll, NY: Orbis.

———. 2000. "Theological Methodologies." In *Dictionary of Third World Theologies*, ed. Virginia Fabella and R. S. Sugirtharajah, 197–201. Maryknoll, NY: Orbis.

Bonhoeffer, Dietrich. 1954. *Life Together*. Trans. John W. Doberstein. San Francisco: HarperSanFrancisco.

Bonk, Jonathan J. 2004. "Orientalism, Occidentalism, and Christian Mission." *International Bulletin of Missionary Research* 28, no. 3 (July): 97.

Bornstein, David. 2004. *How to Change the World: Social Entrepreneurs and the Power of New Ideas*. New York: Oxford University Press.

Bosch, David J. 1980. *Witness to the World: The Christian Mission in Theological Perspective.* London: Marshall, Morgan & Scott.

———. 1991. *Transforming Mission: Paradigm Shifts in Theology of Mission.* Maryknoll, NY: Orbis.

Bowen, Earle, and Dorothy Bowen. 1991. "What Does It Mean to Think, Learn, Teach?" In *Internationalizing Missionary Training: A Global Perspective,* ed. William David Taylor, 203–16. Grand Rapids: Baker.

Bowers, Paul. 2000. "Byang Henry Kato." In *Evangelical Dictionary of World Missions,* ed. A. Scott Moreau, 535–36. Grand Rapids: Baker.

Boyarin, Daniel. 1994. *A Radical Jew: Paul and the Politics of Identity.* Berkeley: University of California Press.

Braaten, Carl E. 1996. "Scripture, Church, and Dogma: An Essay on Theological Method." *Interpretation* 50, no. 2 (April): 142–55.

Bracken, Joseph A. 1995. *The Divine Matrix: Creativity as Link between East and West.* Maryknoll, NY: Orbis.

Brake, Donald L. 1977. "A Historical Investigation of Monophysitism in the Ethiopian Orthodox Church." Th.D. diss., Dallas Theological Seminary.

Brauer, Jerald C. 1971. *The Westminster Dictionary of Church History.* Philadelphia: Westminster.

Brett, Mark. 1996. "Interpreting Ethnicity: Method, Hermeneutics, Ethics." In *Ethnicity and the Bible,* ed. Mark Brett, 3–22. Leiden: Brill.

Bromiley, Geoffrey W. 1978. *Historical Theology: An Introduction.* Grand Rapids: Eerdmans.

———. 1979. "Evangelicals and Theological Creativity." *Themelios* 5 (September): 4–8.

Brown, John Russell. 1995. *The Oxford Illustrated History of the Theater.* Oxford: Oxford University Press.

Brown, Robert K., and Mark R. Norton, eds. 1995. *The One Year Book of Hymns.* Wheaton: Tyndale.

Browning, Don S. 1986. "Globalization and the Task of Theological Education in North America." *Theological Education* 23, no. 1:43–59.

Bruce, F. F. 1988. *The Book of Acts.* Rev. ed. New International Commentary on the New Testament. Grand Rapids: Eerdmans.

Bruce, Steve. 2002. *God Is Dead: Secularization in the West.* Oxford: Blackwell.

Bujo, B. 1992. *African Theology in Its Social Context.* Maryknoll, NY: Orbis.

Bullón, H. Fernando. 2000. *Misión y Desarrollo en América Latina: Desafíos en el Umbral del Siglo 21.* Buenos Aires: Ediciones Kairós.

Burkhart, Louise M. 1989. *The Slippery Earth: Nahua-Christian Moral Dialogue in Sixteenth-Century Mexico.* Tucson: University of Arizona Press.

Buruma, Ian, and Avishai Margalit. 2004. "The Seeds of Revolution." *New York Review of Books* (March 11): 12.

Calenberg, Richard D. 2000. "Panya Baba." In *Evangelical Dictionary of World Missions,* ed. A. Scott Moreau, 103. Grand Rapids: Baker.

Calvin, John. 1975. *Institutes of the Christian Religion.* Trans. H. Beveridge. Grand Rapids: Eerdmans.

Cannell, Linda. 1999. "A Review of Literature on Distance Education." *Theological Education* 36, no. 1:1–72.

Capps, Donald. 1989. *Deadly Sins and Saving Virtues.* Philadelphia: Fortress.

Carrasco, David. 1999. "Uttered from the Heart: Guilty Rhetoric among the Aztecs." *History of Religions* 39:1–31.

Carroll R., M. Daniel. 1992. *Contexts for Amos: Prophetic Poetics in Latin American Perspective.* JSOT Supplement Series 132. Sheffield: Sheffield Academic Press.

———. 2001. "Liberation Theology: Latin America." In *The Oxford Illustrated History of the Bible,* ed. J. Rogerson, 316–29. Oxford: Oxford University Press.

———. 2004. "La Contextualización de los Profetas: Una Reseña de Retos Metodológicos." In *Teología Evangélica para el Contexto Latinoamericano: Ensayos en Honor al Dr. Emilio A. Núñez,* ed. O. Campos, 105–26. Buenos Aires: Ediciones Kairós.

Carson, D. A. 1996. *The Gagging of God: Christianity Confronts Pluralism.* Grand Rapids: Zondervan.

Castañeda, Jorge. 1993. *Utopia Unarmed: The Latin American Left after the Cold War.* New York: Knopf.

Cavalli-Sforza, L. Luca, Paolo Menozzi, and Alberto Piazza. 1994. *The History and Geography of Human Genes.* Princeton: Princeton University Press.

Chandran, J. Russell. 2000. "Epistemological Break." In *Dictionary of Third World Theologies,* ed. Virginia Fabella and R. S. Sugirtharajah, 84. Maryknoll, NY: Orbis.

Chang, Peter S. C. 1984. "Steak, Potatoes, Peas, and Chopsuey: Linear and Nonlinear Thinking." In *Missions and Theological Education in World Perspective,* ed. Harvie M. Conn and Samuel F. Rowan, 113–23. Farmington, MI: Associates of Urbanus.

Chaplin, Jack. 1998. "The Sender Local Church and Mission Agency: What Is the Best Relationship?" *Mission Frontiers* (January–February): 32–35.

Charter, Miriam L. 1997. "Theological Education for New Protestant Church of Russia: Indigenous Judgments on the Appropriateness of Educational Methods and Styles." Ph.D. diss., Trinity Evangelical Divinity School.

Chesnut, R. Andrew. 2003. *Competitive Spirits: Latin America's New Religious Economy.* Oxford: Oxford University Press.

Chesterton, G. K. 1959. *Orthodoxy.* Garden City, NY: Image Books.

Choong, Chee P. 1998. "Samuel Huntington's Clash of Civilizations and Its Implications for Christian Identity in Asia." In *A Global Faith: Essays on Evangelicalism and Globalisation,* ed. Mark Hutchinson and Ogbu Kalu, 214–26. Sydney: Centre for the Study of Australian Christianity.

Chopp, Rebecca S. 1997. "Latin American Liberation Theology." In *The Modern Theologians,* 2nd ed., ed. David Ford, 409–25. Oxford: Blackwell.

Clark, David. 2003. *To Know and Love God: Method for Theology.* Wheaton: Crossway.

Cleary, Edward L., and Hannah W. Stewart-Gambino, eds. 1997. *Power, Politics, and Pentecostals in Latin America.* Boulder: Westview.

Codrington, R. H. 1891. *The Melanesians: Studies in Their Anthropology and Folk-lore.* Oxford: Clarendon.

Coe, Shoki. 1980. "Contextualization as the Way toward Reform." In *Asian Christian Theology: Emerging Themes,* ed. J. Elwood, 48–55. Maryknoll, NY: Orbis.

Colley, Linda. 1992. *Britons: Forging the Nation, 1707–1837.* New Haven: Yale University Press.

———. 2002. *Captives: Britain, Empire, and the World, 1600–1850.* London: Jonathan Cape.

Conn, Harvie M. 1984. *Eternal Word and Changing Worlds: Theology, Anthropology, and Mission in Trialogue.* Grand Rapids: Zondervan.

Cook, Charles A. 2005. "Assessing the Long-term Impact of Intercultural Sojourners: Contributions of the CBC Intercultural Sojourners to Developing and Global Perspective." Ph.D. diss., Trinity International University.

Corbit, J. N. 1998. *Global Awareness Profile.* Yarmouth, ME: Intercultural Press.

Cox, Harvey. 2003. "Christianity." In *Global Religions: An Introduction,* ed. Mark Juergensmeyer, 17–27. New York: Oxford University Press.

Craffert, Peter. 1996. "On New Testament Interpretation and Ethnocentrism." In *Ethnicity and the Bible,* ed. Mark Brett, 449–68. Leiden: Brill.

Crummey, Donald. 1972. *Priests and Politicians: Protestant and Catholic Missions in Orthodox Ethiopia, 1830–1868.* Oxford: Clarendon.

Cunningham, Richard B. 1997. "Theologizing in a Global Context: Changing Contours." *Review and Expositor* 94 (Summer): 351–62.

Davids, Peter H. 2001. "James's Message: The Literary Record." In *The Brother of Jesus: James the Just and His Mission,* ed. Bruce Chilton and Jacob Neusner, 66–87. Louisville: Westminster John Knox.

Davies, Douglas. 2002. *Anthropology and Theology.* Oxford, UK: Berg.

Davies, J. G. 1965. *The Early Christian Church.* London: Weidenfelf & Nicolson.

Davis, John J. 1978. "Contextualization and the Nature of Theology." In *The Necessity of Systematic Theology,* 2nd ed., ed. John J. Davis, 169–85. Grand Rapids: Baker.

———. 1984. *Foundations of Evangelical Theology.* Grand Rapids: Baker.

Deferrari, Roy, ed. 1958. *The Fathers of the Church: Saint Cyprian, Treatises.* New York: Fathers of the Church.

Deiros, Pablo. 2000. "COMIBAM." In *Evangelical Dictionary of World Missions,* ed. A. Scott Moreau, 211–12. Grand Rapids: Baker.

De Ridder, Richard. 1971. *Discipling the Nations.* Grand Rapids: Baker.

De Silva, K. M. 1965. *Social Policy and Missionary Organizations in Ceylon, 1840–1855.* London: Longmans, Green.

de Soto, Hernando. 1989. *The Other Path: The Invisible Revolution in the Third World.* Trans. J. Abbott. New York: Harper & Row.

———. 2000. *The Mystery of Capital: Why Capitalism Triumphs in the West and Fails Everywhere Else.* New York: Basic Books.

Diamond, Jared. 2003. "Domestication and the Evolution of Disease." In *Conformity and Conflict,* 11th ed., ed. James Spradley and David W. McCurdy, 144–57. New York: Allyn & Bacon.

Dollar, David, and Aart Kraay. 2004. "Growth Is Good for the Poor." In *The Globalization Reader,* ed. Frank J. Lechner and John Boli, 177–82. Malden, MA: Blackwell.

Dowsett, Rose. 2001. *The Great Commission.* Grand Rapids: Monarch Books.

Duraisingh, Christopher. 2000. "Syncretism." In *Dictionary of Third World Theologies,* ed. Virginia Fabella and R. S. Sugirtharajah, 192–93. Maryknoll, NY: Orbis.

Dussel, Enrique. 1988. *Ethics and Community*. Trans. R. R. Barr. Liberation and Theology Series 3. Maryknoll, NY: Orbis.

———. 1993a. "Teología de la Liberación y Marxismo." *Ellacuría and Sobrino* 1:115–44.

———. 1993b. *Las Metáforas Teológicas de Marx*. Navarra, Spain: Verbo Divino.

———. 1998. *Ética de la Liberación en la Edad de la Globalización y de la Exclusión*. Colección Estructuras y Procesos; Serie Filosofía. Madrid: Trotta.

Dye, T. Wayne. 1976. "Toward a Cross-cultural Definition of Sin." *Missiology* 4, no. 1 (January): 27–41.

Dyrness, William A. 1990. *Learning about Theology from the Third World*. Grand Rapids: Baker.

———. 1992. *Invitation to Cross-cultural Theology: Case Studies in Vernacular Theologies*. Grand Rapids: Baker.

———, ed. 1994. *Emerging Voices in Global Christian Theology*. Grand Rapids: Eerdmans.

Eastman, Theodore. 1971. *Chosen and Sent: Calling the Church to Mission*. Grand Rapids: Eerdmans.

Eastwood, Cyril C. 1958. "Luther's Conception of the Church." *Scottish Journal of Theology* 11:22–36.

Ebeling, Gerhard. 1964. "Church History as the History of the Interpretation of Scripture." In *The Word of God and Tradition*, 11–31. Philadelphia: Fortress.

Eck, Diana. 2001. *A New Religious America: How a "Christian Country" Has Become the World's Most Religiously Diverse Nation*. New York: HarperCollins.

Edgerton, Robert. 1992. *Sick Societies: Challenging the Myth of Primitive Harmony*. New York: Free Press.

Engel, James F., and William A. Dyrness. 2000. *Changing the Mind of Missions: Where Have We Gone Wrong?* Downers Grove, IL: InterVarsity.

Escobar, Samuel. 2000. "Latin American Mission Boards and Societies." In *Evangelical Dictionary of World Missions*, ed. A. Scott Moreau, 559–60. Grand Rapids: Baker.

———. 2002. *Changing Tides: Latin America and World Mission Today*. Maryknoll, NY: Orbis.

———. 2003. *The New Global Mission: The Gospel from Everywhere to Everyone*. Downers Grove, IL: InterVarsity.

Evans, Alice Frazier, Robert A. Evans, and David Roozen, eds. 1993. *The Globalization of Theological Education.* Maryknoll, NY: Orbis.

Evans-Pritchard, E. E. 1956. "Sin." In *Nuer Religion,* 177–96. Oxford: Clarendon.

Fabella, Virginia. 2000a. "Context." In *Dictionary of Third World Theologies,* ed. Virginia Fabella and R. S. Sugirtharajah, 58. Maryknoll, NY: Orbis.

———. 2000b. "Inculturation." In *Dictionary of Third World Theologies,* ed. Virgina Fabella and R. S. Sugirtharajah, 104–6. Maryknoll, NY: Orbis.

———. 2000c. "Third World." In *Dictionary of Third World Theologies,* ed. Virginia Fabella and R. S. Sugirtharajah, 202–3. Maryknoll, NY: Orbis.

Fee, Gordon D., and Douglas Stuart. 1993. *How to Read the Bible for All Its Worth.* 2nd ed. Grand Rapids: Zondervan.

Feldmeier, Reinhard. 1996. "The 'Nation' of Strangers: Social Contempt and Its Theological Interpretation in Ancient Judaism and Early Christianity." In *Ethnicity and the Bible,* ed. Mark Brett, 241–70. Leiden: Brill.

Fernandez, Eleazar S., and Fernando F. Segovia. 2001. *A Dream Unfinished: Theological Reflections on America from the Margins.* Maryknoll, NY: Orbis.

Ferris, Robert W. 2000a. "Accreditation." In *Evangelical Dictionary of World Missions,* ed. A. Scott Moreau, 33. Grand Rapids: Baker.

———. 2000b. "Theological Education in Non-Western Contexts." In *Evangelical Dictionary of World Missions,* ed. A. Scott Moreau, 945–46. Grand Rapids: Baker.

Flannery, Austin P., ed. 1975. *Documents of Vatican II.* Grand Rapids: Eerdmans.

Foster, George. 1972. "The Anatomy of Envy: A Study in Symbolic Behavior." *Current Anthropology* 13:165–202.

Foster, Richard J. 2003. "Spiritual Formation: A Pastoral Letter." *Heart-to-Heart,* May 2003, http://www.renovare.org/readings_heart_to_heart_2003_may.htm (accessed April 4, 2005).

Freire, Paulo. 1993. *Pedagogy of the Oppressed.* New York: Continuum.

French, Howard W. 2004. *A Continent for the Taking: The Tragedy and Hope of Africa.* New York: Knopf.

Frend, W. H. C. 1972. *The Rise of the Monophysite Movement: Chapters in the History of the Church in the Fifth and Sixth Centuries.* Cambridge: Cambridge University Press.

Freston, Paul. 2001. *Evangelicals and Politics in Asia, Africa, and Latin America*. Cambridge: Cambridge University Press.

Friedland, Roger, and A. F. Robertson. 1990. Introduction to *Beyond the Marketplace*, ed. Roger Friedland and A. F. Robertson, 3–49. New York: Aldine de Gruyter.

Friedman, Thomas L. 1999. *The Lexus and the Olive Tree: Understanding Globalization*. New York: Farrar, Straus & Giroux.

———. 2000. *The Lexus and the Olive Tree: Understanding Globalization*. Rev. ed. New York: Farrar, Straus & Giroux.

———. 2005. *The World Is Flat: A Brief History of the Twenty-first Century*. New York: Farrar, Straus & Giroux.

Frostin, Per. 1985. "The Hermeneutics of the Poor: The Epistemological 'Break' in Third World Theologies." *Studia Theologica* 39, no. 2:127–50.

Fukuyama, Francis. 1992. *The End of History and the Last Man*. New York: Free Press.

Fürer-Haimendorf, Christoph von. 1967. *Morals and Merit: A Study of Values and Social Controls in South Asian Societies*. London: Weidenfeld & Nicolson.

———. 1974. "The Sense of Sin in Cross-cultural Perspective." *Man (N.S.)* 9:539–56.

Gadamer, Hans-Georg. 2002. *Truth and Method*. 2nd rev. ed. Trans. Joel Weinsheimer and Donald G. Marshall. New York: Continuum.

Galadima, Bulus. 2003. "Religion and the Future of Christianity in the Global Village." In *One World or Many? The Impact of Globalisation on Mission*, ed. Richard Tiplady, 191–202. Pasadena: William Carey Library.

Galeano, Eduardo. 1997. *Open Veins of Latin America: Five Centuries of Pillage of a Continent*. 25th anniversary ed. Trans. C. Belfrage. New York: Monthly Review Press.

Galindo, Florencio. 1993. *El 'Fenómeno' de las Sectas: La Conquista Evangélica de América*. Navarra, Spain: Verbo Divino.

García, Ismael. 2001. "The Future of Hispanic/Latino Theology: The Gifts Hispanics/Latinas Bring to the Table." *Journal of Hispanic/Latino Theology* 9, no. 1 (August): 46–56.

Garrard-Burnett, Virginia, and David Stoll, eds. 1993. *Rethinking Protestantism in Latin America*. Philadelphia: Temple University Press.

Garrett, William R., and Roland Robertson. 1991. "Religion and Globalization: An Introduction." In *Religion and the Global Order*, ed. Roland Robertson and William R. Garrett, ix–xxii. New York: Paragon.

Gay, Craig M. 1991. *With Liberty and Justice for Whom? The Recent Evangelical Debate over Capitalism*. Grand Rapids: Eerdmans.

"Gay Bishop Confirmed by Episcopal Church." 2003. *Record Searchlight* (Redding, CA), August 26, sec. A, pp. 1, 8.

Geertz, Clifford. 1973. *The Interpretation of Cultures*. New York: Basic Books.

———. 1977. "'From the Native's Point of View': On the Nature of Anthropological Understanding." In *Symbolic Anthropology: A Reader in the Study of Symbols and Meanings*, ed. Janet Dolgin, David Kemnitzer, and David Schneider, 480–92. New York: Columbia University Press.

———. 1988. *Works and Lives: The Anthropologist as Author*. Stanford: Stanford University Press.

George, Timothy. 1998. "A Theology to Die For." *Christianity Today* 42 (February 9): 49–50.

Gibbs, Eddie. 1994. *In Name Only: Tackling the Problem of Nominal Christianity*. Kent, UK: Monarch.

Giddens, Anthony. 1990. *The Consequences of Modernity*. Stanford: Stanford University Press.

———. 1999. *The Third Way: The Renewal of Social Democracy*. Malden, MA: Polity Press.

Glasser, Arthur F., Paul G. Hiebert, C. Peter Wagner, and Ralph D. Winter, eds. 1976. *Crucial Dimensions in World Evangelization*. Pasadena: William Carey Library.

Globalization and the Classical Theological Disciplines. 1993. Pittsburgh: Association of Theological Schools in the United States and Canada.

Gombrich, Richard, and Gananath Obeysekera. 1988. *Buddhism Transformed: Religious Change in Sri Lanka*. Princeton: Princeton University Press.

Gombrich, Richard F. 1971. *Precept and Practice: Traditional Buddhism in the Rural Highlands of Ceylon*. Oxford: Clarendon.

González, Justo L. 1990. *Mañana: Christian Theology from a Hispanic Perspective*. Nashville: Abingdon.

———. 1993. "Globalization in the Teaching of Church History." *Theological Education* 29, no. 2:49–69.

———, and Catherine G. González. 1994. "An Historical Survey." In *The Globalization of Theological Education*, ed. Alice Frazier Evans, Robert A. Evans, and David Roozen, 13–22. Maryknoll, NY: Orbis.

Goodall, Norman, ed. 1953. *Missions under the Cross*. London: Edinburgh House.

Gould, Stephen Jay. 1996. *The Mismeasure of Man*. New York: Norton.

Gration, John. 1984. "Willowbank to Zaire: The Doing of Theology." *Missiology* 12, no. 3 (July): 297–309.

Gray, John. 2004. "From the Great Transformation to the Global Free Market." In *The Globalization Reader*, ed. Frank J. Lechner and John Boli, 22–28. Malden, MA: Blackwell.

Grayston, Kenneth. 1953a. "A Study of the Word *Sin*, Part 1." *Bible Translator* 4, no. 3:138–40.

———. 1953b. "A Study of the Word *Sin*, Part 2." *Bible Translator* 4, no. 4:149–52.

Grenz, Stanley J. 2000. *Renewing the Center: Evangelical Theology in a Post-theological Era*. Grand Rapids: Baker.

Griffiths, Michael C. 2004. "My Pilgrimage in Mission." *International Bulletin of Missionary Research* 28, no. 3 (July): 122–25.

Grimes, Joseph. 1966. "Sin." *Notes on Translation* 22, no. 1:11–16.

Günther, Wolfgang. 1998. "Gott Selbst Treibt Mission: Das Modell der 'Missio Dei.'" In *Plädoyer für Mission: Beiträge zum Verständnis von Mission Heute*, ed. Klaus Schäffer, 56–63. Weltmission heute 35. Hamburg: Evangelische Missionswerk in Deutschland.

Gutiérrez, Gustavo. 1988. *A Theology of Liberation: History, Politics, and Salvation*. 15th anniversary ed. Trans. and ed. Sister C. Ina and J. Eagleson. Maryknoll, NY: Orbis.

———. 1998. *A Theology of Liberation*. Rev. ed. Maryknoll, NY: Orbis.

Hable Selassie, Sergew. 1972. *Ancient and Medieval Ethiopian History to 1270*. Addis Ababa: United Printers.

Habte, Mariam Worquineh. 1964–65. "The Mystery of the Incarnation." *Greek Orthodox Theological Review* 10, no. 2 (Winter): 154–61.

Haenchen, Ernst. 1971. *The Acts of the Apostles: A Commentary*. Trans. Bernard Noble, Gerald Shinn, Hugh Anderson, and R. McL. Wilson. Philadelphia: Westminster.

Halbfass, W. 1988. *India and Europe*. Albany: SUNY.

Hall, Edward T. 1976. *Beyond Culture*. New York: Anchor.

Hallowell, Irving. 1939. "Sin, Sex, and Sickness in Saulteaux Belief." *British Journal of Medical Psychology* 18:191–97.

Hammer, M. R., M. J. Bennett, and R. Wiseman. 2003. "Measuring Intercultural Sensitivity: The Intercultural Development Inventory." *International Journal of Intercultural Relations* 27:421–43.

Han, Kim Yung, ed. 2002. *The Direction of World Evangelical Theology in the Twenty-first Century*. Seoul: World Life Press.

Hardt, Michael, and Antonio Negri. 2000. *Empire*. Cambridge: Harvard University Press.

———, and Antonio Negri. 2004. *Multitude: War and Democracy in the Age of Empire*. New York: Penguin.

Harries-Jones, Peter. 1985. "From Cultural Translator to Advocated: Changing Circles of Interpretation." In *Advocacy and Anthropology: First Encounters*, ed. Robert Paine, 224–48. St. Johns, Nfld.: Institute of Social and Economic Research.

Harris, Marvin. 1968. *The Rise of Anthropological Theory*. New York: Thomas Y. Crowell.

Harrison, Carl H. 1985. "Summary on the Concept of Sin." *Notes on Translation* 106, no. 1:17–18.

Harrison, Lawrence E. 1985. *Underdevelopment Is a State of Mind: The Latin American Case*. Lanham, MD: Center for International Affairs.

———. 1997. *The Pan-American Dream: Do Latin America's Cultural Values Discourage True Partnership with the United States and Canada?* New York: Basic Books.

Hart, Trevor A., ed. 2000. *The Dictionary of Historical Theology*. Grand Rapids: Eerdmans.

Harvey, David. 1990. *The Condition of Postmodernity*. Cambridge, MA: Blackwell.

Hattaway, Paul. 2003. *Back to Jerusalem: Called to Complete the Great Commission*. Carlisle, UK: Piquant.

Hay, Stephen, ed. 1988. *Sources of Indian Tradition*. Vol. 2. New York: Columbia University Press.

Hedlund, Roger E. 2000. "Indian Mission Boards and Agencies." In *Evangelical Dictionary of World Missions*, ed. A. Scott Moreau, 480–81. Grand Rapids: Baker.

Henry, Carl F. H. 1988. *Twilight of a Great Civilization: The Drift toward Neo-paganism*. Westchester, IL: Crossway.

Herrick, Jim. 1985. "Bradlaugh and Secularism." In *Against the Faith: Some Deists, Sceptics, and Atheists*. London: Glover & Blair.

Hertz, Robert. 1922. "Le Péché e l'Expiation dans les Sociétés Primitives." *Revue de l'Histoire Religions* 86:1–60.

Hesselgrave, David J. 1983. "Missionary Elenctics and Guilt and Shame." *Missiology* 11, no. 4 (October): 461–83.

———, and Edward Rommen. 1988. "Systematic Theology: Who Needs It? With a Response by Kevin J. Vanhoozer." *Trinity World Forum* (Fall): 1–5.

―――, and Edward Rommen. 1989. *Contextualization: Meanings, Methods, and Models*. Grand Rapids: Baker.

Hiebert, Paul G. 1967. "Missions and the Understanding of Culture." In *The Church in Mission*, ed. A. J. Klassen, 251–65. Fresno: Board of Christian Literature, Mennonite Brethren Church.

―――. 1976. "Traffic Patterns in Seattle and Hyderabad: Immediate and Mediate Transactions." *Journal of Anthropological Research* 32, no. 4:326–36.

―――. 1978a. "Conversion, Culture, and Cognitive Categories." *Gospel in Context* 1, no. 4:24–29.

―――. 1978b. "Missions and Anthropology: A Love/Hate Relationship." *Missiology* 6, no. 2 (April): 165–80.

―――. 1982. "The Flaw of the Excluded Middle." *Missiology* 10, no. 1 (January): 35–47.

―――. 1983. "The Category 'Christian' in the Mission Task." *International Review of Mission* 72, no. 287 (July): 421–27.

―――. 1984. "Critical Contextualization." *Missiology* 12, no. 3 (July): 288–96.

―――. 1985. *Anthropological Insights for Missionaries*. Grand Rapids: Baker.

―――. 1987. "Critical Contextualization." *International Bulletin of Missionary Research* 11, no. 3 (July): 104–12.

―――. 1988. "Metatheology: The Step beyond Contextualization." In *Reflection and Projection*, ed. Hans Kasdorf and Klaus Müller, 383–95. Bad Liebenzell, Ger.: Liebenzeller Mission.

―――. 1989. "Form and Meaning in the Contextualization of Theology." In *The Word among Us: Contexualizing Theology for Mission Today*, ed. Dean Gilliland, 101–20. Dallas: Word.

―――. 1991. "Beyond Anti-colonialism to Globalism." *Missiology* 14, no. 3 (July): 263–81.

―――. 1994a. *Anthropological Reflections on Missiological Issues*. Grand Rapids: Baker.

―――. 1994b. "Critical Contextualization." In *Anthropological Reflections on Missiological Issues*, 75–92. Grand Rapids: Baker.

―――. 1994c. "Metatheology: The Step beyond Contextualization." In *Anthropological Reflections on Missiological Issues*, 93–103. Grand Rapids: Baker.

―――. 1999. *Missiological Implications of Epistemological Shifts: Affirming Truth in a Modern/Postmodern World*. Harrisburg, PA: Trinity Press International.

————, R. Daniel Shaw, and Tite Tiénou. 1999. *Understanding Folk Religion: A Christian Response to Popular Beliefs and Practices.* Grand Rapids: Baker.

————, and Tite Tiénou. 2002a. "Missional Theology." *Mission Focus: Annual Review* 10:29–42.

————, and Tite Tiénou. 2002b. "Missions and the Doing of Theology." In *The Urban Face of Mission,* ed. Harvie M. Conn, Manuel Ortiz, and Susan S. Baker, 85–96. Phillipsburg, NJ: P & R.

Hinkelammert, Franz. 1986. *The Ideological Weapons of Death: A Theological Critique of Capitalism.* Trans. P. Berryman. Maryknoll, NY: Orbis.

————. 1992. "La Lógica de la Expulsión del Mercado Capitalista Mundial y el Proyecto de la Liberación." *Pasos* 3:3–21.

————. 1997. "Liberation Theology in the Economic and Social Context of Latin America: Economy and Theology, or the Irrationality of the Rationalized." In *Liberation Theologies, Postmodernity, and the Americas,* ed. D. Batstone, 25–52. New York: Routledge.

Hitchen, John M. 2002. "Relationships between Missiology and Anthropology Then and Now: Insights from the Contribution to Ethnography and Anthropology of Nineteenth-Century Missionaries in the South Pacific." *Missiology* 30, no. 4 (October): 455–78.

Hoefer, Herbert E. 2000. *Churchless Christianity.* Pasadena: William Carey Library.

Hofmeyr, J. W. 1998. "Challenges for Writing African Church History in a Global Age: A Zambian Perspective." In *A Global Faith: Essays on Evangelicalism and Globalization,* ed. Mark Hutchinson and Obgu Kalu, 243–50. Sydney: Centre for the Study of Australian Christianity.

Hollenweger, Walter J. 1986. "Intercultural Theology." *Theology Today* 43, no. 1 (April): 28–35.

————. 2003. "Intercultural Theology: Some Remarks on the Term." In *Towards an Intercultural Theology: Essays in Honour of J. A. B. Jongeneel,* ed. Martha Fredris, Meindert Dijkstra, and Anton Hontepen, 89–95. Zoetermeer, Neth.: Uitgeverij Meinema.

Hopkins, A. G., ed. 2002. *Globalization in World History.* London: Pimlico.

Hopkins, Dwight N., Lois Ann Lorentzen, and Eduardo Mendieta. 2002. *Religions/Globalizations: Theories and Cases.* Durham: Duke University Press.

Howard, David. 2004. "Can a WASP Really Identify with Another Culture?" *Evangelical Missions Quarterly* 40, no. 2 (April): 174–81.

Huber, Evelyne, and Fred Solt. 2004. "Successes and Failures of Neoliberalism." *Latin American Research Review* 39, no. 3:150–64.

Hughes, Robert D. 2000. "Beginning a Theology of Anthropology." In *Anthropology and Theology: God, Icons, and God-talk*, ed. Walter Randolph Adams and Frank A. Salamone, 47–58. Lanham, MD: University Press of America.

Huntington, Samuel P. 1996. *The Clash of Civilizations and the Remaking of World Order*. New York: Simon & Schuster.

Hutchinson, Mark, and Ogbu Kalu, eds. 1998. *A Global Faith: Essays on Evangelicalism and Globalization*. Sydney: Centre for the Study of Australian Christianity.

Hwa, Yung. 1997. *Mangoes or Bananas? The Quest for an Authentic Asian Christian Theology*. Oxford: Regnum Books International.

Hyatt, Harry Middleton. 1928. *The Church of Abyssinia*. London: Luzac.

Imbach, S. R. 1984. "Syncretism." In *Evangelical Dictionary of Theology*, ed. Walter A. Elwell, 1062–63. Grand Rapids: Baker.

Inda, Jonathan Xavier, and Renato Rosaldo, eds. 2002. *The Anthropology of Globalization: A Reader*. Malden, MA: Blackwell.

International Council for Evangelical Theological Education (ICETE). 1990. *ICETE Manifesto on the Renewal of Evangelical Theological Education*. 2nd ed., http://www.icete-edu.org/manifesto.html (accessed May 2, 2005).

———. 2005. "ICETE Affiliated Institutions," http://www.icete-edu.org/directory.html (accessed May 2, 2005).

Irele, Abiola. 1991. "The African Scholar." *Transition* 51:56–69.

Irvin, Dale T., and Scott W. Sunquist. 2001. *History of the World Christian Movement*. Vol 1. Maryknoll, NY: Orbis.

Iwabuchi, Koichi. 2002. *Recentering Globalization: Popular Culture and Japanese Transnationalism*. Durham, NC: Duke University Press.

Jaffarian, Michael. 2002. "The Statistical State of the Missionary Enterprise." *Missiology* 30, no. 1 (January): 15–32.

Jaffrelot, Christophe. 1996. *The Hindu Nationalist Movement in India*. New York: Columbia University Press.

Jayawardena, Kumari. 2000. *Nobodies to Somebodies: The Rise of the Colonial Bourgeoisie in Sri Lanka*. Colombo, Sri Lanka: Social Scientists' Association and Sanjiva Books.

Jenkins, Philip. 2002. *The Next Christendom: The Coming of Global Christianity*. New York: Oxford University Press.

Johnson, Terry. 2005. Personal correspondence, April 13.

Johnson, Todd M., and Sun Young Chung. 2004. "Tracking Global Christianity's Statistical Centre of Gravity, AD 33–AD 2100." *International Review of Mission* 95, no. 369 (April): 166–81.

Johnston, Robert K. 1997. "Orthodoxy and Heresy: A Problem for Modern Evangelicalism." *Evangelical Quarterly* 69, no. 1 (January): 7–38.

Johnstone, Keith. 1989. *Impro: Improvisation and the Theatre.* New York: Routledge.

Johnstone, Patrick. 1998. *The Church Is Bigger than You Think.* Bulstrode, UK: WEC.

———, and Jason Mandryk. 2001. *Operation World: Twenty-first Century Edition.* Carlisle, UK: Pasternoster.

Jones, A. H. M., and Elizabeth Monroe. 1935. *A History of Ethiopia.* Oxford: Clarendon.

Juergensmeyer, Mark. 2003a. *Terror in the Mind of God: The Rise of Religious Violence.* 3rd ed. Berkeley: University of California Press.

———, ed. 2003b. *Global Religions: An Introduction.* New York: Oxford University Press.

Kalilombe, Patrick A. 1998. "How Do We Share 'Third World' Christian Insight in Europe?" *AFER: African Ecclesial Review* 40, no. 1:12–20.

Kane, J. H. 1986. *Wanted: World Christians.* Grand Rapids: Baker.

Kärkkäinen, Veli-Matti. 2002a. *An Introduction to Ecclesiology: Ecumenical, Historical, and Global Perspectives.* Downers Grove, IL: InterVarsity.

———. 2002b. *Pneumatology: The Holy Spirit in Ecumenical, International, and Contextual Perspective.* Grand Rapids: Baker.

———. 2003. *Christology: A Global Introduction.* Grand Rapids: Baker.

———. 2004. *The Doctrine of God: A Global Introduction.* Grand Rapids: Baker.

Kato, Byang H. 1975. *Theological Pitfalls in Africa.* Kisumu, Kenya: Evangel.

Katz, Jack. 1988. *Seductions of Crime: Moral and Sensual Attractions in Doing Evil.* New York: Basic Books.

Kejariwal, O. P. 1988. *The Asiatic Society of Bengal and the Discovery of India's Past, 1784–1838.* Delhi: OUP.

Kelly, J. N. D. 1960. *Early Christian Doctrines.* New York: Harper & Row.

Kelsey, David H. 1999. *Proving Doctrine: The Uses of Scripture in Modern Theology.* Harrisburg, PA: Trinity International Press.

Kemp, Roger, ed. 1994. *Text and Context in Theological Education.* International Council for Evangelical Theological Education, http://www.worldevangelical.org (accessed December 28, 2005).

Kidan, Wolde Kifle. N.d. *Metsehafe Sewasew Weges Wemezegebe Oalat Hadis (New Grammar and Dictionary).* N.p.

King, Richard. 1999. *Orientalism and Religion: Postcolonial Theory, India, and "Mystic East."* London: Routledge.

Kirk, J. Andrew. 1997. *The Mission of Theology and Theology as Mission.* Valley Forge, PA: Trinity Press International.

Korten, David C. 1995. *When Corporations Rule the World.* West Hartford, CN: Kumarian Press.

Korzeniewicz, Roberto Patricio, and William C. Smith. 2000. "Poverty, Inequality, and Growth in Latin America: Searching for the High Road to Globalization." *Latin American Research Review* 35, no. 3:7–54.

Koyama, Kosuke. 1977. *No Handle on the Cross: An Asian Meditation on the Crucified Mind.* Maryknoll, NY: Orbis.

———. 1998. "New Heaven and New Earth: Theological Education for the New Millennium." *Asia Journal of Theology* 12, no. 1 (April): 3–13.

Kraft, Charles H. 1979. *Christianity in Culture: A Study in Dynamic Biblical Theologizing in Cross-cultural Perspective.* Maryknoll, NY: Orbis.

Krieger, David J. 1991. *The New Universalism: Foundations for a Global Theology.* Maryknoll, NY: Orbis.

Kritzinger, J. J. 1996. "The Rwandan Tragedy as Public Indictment against Christian Mission." Paper read at the Annual Congress of the Southern African Missiological Society, http://www.geocities.com/missionalia (accessed December 28, 2005).

Kroeber, Alfred. 1948. *Anthropology.* New York: Harcourt, Brace & World.

Küng, Hans. 1963. *The Living Church.* New York: Shead & Ward.

———. 1971. *The Church.* London: Search Press.

Kuper, Adam. 1973. *Anthropologists and Anthropology: The British School, 1922–1972.* New York: Pica Press.

Lach, Donald F., and Edwin Van Kley. 1993. *Asia in the Making of Europe.* 3 vols. Chicago: University of Chicago Press.

Lambert, Tony. 1999. *China's Christian Millions.* London: Monarch.

Lambeth Commission on Communion. 2004. *The Windsor Report.* Rev. Dr. Robin Eames, archbishop of Armagh, chair. London: Anglican Communion Office, http://www.anglicancommunion.org/windsor2004/index.cfm (accessed December 14, 2004).

Larkin, William J., Jr. 1995. *Acts.* IVP New Testament Commentary Series. Downers Grove, IL: InterVarsity.

Larsen, David L. 2001. *Biblical Spirituality: Discovering the Real Connection between the Bible and Life.* Grand Rapids: Kregel.

Latourette, Kenneth Scott. 1953. *A History of Christianity.* London: Harper & Row.

———. 1967. *A History of the Expansion of Christianity.* Grand Rapids: Zondervan.

Laudin, Larry. 1996. *Beyond Positivism and Relativism: Theory, Method, and Evidence.* Boulder: Westview.

Learman, Linda. 2005. Introduction to *Buddhist Missionaries in the Era of Globalization,* ed. Linda Learman, 1–21. Honolulu: University of Hawaii Press.

Lechner, Frank J., and John Boli. 2004a. General introduction to *The Globalization Reader,* ed. Frank J. Lechner and John Boli, 1–4. Oxford: Blackwell.

———, and John Boli, eds. 2004b. *The Globalization Reader.* 2nd ed. Oxford: Blackwell.

Lee, David Tai Woong. 2000. "Asian Mission Boards and Societies." In *Evangelical Dictionary of World Missions,* ed. A. Scott Moreau, 85–86. Grand Rapids: Baker.

Lee, Jung Young. 1979. *The Theology of Change: A Christian Concept of God from an Eastern Perspective.* Maryknoll, NY: Orbis.

———. 1995. *Marginality: The Key to Multicultural Theology.* Minneapolis: Fortress.

———. 1999. *The Trinity in Asian Perspective.* Nashville: Abingdon.

Leonard, John S. 2004. "The Church in between Cultures: Rethinking the Church in Light of the Globalization of Immigration." *Evangelical Missions Quarterly* 40, no. 1 (January): 62–70.

Levinas, Emmanuel. 1989. "Ethics as First Philosophy." In *A Levinas Reader,* ed. Seán Hand, 75–87. Oxford: Blackwell.

Lewellen, Ted C. 2002. *The Anthropology of Globalization: Cultural Anthropology Enters the Twenty-first Century.* Westport, CN: Bergin & Garvey.

Lewis, Donald M. 1998. "Globalization: The Problem of Definition and Future Areas of Historical Inquiry." In *A Global Faith: Essays on Evangelicalism and Globalisation,* ed. Mark Hutchinson and Ogbu Kalu, 26–46. Sydney: Centre for the Study of Australian Christianity.

Lindbeck, George A. 1984. *The Nature of Doctrine: Religion and Theology in a Postliberal Age.* Philadelphia: Westminster.

Loewen, Jacob A. 1975. *Culture and Human Values: Christian Intervention in Anthropological Perspective.* Pasadena: William Carey Library.

———. 1992. "What Is Happening in Anthropology? An Example for Missionaries and Mission Boards." *Mission Focus* 20, no. 3:47–50.

Lonergan, Bernard. 1972. *Method in Theology.* New York: Seabury.

Lugo, Luis E. 1996. "Caesar's Coin and the Politics of the Kingdom: A Pluralist Perspective." In *Caesar's Coin Revisited: Christians and the Limits of Government*, ed. Michael Cromartie, 1–44. Grand Rapids: Eerdmans.

Luther, Martin. 1955. *Luther's Works*. Philadelphia: Fortress.

Lyman, Stanford M. 1989. *The Seven Deadly Sins: Society and Evil*. Dix Hills, NY: General Hall.

Magesa, Laurent. 2001. "Mission in the Post Cold War Era: Considerations for the Twenty-first Century." *Exchange* 30, no. 3:197–217.

Marshall, I. Howard. 1971. *Luke: Historian and Theologian*. Grand Rapids: Zondervan.

Martey, Emmanuel. 2000. "Liberation Theologies, African." In *Dictionary of Third World Theologies*, ed. Virginia Fabella and R. S. Sugirtharajah, 127–29. Maryknoll, NY: Orbis.

Martin, David. 1990. *Tongues of Fire: The Explosion of Protestantism in Latin America*. Oxford: Blackwell.

Marx, Karl. 1988. *The Communist Manifesto*. New York: W. W. Norton.

Mazrui, Ali A. 1990. *Cultural Forces in World Politics*. London: James Currey.

Mbiti, John S. 1972. "Some African Concepts of Christology." In *Christ and the Younger Churches: Theological Contributions from Asia, Africa, and Latin America*, ed. George F. Vicedom, 51–62. London: SPCK.

———. 1974. "Theological Impotence and the Universality of the Church." *Lutheran World* 21, no. 3:251–60.

———. 1976. "Theological Impotence and the Universality of the Church." In *Mission Trends*, no. 3, ed. Gerald H. Anderson and Thomas F. Stransky, 6–18. Grand Rapids: Eerdmans.

McDonald, J. I. H. 1990. "Hermeneutical Circle." In *A Dictionary of Biblical Interpretation*, ed. R. J. Coggins and J. L. Houlden, 281–82. Philadelphia: Trinity Press International.

McGrane, Bernard. 1989. *Beyond Anthropology: Society and the Other*. New York: Columbia University Press.

McGrath, Alister E. 1990. *The Genesis of Doctrine*. Grand Rapids: Eerdmans.

———. 2000. "Evangelical Theological Method." In *Evangelical Futures: A Conversation on Theological Method*, ed. John G. Stackhouse Jr., 15–37. Grand Rapids: Baker.

McIntosh, John. 2002. "'For It Seemed Good to the Holy Spirit' (Acts 15:28): How Did the Members of the Jerusalem Council Know This?" *Reformed Theological Review* 61, no. 3 (December): 131–47.

McKinney, Lois. 1993. "Missionaries in the Twenty-first Century: Their Nature, Their Nurture, Their Mission." *Missiology* 21, no. 1 (January): 55–64.

Mead, Margaret. 1949. *Coming of Age in Samoa.* New York: New American Library.

Menninger, Karl. 1973. *Whatever Became of Sin?* New York: Hawthorne Books.

Micklethwait, John, and Adrian Wooldridge. 2004. "The Hidden Promise: Liberty Renewed." In *The Globalization Reader,* ed. Frank J. Lechner and John Boli, 9–15. Malden, MA: Blackwell.

Míguez, Néstor Oscar. 2000. "Hermeneutical Circle." In *Dictionary of Third World Theologies,* ed. Virginia Fabella and R. S. Sugirtharajah, 97. Maryknoll, NY: Orbis.

Míguez Bonino, José. 1997. *Faces of Latin American Protestantism.* Trans. E. L. Stockwell. Grand Rapids: Eerdmans.

Milbank, John. 1990. *Theology and Social Theory: Beyond Secular Reason.* Cambridge, MA: Blackwell.

Miller, Christopher L. 1993. "Literary Studies and African Literature: The Challenge of Intercultural Literacy." In *Africa and the Disciplines: The Contribution of Research in Africa to the Social Sciences and the Humanities,* ed. Robert H. Bates, V. Y. Mudimbe, and Jean O'Barr, 213–31. Chicago: University of Chicago Press.

Miller, Ed L., and Stanley Grenz. 1998. *Fortress Introduction to Contemporary Theologies.* Minneapolis: Fortress.

Minear, Paul. 1960. *Images of the Church in the New Testament.* Philadelphia: Westminster.

Moltmann, Jürgen. 1977. *The Church in the Power of the Spirit.* New York: Harper & Row.

———. 1999. *God for a Secular Society: The Public Relevance of Theology.* Minneapolis: Fortress.

Morson, Gary Saul, and Caryl Emerson. 1990. *Mikhail Bakhtin: Creation of a Prosaics.* Stanford: Stanford University Press.

Mouw, Richard J. 1994. *Consulting the Faithful.* Grand Rapids: Eerdmans.

Muller, Richard A. 1991. "The Role of Church History in the Study of Systematic Theology." In *Doing Theology in Today's World: Essays in Honor of Kenneth S. Kantzer,* ed. John D. Woodbridge and Thomas Edward McComiskey, 77–97. Grand Rapids: Zondervan.

Mullick, Sunrit. 1993. "Protap Chandra Majumdar and Swami Vivekananda at the Parliament of Religions." In *A Museum of Faiths:*

Histories and Legacies of the 1893 World's Parliament of Religions, ed. Eric Ziolkowski, 221. Atlanta: Scholars Press.

Murphy, Edward F. 1976. "The Missionary Society as an Apostolic Team." *Missiology* 4, no. 1 (January): 103–18.

Nazir-Ali, Michael. 1991. *From Everywhere to Everywhere: A World View of Christian Witness*. London: Colins.

Nessan, Craig L. 2001. "After the Deconstruction of Christendom: Toward a Theological Paradigm for the Global Era." *Mission Studies* 17:78–96.

Newbigin, Lesslie. 1989. *The Gospel in a Pluralist Society*. Grand Rapids: Eerdmans.

New Indian Express. 2001. May 17, 9.

Nicholls, Bruce J., ed. 1994. *The Unique Christ in Our Pluralistic World*. Grand Rapids: Baker.

Niles, D. T. 1962. *Upon the Earth*. New York: McGraw-Hill.

Noble, Lowell. 1975. *Naked and Not Ashamed: An Anthropological, Biblical, and Psychological Study of Shame*. Jackson, MI: Jackson Printing.

Noll, Mark A. 1997. *Turning Points: Decisive Moments in the History of Christianity*. Grand Rapids: Baker.

Novak, Michael. 1982. *The Spirit of Democratic Capitalism*. New York: Simon & Schuster.

———. 2004. *The Universal Hunger for Liberty: Why the Clash of Civilizations Is Not Inevitable*. New York: Basic Books.

Núñez C., Emilio Antonio. 1997. *Hacia una Misionología Evangélica Latinoamericana: Bases Bíblicas de la Misión (Antiguo Testamento)*. Miami: Unilit.

———, and William David Taylor. 1996. *Crisis and Hope in Latin America: An Evangelical Perspective*. Pasadena: William Carey Library.

Nyamiti, Charles. 1994. "Contemporary African Christologies: Assessment and Practical Suggestions." In *Paths of African Theology*, ed. Rosino Gibellini, 62–77. Maryknoll, NY: Orbis.

O'Donovan, Oliver. 1996. *The Desire of the Nations: Rediscovering the Roots of Political Theology*. Cambridge: Cambridge University Press.

Oestreich, G. 1983. *Neo-Stoicism and the Early Modern State*. Cambridge: Cambridge University Press.

Oliver, Roland Anthony. 1952. *The Missing Factor in East Africa*. London: Longmans.

———. 1956. *How Christian Is Africa?* London: Highway.

Olson, Roger. 1998. "The Future of Evangelical Theology." *Christianity Today* 42 (February 9): 40–42, 44, 47–48.

Olson, Wendy. 2004. "Triangulation in Social Research." In *Developments in Sociology*, ed. M. Holborn. Ormskirk: Causeway Press, http://www.ccsr.ac.uk/methods/festival2004/programme/Sat/pm/MSTheatre/documents/Olsen_000.doc (accessed December 21, 2005).

Osborne, Grant R. 1991. *The Hermeneutical Spiral*. Downers Grove, IL: InterVarsity.

Packer, James I. 2000. "Maintaining Evangelical Theology." In *Evangelical Futures: A Conversation on Theological Method*, ed. John G. Stackhouse Jr., 181–89. Grand Rapids: Baker.

Padilla, C. René. 1980. "Hermeneutics and Culture: A Theological Perspective." In *Down to Earth: Studies in Christianity and Culture*, ed. John R. W. Stott and Robert Coote, 63–78. Grand Rapids: Eerdmans.

————, ed. 1998. *Bases Bíblicas de la Misión: Perspectivas Latinoamericanas*. Buenos Aires: Nueva Creación.

————, and Lindy Scott. 2004. *Terrorism and the War in Iraq: A Christian Word from Latin America*. Buenos Aires: Kairos.

Painter, John. 2001. "Who Was James? Footprints as a Means of Identification." In *The Brother of Jesus: James the Just and His Mission*, ed. Bruce Chilton and Jacob Neusner, 10–65. Louisville: Westminster John Knox.

Palomino, Miguel A. 2005. "Lessons from Latino Missions to Europe." *Evangelical Missions Quarterly* 41, no. 1 (January): 24–29.

Pantoja, Luis, Jr., Sadiri Joy Tira, and Enoch Wan, eds. 2004. *Scattered: The Filipino Global Presence*. Manila: LifeChange.

Park, Timothy Kiho. 2000. "Korean Mission Boards and Societies." In *Evangelical Dictionary of World Missions*, ed. A. Scott Moreau, 546–47. Grand Rapids: Baker.

Parkin, David. 1996. "Sin and Expiation." In *The Dark Side of Humanity: The Work of Robert Hertz and Its Legacy*. Amsterdam, Neth.: Harwood Academic Publishers.

————, ed. 1985. *The Anthropology of Evil*. New York: Blackwell.

Parratt, John, ed. 2004. *An Introduction to Third World Theologies*. Cambridge: Cambridge University Press.

Parshall, Phil. 1998. "Danger! New Directions in Contextualization." *Evangelical Missions Quarterly* 34, no. 4 (October): 404–10.

Pedraja, Luis G. 2003. *Teología: An Introduction to Hispanic Theology*. Nashville: Abingdon.

Peirce, Charles S. 1940. *Philosophical Writings of Peirce*. Ed. J. Buchler. New York: Dover.

Pelikan, Jaroslav. 1971. *The Christian Tradition: A History of the Development of Doctrine*. Vol. 1. Chicago: University of Chicago Press.

———. 2003. *Credo: Historical and Theological Guide to Creeds and Confessions of Faith in the Christian Tradition*. New Haven: Yale University Press.

Peters, George W. 1972. *A Biblical Theology of Missions*. Chicago: Moody.

Peterson, Anna, Manuel Vásquez, and Philip Williams, eds. 2001. *Christianity, Social Change, and Globalization in the Americas*. New Brunswick, NJ: Rutgers University Press.

Peterson, Roger, Gordon Aeschliman, and R. Wayne Sneed. 2003. *Maximum Impact Short-term Mission*. Minneapolis: STEMPress.

Petras, James, and Henry Veltmeyer. 2001. *Globalization Unmasked: Imperialism in the Twenty-first Century*. New York: Zed Books.

Petrella, Ivan. 2004. *The Future of Liberation Theology: An Argument and Manifesto*. Aldershot, UK: Ashgate.

Phan, Peter C. 2003. *Christianity with an Asian Face: Asian American Theology in the Making*. Maryknoll, NY: Orbis.

Pieris, Aloysius. 1988. *Towards an Asian Theology of Liberation*. Maryknoll, NY: Orbis.

Piet, John. 1970. *The Road Ahead: A Theology for the Church in Mission*. Grand Rapids: Eerdmans.

Pike, Kenneth. 1979. "Christianity and Culture: Conscience and Culture." *Journal of the American Scientific Affiliation* 31:8–12.

Plueddemann, James E. 1991. "Culture, Learning, and Missionary Training." In *Internationalizing Missionary Training*, ed. William David Taylor, 217–30. Grand Rapids: Baker.

———. 1995. "Measurable Objectives, No: Faith Goals, Yes." *Evangelical Missions Quarterly* 31, no. 2 (April): 184–87.

Plueddemann, Jim. 2000. "Spiritual Formation." In *Evangelical Dictionary of World Missions*, ed. A. Scott Moreau, 901–2. Grand Rapids: Baker.

Pobee, John S. 1997. "Theology in the Context of Globalization." *Ministerial Formation* 49 (October): 18–26.

Poladian, Bishop Terenig. 1964. "The Doctrinal Position of the Monophysite Churches." *Ethiopian Observer* 7 (Fall): 257–64.

Polhill, John B. 1992. *Acts*. New American Commentary. Vol. 26. Nashville: Broadman.

Poythress, Vern S. 1987. *Symphonic Theology: The Validity of Multiple Perspectives in Theology*. Grand Rapids: Zondervan.

Priest, Robert J. 1993. "Cultural Anthropology, Sin, and the Missionary." In *God and Culture*, ed. D. A. Carson and John Woodbridge, 85–105. Grand Rapids: Eerdmans.

———. 1994. "Missionary Elenctics: Culture and Conscience." *Missiology* 22, no. 3 (July): 291–315.

———. 1997. "Culture and the Victorious Christian Life." In *Free and Fulfilled: Victorious Living in the Twenty-first Century*, ed. J. Robertson McQuilkin, 128–42. Nashville: Thomas Nelson.

———. 2000. "Christian Theology, Sin, and Anthropology." In *Anthropology and Theology: God, Icons, and God-talk*, ed. Walter Adams and Frank Salomone, 59–75. Lanham, MD: University Press of America.

———. 2003. "I Discovered My Sin!" In *The Anthropology of Religious Conversion*, ed. Andrew Buckser and Stephen Glazier, 95–108. Lanham, MD: Rowman & Littlefield.

Proctor, John. 1996. "Proselytes and Pressure Cookers: The Meaning and Application of Acts 15:20." *International Review of Mission* 85, no. 339 (October): 469–83.

Quéau, Philippe. 2001. "Un Mythe Fondateur pour la Mondialisation." *Le Monde* (samedi 17 février): 14.

Ramachandra, Vinoth. 1999. *Faiths in Conflict? Christian Integrity in a Multicultural World*. Downers Grove, IL: InterVarsity.

Ramm, Bernard. 1959. *The Pattern of Religious Authority*. Grand Rapids: Eerdmans.

Ranger, Terence O. 2002. "Evangelical Christianity and Democracy in Africa." *Transformation* 19, no. 4 (October): 265–67.

Raschke, Carl. 2004. *The Next Reformation: Why Evangelicals Must Embrace Postmodernity*. Grand Rapids: Baker.

Raychaudhuri, Tapan. 1995. "The Pursuit of Reason in Nineteenth-century Bengal." In *Mind, Body, and Society: Life and Mentality in Colonial Bengal*, ed. Rajat Kanta Ray. Calcutta: OUP.

Reat, N. Ross, and Edmund F. Perry. 1991. *A World Theology: The Central Spiritual Reality of Humankind*. Cambridge: Cambridge University Press.

Redford, Shawn. 1999. "Facing the Faceless Frontier." In *Footprints of God: A Narrative Theology of Mission*, ed. Charles Van Engen, Nancy Thomas, and Rob Gallagher, 215–24. Monrovia: MARC, World Vision.

Reisz, H. Frederick. 2003. "Assessing Spiritual Formation in Christian Seminary Communities." *Theological Education* 39, no. 2:29–40.

Reventlow, H. G. 1984. *The Bible and the Rise of the Modern World.* London: SCM.

Richards, Lawrence O. 1985. *Expository Dictionary of Bible Words.* Grand Rapids: Zondervan.

Rightmire, R. David. 1996. "Apostle." In *Baker Theological Dictionary of the Bible,* ed. Walter Elwell, 33–35. Grand Rapids: Baker.

Ro, Bong Rin, and Ruth Eshenaur, eds. 1984. *The Bible and Theology in Asian Contexts: An Evangelical Perspective on Asian Theology.* Taichung, Taiwan: Asia Theological Association.

Robbins, Joel. 1998. "Becoming Sinners: Christianity and Desire among the Urapmin of Papau New Guinea." *Ethnology* 37, no. 4:299–316.

———. 2004. *Becoming Sinners: Christianity and Moral Torment in a Papua New Guinea Society.* Berkeley: University of California Press.

Robert, Dana L. 2000. "Shifting Southward: Global Christianity since 1945." *International Bulletin of Missionary Research* 24, no. 3 (April): 50–58.

Robertson, Roland. 1991. "Globalization, Modernization, and Postmodernization: The Ambiguous Position of Religion." In *Religion and Global Order,* ed. Roland Robertson and William Garrett, 281–91. New York: Paragon.

———. 1992. *Globalization: Social Theory and Global Culture.* Newbury Park, CA: SAGE.

———. 1995. "Glocalization: Time-Space and Homogeneity-Heterogeneity." In *Global Modernities,* ed. Mike Featherstone, Scott Lash, and Roland Robertson, 25–44. Thousand Oaks, CA: Sage Publications.

———. 2000. "Globalization and the Future of 'Traditional Religion.'" In *God and Globalization: Religion and the Powers of the Common Life,* ed. Max L. Stackhouse, with Peter J. Paris, 53–68. Harrisburg, PA: Trinity Press International.

———. 2003. "Antiglobal Religion." In *Global Religions: An Introduction,* ed. Mark Juergensmeyer, 110–23. New York: Oxford University Press.

Rosenau, James N. 2003. *Distant Proximities: Dynamics beyond Globalization.* Princeton: Princeton University Press.

Royal, Robert. 1998. "Who Put the West in Western Civilization?" *Intercollegiate Review* 33, no. 2 (Spring): 3–17.

Runia, Klaas. 1993. "The Challenge of the Modern World to the Church." *European Journal of Theology* 2:2.

Rynkiewich, Michael A. 2002a. "Person in Mission: Social Theory and Sociality in Melanesia." *Missiology* 31, no. 2 (April): 155–68.

———. 2002b. "The World in My Parish: Rethinking the Standard Missiological Model." *Missiology* 30, no. 3 (July): 301–21.

Saayman, Willem. 2000. "Missionary by Its Very Nature. *Missionalia*, http://www.geocities.com/missionalia/saayma00.htm (accessed April 11, 2006).

Sachs, Jeffrey D. 2005. *The End of Poverty: Economic Possibilities for Our Time*. New York: Penguin.

Sacks, Jonathan. 2002. *The Dignity of Difference*. London: Continuum.

Sahlins, Marshall. 1996. "The Sadness of Sweetness: The Native Anthropology of Western Cosmology." *Current Anthropology* 37:395–428.

Said, Edward. 1995. *Orientalism: Western Conceptions of the Orient*. London: Penguin.

Samuel, V. C. 1970. "The Faith of the Church." In *The Church of Ethiopia: A Panorama of History and Spiritual Life*, ed. Sergew Hable Selassie. Addis Ababa: Haile Selassie I University Press.

Samuel, Vinay, and Chris Sugden, eds. 1983. *Sharing Jesus in the Two Thirds World: Evangelical Christologies from the Contexts of Poverty, Powerlessness, and Religious Pluralism*. Grand Rapids: Eerdmans.

Sanneh, Lamin. 1989. *Translating the Message: The Missionary Impact on Culture*. Maryknoll, NY: Orbis.

———. 1993. *Encountering the West: Christianity and the Global Cultural Process: The African Dimension*. Maryknoll, NY: Orbis.

———. 1995. "The Gospel, Language, and Culture: The Theological Method in Cultural Analysis." *International Review of Mission* 84, no. 332 (January–April): 47–64.

———. 1997. "Missionary Enterprise." In *Encyclopedia of Africa South of the Sahara*, ed. John Middleton. New York: Charles Scribner's Sons.

———. 1998. "The 1998 Lambeth: Conflict and Consensus." *Christians & Scholarship* 2, no. 3:1–2, 4–5.

———. 2003. *Whose Religion Is Christianity? The Gospel beyond the West*. Grand Rapids: Eerdmans.

Sassen, Saskia. 2002. *Global Networks, Linked Cities*. London: Routledge.

Savarkar, V. D. 1999. *Hindutva: Who Is a Hindu?* Mumbai: Swatantryaveer Savarkar Rashtriya Smarak, Pandit Bakhle.

Sayers, Dorothy L. 1969. *Christian Letters to a Post-Christian World*. Grand Rapids: Eerdmans.

———. 1980. "Creed or Chaos?" In *The Necessity of Systematic Theology*, 2nd ed., ed. John Jefferson Davis, 27–47. Grand Rapids: Baker.

Schaff, Philip. 1877a. *The Creeds of Christendom*. New York: Harper & Bros.

————. 1877b. *The Creeds of Christendom with a History and Critical Notes*. Vol. 2, *The Greek and Latin Creeds with Translations*. Grand Rapids: Baker.

————. 1950. *History of the Christian Church*. Grand Rapids: Eerdmans.

————, and H. Wace, eds. 1974. *Nicene and Post-Nicene Fathers*. Grand Rapids: Eerdmans.

Schechner, Richard. 1989. *By Means of Performance: Intercultural Studies of Theater and Ritual*. Cambridge: Cambridge University Press.

Schimmel, Solomon. 1992. *The Seven Deadly Sins: Jewish, Christian, and Classical Reflections on Human Nature*. New York: Free Press.

Schlatter, Tim. 2002. "The Biblical Concept of Sin Relative to Animistic Worldview: A Case Study for Translating 'Sin' in the Tabo Language of Papua New Guinea." *Melanesian Journal of Theology* 18, no. 1:36–142.

Schmetzer, U. 2001. "Leader Says Islam Is Inferior to West." *Chicago Tribune*, September 28, sec. 1, p. 9.

Schnabel, Eckhard J. 2004. *Early Christian Mission: Jesus and the Twelve*. Vol. 1. Downers Grove, IL: InterVarsity.

Schoeck, Helmut. 1969. *Envy: A Theory of Social Behaviour*. New York: Harcourt, Brace & World.

Schreiter, Robert J. 1985. *Constructing Local Theologies*. Maryknoll, NY: Orbis.

————. 1993. "Contextualization from a World Perspective." *Theological Education* 30, supp. 1:63–86.

————. 1997. *The New Catholicity: Theology between the Global and the Local*. Maryknoll, NY: Orbis.

————. 2002. "Globalization, Postmodernity, and the New Catholicity." In *For All People: Global Theologies in Contexts*, ed. Else Marie Wiberg Pedersen, Holger Lam, and Peter Lodberg, 13–31. Grand Rapids: Eerdmans.

Scott, Allen J., ed. 2001. *Global City-Regions: Trends, Theory, Policy*. Oxford: Oxford University Press.

Scruggs-Leftwich, Yvonne. 2001. "Racism, Terror: A Connection?" *Chicago Tribune*, September 26, sec. 8, p. 6.

Segovia, Fernando F. 1996. "Racial and Ethnic Minorities in Biblical Studies." In *Ethnicity and the Bible*, ed. Mark G. Brett, 469–92. Leiden: Brill.

Segundo, Juan Luis. 1975. *The Community Called Church*. Maryknoll, NY: Orbis.

————. 1976. *The Liberation of Theology*. Maryknoll, NY: Orbis.

Sen, Amartya. 2004. "How to Judge Globalism." In *The Globalization Reader*, ed. Frank J. Lechner and John Boli, 16–21. Malden, MA: Blackwell.

Seoul Declaration. 1982. In *Toward an Evangelical Theology for the Third World*. Taichung, Taiwan: Asia Theological Association.

Severn, Frank M. 2000. "Mission Societies: Are They Biblical?" *Evangelical Missions Quarterly* 36, no. 3 (July): 320–26.

Shearer, Roy E. 1966. *Wildfire: Church Growth in Korea*. Grand Rapids: Eerdmans.

Shelton, James B. 2000. "Epistemology and Authority in the Acts of the Apostles: An Analysis and Test Case Study of Acts 15:1–29." *Spirit & Church* 2, no. 2 (November): 231–47.

Shenk, Wilbert R. 1996. "Toward a Global Church History." *International Bulletin of Missionary Research* 20, no. 2 (April): 50–57.

————. 2001. "Recasting Theology of Mission: Impulses from the Non-Western World." *International Bulletin of Missionary Research* 25, no. 3 (July): 98–107.

Sherman, Amy L. 1992. *Preferential Option: A Christian and Neoliberal Strategy for Latin America's Poor*. Grand Rapids: Eerdmans.

Shweder, Richard, Manamohan Marapatra, and Joan Miller. 1990. "Culture and Moral Development." In *Cultural Psychology: Essays on Comparative Human Development*, ed. James W. Stigler, Richard Shweder, and Gilbert Herdt, 130–204. Cambridge: Cambridge University Press.

Simbitti, Joel. 2003. *Africa Inland Church (Tanzania) and Missions*, #12552. Network for Strategic Missions, http://www.strategicnetwork.org (accessed December 28, 2005).

Singgih, E. G. 2000. "Globalization and Contextualization: Towards a New Awareness of One's Own Reality." *Exchange* 29, no. 4:361–72.

Smart, Ninian, and Steven Konstantine. 1991. *Christian Systematic Theology in a World Context*. Minneapolis: Fortress.

Smith, Adam. 1966. *The Theory of Moral Sentiments*. New York: Augustus M. Kelley.

Smith, David. 2003. *Hinduism and Modernity*. Oxford: Blackwell.

Smith, David J. 1992. *A Handbook of Contemporary Theology*. Wheaton: BridgePoint/Victor.

Smith, Huston. 1982. *Beyond the Post-modern Mind*. New York: Crossroad.

Smith, Wilfred Cantwell. 1981. *Towards a World Theology*. Maryknoll, NY: Orbis.

Song, Choan-Seng. 1984. *Tell Us Our Names: Story Theology from an Asian Perspective.* Maryknoll, NY: Orbis.

———. 1990a. *Jesus, the Crucified People.* New York: Crossroad.

———. 1990b. *Third-Eye Theology.* Rev. ed. Maryknoll, NY: Orbis.

———. 1999. *The Believing Heart: An Invitation to Story Theology.* Minneapolis: Fortress.

Sparks, Kent. 2004. "The Sun Also Rises: Accommodation in Inscripturation and Interpretation." In *Evangelicals and Scripture: Tradition, Authority, and Hermeneutics,* ed. Vincent Bacote, Laura C. Miguélez, and Dennis L. Okholm, 112–32. Downers Grove, IL: InterVarsity.

Spencer, Aida Besançon, and William David Spencer, eds. 1998. *The Global God: Multicultural Evangelical Views of God.* Grand Rapids: Baker.

Spiritual Formation Forum. 2003. *SFF Mission and Values,* http://www.spiritualformationforum.org/sff_mission.html (accessed April 4, 2005).

Sprinker, Michael, ed. 1992. *Edward Said: A Critical Reader.* Oxford: Blackwell.

Stackhouse, John G., Jr., ed. 2000. *Evangelical Futures: A Conversation on Theological Method.* Grand Rapids: Baker.

Stackhouse, Max L. 1988. *Apologia: Contextualization, Globalization, and Mission in Theological Education.* Grand Rapids: Eerdmans.

———. 1991. "Globalization and Theology in America Today." In *World Order and Religion,* ed. Wade Clark Roof, 247–63. Albany: State University of New York.

———, Tim Dearborn, and Scott Paeth, eds. 2000. *The Local Church in a Global Era: Reflections for a New Century.* Grand Rapids: Eerdmans.

Steenbergen, Gerrit van. 1991. "Translating 'Sin' in Pökoot." *Bible Translator* 43, no. 4:431–37.

Stiglitz, Joseph E. 2002. *Globalization and Its Discontents.* New York: W. W. Norton.

———. 2004. "Globalism's Discontents." In *The Globalization Reader,* ed. Frank J. Lechner and John Boli, 200–207. Malden, MA: Blackwell.

Stinton, Diane. 2004. "Africa, East and West." In *An Introduction to Third World Theologies,* ed. John Parratt, 105–36. Cambridge: Cambridge University Press.

Stott, John R. W. 1979. *The Message of Ephesians.* Downers Grove, IL: InterVarsity.

———, ed. 1997. *Making Christ Known: Historic Mission Documents from the Lausanne Movement, 1974–1989.* Grand Rapids: Eerdmans.

————, and Robert Coote, eds. 1980. *Down to Earth: Studies in Christianity and Culture.* Grand Rapids: Eerdmans.

Strand, Mark. 2000. "Explaining Sin in a Chinese Context." *Missiology* 28, no. 4 (October): 427–41.

Strauss, Stephen J. 1997. "Perspectives on the Nature of Christ in the Ethiopian Orthodox Church: A Case Study in Contextual Theology." Ph.D. diss., Trinity Evangelical Divinity School.

Stromberg, Peter. 1985. "The Impression Point: Synthesis of Symbol and Self." *Ethos* 13:56–74.

Sugirtharajah, Rasiah S. 2002. *Postcolonial Criticism and Biblical Interpretation.* Oxford: Oxford University Press.

————. 2003. *Postcolonial Reconfigurations: An Alternative Way of Reading the Bible and Doing Theology.* St. Louis: Chalice.

Sumner, George. 2004. *The First and the Last: The Claim of Jesus Christ and the Claims of Other Religious Traditions.* Grand Rapids: Eerdmans.

Sweet, Leonard. 1999. *Soul Tsunami: Sink or Swim in the New Millennium Culture.* Grand Rapids: Zondervan.

Taber, Charles R. 1991. *The World Is Too Much with Us: "Culture" in Modern Protestant Missions.* Macon, GA: Mercer University Press.

Taddesse, Tamrat. 1972. *Church and State in Ethiopia: 1270–1527.* Oxford: Clarendon.

Tai, Susan H. C., and Y. H. Wong. 1998. "Advertising Decision Making in Asia: 'Glocal' versus 'Regcal' Approach." *Journal of Managerial Issues* 10 (Fall): 318–19.

Tanner, Kathryn. 1997. *Theories of Culture: A New Agenda for Theology.* Minneapolis: Augsburg Fortress.

Tano, Rodrigo D. 1981. *Theology in the Philippine Setting.* Quezon City, Philippines: New Day.

Taylor, Mark. 2000. "Spirit in the Researching of Cultural Worlds: On Theology's Contributions to Anthropology." In *Anthropology and Theology: God, Icons, and God-talk,* ed. Walter Randolph Adams and Frank A. Salamone, 33–46. Lanham, MD: University Press of America.

Taylor, William D. 2000a. "Drawing to a Close: Inviting Reflective, Passionate, and Globalized Practitioners." In *Global Missiology for the Twenty-first Century,* ed. William D. Taylor, 549–56. Grand Rapids: Baker.

————, ed. 2000b. *Global Missiology for the Twenty-first Century: The Iguassu Dialogue.* Grand Rapids: Baker.

Templeton, Alan R. 1999. "Human Races: A Genetic and Evolutionary Perspective." In *The Biological Basis of Human Behavior: A Critical*

Review, ed. Robert W. Sussman, 180–92. Upper Saddle River, NJ: Prentice Hall.

Tesfazghi, Uqbit. 1973. *Current Christological Positions of Ethiopian Orthodox Theologians.* Rome: Pontifical Institutum Studiorum Orientalium.

Thistelwaite, Susan B. 1994. "Beyond Theological Tourism." In *Beyond Theological Tourism: Mentoring as a Grass Roots Approach to Theological Education,* ed. Susan B. Thistelwaite and George F. Cairns, 3–15. Maryknoll, NY: Orbis.

Thomas, John Christopher. 1994. "Women, Pentecostals, and the Bible: An Experiment in Pentecostal Hermeneutics." *Journal of Pentecostal Theology* 5:41–56.

Thomas, M. M. 1976. *The Acknowledged Christ of the Indian Renaissance.* 2nd ed. Madras: CLS.

Tiénou, Tite. 1982. "Biblical Foundations for African Theology." *Missiology* 10, no. 4 (October): 435–48.

———. 1993. "Forming Indigenous Theologies." In *Toward the Twenty-first Century in Christian Mission,* ed. James M. Phillips and Robert T. Coote, 245–52. Grand Rapids: Eerdmans.

———, and Paul Hiebert. 2002. *Missional Theology.* Unpublished manuscript.

Tinker, Hugh. 1974. *A New System of Slavery: The Export of Indian Labour Overseas, 1830–1920.* New York: Oxford University Press.

———. 1979. *The Ordeal of Love: C. F. Andrews and India.* Oxford: Oxford University Press.

Tiplady, Richard, ed. 2003. *One World or Many? The Impact of Globalisation on Mission.* Pasadena: William Carey Library.

Tocqueville, Alexis de. 2000. *Democracy in America.* New York: Bantam Books.

Tomlinson, John. 1999. *Globalization and Culture.* Chicago: University of Chicago Press.

Torres, Sergio, and Virginia Fabella, eds. 1978. *The Emergent Gospel: Theology from the Developing World.* London: Geoffrey Chapman.

Travis, John. 1998. "The C1 to C6 Spectrum: A Practical Tool for Defining Six Types of 'Christ-Centered Communities' ('C') Found in the Muslim Context." *Evangelical Missions Quarterly* 34, no. 4 (October): 407–8.

Tshibangu, Tshishiku. 1987. *La Théologie Africaine: Manifeste et Programme pour le Développement des Activités Théologiques en Afrique.* Limete/Kinshasa: Editions Saint Paul Afrique.

Turner, Harold E. W. 1952. *The Patristic Doctrine of Redemption.* London: A. R. Mowbray.

Turner, Victor. 1982. *From Ritual to Theater: The Human Seriousness of Play*. New York: *Performing Arts Journal* Publications.

United Nations Center for Human Settlements (Habitat). 2001. *Cities in a Globalizing World: Global Report on Human Settlements 2001*. London: Earthscan.

van der Jagt, Krijn. 2002. *Anthropological Approaches to the Interpretation of the Bible*. New York: United Bible Society.

Van der Veer, Peter. 2001. *Imperial Encounters: Religion and Modernity in India and Britain*. Princeton: Princeton University Press.

Van Engen, Charles. 1981. *The Growth of the True Church: An Analysis of the Ecclesiology of the Church Growth Movement*. Amsterdam: Rodopi.

———. 1991. *God's Missionary People*. Grand Rapids: Baker.

———. 1996. *Mission on the Way: Issues in Mission Theology*. Grand Rapids: Baker.

———.1997. "Mission Theology in the Light of Postmodern Critique." *International Review of Mission* 86, no. 343 (October): 437–61.

Vanhoozer, Kevin J. 1995. "Exploring the World; Following the Word: The Credibility of Evangelical Theology in an Incredulous Age." *Trinity Journal* 16:3–27.

———. 2000. "The Voice and the Actor." In *Evangelical Futures: A Conversation on Theological Method*, ed. John G. Stackhouse Jr., 61–106. Grand Rapids: Baker.

———. 2002. "The Trials of Truth: Mission, Martyrdom, and the Epistemology of the Cross." In *First Theology: God, Scripture, and Hermeneutics*, ed. Kevin J. Vanhoozer, 337–73. Downers Grove, IL: InterVarsity.

———. 2005a. "Discourse on Matter: Hermeneutics and the 'Miracle' of Understanding." *International Journal of Systematic Theology* 7:5–37.

———. 2005b. *The Drama of Doctrine: A Canonical-Linguistic Approach to Christian Theology*. Louisville: Westminster John Knox.

———. 2005c. "Lost in Interpretation? Truth, Scripture, and Hermeneutics." *Journal of the Evangelical Theological Society* 48, no. 1 (March): 89–114.

———. 2005d. "Pilgrim's Digress: Christian Thinking on and about the Post/modern Way." In *Christianity and the Postmodern Turn*, ed. Myron Penner, 71–103. Grand Rapids: Brazos.

Vásquez, Manuel A., and Marie F. Marquardt. 2003. *Globalizing the Sacred: Religion across the Americas*. New Brunswick: Rutgers University Press.

Virkler, Henry A. 1981. *Hermeneutics: Principles and Processes of Biblical Interpretation*. Grand Rapids: Baker.

Viswanathan, Gauri. 1998. *Outside the Fold: Conversion, Modernity, and Belief*. Princeton: Princeton University Press.

Volf, Miroslav. 1996. *Exclusion and Embrace: A Theological Exploration of Identity, Otherness, and Reconciliation*. Nashville: Abingdon.

Vulpe, T. D. Kealey, D. Protheroe, and D. MacDonald. 2001. *A Profile of the Interculturally Effective Person*. Ottawa: Canadian Foreign Service Institute.

Wallerstein, Immanuel. 1979. *The Capitalist World-Economy*. Cambridge: Cambridge University Press.

Walls, Andrew F. 1982. "The Gospel as the Prisoner and Liberator of Culture." *Missionalia* 10, no. 3:93–105.

———. 1989. *The Significance of African Christianity*. Church of Scotland: St. Colm's Education Centre and College.

———. 1991. "Structural Problems in Mission Studies." *International Bulletin of Missionary Research* 15, no. 4 (October): 146–55.

———. 1996. *The Missionary Movement in Christian History: Studies in the Transmission of Faith*. Maryknoll, NY: Orbis.

———. 1997. "Old Athens and New Jerusalem: Some Signposts for Christian Scholarship in the Early History of Mission Studies." *International Bulletin of Missionary Research* 21, no. 4 (October): 146–50, 152–53.

———. 2002a. "Christian Scholarship in Africa in the Twenty-first Century." *Transformation* 19, no. 4 (October): 217–28.

———. 2002b. *The Cross-cultural Process in Christian History*. Maryknoll, NY: Orbis.

Walton, Michael. 2004. "Neoliberalism in Latin America: Good, Bad, or Incomplete?" *Latin American Research Review* 39, no. 3:165–83.

Warneck, Gustav. 1901. *Outline of a History of Protestant Missions*. New York: Revell.

Warner, R. Stephen. 2004. "Coming to America." *Christian Century* (February 8): 20–23.

Waters, Malcolm. 2001. *Globalization*. 2nd ed. New York: Routledge.

Weber, Max. 1976. *The Protestant Ethic and the Spirit of Capitalism*. New York: Charles Scribner's Sons.

Wells, David. 1993. *No Place for Truth: Or Whatever Happened to Evangelical Theology?* Grand Rapids: Eerdmans.

Wells, Samuel. 2004. *Improvisation: The Drama of Christian Ethics*. Grand Rapids: Brazos.

Whiteman, Darrell L. 1997. "Contextualizing the Gospel." *Missiology* 25, no. 1 (January): 3–4.

Wiarda, Timothy. 2003. "The Jerusalem Council and the Theological Task." *Journal of the Evangelical Theological Society* 46, no. 2 (June): 233–48.

Wijsen, Frans. 2004. "Intercultural Theology Instead of Missiology: New Wine in Old Wineskins?" *SEDOS Bulletin* 36, no. 718 (July–August): 171–80.

Wiles, Maurice, and Mark Santer, eds. 1975. *Documents in Early Christian Thought*. London: Cambridge University Press.

Willard, Dallas. N.d. "Spiritual Formation: What It Is, and How It Is Done," http://www.dwillard.org/articles/artview.asp?artID=58 (accessed April 4, 2005).

Williams, Stephen N. 1995. *Revelation and Reconciliation: A Window on Modernity*. Cambridge: Cambridge University Press.

———. 2000. "The Theological Task and Theological Method: Penitence, Parasitism, and Prophecy." In *Evangelical Futures: A Conversation on Theological Method*, ed. John G. Stackhouse Jr., 159–77. Grand Rapids: Baker.

Wilson, Bryan R., ed. 1970. *Rationality*. New York: Blackwell.

Wilson, Carl. 1989. "What Is a Religious Order?" *Mission Frontiers* 11, nos. 8–9 (August–September): 21–26.

Wilson, Fiona. 2003. "Globalisation from a Grassroots, Two-thirds World Perspective." In *One World or Many? The Impact of Globalisation on Mission*, ed. Richard Tiplady, 167–88. Pasadena: William Carey Library.

Winter, Ralph D. 1971. "Churches Need Missions Because Modalities Need Sodalities." *Evangelical Missions Quarterly* 7, no. 4 (October): 193–200.

Witherington, Ben, III. 1998. *The Acts of the Apostles: A Socio-rhetorical Commentary*. Grand Rapids: Eerdmans.

Wolterstorff, Nicholas. 1996. "The Travail of Theology in the Modern Academy." In *The Future of Theology: Essays in Honor of Jürgen Moltmann*, ed. Miroslav Volf, Carmen Krieg, and Thomas Kucharz, 35–46. Grand Rapids: Eerdmans.

Yeago, David. 1997. "The New Testament and the Nicene Dogma." In *The Theological Interpretation of Scripture: Classic and Contemporary Readings*, ed. Stephen E. Fowl, 87–100. Oxford: Blackwell.

Yesehaq, Archbishop. 1989. *The Ethiopian Tewahedo Church: An Integrally African Church*. New York: Vantage.

Yung, Hwa. 1997. *Mangoes or Bananas? The Quest for an Authentic Asian Christian Theology.* Oxford: Regnum.

Zimmerman, Hans-Jurgens. 1985. *Fuzzy Set Theory and Its Applications.* Boston: Kluwer-Nijhof.

Zwemer, Samuel. 1950. "Calvinism and the Missionary Enterprise." *Theology Today* 8, no. 7 (July): 206–16.

Contributors

M. Daniel Carroll R. celebrates his heritage from both Guatemala and the United States. He is Earl S. Kalland Professor of Old Testament at Denver Seminary. Prior to this appointment, he was professor of Old Testament at El Seminario Teológico Centroamericano in Guatemala City, Guatemala (1982–96), where he remains adjunct professor. He has authored *Contexts for Amos: Prophetic Poetics in Latin American Perspective* and *Amos—the Prophet and His Oracles: Research on the Book of Amos*. He has edited seven other books and regularly publishes in both English and Spanish on issues related to the Old Testament, ethics, and missiology.

Lois McKinney Douglas is professor emerita of mission at Trinity Evangelical Divinity School in Deerfield, Illinois. She is a past president of the American Society of Missiology, previously taught at Wheaton Graduate School, and directed the joint EFMA-IFMA Committee to Assist Ministry Education Overseas, consulting theological educators internationally. She also served as a missionary educator for twenty-three years in Portugal and Brazil. Her publications have appeared in several journals, and she is coeditor of *With an Eye for the Future: Development and Mission in the Twenty-first Century*.

Paul G. Hiebert is distinguished professor of mission and anthropology at Trinity Evangelical Divinity School in Deerfield, Illinois. He taught previously at Fuller Theological Seminary, the University of Washington in Seattle, and Kansas State University in Manhattan, Kansas. He was born in India and later served there as a missionary. His numerous publications include *Cultural Anthropology, Anthropological Insights for*

Missionaries, and *Anthropological Reflections on Missiological Issues,* which have become standard textbooks. He also coauthored *Incarnational Ministry* and *Understanding Folk Religion.*

Eloise Hiebert Meneses is professor of cultural anthropology at Eastern University in St. Davids, Pennsylvania, where she directs the program in missions and anthropology. She has done anthropological field research among "untouchable" women of India and has interests in global economics, ethnicity, and the integration of science and faith.

Harold A. Netland is professor of philosophy of religion and intercultural studies at Trinity Evangelical Divinity School in Deerfield, Illinois. He has served in Japan as a missionary educator and is the author of *Dissonant Voices: Religious Pluralism and the Question of Truth* and *Encountering Religious Pluralism: The Challenge to Christian Faith and Mission.*

Craig Ott is associate professor of mission and intercultural studies at Trinity Evangelical Divinity School in Deerfield, Illinois, occupying the EFCA International Mission chair. He previously served twenty-one years in Germany and Central Europe and was academic dean of the Academy of World Mission in Korntal, Germany (affiliated with Columbia International University). His publications have appeared in various journals and edited volumes.

James E. Plueddemann is professor of mission and intercultural studies at Trinity Evangelical Divinity School in Deerfield, Illinois. He previously served as director of theological education for ECWA in Nigeria, as professor and chair of the department of Christian education and educational ministries at Wheaton College, and as international director of Serving In Mission (SIM). He has taught in many countries and written extensively, including *God's Heart for the World: Missionary Themes from Genesis to Revelation,* coauthored with his wife, Carol.

Robert J. Priest is professor of mission and intercultural studies and director of the Ph.D. program in intercultural studies at Trinity Evangelical Divinity School in Deerfield, Illinois. With interests in race and ethnicity, religious conversion, culture, and moral discourse, he has written for various edited volumes and journals, including "Missionary Positions: Christian, Modernist, Postmodernist" in *Current Anthropology.* He is currently researching short-term missionaries.

Vinoth Ramachandra is from Sri Lanka and lives in Colombo with his Danish wife, Karin. He holds bachelor's and doctoral degrees in nuclear engineering from the University of London. He is the secretary for dialogue and social engagement (Asia) for the International Fellowship of Evangelical Students (IFES). His primary work is helping students and faculty relate the Christian faith to their academic disciplines and to the social and political challenges they face in their local contexts. He has also given lectures at universities, theological colleges, and conferences internationally. He is the author of four books, including most recently *Faiths in Conflict?* and the coauthor of *The Message of Mission.*

Steve Strauss is United States director for Serving In Mission (SIM), adjunct professor of intercultural studies at Columbia International University, and visiting instructor at Gordon-Conwell Theological Seminary in Charlotte, North Carolina. He served with SIM in Liberia and Nigeria and ministered for nineteen years in Ethiopia, where he helped launch the Evangelical Theological College and the Ethiopian Graduate School of Theology and taught contextual theology.

David K. Strong is the Frances P. Owen Distinguished Professor of Missiology, and his wife, **Cynthia A. Strong**, is assistant professor of missiology at Simpson University in Redding, California. They served with the Christian and Missionary Alliance for fifteen years, both in Korea and in the Philippines, where they taught at the Alliance Biblical Seminary in Manila.

Tite Tiénou is senior vice president of education and academic dean of Trinity Evangelical Divinity School in Deerfield, Illinois, where he is also professor of theology of mission. Formerly he served as president and dean of the Faculté de Théologie Evangélique de l'Alliance in Abidjan, Côte d'Ivoire, West Africa, and taught at the Alliance Theological Seminary in Nyack, New York. He was the founding director and professor of the Maranatha Institute in Bobo-Dioulasso, Burkina Faso. He has authored numerous books and articles, including *The Theological Task of the Church in Africa.*

Charles E. Van Engen is Arthur F. Glasser Professor of Biblical Theology of Mission at the Fuller Theological Seminary School of Intercultural Studies. He has served as a missionary in Chiapas, Mexico, and has taught at Western Theological Seminary in Holland, Michigan. His numerous publications include *God's Missionary People, Mission-on-the-Way: Issues in Mission Theology,* and *The Good News of the Kingdom: Mission Theology for the Third Millennium* (coeditor).

Kevin J. Vanhoozer is research professor of systematic theology at Trinity Evangelical Divinity School in Deerfield, Illinois. He previously taught for eight years at the University of Edinburgh and served on the Church of Scotland's Panel on Doctrine. He is the author of *The Drama of Doctrine: A Canonical-Linguistic Approach to Christian Theology* and *Is There a Meaning in This Text? The Bible, the Reader, and the Morality of Literary Knowledge.* He is the editor of the *Dictionary for Theological Interpretation of the Bible* and *The Cambridge Companion to Postmodern Theology.*

Andrew F. Walls worked in Sierra Leone and Nigeria before becoming professor of religious studies at the University of Aberdeen, Scotland, and then director of the Centre for the Study of Christianity in the Non-western World at the University of Edinburgh. He is now honorary professor at both those universities and visiting professor at the Akrofi-Christaller Centre in Ghana. He has been a visiting professor at Yale and Harvard and a guest professor at Princeton Theological Seminary. He is the founding editor of the *Journal of Religion in Africa* and the author of numerous works, including *The Missionary Movement in Christian History* and *The Cross-Cultural Process in Christian History.*

Darrell L. Whiteman is vice president and resident missiologist for the Mission Society in Norcross, Georgia. He was formerly professor of cultural anthropology and dean of the E. Stanley Jones School of World Mission and Evangelism at Asbury Theological Seminary in Wilmore, Kentucky. He has had research and cross-cultural mission experience in Central Africa, the Solomon Islands, and Papua New Guinea. From 1989 to 2002, he served as editor of the journal *Missiology.* He is presently vice president of the American Society of Missiology, president of the International Association for Mission Studies, and chair of the Network of Christian Anthropologists.

Index